The Academy of International Business

Series Editors

Rudolf R. Sinkovics, Adam Smith Business School, University of Glasgow, Glasgow, UK; LUT Business School, LUT University, Lappeenranta, Finland
Olli Kuivalainen, LUT Business School, LUT University, Lappeenranta, Finland

The Academy of International Business – AIB-UKI Chapter book series is dedicated to publish cutting-edge research in International Business (IB) that is of contemporary relevance and at the cusp of conceptual and empirical development. The socio-political environment within which IB activity takes place is reconfigured and transformed with tremendous speed. This book series seeks to close the time-to-market of new findings and offer a solid evidence base and frameworks that helps to understand these changes. Each of the editions curates the work that exists under a special IB theme, bringing together advances by leading authors in the field.

Submissions to the series are double blind peer reviewed. For information on how to submit a proposal for inclusion in the series please visit our website: https://www.palgrave.com/gp/book-authors/publishing-guidelines/submit-a-proposal

Noemi Sinkovics · Rudolf R. Sinkovics ·
Mehdi Boussebaa · Margaret Fletcher
Editors

International Business and SDG 8

Exploring the Relationship between IB and Society

palgrave
macmillan

Editors
Noemi Sinkovics
Adam Smith Business School
University of Glasgow
Glasgow, UK

InnoLab
University of Vaasa
Vaasa, Finland

Rudolf R. Sinkovics
Adam Smith Business School
University of Glasgow
Glasgow, UK

LUT Business School
LUT University
Lappeenranta, Finland

Mehdi Boussebaa
Adam Smith Business School
University of Glasgow
Glasgow, UK

Margaret Fletcher
Adam Smith Business School
University of Glasgow
Glasgow, UK

ISSN 2662-1223 ISSN 2662-1231 (electronic)
The Academy of International Business
ISBN 978-3-031-46801-8 ISBN 978-3-031-46802-5 (eBook)
https://doi.org/10.1007/978-3-031-46802-5

Cover credit: Manop Phimsit/EyeEm

This Palgrave Macmillan imprint is published by the registered company Springer Nature Switzerland AG
The registered company address is: Gewerbestrasse 11, 6330 Cham, Switzerland

Paper in this product is recyclable.

Foreword

The Academy of International Business UK & Ireland Chapter (AIB UK&I) is the leading association of scholars and specialists in the field of international business in the UK and Ireland. The mission of the AIB UK&I is to promote teaching and research in all areas of international business and to act as a forum for the development and exchange of views in international business. To fulfil this mission, the AIB UK&I promotes several initiatives. Please visit our website (http://www.aib-uki.org) or follow us on Facebook or LinkedIn to explore the work of the Chapter and to find out how to become involved. Among the key initiatives of the AIB UK&I are (i) the Annual Conference which provides a platform for scholars to enhance the quantity and quality of their research and foster a sense of community among academics and practitioners interested in international business, (ii) a Doctoral Colloquium which allows doctoral researchers a unique opportunity to present and discuss their research with a panel of distinguished scholars, and (iii) the Palgrave Macmillan book series dedicated to publishing cutting-edge research in international business that is of contemporary relevance and at the cusp of conceptual and empirical development.

This book is part of this series and contains carefully selected papers presented at the 49th Annual Conference held on 13–15 April 2022 at the Adam Smith Business School, University of Glasgow, and papers from authors working on the theme all over the world. The book reflects the theme of the Annual Conference which was 'International Business and Sustainable Development Goal (SDG) 8: Exploring the Relationship between IB and Society' and is articulated in three parts. Part I includes a conceptual piece based on the keynote address that Rob van Tulder gave at the Conference. In his chapter, van Tulder explores why SDG 8 is particularly relevant for reacting to a series of crises that world is facing and zooms in on how to assess the actions of corporations in view of these challenges. The chapter also provides insights on how the international business (IB) profession could contribute to making progress towards achieving the SDG 8 goal. The rest of the book is divided into three further parts, featuring a collection of works providing research, teaching, and practitioners perspectives pertaining to SDG8.

In Part II, twelve contributions explore issues ranging from labour standard provisions in trade policy, corporate commitment to decent work, and modern slavery law. A range of chapters focuses on Global Value Chains (GVCs), including an analysis of their ethical performance, the role of blockchain technology in facilitating economic and social upgrading, circular economy, and decent work. The last four chapters in Part II look at the mechanisms that enable entrepreneurs to pursue sustainable opportunities, agency problems across collaboration types, knowledge transfer, and worker/producer cooperatives to create a sustainable and inclusive economy.

Part III of the volume provides a range of teaching perspectives on the educational aspects at the interface of SDG8 and IB. Chapters in this part focus on inclusive education within diverse societies, providing examples of course and assessment designs, emphasising the importance of the learning context, and applying design thinking principles to support students in examining modern slavery issues in supply chains.

Part IV concludes the volume with a series of invited reflections from practitioners on issues connected to SDG8. These perspectives range from creating local value in Africa's food value chain, the challenges of asylum seekers and the barriers to their integration in host societies, the implication of Brexit for businesses, and the effectiveness of schemes and programmes launched by central and local governments in India in response to SDG8.

This latest addition to the Academy of International Business—AIB-UKI Chapter book series contributes importantly by offering scholarly contributions on SDG8 based on cutting-edge research, alongside teaching perspectives and practitioner reflections on SDG8. The book addresses a range of SDG8 topics and includes educator and practitioner views. The book thus provides a rich view on the complexities and trade-offs involved in pursuing the. Collectively, the book illuminates on how to make international business scholarship more societally engaged and relevant through engagement with stakeholders, students, and policymakers.

Davide Castellani
University of Reading
Reading, UK

Praise for *International Business and SDG 8*

"*International Business and SDG 8: Exploring the Relationship Between IB and Society* provides a comprehensive exploration of the complex relationship between international business and SDG 8, which seeks to foster inclusive and sustainable economic growth, full and productive employment, and decent work for all. The editors have brought together a diverse range of perspectives and a diverse group of IB scholars, skilfully uniting research, teaching, and practitioner insights in one book. Congratulations to the editors and contributors for producing a thought-provoking resource, which will facilitate important conversations and actions toward a more sustainable and inclusive global economy. *International Business and SDG 8* will be a valuable addition to the reading list of anyone seeking to understand the vital links between SDG 8, the global business landscape, and societal well-being."

—Dr. Saba S. Colakoglu, *Senior Lecturer of Organizational Behavior, Georgia Institute of Technology, President, Women in the Academy of International Business*

"In this brilliantly-thought-through volume we have chapters by scholars and practitioners taking us through the intricate (and often untrodden) lanes of how contemporary global crises have impacted or disrupted international business, supply chains, socioeconomic upgrading and, importantly, job prospects in low-income countries. The diverse experiences of subsectors, enterprises, services and layers of governance as buyers and suppliers responded to the unprecedented challenges have been presented in this unique volume both engagingly and convincingly. The volume is rich in insights for industrial and trade policy making that will be responsive to sustainable growth, decent work and creating greater employment opportunities in the global south. The volume reaffirms the value and efficiency of interdisciplinarity in understanding international business dynamics as often mediated through armed conflicts, deadly viruses and even mistrust between stakeholders at the drop of a hat. This is a volume fecund with grounded analyses, innovative propositions, and responsible strategies."

—Professor Keshab Das, *Dean, School of Social, Financial & Human Sciences, KIIT Deemed to be University, Bhubaneswar, India, and Visiting Professor, Institute for Human Development, New Delhi, India*

"Whereas many books provide a general overview of their domains of interest, this latest addition to the Academy of International Business – AIB-UKI Chapter book series provides cutting-edge research focused specifically on the United Nations' Sustainable Development Goal (SDG) 8. This tightly focused book speaks directly to SDG 8 as it is particularly relevant for international management scholars. Further beyond providing this focused view on scholarly perspectives on SDG 8, the book provides a novel section on teaching perspectives on SDG 8 as well as practitioners' reflections. Together, the book develops the notion of making international business scholarship more societally engaged and relevant through engagement with stakeholders, students, and policy makers."

—Professor Anthony Goerzen, *Sobey Professor of International Business, Smith School of Business, Queen's University, Kingston, Ontario, Canada*

"For IB scholars looking to explore, extend and apply sustainable development principles – with a particular focus on United Nations Sustainable Development Goal (SDG) 8 – this collection is invaluable. As you would expect for a collection on International Business and SDG 8, the contributions come from an internationally diverse group of specialist scholars in the field. The scope of the research chapters covers focal and integrative themes, adding up to a rich, broad and encompassing treatment including ESG issues, global value chains and technologies, and the roles of different types of organization. The teaching-focussed chapters in the book – which cover approaches to education as well as key contemporary issues in the field – can help educators to enrich their programmes at all levels. Overall, this is a useful and timely contribution to the field."

—Professor Paul Hibbert, *Professor of Management, University of St Andrews, UK and Honorary Professor, University of Auckland Business School, New Zealand, Editor-in-Chief, Academy of Management Learning & Education, Co-Editor-in-Chief,* British Journal of Management

"Few can doubt the important ambition of SDG 8 to promote sustainable economic growth and decent work for all. Few can also doubt that execution has proved problematic. This book makes an important contribution by demonstrating how the discipline of International Business can contribute to clarifying the issues and articulating solutions. The key strengths of the book are the wide-ranging diversity of the topics addressed, and the inclusion of educator and practitioner views alongside the scholarly debates on issues ranging from labor standard provisions in international trade policy to multinationals and disadvantaged communities in emerging markets. There is a welcome embrace of complexities and highlighting of trade-offs throughout."

—Professor Geoffrey Jones, *Isidor Straus Professor of Business History, Harvard Business School*

"This book is an essential read for anyone passionate about sustainable development, the future of work, and international business. It offers a comprehensive and thought-provoking exploration of the relationship among these three areas in the context of Sustainable Development Goal

8 (SDG8). The book features contributions from knowledgeable and experienced scholars and practitioners, covering important topics such as multinational companies' commitment to decent work and sustainable development, the possible impact of labour standards on international trade, the role of blockchain technology in facilitating economic and social upgrading in developing economies, and the significance of SDG8 for enabling entrepreneurs to pursue sustainable opportunities. Additionally, it addresses the importance of diversity, equity, and inclusion in international business education, among other critical themes. The book emphasizes how these different perspectives interact, highlighting the crucial role of international business in achieving SDG8. I highly recommend this book to anyone seeking to understand the current state of the art and the practical challenges and opportunities of achieving SDG8."

—Professor Fernando S. Oliveira, *Professor of Procurement and Supply Chain Management, Aberdeen Business School, Robert Gordon University*

"How 'decent work' and relevant 'economic growth' can be linked in an inclusive, sustainable and prosperity-enhancing manner, is one of the key challenges of our time. Investing in decent jobs and social protection has been recognized as a promising pathway to synergistically achieve universal access to essential services, reduce inequalities and safeguard human rights and wellbeing. Hence, it can be argued that the relevance of International Business scholarship depends on whether and how it meaningfully addresses this challenge, at all relevant levels of analysis. There are substantial intellectual gaps to be filled in this area, which not only pertain to the search for proper metrics, but also to what theories, research approaches and teaching activities should be developed to yield actionable insights for practitioners and policymakers alike. This book provides an excellent attempt to bring together many state-of-the-art efforts from International Business scholars, highlighting a rich body of SDG8-related topics to serve this need. In many respects, this book presents inspiring work 'in' and 'on' progress for engaged IB scholars!"

—Eveline van Mil and Professor Rob van Tulder, *Authors of* 'Principles of Sustainable Business. Frameworks for Corporate Action on the SDGs' *(2023, Routledge)*

"This book admirably serves the purpose of framing and shaping the public discourse on the important inter-linkages of international business, social justice and the 2030 Agenda. The authors and editors provide an accessible understanding of how SDG#8 and its focus on decent work and economic growth impact international business and conversely how international business can contribute to a successful implementation of the 2030 Agenda.

The current use of international agreements that guide responsible business conduct needs to enable the partners of industrial relations-employers, employees, civil society and governments- to strike the best approach to balancing economic growth while protecting future generations and preserving our planet's resources." This book offers excellent solutions how these essential interlinkages can be understood and strengthened."

—Raymond Saner, Titular Professor, *University of Basel and Director of Diplomacy Dialogue, CSEND, Geneva*

Contents

Notes on Contributors

Omar Al-Tabbaa (Ph.D., The University of Leeds, UK) is Associate Professor in International Business and Director of Research at Leeds University Business School. His key research areas include inter-organisational relationships (including SME co-internationalisation, university–industry ties, global value chains strategy and social co-innovation), business model innovation and scalability of digital platforms, and the methodology of systematic literature review. He serves on number of editorial review boards. https://business.leeds.ac.uk/departments-international-business/staff/1618/dr-omar-al-tabbaa.

Jason Archie–Acheampong (Ph.D., Alliance Manchester Business School) is currently International Commercial Programmes Manager at Producers Direct. His work and fascinations lie at the intersection of sustainable development and global foods systems, with particular interest on how corporations affect development. He has worked across the global agro-foods industry both in the private sector and within development organisations, where he has led agricultural trade partnerships and market access programmes for agribusinesses and smallholder farmers. His research work has been published in leading international business journals and he is currently a member of the Food Ethics Council (UK). https://www.linkedin.com/in/jason-archie-acheampong.

David Audretsch (Ph.D., The University of Wisconsin, USA) is Distinguished Professor and Ameritech Chair of Economic Development at Indiana University, where he also serves as Director of the Institute of Development Strategies. He also serves as Professor of Entrepreneurship and Innovation Management at the University of Klagenfurt in Austria. Prior to that, he served as Director of the Max Planck Institute of Economics in Germany. His research focuses on entrepreneurship and public policy. He is Co-Editor-in-Chief of *Small Business Economics*. https://oneill.indiana.edu/faculty-research/directory/profiles/faculty/full-time/audretsch-david.html.

Muhammad Ayaz is Assistant Professor of Management at the Institute of Business Administration (IBA) in Karachi, Pakistan. His research interests are economic and social upgrading in global value chains, environmental sustainability in global value chains, the role of labour and multilateral organisations in (re)shaping global value chains, and corporate social responsibility in global value chains. https://oric.iba.edu.pk/profile.php?id=muhammadayaz.

Krishna Kumar Balaraman (Ph.D., Indian Institute of Technology Madras, India) is Associate Professor in the Strategic and Public Policy area at the School of Management and Entrepreneurship at Indian Institute of Technology Jodhpur (IITJ), where he heads the Center of Technology Foresight and Policy. He is an associated faculty at IITJ's AIDE School and CETSD. His Ph.D. research considered strategic foresight and alliances. He is an alumnus of IIM Bangalore, NLSIU Bangalore, and University of Madras. He has more than two decades of international leadership experience in developing products and solutions in leading-edge technologies, and advises start-ups on business models and strategies. His research interests include strategic foresight, microfoundations of institutions, international business, sustainability, and corporate governance. He is a member of the editorial review board of *IEEE Transactions on Engineering Management*. https://research.iitj.ac.in/researcher/krishna-kumar-balaraman.

Dhruba Borah (Ph.D., The University of Manchester, UK) is Senior Lecturer in Innovation Management at the University of Liverpool and the Director of Studies for the M.Sc. in Entrepreneurship and Innovation Programme. His research interests include the management of emerging technologies, innovation in emerging economies, and cross-sector collaborations for innovation. He completed his Ph.D. from Alliance Manchester Business School, and he is a recipient of the prestigious RADMA doctoral funding and the dissertation grant from the Strategic Research Foundation (SRF) of the Strategic Management Society. https://www.liverpool.ac.uk/management/staff/dhruba-borah.

Mehdi Boussebaa (Ph.D., University of Warwick, UK) is Professor of International Business at the University of Glasgow, UK, where he also leads the International Business & Enterprise Research Cluster. Prior to joining Glasgow in 2016, he worked at the universities of Bath and Oxford. His research spans the fields of international business and organisation studies and is also informed by postcolonial thought and international political economy. It is mainly concerned with the politics of globalisation, transnational enterprise, and management knowledge. He is Co-Editor-in-Chief of *Critical Perspectives on International Business* and serves on a number of editorial review boards. https://www.gla.ac.uk/schools/business/staff/mehdiboussebaa.

Wilhelm Brunner (Mag. rer.soc.oec., WU-Vienna, Austria) has worked in the field of services for refugees in Austria, Germany, Ireland, Slovakia, and Switzerland for 20 years. Wilhelm is currently Director Business Development—Europe at ORS, which is based in Switzerland and part of Serco Group plc. https://www.ors-group.org.

Brent Malcolm Burmester (Ph.D., University of Auckland, NZ) is Senior Lecturer in International Business and a member of the Centre for Research on Modern Slavery at the University of Auckland Business School in New Zealand. His research interests centre around the origins and application of MNE power, augmenting international business with theories and perspectives from international relations and international law. Recently he has been working with a research team focussing on modern slavery and labour exploitation in New Zealand, both as a human rights challenge to the practice of international business and as a domestic and international policy issue. He is Associate Editor for *Critical Perspectives on International Business*. https://profiles.auckland.ac.nz/b-burmester.

Lisa Callagher (Ph.D., The University of Auckland, NZ) is Senior Lecturer in Innovation and Research Commercialisation at The University of Auckland, NZ. Her research addresses the organisation and management of innovation. Lisa is particularly interested in processual and practice-theoretic explanations of innovation in cooperative and collaborative business models and ownership structures. https://profiles.auckland.ac.nz/l-callagher.

Jayne Cathcart (Ph.D., Queen's University Belfast) is Research Fellow in Strategy and International Business at the University of Birmingham, UK. Her Ph.D. examined Consumer Perceptions of Corporate Social Responsibility in Sweden and the UK. Jayne has experience working as a Teaching Associate at Alliance Manchester Business School, in addition to policy, and business roles in project management and supply chain management. https://research.birmingham.ac.uk/en/persons/jayne-cathcart.

Jorge Carneiro (Ph.D., Federal University of Rio de Janeiro, Brazil) is Associate Professor of Strategy and International Business at FGV Sao Paulo School of Business Administration. His research covers issues of strategic planning and strategy execution, internationalisation of emerging market enterprises, and multinationals and inclusive development. He is Academic Director of OneMBA—global executive MBA, President of AIB-LAC (Academy of International Business—Latin America and the Caribbean chapter), and former board member of EIBA (European International Business Academy) and of BALAS (Business Association of Latin American Studies; Member of the Strategic Committee of Corporate Governance of Amcham Brasil and of the Strategy Committee of IBGC (Brazilian Institute of Corporate Governance); Editor-in-chief of *Revista de Administração de Empresas* and Associate editor of *International Business Review* and *Multinational Business Review*. Before embracing academic life, Carneiro accumulated 16 years of experience in the oil & gas industry and in digital companies. https://www.carneirojorge.com.

Umair Shafi Choksy (Ph.D., University of Manchester) is Senior Lecturer in Management at University of Stirling Management School. His research interests include global value chains, governance, and supply chain resilience. This includes work on the knowledge connectivity, power and governance, absorptive capacity, sustainability, and economic upgrading in global value chains. https://www.stir.ac.uk/people/1834301.

Louise Curran (Ph.D., Manchester Metropolitan University) is Senior Lecturer in International Business in TBS Education in Toulouse in France. Her research interests include the interactions between government policy and global value chains (GVCs), EU trade policy making, especially in relation to sustainability and EU-China trade relations. She is on the Editorial Advisory Board of the *Journal of International Business Policy*, *Critical Perspectives on International Business* and the *Journal of Fashion Marketing and Management*. https://www.tbs-education.com/teacher/curran-louise/.

Antje Fiedler (Ph.D., University of Auckland, NZ) is Senior Lecturer in Management and Deputy Director of the New Zealand Asia Institute at the University of Auckland Business School. Her research interests centre around how Western firms and entrepreneurs can productively engage with Asia. She is an Associate Editor for the *Journal of Small Business Management* and serves on the editorial review boards for *Small Business Economics* and *Critical Perspectives on International Business*. She is also a Director of the Board of the *Small Enterprise Association of Australia and New Zealand* (SEAANZ). https://profiles.auckland.ac.nz/a-fiedler.

Margaret Fletcher is Professor of International Business at the Adam Smith Business School, University of Glasgow, UK. Her research interests include internationalisation, international entrepreneurship, small firm policy, and the financing of small firms. She has numerous journal and book chapter publications. She was Doctoral Convenor of the Academy of International Business (AIB) UK&I leader and currently serves on the executive board as Equality & Diversity officer. https://www.gla.ac.uk/schools/business/staff/margaretfletcher/.

James Francis (M.Sc., Kent Business School, United Kingdom). His M.Sc. dissertation focused on the implications of blockchain technology on economic, social, and environmental outcomes of supply chain participants. His research interests include digital technologies and sustainability in GVCs.

Pervez N. Ghauri (Ph.D., Uppsala University, Sweden) is Professor and Chair of International Business at University of Birmingham, UK. Over the years he has worked at Manchester Business School and King's College London in the UK. His current research includes examining how multinationals from advanced markets can contribute to the achievement of the United Nations Sustainable Development Goals (SDGs) by creatively serving disadvantaged communities in emerging markets, and create competitive advantage at the same time. Pervez has published more than 30 books and more than 150 journal articles in top-level journals. He was founding editor of International Business Review (IBR) and at present he is Consulting Editor for *Journal of International Business Studies and IBR*. Pervez is a Fellow for both the European International Business Academy (EIBA) and the Academy of International Business (AIB), where he was also elected Vice President between 2008 and 2010. https://pervezghauri.com/.

Axèle Giroud (Ph.D., The University of Bradford, U.K.) is Professor of International Business, Head of the Comparative and International Business group at the Alliance Manchester Business School (UK). She is Senior Editor of *International Business Review*, Associate Editor of *Journal of International Business Policy*, and serves on number of editorial review boards. She was previously Senior Economist with the United Nations (UNCTAD) and was President of the Euro-Asia Management Studies Association. Her research interests include MNEs Strategies, Sustainable Development, Knowledge Transfer, Inter-firm Linkages, and Emerging Markets. She currently leads an ESRC-funded Project on MNEs and Marginalised Communities. https://research.manchester.ac.uk/en/persons/axele.giroud.

J. P. Jagdev is the CEO and Managing Director of Parameter Softwares (P) Ltd., a 30-year-old IT and Management Consulting firm based in Bhubaneswar, Odisha, India. He has worked mostly with the UN systems and government departments across various sectors as a consultant and a policy implementation specialist. His organisation is focused on providing solutions in the space of SDG, Sustainability, and ESG. He has interest in research and academics. https://pspl.ind.in/.

Zaheer Khan (Ph.D., The University of Birmingham, UK) is Professor of Strategy & International Business and Founding Director of Africa-Asia Centre of Sustainability Research at the Business School, University of Aberdeen, UK. He is a Fellow of the Academy of Social Sciences (FAcSS). His research focuses on global technology management, international alliances, platform firms, non-market strategy, and internationalisation of firms from emerging markets. He is Associate Editor of *Critical Perspectives on International Business* and serves on number of editorial review boards. https://www.abdn.ac.uk/people/zaheer.khan/.

Jihye Kim (Ph.D., The University of Manchester, UK) is Lecturer of Management and Marketing at the University of Dundee School of Business, UK. She holds an M.Phil. in International Business and a Ph.D. in International Business from the University of Manchester, UK. Her research interests include corporate social responsibility, cross-sector partnership, and sustainability. https://discovery.dundee.ac.uk/en/persons/jihye-kim.

Gary Knight (Ph.D., Michigan State University, USA) is the Helen Jackson Chair in International Management at Willamette University in Salem and Portland, Oregon, USA. Gary is a Fellow of the Academy of International Business and President of the Academy of International Business. His research interests include international entrepreneurship, global strategy, and the role of innovation and technology in internationalisation. https://willamette.edu/mba/faculty/knight/index.html.

Stefan Korber (Ph.D., The University of Auckland, NZ) is Lecturer in Innovation and Entrepreneurship at The University of Auckland, NZ. His research is concerned with the collaborative and relational aspects of innovation and entrepreneurship in a diverse range of settings such as professional services, agriculture cooperatives, and deep-tech. In his work, Stefan draws upon institutional and practice-based perspectives. https://profiles.auckland.ac.nz/s-korber.

Khalid Nadvi (D.Phil., University of Sussex) is a Professor of International Development at the Global Development Institute, School of Environment, Education and Development, University of Manchester. His research focuses on globalisation, trade, industrial development, and sustainability. He has written extensively on small enterprise clusters, global value chains and production networks, global standards, corporate social responsibility, labour, environment, and technological upgrading. His research focuses mainly on South and Southeast Asia, sub-Saharan Africa, and Brazil. He has won various ESRC-funded large grants including the 'Rising Powers, Labour Standards and Governance of Global Production'; and the 'Shifting South: Decent Work and the Governance of Regional Value Chains in sub-Saharan Africa' studies. He has published over 50 leading journal articles and book chapters and is highly cited. He has acted as a consultant for leading international agencies including UNIDO, ILO, UNCTAD, IADB, and the World Bank. https://research.manchester.ac.uk/en/persons/khalid.nadvi.

Swati Nagar (PhD, Auckland University of Technology) is a Senior Lecturer (Education—Focused—Discipline of International Business) at the University of Sydney Business School. Prior to joining the University of Sydney, she was employed at the AUT Business School, where she served as the Head of Department at the Department of International Business, Strategy & Entrepreneurship, AUT Business School, New Zealand. Her current research interests include the Social Impact of Modern Slavery, Sustainable Production and Consumption in the FMCG Industry, and Pedagogical research that explores teaching and learning best practices in a post-COVID education environment. She also serves as the Communication Co-ordinator for the AIB Teaching and Learning SIG and is the VP. Secretary for AIB Oceania. She has published in several outlets, including Routledge, AIB Insights, Cambridge University Press, Palgrave and the Journal of International Business Education.

Renan Oliveira is Research Fellow at FGV Sao Paulo School of Business Administration. He has published in International Marketing Review and holds a Ph.D. degree from the Federal University of Rio de Janeiro (UFRJ), where he studied the influence of the network in the internationalisation process of firms in the oil and gas industry based in Rio de Janeiro. He visited Copenhagen Business School (CBS), and was appointed as External Lecturer in the course of Business Research Methods (BSs International Business in Asia).

Matevž (Matt) Rašković (Ph.D., University of Ljubljana, Slovenia) is Associate Professor of International Business & Strategy at Auckland University of Technology in New Zealand and a Full Professor of International Business (Adjunct) at the School of Economics and Business, University of Ljubljana in Slovenia. Matt is an economic sociologist conducting research at the intersection of international business, society, and policymaking at the macro and organisational levels. He mostly works with social identity theory, institutional theory, and socio-cognitive theory. Matt currently serves as Vice-President Administration at the Academy of International Business, is the founding member of the AIB Diversity & Inclusion taskforce and also serves as Senior Editor at the *European Journal of International Management*. He was a 2017 Fulbright Scholar at Harvard University, FAS Sociology. https://academics.aut.ac.nz/matt.raskovic.

Elizabeth L. Rose (Ph.D., University of Michigan, USA) is Research Chair Professor of Business Policy and Strategy at Indian Institute of Management Udaipur, India. Her previous academic appointments have included positions in Finland, New Zealand, the UK, and the US. A Fellow of the Academy of International Business, her research sits at the intersection of international business, international entrepreneurship, and global strategy, with a focus on internationalisation choices and emerging markets. She is a member of the editorial team for *Journal of International Business Studies* and Co-Editor-in-Chief of *Academy of Management Collections*. https://www.iimu.ac.in/faculty-aamp-research/faculty/full-time-faculty/elizabeth-l-rose.

Asmund Rygh (Ph.D., BI Norwegian Business School, Oslo, Norway) is Senior Lecturer in International Business at Alliance Manchester Business School, University of Manchester, UK. He has diverse research interests within international business, corporate governance and finance (including state ownership), social responsibility and sustainability (including inequality and labour relations), entrepreneurship and innovation. He has published numerous articles and book chapters in international business and related areas and currently serves on the editorial review boards of *Global Strategy Journal* and *Journal of International Business Policy*. https://research.manchester.ac.uk/en/persons/asmund.rygh.

Holly Sherrie (B.A. Economics, Strathclyde University) is a recent graduate who joined Scottish Enterprise as an Economic Researcher this year. Holly has been involved in gathering insights from companies as well as analysing official datasets published by the Scottish Government and ONS.

Frank Siedlok (PhD, University of Strathlyde, UK) is a Senior Lecturer in Strategy at University of St Andrews, St Andrews, UK. His research centres around practices and processes of innovation, knowledge coordination and strategy making in a range of collaborative settings.

Aušrinė Šilenskytė (Ph.D., University of Vaasa, Finland) is Post-Doctoral Researcher and a Program Manager (Bachelor in International Business) at the School of Management, University of Vaasa, Finland. She also serves as a Chair at the Academy of International Business Teaching and Education Shared Interest Group and is a Governing Board member at the AIB-CIBER Doctoral Academy. Her research centres around strategy implementation in multinational corporations, blockchain adoption in International Business (IB) management, and teaching IB. https://www.uwasa.fi/en/person/1082312.

Noemi Sinkovics (Ph.D., The University of Manchester, UK) is Reader in International Business at University of Glasgow, Adam Smith Business School, UK and Visiting Professor at the University of Vaasa, InnoLab, Finland. She previously worked at The University of Auckland, NZ and

The University of Manchester, UK. Her research interests are theoretical and practical issues around entrepreneurship (including international and social entrepreneurship) and social, environmental, and economic upgrading in global value chains. She is Co-Editor-in-Chief for *Data in Brief*, Associate Editor for *Critical Perspectives on International Business* and serves on number of editorial review boards. https://www.sinkovics.com/noemi.

Rudolf R. Sinkovics (Dr.rer.soc.oec., WU-Vienna, Austria) is Professor of International Business at University of Glasgow, Adam Smith Business School, UK, and Visiting Professor at LUT University, Finland. His research covers issues of inter-organisational governance, and the role of ICT, with a current focus on responsible business. He is Co-Editor-in-Chief for *Critical Perspectives on International Business*, Associate editor for *Transnational Corporations* and serves on a number of editorial boards. https://www.sinkovics.com/rudolf.

Jonathan Slow (M.Sc. Economics and Econometrics, University of Southampton) is Economics and Research Manager at Scottish Enterprise. His background is in Economics and Statistics and he has over 20 years experience in public sector policy making. He has a particular research focus on international business and engaged extensively with businesses from all sectors to identify any challenges and opportunities they face.

Ji-Won Song (Ph.D., Stockholm School of Economics, Sweden) is Lecturer of International HRM and Employment Relations at the University of Edinburgh Business School, UK. Prior to Edinburgh, he worked at the University of Greenwich, UK. His research interests include HRM practice transfer in MNEs, diversity management, and comparative institutionalism. https://sites.google.com/view/jiwonsong/.

Rob van Tulder Ph.D. is Emeritus Professor of International Business-Society Management at RSM Erasmus University Rotterdam and Academic Director of the Partnerships Resource Centre. He is co-founder of the department of Business-Society Management, one of the leading departments in the world organising research and education on the way business can create value for society either alone or through cross-sector partnerships. He advises international organisations, governments, multinational enterprises, and international NGOs on issues of sustainability and strategy and has published in leading international journals. He made scientific knowledge practical in a variety of directions, for instance: (1) to help managers assess the transition stage they are in (www.betterbusinessscan.org), (2) to help societal parties and students assess and address wicked problems (wicked problems plaza), (3) to help partnerships identify relevant intervention points and theories of change (www.rsm/prc), (4) to help students apply analytical frameworks to corporate cases and their personal leadership ambitions (posters, checklists and profilers). www.principlesofsustainablebusiness.nl or www.robvantulder.nl.

Joanne Wright (PhD, The University of Auckland, NZ) is a Professional Teaching Fellow in International Business at The University of Auckland, NZ. Her research focuses on the internationalisation of small and medium sized firms (SMEs). Jo is particularly interested in SMEs from small and open economies leverage relationships to drive international growth. https://profiles.auckland.ac.nz/joanne-wright.

Stefan Zagelmeyer (Dr. rer. pol., University of Erlangen-Nuremberg, Germany) is Reader in Comparative and International Business at Alliance Manchester Business School, Manchester, UK. Prior to that, he has held appointments at Manchester School of Management (UK), Université Paris II Panthéon-Assas (France), Turku School of Economics (Finland), and the University of Twente (The Netherlands). He is author of numerous publications in academic and practitioner-oriented journals. His research interests are international business strategy, comparative business and management, international human resource management, and business and human rights. https://research.manchester.ac.uk/en/persons/s.zagelmeyer.

Shasha Zhao (Ph.D., The University of Manchester, United Kingdom) is Associate Professor (Senior Lecturer) of International Business and Innovation at Surrey University Business School, UK. Her research focuses on global innovation strategy and knowledge management of

MNEs and EMNEs, and their implications on sustainability. She is Co-Founder and Co-Chair of Academy of International Business Sustainability Shared Interest Group. Her work has been featured in UNIDO publications. She has published in numerous world-leading journals and is Deputy Editor of Asian Business and Management, as well as being on the editorial board of several elite journals. https://www.surrey.ac.uk/people/shasha-zhao.

List of Figures

Chapter 2

Chapter 3

Chapter 6

Chapter 15

Chapter 17

List of Tables

Chapter 8

Chapter 10

Chapter 14

Chapter 15

Part I

Introduction to International Business and SDG 8

1

International Business and SDG 8: An Introduction to the Theme

Noemi Sinkovics, Rudolf R. Sinkovics, Mehdi Boussebaa, and Margaret Fletcher

1 International Business and SDG 8

Sustainable Development Goal (SDG) 8 aims to promote sustained, inclusive, and sustainable economic growth, full and productive employment, and decent work for all. The twelve associated targets call for action in several interconnected domains that are of great relevance for global governance, international business, and international entrepreneurship.

N. Sinkovics (✉) · R. R. Sinkovics · M. Boussebaa · M. Fletcher
Adam Smith Business School, University of Glasgow, Glasgow, UK
e-mail: noemi.sinkovics@glasgow.ac.uk

R. R. Sinkovics
e-mail: rudolf.sinkovics@glasgow.ac.uk

M. Boussebaa
e-mail: Mehdi.Boussebaa@glasgow.ac.uk

M. Fletcher
e-mail: margaret.fletcher@glasgow.ac.uk

N. Sinkovics et al. (eds.), *International Business and SDG 8*, The Academy of International Business, https://doi.org/10.1007/978-3-031-46802-5_1

However, the Covid-19 pandemic and geopolitical issues such as war, the climate crisis and associated humanitarian catastrophes highlight just how fragile progress towards inclusive and sustainable growth is. German Chancellor Olaf Scholz called the February 24, 2022 invasion of Ukraine a "Zeitenwende" (a revolution). Faced with external shocks, we witness local communities and small firm actors being hit hard. Global disruptions in supply chains and an increase in national protectionism prompt questions about whether global value chains should be shortened and re-localised to reduce risks. The increased need for government support for small and medium enterprises shifts the grounds on which support was traditionally provided. Restrictions to travel and in-person communication prompt businesses to take advantage of digital technologies to ensure business continuity. Disruptions to peace and the weakening of democratic systems raise questions around the responsibility of local and foreign business actors in these regions. Mass migration, forced or voluntary, raises questions around integration mechanisms in host countries including integration into the labour market and through encouraging entrepreneurship.

Against this background, this book offers a collection of chapters that interrogate the complex relationship between international business and SDG8 from various angles. Specifically, we sought to bring together insights from a research, teaching, and practitioner perspective.

2 Contributions to This Volume

The first contribution in this volume under Part I is a conceptual piece by Rob van Tulder (Emeritus Professor of International Business-Society Management, Rotterdam School of Management) based on his keynote address at the 2023 Academy of International Business UK and Ireland

N. Sinkovics
Innolab, University of Vaasa, Vaasa, Finland

R. R. Sinkovics
LUT Business School, LUT University, Lappeenranta, Finland

Chapter conference held at the University of Glasgow. In this opening chapter, he explores why SDG 8 is particularly relevant for reacting to the perfect storm comprising a series of, predominantly man-made, crises that humanity is facing. Further, the chapter zooms in on how to assess the actions of corporations, domestic and multinational, in the face of these challenges and what an engaged IB scholarship should focus on in their research and teaching. Although the chapter concludes that we are not on track to reach SDG8, it charts different avenues for the IB profession to course correct and make progress towards this goal. The rest of the book is divided into three further parts.

2.1 Research Perspectives

Part II takes a research perspective. The twelve contributions explore different issues pertaining to SDG 8 as well as various ways of progressing towards it. Rygh examines labour standards provisions in international trade policy. The chapter argues that social clauses in bilateral, regional, and unilateral trade policy represent a highly relevant topic for IB research. In addition to providing an overview of social clauses and labour standards in international trade, the author provides an assessment of their value and impact. The chapter concludes with an outline of several areas where the IB discipline can contribute. Examples include the implementation of social clauses, the interaction between private and public regulations, their implications for broader MNE strategies, and an increasingly multi-order global economy.

Zagelmeyer takes a more organisational approach and examines the extent of corporate commitment to decent work and sustainable development through a quantitative analysis of corporate reports of DAX 40 MNCs. The results of the text-mining analysis reveal that there may be a separation in issues discussed in sustainability reports and annual reports. Although the insights in this chapter are based on a purely quantitative, keyword-frequency-count-based analysis, the pitfalls of reporting including potential SDG washing practices will need further attention from future research.

Burmester examines the parallels between antitrust and modern slavery law to identify alternative global governance pathways to realising SDG 8.7. The chapter suggests that allying these two approaches, specifically, complementing new thinking in the domain of business and human rights with new thinking in the domain of antitrust provides renewed hope to tackle the issue of modern slavery in supply chains.

Currant and Nadvi zoom in on fashion global value chains. They investigate transparency databases and explore the extent to which they can improve the ethical performance of these value chains. The analysis reveals that transparency initiatives on their own are not sufficient to improve working conditions and wages. The authors call for stronger regulations to complement increased transparency.

Oliveira, Cathcart, Giroud, Carneiro, and Ghauri conduct a thematic literature review to examine how MNEs interact with disadvantaged communities in emerging markets and how such interactions may facilitate the proliferation of decent work opportunities and scaffold economic development (SDG8). They identify valuable examples connected to the various SDG8 targets. Zhao also takes a literature-based conceptual approach to explore the links between MNE FDI, subnational peripheries, and local upgrading. The chapter offers a framework, bringing together several antecedents, mechanisms, and consequences. The chapter also highlights the connection between SDG 8.2 and SDG 8.3.

Choksy, Ayaz, and Francis reflect on the role of blockchain technology in facilitating economic and social upgrading in global value chains. Specifically, the authors explore the trade-offs between economic and social upgrading for developing economy suppliers and theorise about the conditions that aid the mitigation of these trade-offs. The chapter concludes that although blockchain technology can indeed be used to achieve process as well as social upgrading in developing economies, it also has the potential to further increase the power of lead firms that may dampen the technology's potential positive impact.

Al-Tabbaa, Khan, and Knight also take a global value chain perspective. They present a framework that draws on an affordance lens and explores the interface between circular economy principles and dimensions of decent work as specified by the International Labour Organization. The authors illustrate their points with examples.

The last four papers take a somewhat different perspective. Audretsch and Fiedler connect the literature on entrepreneurial ecosystems with international business perspectives. Specifically, they reflect on the mechanisms that enable entrepreneurs to pursue sustainable opportunities. Kim, Song, and Bora adopt a multiple agency lens to conceptualise a typology of cross-sector partnerships. Besides the delineation of five types of collaborations, the authors draw attention to agency problems across the different collaboration types. Balaraman and Rose apply an institutional micro-foundations perspective to knowledge transfer in the arts and crafts industry in India. The last chapter in Part II by Siedlok, Callagher, and Korber provides an overview of different types of worker and producer cooperatives underpinned with illustrative examples. This form of organisation has a key importance in creating a sustainable and inclusive economy.

2.2 Teaching Perspectives

Part III in this volume focuses on the educational aspects at the interface of SDG8 and international business. Šilenskytė and Rašković draw on an OECD framework on inclusive education within diverse societies and reflect on diversity, equity, and inclusion-enabling actions at institutional, programme, course, and individual levels. The authors posit that the rhetoric-vs-action gap can be narrowed by embedding diversity, equity, and inclusion as well as belonging perspectives at the various levels. They provide a specific list of recommended actions for each level.

Whereas the chapter by Šilenskytė and Rašković provides a more bird's eye view perspective, the other two chapters in this part of the book offer concrete examples of course and assessment design. Wright emphasises the importance of the learning context. The institutional environment of the country or region where the educational programme takes place is just as important as the context of the organisations that learners are engaging with within their curriculum. The author uses the example of small and medium-sized enterprises in New Zealand and offers a detailed description of experiential learning activities and assessments. The third chapter in this section by Swati Nagar applies design thinking principles to support students in examining modern slavery issues in supply chains. This chapter again provides hands-on recommendations and illustrative examples.

2.3 Practitioner Reflections

Part IV in this volume comprises invited reflections from practitioners on issues connected to SDG8 within their field of operation. Jason Archie-Acheampong, International Commercial Programmes Manager at Producers Direct, zooms in on creating local value in Africa's food value chains. Wilhelm Brunner, Director of Operations Austria and Director of Business Development Europe of ORS Group, a Serco company, reflects on migration issues in Europe. Specifically, he discusses the challenges of asylum seekers and the systemic barriers to their integration in host societies. Jonathan Slow, Head of Economic Analysis, and Holly Sherrie, Insights and Economics Team Graduate, from Scottish Enterprise delve into the implications of Brexit for Scottish businesses. JP Jagdev, CEO and Managing Director of Parameter Softwares Ltd., reflects on the effectiveness of selected schemes and programmes launched by the central government of India and the state government of Odisha in response to SDG8. He identifies various gaps and provides suggestions for more effective interventions.

2

International Business and SDG8: Are We on Course?

Rob van Tulder

The world is facing a 'perfect storm'—a combination of largely man-made crises that puts the governance of the global economic, political, social and health system as developed since the 1990s under increasing pressure. The perfect storm presents a number of fundamental questions for engaged International Business (IB) scholarship. How to assess the action of (multinational) corporations under these circumstances? How to measure the effectiveness of corporate strategies for sustainable development? Moreover, what could engaged IB scholarship focus on in their research and teaching? Why is SDG 8 (decent work and economic growth) thereby particularly relevant? Are we on course?

R. van Tulder (✉)
Rotterdam School of Management, Erasmus University, Rotterdam, The Netherlands
e-mail: rtulder@rsm.nl

N. Sinkovics et al. (eds.), *International Business and SDG 8*, The Academy of International Business, https://doi.org/10.1007/978-3-031-46802-5_2

1 Organizing in a Perfect Storm, Why the SDGs?

The perfect storm confronts engaged IB scholars in their teaching and research activities with fundamental choices on what phenomena to focus on and how to link their coverage of Multinational strategies to relevant societal outcomes. The challenge for engaged IB scholarship, in essence, boils down to effectively linking macro/systemic problems to the future-resilient micro-strategies of (Multinational) companies, along three lines of argument.

First, acknowledge the systemic nature of the present crisis. The shape of recent events is closely related to the way globalization has been governed/organized since 1995. With the World Trade Organization (WTO) prioritizing 'free trade' over 'fair trade', globalization, on the one hand, has triggered remarkable progress in many areas of sustainable development (see e.g. Rosling et al., 2018). Witnessing the characteristics of the perfect storm, on the other hand, however, suggests that this version of globalization has reached a key turning point in which negative trends are starting to prevail over positive trends. The systemic nature of present global governance problems is increasingly acknowledged, though. Consecutive Global Risks Reports by the World Economic Forum (WEF), for instance, not only show an increasing number of risks, but note that these risks (ecological, social, financial, economic) are increasingly interconnected and can therefore not be addressed separately. The WEF (2023) qualifies this situation as a 'poly-crisis'—a cluster of related present and future global risks with compounding effects, such that the overall (negative) impact exceeds the sum of each part. A poly-crisis, if not treated properly, could have catastrophic consequences including armed conflict. The United Nations in its Global Sustainable Development Report (UN, 2023) uses another qualification—a 'cascade of crises'—as an explanation for the relative stagnation and even reversal of (largely positive) sustainable development trends since 2015.

Second, consider the extent to which Multinational Enterprises have contributed to these crises (the root causes). Sustained and accumulative crises are not only a sign of a fragile global economic system, consisting of increasingly fragile societies (signaling for instance a clash between democracy and autocracy), but also of prevalence of fragile business models (exploitative rather than innovative), increasingly fragile international value chains (favoring efficiency and speed over resilience), facilitated by increasingly fragile financial systems (favoring speculative over productive capital). At the level of corporations, a relatively new phenomenon appears as a sign of increased global fragility: 'zombie companies'—companies that will collapse at the slightest set-back.[1] According to research by the Bank of America, around one-fifth of US and EU companies can (already) be considered 'zombie' companies. The Bank for International Settlement (BIS) calculated that the number of zombie companies around the world increased from two percent by the end of the 1980s, to 12 percent of all companies in 2016 (Banerjee & Hofman, 2018). The aftermath of the Corona pandemic in many developed countries also revealed a growing uneasiness with the way companies have organized their work-related activities: [1] The "Great Resignation" relates to workers that after corona don't want to go back to their previous (underpaid) jobs; [2] 'Quiet Quitting' involves workers that keep working for a company but without commitment; [3] increased skill gaps lead to labor shortages for jobs in vital sectors such as care, education and other public utilities; [4] which is reinforced by the preferences of Gen-Z that looks for companies with a purpose rather than (only) profit orientation.

Thirdly, consider ways in which frontrunner Multinationals are trying to deal with these phenomena. A dominant trend in the media and parts of the scientific discourse is to concentrate thereby on reactive approaches that either feed into the idea that MNEs don't take up responsibility and are not willing/capable of addressing the root-causes of global problems (stressing Green-washing activities of particular Multinationals). This approach then stresses the importance of a moral/ethical leadership with companies and stricter regulation with governments. Another line of observations stresses that frontrunner companies are actually taking up responsibility, see major opportunities also in systems change, but face considerable implementation problems in volatile and complex world

[1] The OECD defines 'zombie firms' as those aged ten years or older, with an interest-coverage ratio (the ratio of operating income to interest expenses) of less than one, in each of the preceding three years (Andrews et al., 2017).

economy. International company coalitions like the World Business Council for Sustainable Development (WBSCD) introduced the need for a systems reboot (the big reset) by focusing on 'just and regenerative business' models. Frontrunner business leaders formulated statements like: "in a system that fails, I cannot do business" or "inaction is not an option".

Engaged IB scholarship takes these three phenomena seriously and tries to come up with balanced research and teaching approaches. Dealing with the poly-crisis in an integrated, positive and productive way for companies, thus, focuses on two sides of the equation: mitigating risks, while seizing opportunities on the basis of common (global) goals that address the root causes of the poly-crisis through innovative and scalable strategies.

1.1 Why (Still) the SDGs?

The most prolific and integrated effort to date on this combined challenge has arguably become the formulation of the Sustainable Development Goals (Van Tulder & Van Mil, 2023). Agreed upon in 2015, as a dashboard approach to sustainable development (with 17 goals, 169 interrelated targets and 230 indicators), the SDGs form an integrated effort to create a 'global agenda' through which positive change efforts can be coordinated and navigated and in which the private sector should play a major role—either alone or in partnerships. From their inception, the SDGs were supported by all countries, major frontrunner companies, NGOs and scientific institutes as a common positive change agenda, based on a (hybrid) governance logic, supported by common efforts to accumulate relevant statistics to keep track of progress or regress and identify ways to move beyond global crises like COVID-19 (Van Zanten & Van Tulder, 2020) and fill the global governance gap with principles-based initiatives (Young, 2017).

Notwithstanding serious set-backs over the 2019–2022 period, due in particular to the COVID-19 pandemic and the Ukraine war, the SDG agenda and frame can still be considered a success in mobilizing actors around the world. There are four reasons for this positive assessment (cf. Van Tulder, 2024; Van Tulder & van Mil, 2023 in Goetze (ed)):

1. Governments have started to develop and document national SDG policies (through Voluntary National Reports). This makes policies and initiatives comparable and thus risk-responsibility assessment feasible for MNEs.
2. International organizations have aligned their own initiatives on the basis of the SDG frameworks, such as: UNCTAD (Investment Policy Framework) or the European Union (EU Corporate Social Reporting Directive).
3. Coordinated efforts of 'custodian agencies' like the World Bank, IMF, OECD or IOM created increased harmonization and elaboration of relevant data necessary to support a dashboard approach that covers many relevant dimensions of sustainable development. The SDG approach has increased the 'collective intelligence' of the world to deal with complex sustainability issues. Over the 2015–2022 period the coverage of Tier 1 indicators (based on established methodology and regularly updated data) increased from 50 to 56 percent, while Tier 3 data (for which no internationally established methodology or standard was available) decreased from 11 to 2 percent.
4. The number of frontrunner companies (mostly MNEs) that used the SDG agenda to upgrade their sustainability strategies—prioritizing SDGs and establishing partnerships with societal actors—has increased over the years.

The role of the SDGs as strategic 'navigating' instrument for companies has seriously improved, not in the least because of the wealth of platforms that developed like SDG Dashboards, SDG Financing Lab or SDG knowledge platforms. Important initiatives that have converged around the SDG lens have materialized in 'value accounting', reporting standards and dedicated networks that specified SDG-related principles such as the 'international capital market association bond principles' or the 'CFO Principles on Integrated SDG Investment and Finance'. The opportunities and relevance for engaged IB scholarship to contribute to the SDG agenda have consequently seriously increased. The complexity of the perfect storm and the dashboard approach of the SDGs presents an opportunity as well as a challenge for IB scholars. Taking all possible goals, targets, indicators and their thousands of potential cross-linkages into account, what to prioritize? This paper argues in favor of prioritizing SDG8 (decent work and economic growth) for engaged IB research and teaching.

2 Dealing with Complexity: Why SDG8?

The experts consulted by the WEF (2023) in its annual Global Risks Perception Survey (GRPS) distinguish between future and immediate risks. Climate-related risks are considered the biggest *future* threat facing the world. The 'cost-of-living' crisis, however, is considered the most *immediate* and severe global risk. This finding resonates one of the fundamental trade-offs that exist in sustainable development: people that don't earn an income that covers for the cost-of-living today will not be supportive for addressing climate change. The relationship between present and future risks gets further mediated by the pace, nature and shape of (endogenous) 'economic growth' in countries: (1) a decent cost-of-living cannot be achieved without sufficient and sustainable economic growth, (2) but economic growth that is based upon unsustainable practices leads to increased social unrest and ultimately also debilitates effective approaches to climate problems. The latter argument also refers to the concept of 'climate justice' which connects the climate crisis to the social and racial issues in which it is deeply entangled and without which climate change cannot be resolved.

2.1 Cost-of-Living and Economic Growth

Support for the first relationship comes from various sources. Historical macro-economic research shows that sustainable economic progress can only be achieved if countries adopt *inclusive* growth policies and inclusive development strategies. Inequalities represent economic power imbalances that not only undermine economic performance, but also run the risk of becoming politically entrenched. Inequality and exclusion are, therefore, indicators of impending social unrest, crumbling social cohesion and instability. A study by the International Monetary Fund (Dabla-Norris et al., 2015) of 159 economies for the 1980–2012 period found three trends that are pivotal in this light: (1) growing income inequality had a *negative* effect on economic growth; (2) increasing the income share of the poor and middle class had actually increased economic growth; and (3) a rising income share of the top 20 percent resulted in lower growth. In other words, when the rich get richer, the poor do not automatically profit. Wealth does not trickle down. Inclusiveness, reducing income inequality and the provision of a minimum threshold of a 'living income' for all are necessary preconditions for sustained progress. They provide the crucial conditions for enhancing human capabilities and agency—through education, health, living standards, dignity and acknowledgment of human rights—that are vital drivers for enhancing productivity and prosperity, but also increase the awareness and capabilities to address ecological issues and ultimately climate change.

Already Adam Smith, in his 'wealth of nations' (1776; Book I, chapter 8) acknowledged the relevance of rising real wages that can lead to the "improvement in the circumstances of the lower ranks of people" and are therefore an advantage to society. Smith advocated that labor should receive an equitable share of what labor produces. For Smith, this equitable share amounted to more than subsistence. He reasoned that as wages [and rents related to land] rise, as a result of higher productivity, societal growth will occur, thus increasing the quality of life for the greater part of its members. The French 'regulation school' in this context points to the constituting parts of *exploitative* business models and *accumulation regimes* (based on low wages and what would now be called a 'race to the bottom') that trigger 'vicious growth cycles' versus the creation of explorative business models (based on higher wages as in Fordism aimed at a 'race to the top') that triggers "virtuous growth cycles" (Ruigrok & Van Tulder, 1995, pp. 17ff.). Piketty (2014) adds longitudinal data to this observation from which it becomes clear that the rising inequality of capital ownership and labor income creates 'grand dynamics' that can be considered negative for the prospects of sustainable development and growth.

2.2 Sustainable Economic Growth Requires a Dashboard Approach

Support for the second relationship comes from a variety of complementary sources, that have increasingly criticized the practice of considering 'Gross Domestic Product (GDP) growth' as a single-indicator measure of prosperity and well-being. Raworth (2017, p. 26) summarizes this argument as follows: "the conventional economic paradigm, with a fixed focus on GDP-growth as the single leading measure of societal success, has led to an untenable yet dominant steering principle in which economies have to grow, whether or not they make us thrive". What we need instead, Raworth argues, are "economies that make us thrive, whether or not they grow" (ibid., p. 26). By introducing 17 goals, 169 targets and 230 indicators, the SDGs present a 'dashboard' approach to measuring 'progress' that help in adopting the "decoupling principle": decouple growth from environmental impact, including through circularity, dematerialization and the re-use of (natural) resources. For a sustainable future, goals of human progress and a healthy environment need to be *re*coupled. The dashboard approach of the SDGs can be analyzed as a long-overdue paradigm break with previous economic thinking that focused on a narrow conceptualization of development.[2] A dashboard approach, on the other hand, allows for a variety of indicators to assess progress, monitor developments and identify strengths, weaknesses and priorities for action. As a dashboard is composed of a set of separate relevant indicators, it provides a more diversified picture of parallel developments and, therefore, richer information for policymakers to steer and adjust. The approach reckons that not all dimensions of an issue are (yet) entirely known and that the exact interplay between

[2] Van Tulder and Van Mil (2023) provide a historical overview of the efforts of scholars to broaden national accounts in which 'well-being' and 'welfare growth' metrics rather than economic growth alone are covered as measure of progress/development.

dimensions may also be unclear—for instance, when taking different contextual circumstances into account—and need to be studied further. But a dashboard approach is also susceptible to compromise and depends on the way new insights can be used for learning and further upgrading of targets and indicators. As noted by MacFeely (2019, p. 8): "the composition of this dashboard will effectively determine whether the 2030 Agenda adopts an orthodox or heterodox view of the global economy."

2.3 Limitations of SDG8

Within the SDG framework, arguably SDG8 ('Decent work and economic growth') provides the most relevant and explicit intervention angle for the ambition to link decent (real) income and virtuous economic growth cycles. The official demarcation of SDG8 reads as follows: "promote sustained inclusive and sustainable economic growth, full and productive employment and decent work for all." SDG8 suggests a direct relationship between entrepreneurship and job creation "[to achieve] full and productive employment and decent work for all women and men by 2030." The UN thereby adopted the 'decent work agenda' of the International Labour Organization (ILO) and made explicit links to this agenda in other development targets such as reducing poverty (SDG1) and increasing access to education (SDG4).

Unfortunately, in particular for SDG8, the negotiators of the SDG-agenda compromised on the identification of relevant data and the way they could be gathered. Applying the SDG8 agenda as framework for IB scholarship, therefore, comes with two research and measurement challenges:

- ***Covering 'Relevant' Economic Growth.*** Two targets introduced in SDG8 to cover for relevant economic growth are Targets 8.1 ("sustain per capita economic growth in accordance with national circumstances and, in particular, at least 7 per cent gross domestic product growth per annum in the least developed countries") and 8.2 ("achieve higher levels of economic productivity through diversification, technological upgrading and innovation, including through a focus on high-value added and labor-intensive sectors"). In both cases the UN uses annual growth rate of "real GDP" either per capita or per employed person as sole (Tier I) metrics for progress. SDG8 has become one of the most popular SDGs primarily because of its obvious reference to 'economic growth' (much less to decent work). UN Global Compact (2022) identified this mechanism as 'cherry picking' that can lead to a superficial use of the full potential of the SDG agenda. GDP growth does not necessarily measure 'relevant (sustainable) economic growth'. This flaw in the specific elaboration of SDG8 presents considerable measurement challenges for IB scholars. It has also consequences for the way scholars engage in the debate around 'de-growth'. The essence of that debate is not necessarily that all countries (and certainly not developing countries) should reduce consumption and production, but that GDP should be replaced with social and environmental well-being as the indicator of prosperity. Fortunately, the SDG agenda recognizes important negative/positive spill-over effects that link SDG8 with other SDGs. This so-called 'nexus' effect enables a broader definition of economic growth—which could be defined as '*relevant/inclusive* economic growth'. *The first challenge for engaged IB scholarship therefore concerns how to deal with the nexus between SDG8 and other SDGs at the level of individual companies.*

- ***Covering 'Decent Work'***. The SDG agenda contained another compromise in its search for relevant metrics by the way it defined 'decent work'. The ILO serves as the custodian agency for these metrics, but uses a rather vague definition of decent work as 'employment' that "respects the fundamental rights of the human person as well as the rights of works in terms of conditions of work safety and remuneration... Respect for the physical and mental integrity of the workers in the exercise of his/her employment." Consequently, in the negotiations on measuring decent work (in particular related to SDGs 8.3.1 and 8.5.1), it was decided to use relatively vague descriptions for each of these indicators at a relatively low level of quality and comparability (Tier II). Over the 2015–2023 period, the quality of other metrics in the SDG agenda was increased (see above), but not for decent work, which remained a Tier II indicator. Saner and Yiu

(2019) criticize the chosen compromise. They note that solid metrics on 'minimum wage' (MW) and 'living wage' (LW) had already been developed 100 years ago as part of the ILO mandate. But there is no mention of minimum wage nor of living wage as relevant metrics in the SDG framework, which would have made it much easier for scholars to cover for progress in this vital area. This circumstance is the more relevant because, according to Wage Indicator Foundation (2023) estimates, in particular, 'living wage' more than 'minimum wage' presents an important condition under which economic development can be triggered. *The 'living wage' level* reflects the minimum income, at the local living standard, needed for an individual and her/his family to meet basic needs. A living wage reckons with the costs of food, water, housing, transport, education, health care, phone costs, clothing, and other essential needs. As such, it indicates that workers earning above this income level are out of absolute poverty and can afford a modest yet decent life in dignity. Many countries take the standpoint that the minimum wage should be sufficient for a "decent income". However, for many countries the Minimum Wage and Living Wage reveal large disparities. In 2022, only 17 countries out of a total of 151 countries registered a monthly Nationally Applicable Minimum Wage higher than the monthly Living Wage.[3] Large discrepancies also appear between different regions in the same country. For 2021, across high-income countries the Minimum Wages are on average 122 percent of the Living Wage, whereas across low-income countries the Minimum Wages only represent 28 percent of the Living Wage. Living wage consequently presents a perfect metric for Multinational Enterprises to assess the extent to which they contribute to vicious or virtuous growth regimes in the countries where are active or from where they source. *The second challenge for engaged IB scholarship therefore concerns dealing with the coverage of*

[3] According to Wage Indicator Foundation data, these countries are: Andorra, Australia, Austria, Belgium, Canada, France, Germany, Hungary, Luxembourg, Netherlands, New Zealand, Poland, South Korea, Spain, Switzerland, Taiwan, United Kingdom. High Income countries like the United States (with minimum wage at 59 percent of living wage) trail behind. The same applies a fortiori for most developing/low-income countries.

living wage (Tier 1) across countries and the how Multinational organization can actively overcome the gap between minimum wage and living wage within their own operations (so-called Scope 1 activities), in their value chains (Scope 2) and towards local (host) communities (Scope 3). The latter ambition also requires a better understanding of the way 'living wage' creates positive nexus effects to other SDGs.

3 Are We on Course? Challenges for IB Scholars

There are three sides to the main question of this paper: are we on track for SDG8; have SDG-related questions been sufficiently covered by IB research and what challenges and opportunities remain for engaged IB scholarship on SDG8?

3.1 We Are Not on Track

Information drawn from database of the UN (2023)[4] on SDG8 provides a sobering picture of the state of the world. COVID-19 has had major negative impact on a number of key indicators that all seem to indicate at an increasingly 'fragile' global system in which the link between 'decent work' and 'economic growth' (as defined by the UN) has been weakened:

- "After the worst economic crisis in decades due to COVID-19, the global economy remains fragile and recovery uneven. Globally, real gross domestic product (GDP) per capita for LDCs was projected to rise by 4.0 per cent in 2022, and 5.7 per cent in 2023, which is still well below the 7 per cent target envisioned in the 2030 Agenda for Sustainable Development."

---

[4] *Source* Progress Towards Sustainable Development Goals—Report of the Secretary General (https://documents-dds-ny.un.org/doc/UNDOC/GEN/N22/335/13/PDF/N2233513.pdf?OpenElement).

- "The impact of COVID-19 has resulted in unprecedented and volatile shifts in global labor productivity. Lower-productivity firms and sectors and lower-paid workers were disproportionately affected by the pandemic, while high-productivity enterprises and high earners saw far less damage. Many small firms are disadvantaged, with limited capacity to remain viable over an extended period."
- "The global unemployment rate is projected to remain above its 2019 level of 5.4 per cent, at least until 2023. The groups that were disproportionately impacted since the onset of the pandemic—women, youth and persons with disabilities—are having the hardest time recovering."
- "In 2019, 2 billion people worldwide (60 per cent of global employment) worked in the informal sector…. "Rather than become unemployed or shift to informal jobs, as in previous crises, laid-off employees and self-employed workers alike [during COVID-19] left the labour force. A disproportionate impact on informal workers was reflected in a decline in the informal employment rate in some countries at the height of the crisis, which has left informal workers and their families in a highly precarious position, exposed to sudden income losses and heightened risks of falling into poverty."
- "Worldwide, 160 million children (63 million girls and 97 million boys) were (still) engaged in child labour at the beginning of 2020. This is an increase of 8.4 million children since 2016, translating to almost 1 out of 10 children engaged in child labour worldwide."
- "The proportion of the world's youth *not* engaged in either education, employment or training (NEET) increased […] to 23.3 per cent in 2020. The development and implementation of national youth employment strategies are increasing across most regions. Out of 81 countries reporting in 2021, more than half have operationalized such strategies."

Faced with these (and related statistics on most SDGs), the conclusion of Secretary General Antonio Guterres was twofold: in 2019 he stated "We are not on track" to be followed in 2022 by "Rescuing globalization, necessitates rescuing the SDGs".

3.2 IB SDG Scholarship Is Increasing, But Remains Relatively Fragmented

Even recognizing that there are considerable flaws in the SDG framework, these findings—the result of coordinated data gathering by a large number of platforms and initiatives—reiterate the relevance of the SDG Agenda as the most relevant benchmark of progress in sustainable development. In a way it is the only framework the world has (Van Tulder & Van Mil, 2023). More specifically, the framework creates 'SDG logics' (Van Zanten & Van Tulder, 2020) that help (Multinational) enterprises to align their individual strategies with that of the global community and invest in optimizing positive change (stimulating a race to the top), rather than mitigating negative change (or limiting a 'race to the bottom'). Has IB scholarship contributed to the general plea of Guterres? A recent systematic literature review on the way the SDGs have been integrated in extant IB and management research makes the following observations (Almeida et al., 2023):

- The SDGs with their emphasis on private sector engagement have had a positive effect on the number and quality of IB related studies. The Millennium Development Goals (the predecessor of the SDGs) largely focused on public interventions and consequently hardly triggered any relevant IB research.
- Extant research trails behind practice. The potential of the IB research and business scholarship, to unlock the potential of MNEs as powerful players to implement the transformational potential of the SDGs, has yet to be realized.
- Research is also concentrated in a relatively small number of journals, concentrated in special issues and with a limited (but growing) number of scholars.
- The most important barriers for implementing the SDGs as identified by extant research are: (1) implementation barriers and the test of practical steps to implement SDGs, (2) measuring and reporting challenges; (3) SDG complexity and difficulty in understanding their nexus approach; (4) activate and develop partnerships.

The way forward for the IB profession is to further gain insights into the conditions under which MNEs can adopt relevant SDGs, make them actionable for functional areas of management, implement them into their operations (in various country constellations) and use them as leverage for sophisticated cross-sectoral partnership strategies. A number of recent special issues have brought together first efforts to solicit IB, Ethical and strategic coverage of the SDGs (cf. Nonet et al., 2022; Sinkovics et al., 2022; Van Tulder et al., 2021, 2023). The book 'Principles of Sustainable Business' integrates all relevant areas of international management and develops actionable frames and tools to navigate further progress in research and management of the SDGs (Van Tulder & Van Mil, 2023).

3.3 What Challenges to Focus on for SDG8?

Developing further insights on the conditions under which MNEs can adopt SDG8-related strategies will arguably provide one of the most relevant points of entry to interrogate the complex relationship between international business (IB) and society. The number of dedicated studies on SDG8 as yet remains rather limited. A number of more general/framing exercises have been introduced in which SDG8 has been included (cf. e.g. the Matrix introduced by Sinkovics et al., 2021, or the list of actionable targets as introduced by Van Zanten & Van Tulder, 2018). IB-relevant studies that focused on global value chains and the SDGs including SDG8 adopted a narrow focus on SDG8 as a means to 'increase wealth' (cf. Montiel et al., 2021). Somewhat broader studies on global value chains combine a focus on SDG8 and SDG13 as part of 'just transitions' (cf. Andrews et al., 2023). Other studies have tried to take a more regional approach by exploring the link between company strategies and city performance in attaining SDG8-12—and thus focus primarily on economic nexus effects (Yang Gao et al., 2023). Witnessing the relatively slow progress in engaged IB scholarship on SDG8, it can be argued, that progress in IB scholarship on a key mechanism of the SDG agenda depends on further development and testing of the two bottlenecks in the SDG8 design (a) how to broaden 'economic growth' to ‘relevant/inclusive economic growth’ for sustainable development; (b) how to operationalize and measure decent work as ‘living wage’ and assess related nexus effects.

4 Covering Relevant/Inclusive Economic Growth: Nexus Effects at Goal Level

The first challenge for engaged IB scholarship concerns dealing with the nexus between SDG8 and other SDGs at the level of individual companies. From a research perspective this particular nexus effect can be based upon two mechanisms:

- As embedded in the design of the SDG agenda (Fig. 1a) which shows how ‘macro-economic’ nexus effects can be measured and leveraged. The original SDG design—as covered by ECOSOC in 2016—distinguishes between explicit and substantive SDG interactions. Explicit links are those connections that follow directly from how targets have been formulated within the SDG framework (‘linkage by design’); substantive links are those connections that can be expected to generate interaction effects. The explicit links in the SDG dashboard reveal the way the SDGs have adopted a relatively broad definition of economic growth (addressing poverty, education, gender and infrastructure, but also living below water and peace).
- A separate research agenda on sustained nexus effects has also been proposed to cover for other types of linkages that are embedded in the ‘governance logic’ that the SDG agenda provides (Van Zanten & Van Tulder, 2020) or linked to way the SDG agenda is linked to the strategies of companies (Van Zanten & Van Tulder, 2021a, 2021b). Four types of economic activities have been distinguished that companies might undertake with different bearing on the SDGs and thus on relevant economic growth: activities that are core to the SDG

a b

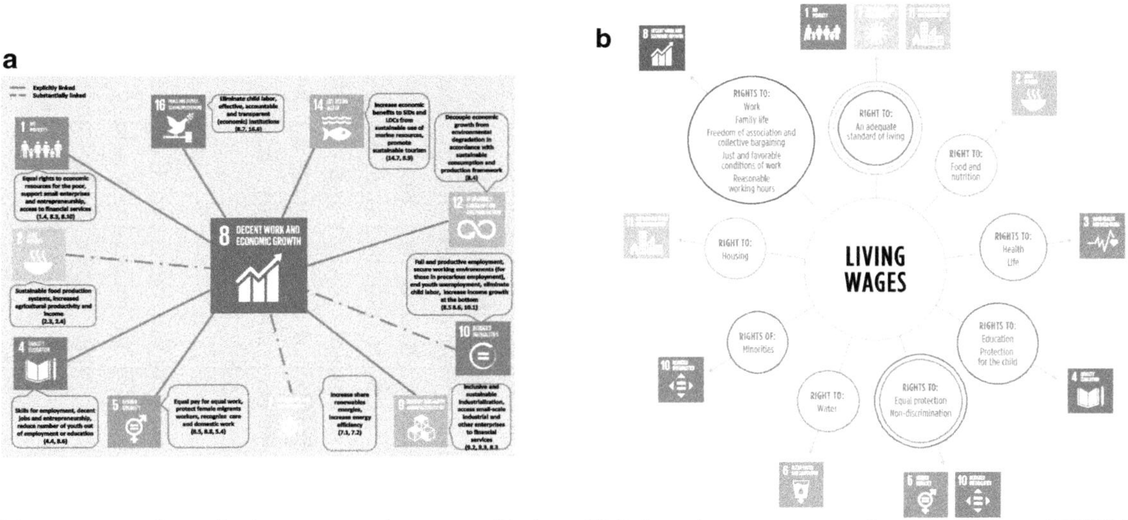

Fig. 1 Macro-economic and micro-economic nexus effects. **a** SDG 8 and macro-economic nexus (*Source* ECOSOC, 2016). **b** Living wage and micro-economic nexus (*Source* Shift & WBCSD, 2018)

agenda, mixed activities, opposed activities and peripheral activities.[5] The more companies can link SDG8 to other SDGs (through either substantive or explicit nexus linkages) and integrate that in their core activities, the more companies can claim to aim at a positive impact on a broad interpretation of 'sustainable development'.

5 Covering Living Wage as Litmus Test for Progress on SDG8 and Sustainable Development

The second challenge for engaged IB scholarship concerns dealing with the coverage of living wage (Tier 1) across countries in which Multinational organization operate and the nexus with other SDG at the level of individual companies.

Providing people with decent working conditions and paying them a living wage underpins many of the wider (nexus) ambitions represented by the SDGs, including good health and well-being, quality education and gender equality. *The 'living wage' level* reflects the minimum income, at the local living standard, needed for an individual and her/his family to meet basic needs. A living wage reckons with the costs of food, water, housing, transport, education, health care, phone costs, clothing and other essential needs. As such, it indicates that workers earning above this income level are out of absolute poverty and can afford a modest yet decent life in dignity. A number of developments can help IB scholars to get engaged in either more general/comparative studies or more specific (management-oriented) research.

- Reporting initiatives such as the European Corporate Sustainability Reporting Directive (CSRD) are increasingly asking for relevant data on the provision of living wage within the company (Scope 1) and along the value chain (Scopes 2 and 3). This has prompted value

[5] On the website of the book 'Principles of Sustainable Business', the nexus project is further elaborated: https://www.principlesofsustainablebusiness.nl/wp-content/uploads/2021/05/nexus.pdf.

accounting networks and the Capitals coalition—to create standardized frameworks to understand, measure and valuate natural, social and human capital in order to inform actionable and holistic (corporate) decisions "that create value for nature, people and society alongside businesses and the economy." 'Accounting for a Living Wage' is the Coalition's next step in fueling the practice of 'value accounting'. A number of coalitions are formed at the moment to create and continuously update relevant data on a global scale on living wage measures. The most advanced database—that also delivers the data to an increasing number of frontrunner companies and multilateral organization—is the Wage Indicator Foundation (WIF; Guzi et al., 2023). Anno 2023, the Foundation measures Living Wage for around 2500 regions in the world, which can help MNEs adopt much more sophisticated accounting/reporting practices for their living wage strategies.[6] The gathering of basic data on living wage further helps platforms like UN Global Compact to make action on living wage a priority (UNGC, 2023).

- In the area of HRM and personal management, the better performance of purpose-driven companies that take societal issues and crises seriously has been documented extensively (cf. Van Tulder & Van Mil, 2023). Increasingly an SDG-nexus approach through 'human rights' connections has been documented as particularly effective. In 2018, Shift—the leading center of expertise on the UN Guiding Principles on Business and Human Rights (UNGPs)—and the World Business Council for Sustainable Development (WBSCD) published a compendium on the potential of companies to contribute to the SDG-agenda by taking a people-centered, human rights-based approach as part of a 'holistic SDG strategy'. The principal argument: "*Business respect for human rights is more than a requirement to 'do no harm'. By proactively implementing the key tenets of the UNGPs companies have the potential to break down significant barriers to development and positively impact the lives of millions of the most vulnerable individuals in*

[6] Regional findings for July 2023 by WIF for instance indicate (1) that in only 12 countries in the world is the Minimum Wage (MW) in all regions higher than the Living Wage LW); (2) in 24 countries at least one region has defined a MW that is higher then LW; (3) in 228 (out of 2327 regions) MW is higher than LW. See: https://wageindicator.org/salary/living-wage.

society" (2018, p. 4). Living wage (as well as gender equality) will not only positively impact people's lives and contribute to the 'People' part of the SDGs (Fig. 1b), but also benefit HRM purposes through "improved recruitment and retention of staff; increased productivity and business continuity; a more secure and enhanced reputation; and the opportunity to become an investment, a business partner and a brand of choice" (Shift & WBCSD, 2018, p. 7).

Taking these two dimensions into account, it should become clear that Living Wage presents an increasingly relevant *litmus test* for measuring progress in the way Multinational Enterprises contribute to the whole SDG agenda: it can be measured across countries and can become a core intervention point for Multinationals through which they can show how they can contribute to sustainable development and virtuous growth cycles, through the active management of positive nexus effects linked to SDG8 and living wage.

References

Abord-Hugon Nonet, G., Goesling, T., Van Tulder, R., & Bryson, J. (2022). Multi-stakeholder engagement for the sustainable development goals: Strategic and organizational challenges for principles-based approaches. *Journal of Business Ethics, 180*, 945–957.

Andrews, D., McGowan, M., & Millot, V. (2017, December). *Confronting the Zombies: Policies for productivity revival* [OECD Economic Policy Papers, No. 21].

Andrews, K., Sinkovics, N., & Sinkovics, R. (2023). Tensions on the road toward just transitions in the Latin American Coffee Value chain. In *International business and sustainable development goals progress in international business research* (Vol. 17, pp. 309–323). Emerald Publishing Limited.

Banerjee, R., & Hofman, B. (2018, September). The rise of zombie firms: Causes and consequences. *BIS Quarterly Review*, pp. 67–78.

Dabla-Norris, E., Kochhar, K., Suphaphiphat, N., Ricka, F., & Tsounta, E. (2015, June 15). *Causes and consequences of income inequality: A global perspective*. IMF Staff Discussion Note, Strategy, Policy, and Review Department, SDN/15/13.

De Almeida, F. P., van Tulder, R., & Rodrigues, S. B. (2023). Walking the talk: Making the SDGs core business—An integrated framework. In R. van Tulder, E. Giuliani, & I. Álvarez (Eds.), *International business and sustainable development goals* (Progress in international business research, Vol. 17, pp. 49–82). Emerald Publishing Limited.

ESOSOC. (2016). *A nexus approach for the SDGs. Interlinkages between the goals and targets*. https://www.un.org/ecosoc/sites/www.un.org.ecosoc/files/files/en/2016doc/interlinkages-sdgs.pdf

Gao, Y., Turkina, E., & Van Assche, A. (2023). The nexus between cultural and creative sectors and the sustainable development goals—A network perspective. In *International business and sustainable development goals: Progress in international business research* (Vol. 17, pp. 151–176). Emerald Publishing Limited. https://doi.org/10.1108/S1745-886220230000017009

Guzi, M., Amanquarnor, N. A., Ceccon, D., Kahanec, M., Osse, P., & Tijdens, K. G. (2023). *Living wages worldwide, update February 2023*. Wage Indicator Foundation.

MacFeely, S. (2019, June). *The political economy of measuring the sustainable development goals* [UNCTAD Research Paper No. 32, UNCTAD/SER.RP/2019/4].

Montiel, I., Cuervo-Cazurra, A., Park, J., Antolín-López, R., & Husted, B. W. (2021). Implementing the United Nations' sustainable development goals in international business. *Journal of International Business Studies, 52*, 999–1030.

Piketty, T. (2014). *Capital in the twenty-first century*. Belknap Press of Harvard University

Raworth, K. (2017). *Doughnut economics. Seven ways to think like a 21st-century economist*. Cornerstone.

Rosling, H., with Rosling, O., & Ronnlund, R. (2018) *Factfulness: Ten reasons we're wrong about the world—And why things are better than you think*. Flatiron Books.

Ruigrok, W., & Van Tulder, R. (1995). *The logic of international restructuring*. Routledge.

Saner, R., & Yiu, L. (2019). Living wage and sustainable development goal #8. In *Paper for the 6th Conference of the Regulating for Decent Work Network*. ILO.

Shift & WBCSD. (2018). *The Human Rights Opportunity. 15 real-life cases of how business is contributing to the Sustainable Development Goals by putting people first*. Shift.
Sinkovics, N., Sinkovics, R. R., & Archie-Acheampong, J. (2021). The business responsibility matrix: A diagnostic tool to aid the design of better interventions for achieving the SDGs. *Multinational Business Review, 29*(1), 1–20.
Sinkovics, N., Vieira, L. M., & van Tulder, R. (2022). Working toward the sustainable development goals in earnest—Critical international business perspectives on designing and implementing better interventions. *Critical Perspectives on International Business, 18*(4), 445–456.
Smith, A. (1776). *The wealth of nations*. W. Strahan and T. Cadell.
United Nations. (2023). *Global sustainable development report*. UN.
United Nations Global Compact. (2023). *Moving living wage forward faster*. Action Guide. UN.
Van Tulder, R. (2024). The way forward: Mapping the governance logic of international CSR pathways. In A. Goerzen (Ed.), *Research handbook on international corporate social responsibility* (pp. 480–502). Edward Elgar Publishing.
Van Tulder, R., Giuliani, E., & Alvares, I. (Eds.). (2023). *International business and the sustainable development goals*. Progress in International Business Research (Vol. 17). Emerald.
Van Tulder, R., Rodrigues, S. B., Mirza, H., & Sexsmith, K. (2021). The UN's sustainable development goals: Can multinational enterprises lead the decade of action? *Journal of International Business Policy, 4*, 1–21.
Van Tulder, R., & Van Mil, E. (2023). *Principles of sustainable business: Frameworks for corporate action on the SDGs*. Routledge.
Van Zanten, J., & Van Tulder, R. (2021a). Analyzing companies' interactions with the SDGs through network analysis: Four corporate sustainability imperatives. *Business Strategy and the Environment, 30*(5), 2396–2420.
Van Zanten, J. A., & Van Tulder, R. (2021b). Improving companies' impacts on sustainable development: A nexus approach to the SDGs. *Business Strategy and the Environment, 30*(8), 3703–3720.
Van Zanten, J., & Van Tulder, R. (2020). Beyond COVID-19: Applying "SDG logics" for resilient transformations. *Journal of International Business Policy, 3*(4), 451–464.
Van Zanten, J., & Van Tulder, R. (2018). Multinational enterprises and the sustainable development goals: An institutional approach to corporate engagement. *Journal of International Business Policy, 1*, 208–233.

World Economic Forum (WEF). (2023). *Global risks reports 2023*. WEF.

Young, O. R. (2017). Conceptualization: Goal setting as a strategy for earth system governance. In N. Kanie & F. Biermann (Eds.), *Governing through goals: Sustainable development goals as governance innovation* (pp. 31–52). The MIT Press.

Part II

Research Perspectives on SDG 8

3

Labour Standards Provisions in International Trade Policy: An International Business Perspective

Asmund Rygh

1 Introduction

Decent Work, part of Sustainable Development Goal (SDG) 8, remains a daunting challenge for international business (IB), with persistent issues such as forced labour, child labour and unsafe working conditions (Holzberg, 2020). The lack of an effective multilateral governance framework for labour standards and the huge variation in labour standards worldwide has led to concerns that weak labour regulation could be used to gain competitive advantage in international trade and investment (Donaghey et al., 2014). Proposals to establish labour standards provisions within World Trade Organisation (WTO) agreements through a so-called *social clause* that would link market access to the respect of

A. Rygh (✉)
Alliance Manchester Business School, University of Manchester, Manchester, UK
e-mail: asmund.rygh@manchester.ac.uk

N. Sinkovics et al. (eds.), *International Business and SDG 8*, The Academy of International Business, https://doi.org/10.1007/978-3-031-46802-5_3

labour standards have so far failed, largely due to opposition from developing countries fearing it would remove their comparative advantage in low-cost production (Sanyal, 2001).

One response to the labour governance gap has been private regulation by multinational enterprises (MNEs) through codes of conduct and monitoring of working conditions in supplier factories abroad (Donaghey et al., 2014; Locke, 2013). IB scholars have also contributed to our understanding of such private initiatives and their strengths and limitations (Holzberg, 2020; Kolk & Van Tulder, 2004, 2005; Narula, 2019; Scherer & Smid, 2000; Sinkovics et al., 2016; Van Assche & Narula, 2023; Van Tulder & Kolk, 2001). In contrast, so far IB research has paid little attention to the fact that while there is no multilateral framework for labour standards, social clauses are included in numerous bilateral and regional agreements, as well as in unilateral trade preference schemes (Campling et al., 2016; Cuyvers & De Meyer, 2012; Postnikov & Bastiaens, 2014). Despite the focus on national institutions in IB research (Peng et al., 2008), the implications of this specific *supranational institution* (Hartmann et al., 2022) for MNEs' strategies remain largely unknown. Similarly, while IB policy and global value chain (GVC) scholars have built up a good understanding of various roles that state policy can play for suppliers' upgrading in GVCs, including social upgrading related to labour standards (De Marchi & Alford, 2022; Pietrobelli et al., 2021), this literature has also largely overlooked bilateral and regional regulation of labour standards through FTAs.

The present chapter proposes that social clauses in bilateral, regional and unilateral trade policy represent a highly relevant topic for IB research, and that the IB discipline is uniquely positioned to contribute to our understanding of such social clauses. IB's deep understanding of national institutions can be extended to understand not only the effect of this supranational labour institution on MNE strategies, but also how MNEs may influence labour provisions in trade agreements (Hartmann et al., 2022). In turn, this can help understand labour standards outcomes from social clauses, addressing the somewhat mixed findings in existing literature (Raess, 2022). The current GVC agenda in IB, already providing useful insights on the role of policy, provides a strong basis for understanding the impact of social clauses. Finally, IB studies on private regulation and how such initiatives interact with national regulation can provide useful policy implications for the implementation of labour provisions.

Section 2 briefly reviews labour standards, the social clause proposal in WTO and current trends with social clauses in bilateral or regional trade agreements. Section 3 presents some relevant theory and empirical evidence on social clauses. Section 4 outlines areas where IB research could particularly contribute to the social clause debate. Brief concluding remarks are offered in Sect. 5.

2 Social Clauses and Labour Standards in International Trade

Labour standards come in different categories (Brown & Stern, 2008). Some standards relate to civil and human rights, including prohibitions of forced labour and (some forms of) child labour; non-discrimination based on characteristics such as gender, race or religion; and industrial relations standards such as freedom of association, collective bargaining and the right to strike. Outcome standards include (minimum) wages, working hours, voluntary and paid overtime, leave and protection against dismissal. Social protection standards include provisions for old age pensions, unemployment, and sickness and disability. Another distinction is often made between enabling rights and outcomes. For instance, collective bargaining rights can allow workers to improve outcomes such as wages. Four "core" labour standards outlined in ILO's 1998 Declaration on Fundamental Principles and Rights at Work (McCrudden & Davies, 2000) play a particularly prominent role, being cited in some bilateral and regional free trade agreements, company codes of conduct (Hassel, 2008) and multilateral initiatives such as OECD's Guidelines for MNEs and the UN Global Compact (Doumbia-Henry & Gravel, 2006):

1. Freedom of association and effective recognition of the right to collective bargaining;
2. Elimination of all forms of forced or compulsory labour;

3. Effective abolition of child labour;
4. Elimination of discrimination with respect to employment and occupation.

Labour standards could affect international business if such standards tend to increase firms' costs and reduce competitiveness. The idea that labour standards matter for trade has a long history, raised among others by English industrialists in the nineteenth century and forming part of the motivation for creating the International Labour Organisation (ILO) as part of the League of Nations in 1919, now part of the United Nations (McCrudden & Davies, 2000). The ILO, a tripartite organisation involving governments, business associations and trade unions, establishes labour standards through recommendations (providing guidance to member states) as well as "conventions" (that have the status of treaties and that in principle are binding on the member states) (Block et al., 2001). Although a key source of norms and approaches related to labour standards, ILO's power is limited, as ratification of conventions is voluntary, there are no sanctions for countries that are not complying, and there is significant flexibility in the implementation of conventions (Block et al., 2001).

This has led some actors to attempt to use international trade institutions such as the General Agreement on Trade and Tariffs (GATT) and the later WTO to promote global labour standards, building on these organisations' ability to enforce trade rules through sanctions. The original proposal for a social clause in WTO agreements envisaged that countries not respecting labour standards would be subject to fines or trade sanctions similar to those imposed following transgressions of other WTO rules. Unsurprisingly, the proposal met with opposition not only from MNEs and import-oriented companies, but also from developing countries who saw it as covert protectionism aiming to weaken their competitive advantage in low-cost production (Sanyal, 2001). Ultimately, WTO's 1996 Singapore Declaration strongly rejected the social clause proposal and assigned ILO as the competent organisation to deal with labour matters, without, however, granting ILO additional powers of enforcement.

The failure to establish a multilateral enforceable framework for labour standards has instead led to a diverse patchwork of labour provisions and social clauses in regional and bilateral trade free trade agreements (FTAs) and unilateral trade preference schemes (Postnikov & Bastiaens, 2014; Raess, 2022; Raess & Sari, 2018). A prominent early example was the 1994 regional North American Free Trade Agreement (NAFTA) between Canada, the US and Mexico, which included a side-agreement on labour (Siroen, 2013). Subsequently, various forms of labour provisions have been included in numerous bilateral and regional FTAs. According to Araujo (2018, p. 233), "[t]he requirement to adopt minimum labour standards is now standard practice in free trade agreements (FTAs) negotiated by major trading powers such as the EU and US". Figure 1 from the online ILO Labour Provisions in Trade Agreements Hub shows the strong growth in the number of free trade agreements (FTAs) in general, and FTAs including labour provisions specifically.

Recent literature also identifies important variations between FTAs in terms of the scope of their labour provisions and implementation and enforcement mechanisms. Many FTAs, such as the labour side-agreement to NAFTA, do not aim to harmonise standards between countries and essentially only require partners to enforce their own

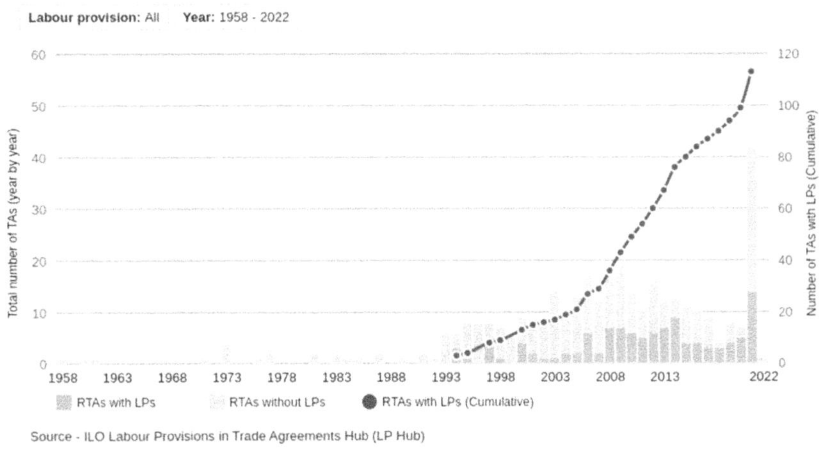

Fig. 1 Labour provisions in trade agreements (*Note* Created from https://www.ilo.org/LPhub/#home. Reproduced with permission)

labour laws (Cuyvers & De Meyer, 2012; Siroen, 2013). Other FTAs, including some US FTAs, refer to ILO's "core labour standards", and some mention outcome standards such as minimum wages and safety standards (Postnikov & Bastiaens, 2014). Some scholars distinguish US FTAs, where labour provisions are often in principle enforceable through sanctions; from EU FTAs, which are generally based on a softer approach and "rely on dialogue with trading partners as a means of enforcing and implementing labor provisions" (Postnikov & Bastiaens, 2014, p. 924). US FTAs specify a dispute settlement process including an independent third party, which may end with the withdrawal of trade access if a partner is determined not to be respecting labour standards. In contrast, EU FTAs do not include potential sanctions in case of failure to respect labour standards, instead relying on consultation with civil society on the implementation of labour provisions. Following the EU-South Korea FTA in 2010, labour provisions within an extensive Sustainable Development chapter were made legally binding and subject to dispute settlement, but the outcomes from these panels still served as recommendations and not a basis for sanctions (Postnikov & Bastiaens, 2014). Some authors argue the distinction between US and EU FTAs is somewhat exaggerated (Raess & Sari, 2018). EU FTAs are currently developing towards greater enforceability, while both the US and the EU have been argued to be unable or unwilling to enforce labour provisions in practice (Araujo, 2018). In one case where the US attempted to enforce labour provisions towards Guatemala within the Central American FTA (CAFTA), the US lost (Paiement, 2017). While the US was able to demonstrate that Guatemala did not uphold labour standards, the panel did not agree that this fact had affected trade.

Other countries such as Canada also have FTAs with labour provisions. Like the US' FTAs, Canada's include references to transparent dispute settlement involving an independent third party. The Canada-Chile FTA outlines a restrictive set of conditions related to selected labour standards such as child labour and demonstrating that the issue is trade-related, leading to a monetary fine that is transferred to a fund to help improve labour standards. The agreement also refers to cooperation activities including "seminars, technical assistance, joint research projects and working groups" (Siroen, 2013, p. 90). As discussed by

Siroen (2013) partners in the regional MERCOSUR agreement (Brazil, Argentina, Paraguay and Uruguay) also make reference to labour provisions in a declaration, but the agreement does not contain any dispute settlement mechanism. In general, FTAs between emerging markets, including those led by China and the African Continental Free Trade Area (AfCFTA) (Pasquali et al., 2021) are less likely to include labour provisions.

Labour provisions also appear in some Generalised System of Preferences (GSP) schemes. Such schemes unilaterally offer market access to certain partners above and beyond WTO agreements, conditional on respecting labour standards and human rights. EU has a "GSP+ incentive scheme for the respect of labour, human, environmental and good governance rights and rule" (Siroen, 2013, pp. 93–94). Trade preferences received by typically less developed partner countries may be (temporarily) withdrawn in the case of serious and systematic violations of international conventions. In the US GSP scheme, countries may similarly be excluded or suspended from trade preferences. Compared to bilateral FTAs, which often only require partners to enforce their own labour laws, GSP schemes are typically more demanding on the respect of international labour standards. Also, while sanctions have rarely been used for FTAs, there are examples of suspension of trade privileges in GSPs (Siroen, 2013).

3 Theory and Evidence on Labour Provisions in International Trade

The linkage of labour standards and trade involves many complex theoretical and empirical issues that can only be briefly covered here. The debate can be decomposed into three key questions: (1) Are labour standards desirable? (2) Do labour standards matter for trade and investment? (3) What are the effects of labour provisions in international trade policy? These are discussed in turn below.

3.1 Are Labour Standards Desirable?

Some opponents of labour provisions doubt the usefulness of labour market institutions and regulations as such. Many economists argue that minimum wages, while increasing income for some workers, will have negative effects for others by reducing overall employment, as firms substitute labour for other inputs such as capital and labour-saving technologies, or reduce output. Broadly, these economists also assume that other labour market institutions (including unions, restrictions on firing and rules to protect worker safety) have a similar effect as minimum wages, by increasing costs for employers. Empirical studies, however, are less conclusive (Betcherman, 2012). Research on minimum wages finds that effects on employment are not consistently negative, and that negative effects are generally modest, although certain groups such as younger workers tend to be more affected. Theoretically, a minimum wage could increase both wages and employment in a situation where employers have market power on wages (so-called monopsony). Similarly, unions may have further functions such as improving coordination, while employment protection can increase firms' and workers' incentives to increase skill and human capital levels and hence productivity (Block et al., 2001).

Other opponents of social clauses support labour standards in principle but are concerned that standards can be "too high" for certain stages in a country's development. More developed countries can better absorb the costs of standards with higher productivity (Araujo, 2018), and citizens have higher willingness to pay for standards. For developing countries characterised by large informal sectors (Narula, 2019), a concern has been that higher labour standards would push a greater share of activity into the informal sector. Interestingly, however, some research found higher minimum wages to have positive spillovers to the informal sector by increasing wages there as well ("lighthouse effect") (Betcherman, 2012).

3.2 Do Labour Standards Influence Trade and Investment?

Although the implications of standards are debated, an assumption among both proponents and opponents of a social clause is that countries having low labour standards would (all else equal) have lower costs and perform better in terms of exports or attracting FDI. Again, the evidence is inconclusive. Several empirical studies found that higher labour standards attract rather than deter FDI (Busse et al., 2011; Kucera, 2002), while others found the opposite (Olney, 2013). Similarly, while some studies find that non-respect of core labour standards increases exports from South to North (Granger, 2005), others do not find such an effect (Hasnat, 2002). Mosley and Uno (2007) find that while labour standards attract FDI, outsourcing is associated with lower standards.

While this takes labour standards as given to examine how they affect trade and investment patterns, more directly related to the question of whether there is a "race to the bottom" or "race to the top", is how international trade and investment affect labour standards. A negative effect could arise if countries competitively devalue their labour standards to attract FDI. Even if labour standards do not actually affect firms' decisions, it could be that governments *perceive* this to be the case and decide their labour standards policies based on this perception. Again, evidence exists both ways. Some studies focused on how countries' policies are affected by those of their peers, finding some evidence for a race to the bottom in this sense (Davies & Vadlamannati, 2013; Olney, 2013). Conversely, a positive effect of trade on labour standards could work indirectly by trade raising a country's income (in turn improving labour standards), or directly through diffusion effects from trade partners (Greenhill et al., 2009), where consumers may demand higher standards. Trade openness has often also been found to be positively associated with labour standards (Martinez-Zarzoso & Kruse, 2019).

Whereas early literature focused on MNEs from developed economies, some recent studies considered MNEs from emerging markets, where labour standards at home are lower and there may be less pressure from stakeholders to respect labour standards abroad (Duanmu, 2014). The rise of emerging markets as trading partners also provides alternative export destinations, meaning that developing countries can export their products without having to comply with labour standards (Pasquali et al., 2021).

3.3 Effects of Labour Provisions

Theoretical arguments for both positive and negative effects of a social clause exist. Fundamentally, standards aim to promote coordination between actors and ensure a minimum level. Multilateral labour provisions could help address Prisoner's dilemma type dynamics for international labour standards (Palley, 2004). Even if two countries would both be better off having high standards, in a situation where having a high standard yourself while your neighbour does not will mean that all firms will migrate to the neighbour, two uncoordinated countries would both choose suboptimal low standards. Importantly, while raising standards unilaterally might lead one developing country to lose out in competition with others, if all countries raised standards this competitive effect would be neutralised. In theory, a social clause could mitigate this collective action problem.

Nevertheless, there are potential limitations with using trade policy to address labour standards. Firstly, policy focusing on the effects of labour standards on international trade and investment would not directly address labour standards in industries and firms that do not participate in international business. Indeed, evidence suggests that standards are better in MNE subsidiaries and export-oriented sectors than in the rest of the domestic economy. Secondly, applying sanctions at the country level would penalise also relatively well-performing firms in the country (Moran, 2002). In general, an issue with sanctions is also that by reducing exports, they could lead firms in the sanctioned country to reduce employment. Thus, at least in the short term, sanctions could have the effect of pushing laid-off workers into worse alternatives.

Lastly, while there may be some agreement among countries on the broader aspects of labour standards, determining whether a specific labour standard has been transgressed raises challenges in terms of monitoring, as well as in determining the exact form and level of standards

(Moran, 2005). An example is freedom of association. The US, a main proponent for social clauses, is itself argued to restrict the right to strike by allowing permanent replacement of striking workers (Brown & Stern, 2008). Measuring labour standards is not a trivial task and would be particularly contentious if the results might be used as a basis for trade sanctions.

Absent multilateral regulation of labour standards, the available empirical evidence on the effects of social clauses comes from a relatively small literature on regional, bilateral and unilateral labour provisions, and is again somewhat mixed (Raess, 2022). Kim (2012) found that labour clauses in US FTAs led trade partners to improve their labour standards before the agreements entered into force, reflecting that labour clauses have become a precondition for FTAs passing in the US Congress (Cezar, 2022b). As noted earlier, it has been argued that whereas US FTAs are based on enforcement and potential trade sanctions, EU FTAs are based on positive incentives and policy learning (Campling et al., 2016). Postnikov and Bastiaens (2014) hence expect that compared to US FTAs, where improvements take place *ex ante*, for EU FTAs, improvements in labour standards occur mostly *ex post*, as consultation and dialogue with stakeholders and civil society take place to address labour standards issues. Their empirical analysis finds evidence of improvements ex ante, but even more so ex post. Martinez-Zarzoso and Kruse (2019) find that FTAs in general improve labour standards in partner countries, while the inclusion of labour provisions is in addition associated with higher minimum wages and a better coverage ratio. Dewan and Ronconi (2018) find that FTAs with the US strengthen labour enforcement through increasing the number of labour inspectors and inspections.

Other studies do not find similar positive impacts on labour standards. Using qualitative comparative analysis, Giumelli and van Roozendaal (2017) do not find that stringent labour provisions in 13 US FTAs with 17 countries have generally led to an improvement in country labour standards. Francois et al. (2023) using a large sample find that labour provisions do not have a consistent and clear impact on labour standards in partner countries. Binding labour provisions in EU FTAs specifically are weakly positively associated with an indicator of collective labour rights, but negatively associated with a broader measure of labour standards, including occupational health and safety, work hours and minimum age for child labour. As the countries with FTAs including labour provisions are compared to countries not signing such FTAs (i.e. also countries without FTAs altogether), the authors interpret the results as suggesting that FTAs create pressures on labour and environmental standards, and that the provisions in FTAs are not able to fully mitigate these pressures (Francois et al., 2023). Harrison et al. (2019, p. 264) provide a further critique of labour provisions in Trade and Sustainable Development (TSD) chapters in EU FTAs. Through three case studies, their analysis focuses on "the institutionalized practices of dialogue and co-operation which are meant to flow from the implementation phase" of these chapters. They argue that there is no evidence that the TSD chapters have led to improved labour standards governance, with one reason being that the EU's "one size fits all" model does not engage with the most salient labour issues for each partner.

Among other outcomes of interest, through a survey experiment Bastiaens and Postnikov (2020) find that respondents in advanced countries display more positive attitudes towards free trade when FTAs include social standards. Càrrere et al. (2022) find that labour clauses in FTAs are associated with greater exports from low- and middle-income countries to advanced markets, but that this is driven by FTAs with institutionalised cooperation mechanisms, while the effect is insignificant for FTAs with enforcement mechanisms. Timini et al. (2022) present somewhat consistent findings in that labour clauses tend to increase export effects from FTAs, but exports from South to North are only increased when FTAs have no or weak labour provisions, a difference that is stronger in labour-intensive sectors. Labour provisions have been found to affect FDI flows differently depending on whether the firm relies on high-skill labour versus low-skill labour (Lechner, 2018).

4 Labour Provisions and International Business Research

This section presents five areas where the IB discipline can contribute to our understanding of social clauses: Lessons from private regulation for the implementation of a social clause: Implications of interaction between private and public regulation; implications of social clauses for MNE strategies more broadly; corporate political activity in relation to social clauses in trade agreements; and finally potential implications of an increasingly multi-order global economy.

4.1 Private Regulation of labour standards by MNEs

Private regulation of labour standards typically takes the form of (company or industry) "codes of conduct" specifying requirements for suppliers in areas such as wages, health and safety issues, freedom of association, and child labour. The logic behind this private regulation model, by many preferred to regulation through a social clause (Moran, 2002), is that consumer and investor pressure would incentivise reputation-conscious MNEs to promote labour standards in their suppliers abroad. MNEs monitor suppliers against the code of conduct, with the suppliers themselves argued to be facing economic incentives to comply since they could otherwise lose orders from MNEs. However, this *compliance model* (Locke et al., 2009) has faced challenges. Questions have been raised about the effectiveness and credibility of MNEs' monitoring of their suppliers (O'Rourke, 2003). Even with recent movements towards greater transparency and involvement of multiple stakeholders (Doorey, 2011), challenges remain with factory managers becoming increasingly adept at tricking inspectors, some labour standards such as freedom of association being inherently more difficult to monitor, and less ability to reach sub-suppliers in lower tiers of the supply chain (Locke, 2013; Nadvi & Raj-Reichert, 2015; Narula, 2019; Sinkovics et al., 2016).

IB scholars have also made important contributions to this research, building on core IB theories such as internalization theory. In practice, due to the costs of achieving full value chain compliance, MNEs have used a "cascading compliance" approach, whereby first-tier suppliers are assigned the task of monitoring standards in their own suppliers; combined with some re-internalization of outsourced activities that may make monitoring and control easier (Narula, 2019; Van Assche & Narula, 2023). One effect of this has been consolidation of supply chains, dropping non-compliant suppliers or suppliers in the informal sector where monitoring compliance is too costly. This has led to some of the same negative consequences that a social clause was argued to have, e.g., in terms of loss of employment.

However, it has been possible to overcome some of these limitations of private regulation by focusing on assistance, capacity building and long-term relationships; what Locke et al. (2009) call the *commitment model*. Their study found that compliance inspectors actively helped supplier factories achieve compliance through technical assistance and by suggesting low-cost solutions to labour standards problems that factory owners were actually able to implement; in some cases having observed these solutions at other factories they inspected. These findings may suggest useful lessons for the implementation of social clauses too, in that financial and technical assistance are likely to be important preconditions for positive results.

4.2 Interactions Between Private and Public Regulation

Another finding from private regulation literature is that national regulation remains an important determinant of labour standards (Locke et al., 2007), sometimes also interacting with private regulation to achieve improvements (Amengual, 2010). Locke et al. (2013) find that in Mexico, private labour regulation largely *substituted* for ineffective government regulation, while in the Czech Republic the private regulation built upon national regulation, was legitimized by it, and thus *complementary*. The strong institutional tradition in IB could contribute insights here. An interesting question is how private regulation could also interact with supranational regulation in the forms of labour provisions in bilateral and regional FTAs. Such agreements could change the incentive structure for both MNEs and local actors and mitigate collective action problems. Complaint procedures could lead MNEs to allocate more resources to addressing labour standards to avoid negative publicity from being named in dispute settlement cases (Valor, 2006). Moreover, if FTAs with labour provisions can also provide a forum for dialogue and assistance, they could help overcome resource and capability constraints that tend to characterise local governments in emerging markets (Narula, 2019).

Evidence on such interactions between international public regulation and private regulation is still scarce, but a frequently cited case from Cambodia suggests potential complementarity between private and supranational regulation as well. The social clause in the US-Cambodian bilateral agreement has been seen as one important factor in improving conditions in the Cambodian apparel industry, along with qualified ILO monitoring, private self-regulation and clever national regulation (Polaski, 2006). The bilateral agreement meant that if Cambodia could ensure compliance with specified targets on national labour laws and international labour standards in its textile sector, textile quotas would increase annually. Monitoring was carried out by the ILO, with information from these audits used to decide on quotas. Since quotas were awarded for the country as a whole, while participation in the ILO monitoring program was voluntary, individual factories had the incentive not to participate, and instead free-ride on the efforts of others. To avoid this, Cambodian government made participation in the monitoring program mandatory to receive export quotas, leading all factories to participate. An important additional effect was that also MNE buyer firms benefitted from information from ILO monitoring for their sourcing decisions.

GVC literature also highlights the various roles that government can play in upgrading efforts, including social upgrading (De Marchi & Alford, 2022). However, we know less about how international regulation through labour provisions in FTAs may intersect at various governance points in GVCs. MNEs may lead GVCs where some parts of the value chain are covered by FTAs with labour provisions, while others are not. Studying the complex effects of this could also be a promising line of research for IB.

4.3 Social Clauses and MNEs International Strategies

Social clauses in FTAs may also affect MNE decisions such as host-country location. A social clause in an FTA between the MNE's home country and a host country could affect labour standards, and in turn labour cost and productivity. A handful of IB studies have already considered how labour standards affect foreign direct investment (FDI) and trade (Duanmu, 2014; Hasnat, 2002; Maggioni et al., 2019), and further studies could extend the work of scholars such as Lechner (2018) by considering how different motives for FDI (Dunning & Lundan, 2008) determine the impact of social clauses on decisions such as location. Efficiency-seeking MNEs might display greater sensitivity to labour provisions in FTAs, as these could lead to higher costs, while strategic asset-seeking MNEs might even benefit from labour regulations protecting high-skill workers (Alimov, 2015). The web of bilateral and regional FTAs with labour provisions could also have complex effects on export platform strategies and location of GVC stages, which IB's expertise in international strategies can help us better understand.

4.4 MNE Political Activity Towards Social Clauses

IB also has a research tradition on MNEs' political activity, building on insights from institutional theory and the resource-based view (Sun et al., 2021). IB scholars could also contribute to the understanding of under what conditions firms will support, oppose or otherwise shape the inclusion of social clauses in FTAs, adding to a small but insightful body of literature in political science (Cezar, 2022a, 2022b; Poletti et al., 2021). Intuitively, MNEs and importers (including GVC lead firms) have incentives to oppose social clauses, to the extent that the latter are expected to increase their costs. However, research indicates that firms are taking a more pragmatic stance, given potential reputational costs of publicly opposing social clauses, and with social clauses often being a necessary concession to have trade agreements ratified (Cezar, 2022b). Instead, firms may seek to limit the strength of labour provisions. IB research could build on this work to explore, among others, how MNEs from different countries may coordinate their efforts internationally (Hartmann et al., 2022), as well as the political resources different MNEs are able to bring to their political activity in this area. The development seems to be towards stronger provisions, as Curran (2022) discusses in the case of EU, creating unpredictable challenges but also opportunities for trade-dependent companies.

4.5 The Future of Social Clauses in the World Trading System

The last suggested research area concerns the different scenarios for social clauses, i.e. whether or not they are likely to continue to grow within regional and bilateral FTAs, and whether there could at some point be a new push towards greater multilateralism in labour provisions. Here, two developments that have received extensive attention by IB researchers are likely to be of importance. The first is the growth over the last decades of MNEs from emerging market "rising powers" (Nadvi, 2014), in particular China, India and Brazil. The second is current geopolitical tensions and de-globalisation trends that are argued to lead to an increasingly "fractured" global economy (Buckley, 2022). As discussed in Araujo (2018), the EU and US proposed to include more substantial labour standards provisions in "mega-regional" agreements such as the Trans-Pacific Partnership (TPP) and the Transatlantic Trade and Investment Partnership (TTIP). While both these agreements stalled, Araujo (2018, p. 234) argues that they set out, at least on paper, a "grand vision" for labour standards in future agreements. In contrast, China generally does not include labour provisions in its FTAs, and the China-led Regional Comprehensive Economic Partnership (RCEP) mostly omits labour standards and other regulatory aspects. Should the global economy continue to separate into distinct blocs, it is likely that these blocs would also differ substantially on labour provisions. The implications of this for MNEs and their stakeholders is another relevant area for IB research.

5 Conclusion

Social clauses in bilateral, regional and unilateral FTAs represent a relevant form of supranational institution in IB. The IB discipline can make unique contributions to research on the antecedents and implications of such clauses, based on its expertise in MNEs and their interplay with institutions, in the process also addressing broader agendas on supranational institutions in IB (Hartmann et al., 2022) and IB's social impact.

References

Alimov, A. (2015). Labor market regulations and cross-border mergers and acquisitions. *Journal of International Business Studies, 46*, 984–1009.

Amengual, M. (2010). Complementary labor regulation: The uncoordinated combination of state and private regulators in the Dominican Republic. *World Development, 38*(3), 405–414.

Araujo, B. M. (2018). Labour provisions in EU and US mega-regional trade agreements: Rhetoric and reality. *International & Comparative Law Quarterly, 67*(1), 233–253.

Bastiaens, I., & Postnikov, E. (2020). Social standards in trade agreements and free trade preferences: An empirical investigation. *The Review of International Organizations, 15*, 793–816.

Betcherman, G. (2012). *Labor market institutions: A review of the literature* World Bank Policy Research Working Paper 6276.

Block, R. N., Roberts, K., Ozeki, C., & Roomkin, M. J. (2001). Models of international labor standards. *Industrial Relations: A Journal of Economy and Society, 40*(2), 258–292.

Brown, A. G., & Stern, R. M. (2008). What are the issues in using trade agreements to improve international labor standards? *World Trade Review, 7*(2), 331–357.

Buckley, P. J. (2022). Corporate reactions to the fracturing of the global economy. *International Business Review,* 102014.
Busse, M., Nunnenkamp, P., & Spatareanu, M. (2011). Foreign direct investment and labour rights: A panel analysis of bilateral FDI flows. *Applied Economics Letters, 18*(2), 149–152.
Campling, L., Harrison, J., Richardson, B., & Smith, A. (2016). Can labour provisions work beyond the border? Evaluating the effects of EU free trade agreements. *International Labour Review, 155*(3), 357–382.
Càrrere, C., Olarreaga, M., & Raess, D. (2022). Labor clauses in trade agreements: Hidden protectionism? *The Review of International Organizations, 17*, 453–483.
Cezar, R. F. (2022a). Dispute settlement, labor and environmental provisions in PTAs: When will business interests shift positions? *Business and Politics, 24*(2), 221–240.
Cezar, R. F. (2022b). The intricacies of firms' support for labor provisions in US trade agreements. *Global Policy, 13*(4), 483–494.
Curran, L. (2022). Future challenges to trade policy in support of international business. In A. Karhu & E. Haaja, (Eds.), *Global trade and trade governance during de-globalization: Transforming trade policy for not-so-united world* (pp. 161–179). Springer.
Cuyvers, L., & De Meyer, T. (2012). Market-driven promotion of international labour standards in Southeast-Asia–the corporatization of social justice. In A. Marx, M. Maertens, F. S. Johan, & J. Wouters (Eds.), *Private standards and global governance* (pp. 114–149). Edward Elgar Publishing.
Davies, R. B., & Vadlamannati, K. C. (2013). A race to the bottom in labor standards? An empirical investigation. *Journal of Development Economics, 103*(July), 1–14.
De Marchi, V., & Alford, M. (2022). State policies and upgrading in global value chains: A systematic literature review. *Journal of International Business Policy, 5*(1), 88–111.
Dewan, S., & Ronconi, L. (2018). US free trade agreements and enforcement of labor law in Latin America. *Industrial Relations: A Journal of Economy and Society, 57*(1), 35–56.
Donaghey, J., Reinecke, J., Niforou, C., & Lawson, B. (2014). From employment relations to consumption relations: Balancing labor governance in global supply chains. *Human Resource Management, 53*(2), 229–252.
Doorey, D. J. (2011). The transparent supply chain: From resistance to implementation at Nike and Levi-Strauss. *Journal of Business Ethics, 103*(4), 587–603.

Doumbia-Henry, C., & Gravel, E. (2006). Free trade agreements and labour rights: Recent developments. *International Labour Review, 145*, 185.
Duanmu, J.-L. (2014). A race to lower standards? Labor standards and location choice of outward FDI from the BRIC countries. *International Business Review, 23*(3), 620–634.
Dunning, J. H., & Lundan, S. M. (2008). *Multinational enterprises and the global economy*. Edward Elgar Publishing.
Francois, J., Hoekman, B., Manchin, M., & Santi, F. (2023). *Pursuing environmental and social objectives through trade agreements.* World Bank Policy Research Working Paper 10323.
Giumelli, F., & van Roozendaal, G. (2017). Trade agreements and labour standards clauses: Explaining labour standards developments through a qualitative comparative analysis of US free trade agreements. *Global Social Policy, 17*(1), 38–61.
Granger, C. (2005). Normes de travail fondamentales et échanges Sud-Nord. *Economie Internationale, 1*, 47–62.
Greenhill, B., Mosley, L., & Prakash, A. (2009). Trade-based diffusion of labor rights: A panel study, 1986–2002. *American Political Science Review, 103*(4), 669–690.
Harrison, J., Barbu, M., Campling, L., Richardson, B., & Smith, A. (2019). Governing labour standards through free trade agreements: Limits of the European Union's trade and sustainable development chapters. *Journal of Common Market Studies, 57*(2), 260–277.
Hartmann, S., Lindner, T., Müllner, J., & Puck, J. (2022). Beyond the nation-state: Anchoring supranational institutions in international business research. *Journal of International Business Studies, 53*(6), 1282–1306.
Hasnat, B. (2002). The impact of core labour standards on exports. *International Business Review, 11*(5), 563–575.
Hassel, A. (2008). The evolution of a global labor governance regime. *Governance, 21*(2), 231–251.
Holzberg, B. (2020). Crossvergence of socially (ir) responsible employment practices in supplier firms. *Critical Perspectives on International Business, 16*(3), 305–324.
Kim, M. (2012). Ex ante due diligence: Formation of PTAs and protection of labor rights. *International Studies Quarterly, 56*(4), 704–719.
Kolk, A., & Van Tulder, R. (2004). Ethics in international business: Multinational approaches to child labor. *Journal of World Business, 39*(1), 49–60.
Kolk, A., & Van Tulder, R. (2005). Setting new global rules? TNCs and codes of conduct. *Transnational Corporations, 14*(3), 1–27.

Kucera, D. (2002). Core labour standards and foreign direct investment. *International Labour Review, 141*(1–2), 31–69.

Lechner, L. (2018). Good for some, bad for others: US investors and non-trade issues in preferential trade agreements. *The Review of International Organizations, 13*(2), 163–187.

Locke, R. M. (2013). *The promise and limits of private power: Promoting labor standards in a global economy*. Cambridge University Press.

Locke, R. M., Amengual, M., & Mangla, A. (2009). Virtue out of necessity? Compliance, commitment, and the improvement of labor conditions in global supply chains. *Politics & Society, 37*(3), 319–351.

Locke, R. M., Qin, F., & Brause, A. (2007). Does monitoring improve labor standards? Lessons from Nike. *Industrial & Labor Relations Review, 61*(1), 3–31.

Locke, R. M., Rissing, B. A., & Pal, T. (2013). Complements or substitutes? Private codes, state regulation and the enforcement of labour standards in global supply chains. *British Journal of Industrial Relations, 51*(3), 519–552.

Maggioni, D., Santangelo, G. D., & Koymen-Ozer, S. (2019). MNEs' location strategies and labor standards: The role of operating and reputational considerations across industries. *Journal of International Business Studies, 50*, 948–972.

Martinez-Zarzoso, I., & Kruse, H. W. (2019). Are labour provisions in free trade agreements improving labour conditions? *Open Economies Review, 30*, 975–1003.

McCrudden, C., & Davies, A. (2000). A perspective on trade and labor rights. *Journal of International Economic Law, 3*(1), 43–62.

Moran, T. H. (2002). *Beyond sweatshops: Foreign direct investment and globalization in developing countries*. Brookings Institution Press.

Moran, T. H. (2005). Monitoring compliance with international labor standards: How can the process be improved, and what are the implications for inserting labor standards into the WTO? *Journal of Business Ethics, 59*, 147–153.

Mosley, L., & Uno, S. (2007). Racing to the bottom or climbing to the top? Economic globalization and collective labor rights. *Comparative Political Studies, 40*(8), 923–948.

Nadvi, K. (2014). "Rising powers" and labour and environmental standards. *Oxford Development Studies, 42*(2), 137–150.

Nadvi, K., & Raj-Reichert, G. (2015). Governing health and safety at lower tiers of the computer industry global value chain. *Regulation & Governance, 9*(3), 243–258.

Narula, R. (2019). Enforcing higher labor standards within developing country value chains: Consequences for MNEs and informal actors in a dual economy. *Journal of International Business Studies, 50*, 1622–1635.

O'Rourke, D. (2003). Outsourcing regulation: Analyzing nongovernmental systems of labor standards and monitoring. *Policy Studies Journal, 31*(1), 1–29.

Olney, W. W. (2013). A race to the bottom? Employment protection and foreign direct investment. *Journal of International Economics, 91*(2), 191–203.

Paiement, P. (2017). Leveraging trade agreements for labor law enforcement: Drawing lessons from the US-Guatemala CAFTA dispute. *Georgetown Journal of International Law, 49*, 675.

Palley, T. I. (2004). The economic case for international labour standards. *Cambridge Journal of Economics, 28*(1), 21–36.

Pasquali, G., Godfrey, S., & Nadvi, K. (2021). Understanding regional value chains through the interaction of public and private governance: Insights from Southern Africa's apparel sector. *Journal of International Business Policy, 4*, 368–389.

Peng, M. W., Wang, D. Y., & Jiang, Y. (2008). An institution-based view of international business strategy: A focus on emerging economies. *Journal of International Business Studies, 39*(5), 920–936.

Pietrobelli, C., Rabellotti, R., & Van Assche, A. (2021). Making sense of global value chain-oriented policies: The trifecta of tasks, linkages, and firms. *Journal of International Business Policy, 4*(3), 327–346.

Polaski, S. (2006). Combining global and local forces: The case of labor rights in Cambodia. *World Development, 34*(5), 919–932.

Poletti, A., Sicurelli, D., & Yildirim, A. B. (2021). Promoting sustainable development through trade? EU trade agreements and global value chains. *Italian Political Science Review, 51*(3), 339–354.

Postnikov, E., & Bastiaens, I. (2014). Does dialogue work? The effectiveness of labor standards in EU preferential trade agreements. *Journal of European Public Policy, 21*(6), 923–940.

Raess, D. (2022). Evidence on the impact of labor provisions in preferential trade agreements. In K. A. Elliott (Ed.), *Handbook on globalisation and labour standards* (pp. 226–243). Edward Elgar Publishing.

Raess, D., & Sari, D. (2018). Labor provisions in trade agreements (LABPTA): Introducing a new dataset. *Global Policy, 9*(4), 451–466.

Sanyal, R. N. (2001). The social clause in trade treaties: Implications for international firms. *Journal of Business Ethics, 29*, 379–389.

Scherer, A. G., & Smid, M. (2000). The downward spiral and the US model business principles-Why MNEs should take responsibility for the improvement of world-wide social and environmental conditions. *Management International Review, 40*, 351–371.

Sinkovics, N., Hoque, S. F., & Sinkovics, R. R. (2016). Rana Plaza collapse aftermath: Are CSR compliance and auditing pressures effective? *Accounting, Auditing & Accountability Journal, 29*(4), 617–649.

Siroen, J. M. (2013). Labour provisions in preferential trade agreements: Current practice and outlook. *International Labour Review, 152*(1), 85–106.

Sun, P., Doh, J. P., Rajwani, T., & Siegel, D. (2021). Navigating cross-border institutional complexity: A review and assessment of multinational nonmarket strategy research. *Journal of International Business Studies, 52*(9), 1818–1853.

Timini, J., Cortinovis, N., & López Vicente, F. (2022). The heterogeneous effects of trade agreements with labour provisions. *The World Economy, 45*(9), 2820–2853.

Valor, C. (2006). What if all trade was fair trade? The potential of a social clause to achieve the goals of fair trade. *Journal of Strategic Marketing, 14*(3), 263–275.

Van Assche, A., & Narula, R. (2023). Internalization strikes back? Global value chains, and the rising costs of effective cascading compliance. *Journal of Industrial and Business Economics, 50*(1), 161–173.

Van Tulder, R., & Kolk, A. (2001). Multinationality and corporate ethics: Codes of conduct in the sporting goods industry. *Journal of International Business Studies, 32*(2), 267–283.

4

Corporate Commitment to Decent Work and Sustainable Development: A Quantitative Analysis of Corporate Reports of DAX 40 MNCs

Stefan Zagelmeyer

1 Introduction

The United Nations' (UN) 2030 Agenda for Sustainable Development (2030 Agenda) ascribes specific roles to business organizations and has reinvigorated the discussions on the link between multinational corporations (MNCs) and international development. Among the 17 Sustainable Development Goals (SDGs), SDG 8 aims to promote sustained, inclusive, and sustainable economic growth, full and productive employment, and decent work for all. Thus, the 2030 Agenda establishes an explicit connection to the Decent Work Agenda of the International Labour Organisation (ILO) to address the societal challenges of globalisation by ensuring human-oriented development.

From the perspective of corporations, the SDGs can provide a framework for business to address the Grand Societal Challenges and develop strategies to create a better world (PWC, 2019). Yet, despite the relevance

S. Zagelmeyer (✉)
Alliance Manchester Business School, Manchester, UK
e-mail: s.zagelmeyer@manchester.ac.uk

N. Sinkovics et al. (eds.), *International Business and SDG 8*, The Academy of International Business, https://doi.org/10.1007/978-3-031-46802-5_4

for both the ILO's Decent Work Agenda and the UN's 2030 Agenda, international business research on the links between MNCs and sustainable development has largely ignored the topic of decent work (Sinkovics et al., 2022; Van Tulder et al., 2021).

This chapter analyses the incidence and extent of corporate commitment to decent work and sustainable development, as measured through word frequency analysis and text-mining methods, drawing on annual reports and sustainability reports published in 2010 and 2020 of MNCs listed on the DAX-40 stock market index. It seeks to explore (i) the incidence and variation in decent work- and sustainability-related corporate reporting across companies, and (ii) the changes in decent work and sustainability reporting over time.

2 Business, Decent Work and Sustainable Development

2.1 The Decent Work Agenda

In 1999 the International Labour Organisation (ILO) announced the Decent Work Agenda (ILO, 1999), its signature strategy to address the social challenges of globalisation to ensure human-oriented development, i.e. to give a 'human face to the global economy' (ILO, 1999, p. 4), and to achieve full and productive employment and decent work for all at the global, regional, national, sectoral and local levels (ILO, 2007; Rantanen, Muchiri, & Lehtinen, 2020).

The ILO defines decent work as 'productive work for women and men in conditions of freedom, equity, security and human dignity' (ILO, 2007, p. vi).

> Decent Work involves opportunities for work that is productive and delivers a fair income, provides security in the workplace and social protection for workers and their families, offers prospects for personal development and encourages social interaction, gives people the freedom to express their concerns, and organise and participate in decisions

> affecting their lives and guarantees equal opportunities and equal treatment for all. (ILO, 2007, p. vi)

The Decent Work Agenda includes the following strategic objectives and programs to achieve them: (i) employment, (ii) fundamental principles and rights at work, (iii) social protection (social security and occupational safety and health) and (iv) social dialogue (ILO, 1999).

With respect to international labour and social policy, the development of decent work strategy of the ILO has evolved in several steps. In 1998, the Declaration on Fundamental Principles and Rights at Work was agreed at the International Labour Conference, covering all 187 member states of the ILO, and emphasising (i) freedom of association and right to collective bargaining; (ii) the elimination of forced or compulsory labour; (iii) the abolition of child labour; and (iv) the elimination of discrimination in employment and occupation (Rantanen et al., 2020). Decent work then played a central role at the 2005 World Summit of the United Nations General Assembly, heads of state and government, and in the meantime is advocated by the entire United Nations system (ILO, 2007).

Yet, the Decent Work Agenda must be considered in a broader context. Around the time the ILO announced the Decent Work Agenda in 1999, several initiatives under the United Nations Secretary-General Kofi Annan were initiated, such as the United Nations Global Compact (1999), the Millennium Declaration (2000) and the subsequent 2030 Agenda on Sustainable Development (2015), and the debate on business and human rights which later led to the United Nations Guiding Principles on Business and Human Rights (2011).

2.2 Decent Work and Sustainable Development

While the ILO's decent work strategy can be discussed as a stand-alone strategy, the concept of decent work has been a focal point in the broader discussions on social and economic development among public policy makers and in academia since the end of the 1980s, centring on the question how to respond to the social challenges of the increasing economic globalisation (World Commission on the Social Dimension of Globalization, 2004).

Overall, the decent work debate has been firmly intertwined with the discussion of the role of work and employment in economic and social development, starting with a focus on labour standards at the 1995 World Summit on Social Development and the WTO Ministerial Conference in 1996 and the inclusion of labour standards into the UN Global Compact 1999 as well as in the revised OECD Guidelines for multinational corporations in the year 2000. Subsequently, the debate shifted towards decent work, triggered by the ILO Director-General's report of 1999 and continued at subsequent International Labour Conferences (Fields, 2003).

International development policy entered a new stage when in 2000 the UN Millennium Declaration (United Nations, 2000) set out a strategic vision to work towards the achievement of eight Millennium Development Goals (MDG) until the year 2015. The MDGs are aimed at supporting human capabilities and development by emphasising human capital, infrastructure, and human rights. In 2015 the UN General Assembly adopted Agenda 2030 on Sustainable Development, which encompasses 17 goals, known as the SDGs (United Nations, 2015a, 2015b). They provide orientation for global development efforts for the period 2016–2030 and build on the MDGs (Pogge & Sengupta, 2016). In contrast to the MDGs, the SDG agenda is more comprehensive and more universal, addressing all countries' sustainability needs instead of focusing on developing countries.

The Millennium Development Goals (MDGs) included an explicit reference to decent work in MDG target 1B, i.e. to eradicate extreme poverty and hunger through achieving full and productive employment and decent work for all, including women and young people (Renwick, 2011). This goal was further developed in the 2030 Agenda, in which SDG 8 includes the promotion of inclusive and sustainable economic growth, full and productive employment and decent work for all, taking an integrated approach to international economic policy and international social policy, advocating the ILO's Decent Work Agenda at the highest level, and extending its reach until 2030 and beyond (Fields, 2003; ILO, 2017).

2.3 The Role of Business in Sustainable Development

The links between MNCs and sustainable development can be discussed at several levels. The MDGs emphasise the role of partnerships between the public sector, the private sector and civil society in the pursuit of development (United Nations, 2000). The SDGs aim at 'bringing together governments, the private sector, civil society, the United Nations system and other actors' to mobilise 'all available resources' (United Nations, 2015a, p. 10), explicitly mentioning micro-enterprises, cooperatives and multinationals 'as drivers of productivity, inclusive economic growth and job creation' (United Nations, 2015a, p. 29). SDGs target 12.6 encourages the adoption of sustainable practices and the engagement in sustainability reporting for companies. SDGs 8 and 9 emphasise the role of small and medium-sized companies for economic growth and decent work. The SDG Compass (Global Reporting Initiative et al., 2015) provides a detailed guide of indicators and tools to assist companies in contributing to the achievement of the SDGs.

Both the MDGs and the SDGs have led business organisations as well as non-governmental organisations to address and discuss the link between business and sustainability. A joint statement of the Global Agenda Councils of the World Economic Forum endorses the idea of business contributing to sustainable development by, among others, 'offering an image of business sustainability that can begin to inform business decisions and the creation of new business models' (World Economic Forum, 2014, p. 10).

3 Corporate Reporting on Sustainable Development and Decent Work

3.1 Corporate Reporting, Decent Work and the SDGs

The SDGs encourage corporations to commit to sustainable development and on their sustainable development activities. SDG target 12.6 explicitly encourages the adoption of sustainable practices and engagement in sustainability reporting. Corporate reporting involves the disclosure of financial and non-financial information and can take many forms: financial reporting, corporate governance reporting, corporate social responsibility reporting, sustainability reporting and human rights reporting (Michelon et al., 2022). While financial reporting may be a regulatory requirement, voluntary non-financial reporting has increasingly become common practice, especially by larger corporations, responding to the expectations and 'demands of various stakeholder groups—investors, employees, consumers, communities, and regulators' (Shoaf et al., 2018, p. 1). Non-financial reporting usually addresses broad topics related to environmental, social, and governance (ESG) concerns, but can also involve sustainability reporting (Shoaf et al., 2018) and human rights reporting (Zagelmeyer, 2019).

Most companies, especially those listed on the stock market, publish annual reports that provide a general view of company data, and may include information on management, strategy, the financial situation, and environmental and/or social issues. Other types of reports, such as sustainability reports, CSR reports or human rights reports, take a more focused approach, but frequently vary in terms of format, structure, content and publication frequency. Over the years, sustainability reports and CSR reports—companies usually choose either label—have become established as a second pillar of corporate reporting, with many companies publishing a sustainability report or CSR report on an annual basis. More recently, some companies have moved towards integrated reporting, i.e., to include non-financial information in their annual reports (Maniora, 2017; Velte, 2021).

Since the publication of the 2030 Agenda for Sustainable Development, corporate reporting on the SDGs has been experiencing considerable growth. Research on SDG reporting at more than 1100 companies on all continents published in 2019 by PWC (2019) shows that 72 percent of all companies mentioned the SDGs in their reports, 65 percent referred to specific SDGs, 25 percent of companies included the SDGs in their published strategy, and one percent of companies reported that they measured the performance on SDG targets. As far as the coverage of specific SDGs in corporate disclosure is concerned, 86 percent of the companies explicitly mentioned SDG 8 (decent work and economic growth), the most frequently mentioned SDG in the analysis. Similar research is available for different years (PWC, 2017, 2018) and by other companies, e.g., KPMG (2016).

3.2 Analytical Framework

The literature on non-financial and/or social reporting is dominated by three approaches, namely legitimacy theory, stakeholder theory, and signalling theory. 'Legitimacy is a generalised perception or assumption that the actions of an entity are desirable, proper or appropriate within some socially constructed system of norms, values, believes and definitions' (Tan et al., 2016, p. 12). Legitimacy theory argues that in order to obtain a 'social licence to operate' (Deegan, 2002, 2014), corporations need to comply with values and norms that prevail in a particular institutional setting (Hahn & Kühnen, 2013), which is a necessary resource and prerequisite for the corporation's existence and success. Non-financial reporting, including sustainability reporting and human rights reporting, seeks to influence the perception of the corporation by its stakeholders by signalling how it meets the expectations, demands and requirements for being considered legitimate.

The stakeholder approach argues that the corporation is not only acting in the interests of the owners and investors, but that it has to 'balance a multiplicity of stakeholder interests that can affect or be affected by the firm's actions' (Thorne et al., 2014, p. 689). This is a political process in which different stakeholders urge the corporation to act in ways that are conducive to their interests and expectations. Following the instrumental approach to stakeholder theory, one may distinguish stakeholders who are internal or external to the organisation. Internal stakeholders include, among others, the owners of the company, the workforce or different actors from within the company, such as works councils. External stakeholders include actors in the external environment of business organisations, such as NGOs, government, consumers or suppliers.

The third approach focusses on signalling. Based on the assumption of information asymmetries in the relationship of two parties—which may involve a market relationship or another type of cooperation—signalling theory suggests that the informational situation and credibility can be improved by one party sending signals (i.e. relevant information) to the other party, improving decision-making and cooperation between the two parties and avoiding adverse selection when it comes to choice of cooperation partners (Drover et al., 2018; Spence, 1974). As far as social reporting is concerned, this perspective suggests that companies signal their behavioural values and other information they consider relevant to the respective stakeholders to improve their reputation and gain approval and thus legitimacy. While some corporations may use several reporting channels and a higher intensity of reporting to signal their human rights commitment to different stakeholders, other companies try to hide or selectively disclose information (Hahn & Kühnen, 2013).

4 Methods, Data and Analysis

4.1 Research Objectives and Dataset

In line with the analytical framework outlined above, corporate disclosure information is assumed to indicate the commitment of business organisations to goals that align with the expectations of relevant stakeholders. We thus assume that corporate disclosure information concerning sustainable development and the SDGs serve the purpose of signalling commitment to the expectations of the respective stakeholders. While this may require a specific configuration of reporting activities, potentially involving multi-channel reporting, one may assume that the decisions on the channel-configuration and the information included in corporate disclosure are based on a cost–benefit analysis and serve a strategic business purpose.

Against this background, the empirical part of this paper analyses the extent to which multinational companies engage in disclosing information related to the sustainable development goals. The analysis draws on the annual reports and sustainability reports of German multinational corporations listed in the DAX 40 stock market index in 2021. The reason for choosing to analyse DAX 40 companies is the extensive discussion of both the decent work agenda (Trebilcock, 2018) and corporate sustainability (Patrick & Bernd, 2012) in Germany. Beyond describing the incidence and development of reporting on sustainability-related topics and themes, the empirical analysis also seeks to map the relative intensity of SDG-related reporting, especially comparing corporate disclosure information on SDG 8 to the coverage of other SDGs. Finally, the paper seeks to analyse corporate disclosure on sustainability reporting over time.

The dataset includes two types of corporate disclosure documents, annual reports and sustainability reports, for 2010 and 2020. Reports were collected from different sources, including the EIKON Refinitiv database and corporate websites. Table 1 provides an overview of all reports included in the dataset. All companies included in the dataset published an annual report in the year 2020. Seven of the companies did not exist in 2010, and thus did not publish an annual report. Sustainability reports have become very popular among corporations. However, there is considerable variation with respect to title, format, content, and detail. Most companies publish this type of report annually, and usually with the title of 'sustainability report', 'corporate social responsibility report' or 'CSR report', but some companies use alternative titles such as 'citizenship report' or 'social performance report'. As social reporting can take many forms, from full-text reports of several hundred pages to presentation-style or handout-style documents, each of the downloaded potential documents was checked for content and included in the dataset only if the document covered information on management structures, corporate CSR/sustainability strategy, and policies and practices concerning sustainability and/or corporate social responsibility. Business presentation-style documents were not included in the analysis. 18 of the corporations published a sustainability report in 2010, increasing to 25 corporations in 2020. Seven of the 33 corporations that existed in both years did not publish any sustainability report at all, while six of these corporations published a sustainability report only in 2010 and moved to integrated reporting, i.e. including sustainability and CSR-related information in the annual report only, in 2020.

4.2 Overview of the Structure of the Empirical Analysis

The empirical analysis involved both word frequency analysis and text-mining processes, using the Provalis WordStat software. The following section provides an introduction to and overview of the different steps of the analysis.

4.2.1 Word Frequency Analysis and Text Mining Analysis

With respect to the sustainable development goals, word frequency analysis included searching for the following keywords and phrases: 'millennium development goal', 'millennium development goals', 'MDG', 'MDGs', 'sustainable development goal', 'sustainable development goals', 'SDG' and 'SDGs'. The obtained word frequency data for the different search terms were then added to yield the total number of count data for the word frequency variable 'MDG'/'SDG'. As the analysis in this paper focuses on decent work, as included in SDG8, the word frequency analysis also searched for the phrase 'decent work'.

The text-mining part of the analysis included the following. To measure aspects related to the sustainable development goals in text documents, the University of Auckland has developed a mapping tool, which allows scholars to analyse text data with respect to SDGs 1 to 16, i.e., all SDGs except for SDG 17 (partnerships). This mapping tool includes a total of over 2300 keywords, which were transformed into a

Table 1 Corporate reports of DAX 40 corporations (2010 and 2020)

	Annual reports		Sustainability reports	
	2010	2020	2010	2020
Adidas	×	×	×	
Airbus	×	×		
Allianz	×	×	×	×
BASF	×	×		
Bayer	×	×	×	×
BMW	×	×	×	
Beiersdorf	×	×	×	×
Brenntag	×	×		×
Continental	×	×		×
Covestro		×		×
Daimler	×	×	×	×
Delivery Hero		×		
Deutsche Bank	×	×		
Deutsche Boerse	×	×	×	
Deutsche Post	×	×	×	
Deutsche Telekom	×	×	×	×
Deutsche Wohnen	×	×		×
E.ON	×	×	×	×
Fresenius Medical Care	×	×		
Fresenius	×	×		
Heidelberg Cement	×	×		×
HelloFresh		×		×
Henkel	×	×	×	×
Infineon	×	×		×
Linde	×	×	×	×
Merck	×	×		×
MTU	×	×		×
Muenchener Rueck	×	×		×
Puma	×	×		
Qiagen	×	×	×	
RWE	×	×	×	×
SAP	×	×	×	
Sartorius	×	×		
Siemens	×	×	×	×
Siemens Energy		×		×
Siemens Health		×		
Symrise	×	×	×	×
Volkswagen	×	×	×	×
Vonovia		×		×

(continued)

Table 1 (continued)

	Annual reports		Sustainability reports	
	2010	2020	2010	2020
Zalando		×		×
Number of reports	*33*	*40*	*18*	*25*

WordStat-compatible dictionary to measure the extent to which the text documents cover SDG-related terms and topics.

Frequency data measuring the total number of keywords or topics occurring in a text is a useful first step in text analysis, showing whether and how frequently specific terms, phrases or topics occur in the analysed text corpus. The next step in the analysis was then to measure the relative importance of a particular concept of phrase by calculating the frequency in relation to the total number of words in the respective original document, e.g. annual report or sustainability report. For this purpose, we identified and used the total number of words included in the respective document, as calculated by Microsoft Word. As some of the analysed documents included several hundred thousand words, the following sections report the relative frequency scores per 10,000 words of the respective document or set of documents.

4.2.2 Structure of the Analysis

The analysis proceeded in four stages. Stage I included the separate word frequency analysis of the annual reports and the sustainability reports for 2010 and 2020 with respect to both the SDG and decent work keywords. For those companies which published annual reports in 2010 and 2020, word frequency differences between both data points were calculated. This information was used to identify increases, decreases or no change with respect to word frequency. Finally, this stage involved aggregating word frequency data by adding the word frequency scores for annual reviews and sustainability reviews for 2010 and 2020.

Stage II involved the calculation of a relative word frequency score that measures the relative word count frequency of the respective SDG or decent work keywords per 10,000 words of the respective document.

This provides information on the relative importance of the keywords in relation to the length of the document. As a standard measure applied to all documents, this variable also allows us to compare the relative importance of keywords across companies and across time. Then, the differences between both data points in 2010 and 2020 were calculated for each corporation to capture whether the relative frequency of the keywords had increased, decreased or remained constant. Last, like in stage I, a score was calculated for the analysis of both annual reports and sustainability reports together.

Stage III involved the text-mining analysis in WordStat, drawing on the SDG dictionary. The analysis yielded topical theme-related word frequency scores for the 16 SDGs, for both types of reports published in 2010 and 2020. Similar to stages I and II, calculating the difference of work frequency scores between two years allows for comparisons over time and the identification of changes. Finally, the data was then aggregated for both types of reports.

Stage IV used the word frequency scores generated during stage III and related these values to the total length (in words) of the respective document, generating a word frequency score per 10,000 words of each document (annual report and sustainability report), and for both documents combined.

5 Empirical Findings

5.1 Word Frequency Analysis

5.1.1 Stage I: Total Number of Keywords

The following sections report on the most important findings of the word frequency analysis (stage I) analysis, covering (i) the annual reports, (ii) the sustainability reports and (iii) both reports together. Starting with the analysis of annual reports, in 2010 Siemens AG was the only of the then 33 corporations in the dataset to include a reference to the MDGs/SDGs. By 2020, 24 of the 40 corporations in the dataset included between one and 58 references to the MDGs/SDGs in their annual reports. Of the 33 companies that published annual reports in both years, 2010 and 2020, 20 companies had moved from zero references to include information on the SDGs, and one corporation (Siemens AG) stopped referring to the SDGs explicitly.

Six of the 18 sustainability reports published in 2010 refer explicitly to the MDGs/SDGs. By 2020, this number increased to 24 of the 25 corporations publishing sustainability reports, with all 12 companies with sustainability reports in 2010 and 2020 increasing the frequency of using the MDGs/SDGs in their reports. As far as the aggregate analysis for both types of reports combined is concerned, in 2010 six of the 33 corporations in the sample included references to the MDGs/SDGs, increasing to 36 of the 40 corporations in 2020, with overall 31 corporations of 33 with reports in both years increasing the number of references to the MDGs/SDGs.

Turning to decent work, none of the 33 annual reports published in 2010 included any explicit reference to decent work, increasing to 11 out of 40 in 2020. Looking at sustainability reports, 7 of the 18 corporations included in the sample for 2010 refer to decent work. This number increased to 16 out of 25 in 2020. All 12 companies with sustainability reports in 2010 and 2020 increased the number of references to decent work over the observation period. As far as the aggregate analysis for both types of reports together is concerned, 7 of the 33 corporations included references to decent work in 2010, increasing to 27 out of 40 in 2020. For companies with reports in both years, 21 of the 33 corporations increased the number of references to decent work, with one corporation (Deutsche Post) stopping to refer to decent work.

5.1.2 Stage II: Relative Proportion of Keywords

While the total number of words gives the first indication of whether corporate disclosure information covers particular concepts and phrases, it is an imperfect measure as it does not take into consideration the specific format and length of the respective documents. For example, the length of the annual report documents in the sample ranges from 19,950 words (Deutsche Wohnen, 2010) to 282,488 words (Deutsche

Bank, 2020). The respective figures for sustainability reports are 7,573 (Covestro, 2020) to 124,601 (Deutsche Telekom, 2010).

5.2 Text-Mining Analysis

To improve the comparability between documents of the same category, Table 2 includes information on the total number of keywords in relation to the length of the document, measured by keywords per 10,000 words in the document. To illustrate the point: even though Covestro's sustainability report for 2020 is short in terms of word count (7,573) compared to other reports, the values for the relative keyword score (keywords per 10,000 words) are relatively high with, 3.9 for SDGs and 4.0 for decent work, while the respective score for the 2020 annual report of Deutsche Bank (length: 282,488 words) is much lower at 0.0 for both SDGs and for decent work. Yet, this type of analysis is limited in that it measures the relative quantity of keywords and does not allow for any more sophisticated interpretation of the content of the report.

Without going into every detail, the analysis of annual reports with respect to the relative frequency of keywords related to the SDGs and decent work in annual reports and sustainability reports for both years of observation is relatively consistent with the analysis of the absolute frequency of keywords reported in the previous section. Yet, the analysis of the development of the relative keyword quantity provides for some more nuanced findings with respect to changes of overall reporting (annual reports and sustainability reports combined) on decent work. In contrast to the total word count analysis, which reveals that 21 of the 33 companies in the sample operating in 2010 and 2020 have increased the use of the term 'decent work', with one company reducing the use of the keyword of decent work. This trend is more pronounced when looking at the changes with respect to relative quantity of keywords in corporate disclosure: while none of the corporations had reduced the relative quantity of SDG-related keywords, three corporations reduced the relative quantity of decent work-related keywords between 2010 and 2020.

Table 2 Scores of the word frequency analysis (per 10,000 words)

	Annual reports				Sustainability reports				Annual and sustainability reports			
	MDG/ SDG		Decent work		MDG/ SDG		Decent work		MDG/ SDG		Decent work	
	2010	2020	2010	2020	2010	2020	2010	2020	2010	2020	2010	2020
Adidas	0.00	0.37	0.00	0.15	0.00		0.17		0.00	0.37	0.06	0.15
Airbus	0.00	1.74	0.00	0.45					0.00	1.74	0.00	0.33
Allianz	0.00	0.00	0.00	0.00	0.00	6.71	0.00	0.13	0.00	2.60	0.00	0.05
BASF	0.00	2.47	0.00	0.07					0.00	2.47	0.00	0.06
Bayer	0.00	0.49	0.00	0.00	0.63	2.37	0.00	0.18	0.19	1.07	0.00	0.06
BMW	0.00	0.60	0.00	0.00	0.34		0.00		0.13	0.66	0.00	0.00
Beiersdorf	0.00	1.31	0.00	0.00	0.00	19.11	0.00	0.55	0.00	4.09	0.00	0.09
Brenntag	0.00	0.00	0.00	0.00		3.93		0.30	0.00	1.01	0.00	0.08
Continental	0.00	0.00	0.00	0.00		1.40		0.16	0.00	0.48	0.00	0.05
Covestro		3.92		0.07		25.09		0.00		5.13		0.08
Daimler	0.00	0.32	0.00	0.00	0.00	2.44	0.00	0.29	0.00	1.15	0.00	0.11
Delivery Hero		0.43		0.00						0.43		0.00
Deutsche Bank	0.00	0.04	0.00	0.00					0.00	0.04	0.00	0.00
Deutsche Boerse	0.00	2.56	0.00	0.37	0.00		0.44		0.00	2.56	0.07	0.43
Deutsche Post	0.00	0.54	0.00	0.00	0.23		0.12		0.10	1.30	0.05	0.00
Deutsche Telekom	0.00	3.04	0.00	0.15	0.00	8.40	0.08	0.13	0.00	4.55	0.04	0.11
Deutsche Wohnen	0.00	0.00	0.00	0.00		2.92		0.00	0.00	1.10	0.00	0.00
E.ON	0.00	0.23	0.00	0.00	0.26	2.68	0.00	0.00	0.07	1.02	0.00	0.00
Fresenius Medical Care	0.00	0.00	0.00	0.00					0.00	0.00	0.00	0.00
Fresenius	0.00	0.38	0.00	0.07					0.00	0.38	0.00	0.05
Heidelberg Cement	0.00	0.00	0.00	0.00		0.54		0.00	0.00	0.12	0.00	0.00
HelloFresh		0.00		0.00		6.18		0.00		1.39		0.00
Henkel	0.00	0.00	0.00	0.00	1.32	5.36	0.00	0.12	0.30	2.21	0.00	0.05
Infineon	0.00	0.00	0.00	0.00		4.25		0.39	0.00	0.78	0.00	0.07
Linde	0.00	0.00	0.00	0.00	0.00	4.26	0.00	1.16	0.00	2.08	0.00	0.57
Merck	0.00	1.11	0.00	0.07		2.66		0.11	0.00	1.70	0.00	0.09
MTU	0.00	0.00	0.00	0.00		25.74		1.50	0.00	8.12	0.00	0.47

(continued)

Table 2 (continued)

	Annual reports				Sustainability reports				Annual and sustainability reports			
	MDG/ SDG		Decent work		MDG/ SDG		Decent work		MDG/ SDG		Decent work	
	2010	2020	2010	2020	2010	2020	2010	2020	2010	2020	2010	2020
Muenchener Rueck	0.00	0.00	0.00	0.00		1.95		0.00	0.00	0.58	0.00	0.00
Puma	0.00	1.54	0.00	0.07					0.00	1.54	0.00	0.11
Qiagen	0.00	0.11	0.00	0.00	0.00		0.00		0.00	0.11	0.00	0.00
RWE	0.00	3.90	0.00	0.00	0.00	3.22	0.33	0.20	0.00	3.67	0.08	0.07
SAP	0.00	0.71	0.00	0.15	0.00		0.00		0.00	0.71	0.00	0.13
Sartorius	0.00	0.00	0.00	0.22					0.00	0.00	0.00	0.35
Siemens	0.06	0.00	0.00	0.00	0.24	13.87	0.00	1.40	0.09	5.07	0.00	0.51
Siemens Energy		0.11		0.00		21.41		2.14		5.86		0.58
Siemens Health		0.00		0.00						0.00		0.00
Symrise	0.00	6.98	0.00	0.07	0.00	5.42	0.38	0.00	0.00	6.00	0.11	0.11
Volkswagen	0.00	0.12	0.00	0.00	0.00	2.21	0.36	0.18	0.00	0.63	0.07	0.04
Vonovia		1.01		0.07		2.96		0.00		1.63		0.05
Zalando		0.00		0.00		0.00		0.00		0.00		0.00
Number of reports	*33*	*40*	*33*	*40*	*18*	*25*	*18*	*25*	*33*	*40*	*33*	*40*

5.2.1 Stage III: Total Number of Keywords

In contrast to word frequency analysis, which accounts for the occurrence of specific keywords in a particular document, text-mining analysis is more sophisticated in that it seeks to capture the extent to which particular topics, measured through a set of related words of a (ideally validated) topic-related dictionary, are covered in the content of a particular document. Even though text-mining analysis includes a range of different analytical methods and tools (Aggarwal & Zhai, 2018; Kwartler, 2017), the reported analysis has taken the relatively simple approach of using an existing dictionary to map the incidence SDG-related reporting in annual reports and sustainability reports in 2010 and 2020.

In contrast to the keyword search reported above, which searched for a small number of keywords or phrases directly mapping concepts such as 'sustainable development goals' and 'decent work', using dictionaries with several hundred of words to search for topical themes yields far higher numbers of 'hits' in the respective documents. Thus, the findings reported in the subsequent sections cannot be directly compared to the word frequency analysis.

Similar to the structure of the report on word frequency analysis, the following sections will outline the most important observations of the text-mining analysis, starting first with the analysis of annual reports, then of sustainability reports, and, finally, the analysis for both types of reports combined in 2010 and 2020.

Overall, in both 2010 and 2020, all annual reports and sustainability reports in the sample, and thus also both reports combined, covered material related to the SDGs and decent work, as specified by the University of Auckland dictionary (Wang, Kang, & Mu, 2023). Although this finding does not seem spectacular, it is noteworthy that apparently even annual reports of all companies cover material related to the SDGs and decent work. Instead of reporting on descriptive information on specific companies or elaborating on the summary statistics for cross-sectional data, which, for example, would show considerable variation in coverage across companies, the following paragraphs will focus on the changes between 2010 and 2020.

With respect to SDG coverage in annual reports, the reported count values have increased for 31 of the 33 companies, while the respective values decreased for two (Linde AG and Siemens). Focusing on SDG 8 (decent work and economic growth), 23 corporations increased in terms of quantity of reporting, while 10 companies decreased the quantity of reporting.

Focusing on sustainability reports, SDG reporting intensity increased for 11 companies for which sustainability reports existed in 2010 and 2020, while one company (Deutsche Telekom) reduced the quantity of reporting. With respect to SDG 8 (decent work and economic growth), all 12 companies increased the quantity of reporting. As far as the analysis of both annual reports and sustainability reports combined is concerned,

30 (3) of the 33 companies increased (decreased) SDG reporting, while 29 (4) increased (decreased) SDG 8 reporting.

5.2.2 Stage IV: Relative Proportion of Keywords

Similar to word frequency analysis, focusing on count data in text-mining allows for the identification of the presence of particular topical themes in documents. However, given the variation in terms of format, structure and length, relative count data (i.e. words or phrases per 10,000 words in the document) provides information on the relative quantitative importance of different topical themes across corporations in the respective document or set of documents, and changes thereof over time. Table 3 provides an overview of the text-mining analysis, reporting on the overall frequency of words per 10,000 words in the document.

With respect to SDG reporting, the analysis of annual reports and sustainability reports separately shows relatively similar characteristics as compared to the analysis in the previous section. However, when looking at reporting changes in the sustainability reports, it is now all companies (12 compared to 11 reported in the previous section) increasing the relative quantity of SDG reporting between 2010 and 2020. With respect to the combined analysis of the annual reports and the sustainability reports, it is now 32 (instead of 31) of the 33 companies increasing the relative reporting intensity.

As far as SDG 8-related reporting in annual reports, sustainability reports and the combination of the two reports are concerned, all companies in the respective samples cover aspects related to decent work. However, when looking at changes over time, it is noteworthy that 15 out of 33 companies have reduced the quantity of decent work-related material in annual reports between 2010 and 2022. When analysing sustainability reports, however, all companies increased the relative reporting intensity. Finally, when analysing the relative quantity of SDGs-related and SDG 8-related reporting for the combined set of documents (annual reports and sustainability reports together), SDG-related reporting was reduced at 2 out of 33 companies, while SDG 8-related reporting decreased at 4 out of 33 corporations.

Table 3 Score of the text-mining analysis (per 10,000 words)

	Annual reports				Sustainability reports				Annual & sustainability reports			
	MDG/SDG		Decent Work		MDG/SDG		Decent Work		MDG/SDG		Decent Work	
	2010	2020	2010	2020	2010	2020	2010	2020	2010	2020	2010	2020
Adidas	23.3	39.3	3.1	1.6	961.4		104.8		484.3	392.8	56.2	15.7
Airbus	35.1	59.5	2.7	5.7					351.2	595.0	27.0	41.2
Allianz	14.4	43.8	0.7	1.9	1277.0	1963.0	0.0	65.8	390.6	1029.0	5.2	38.5
BASF	55.2	85.0	2.7	8.7					551.6	849.8	27.0	68.3
Bayer	35.5	66.2	0.5	0.5	1087.2	1942.5	12.6	42.0	572.8	1056.2	7.5	16.9
BMW	19.9	54.6	1.7	4.0	1046.1		32.5		516.7	546.0	23.1	35.2
Beiersdorf	17.4	76.5	2.0	3.4	1001.5	1922.1	22.1	125.6	394.0	946.0	20.6	58.8
Brenntag	13.7	32.9	0.9	0.3		1128.2		48.4	137.2	533.7	9.4	15.5
Continental	17.1	31.3	4.1	1.9		688.0		54.6	171.4	441.9	41.3	32.3
Covestro		103.2		13.8		2178.8		224.5		1097.7		151.6
Daimler	19.2	37.7	1.6	2.2	841.9	1168.2	28.0	30.3	366.6	687.3	19.4	23.4
Delivery Hero		35.0		1.0						350.3		15.0
Deutsche Bank	12.4	27.6	1.4	3.9					124.2	276.5	13.7	18.4
Deutsche Boerse	12.4	26.1	1.4	1.7	658.4		39.2		211.0	261.5	18.5	19.7
Deutsche Post	10.8	42.0	1.5	1.6	1103.1		31.4		555.3	419.8	22.5	23.9
Deutsche Telekom	14.0	28.5	2.3	3.5	809.0	1223.9	20.9	66.7	485.3	550.2	21.9	36.5

	Annual reports				Sustainability reports				Annual & sustainability reports			
	MDG/SDG		Decent Work		MDG/SDG		Decent Work		MDG/SDG		Decent Work	
	2010	2020	2010	2020	2010	2020	2010	2020	2010	2020	2010	2020
Deutsche Wohnen	20.6	45.7	3.0	2.3		1703.2		111.4	205.5	927.1	30.1	63.4
E.ON	32.1	43.2	1.2	1.9	1019.3	1147.8	7.7	22.0	517.8	663.9	10.9	19.9
Fresenius Medical Care	42.5	71.2	1.2	0.5					425.3	711.9	12.0	4.6
Fresenius	60.5	104.0	1.0	1.1					604.6	1040.1	9.8	8.2
Heidelberg Cement	28.7	46.9	4.6	4.8		1514.3		117.7	286.9	711.8	45.7	67.1
HelloFresh		25.2		1.2		2336.4		34.4		721.7		32.5
Henkel	19.2	54.4	3.6	2.3	906.5	1583.5	44.0	186.9	353.7	972.3	37.9	92.2
Infineon	29.4	32.9	1.8	0.7		1630.0		65.7	294.1	567.7	18.2	19.1
Linde	30.8	19.7	1.0	0.1	1211.8	1644.6	46.9	75.5	456.5	903.4	16.2	37.8
Merck	47.6	56.1	0.9	1.0		1372.8		50.9	475.5	873.0	9.0	25.1
MTU	18.0	39.7	1.2	0.7		1647.6		137.3	179.7	791.4	11.6	49.4
Muenchener Rueck	19.9	40.5	1.6	0.6		1635.8		71.6	198.8	769.6	15.7	26.3
Puma	58.0	82.4	3.3	3.6					579.9	824.4	32.5	52.8
Qiagen	35.2	45.9	0.8	0.8	1252.4		0.0		426.2	459.3	7.0	12.3

(continued)

Table 3 (continued)

	Annual reports				Sustainability reports				Annual & sustainability reports			
	MDG/SDG		Decent Work		MDG/SDG		Decent Work		MDG/SDG		Decent Work	
	2010	2020	2010	2020	2010	2020	2010	2020	2010	2020	2010	2020
RWE	38.6	57.2	0.5	0.5	1057.6	1413.9	20.1	36.2	551.6	846.5	9.1	16.4
SAP	25.6	73.3	1.6	4.9	1129.2		27.2		446.3	733.1	18.4	41.7
Sartorius	27.8	49.2	2.8	1.8					277.9	492.0	28.3	28.3
Siemens	36.3	27.9	1.9	0.6	1360.3	1517.3	29.3	105.4	553.8	731.7	21.0	43.6
Siemens Energy		58.9		0.7		1831.7		107.0		924.4		36.3
Siemens Health		32.0		0.9						319.8		14.6
Symrise	33.3	104.6	3.5	1.4	590.6	1540.1	11.4	57.8	404.3	1355.9	28.4	57.7
Volkswagen	20.1	46.0	1.4	1.9	774.4	1475.9	61.5	174.8	311.5	707.2	23.0	54.2
Vonovia		52.6		2.3		1566.5		62.5		858.8		36.3
Zalando		25.2		0.5		1655.6		98.9		588.2		30.9
Number of reports	*33*	*40*	*33*	*40*	*18*	*25*	*18*	*25*	*33*	*40*	*33*	*40*

6 Discussion and Conclusions

This chapter analysed corporate disclosure information published in annual reports and sustainability reports of multinational corporations listed in the DAX 40 stock market index in 2010 and 2020 to capture the commitment of business organisation to both the UN's sustainable development agenda and to the ILO's decent work agenda.

Even though word frequency analysis and text-mining analysis do not allow for interpretation with respect to the content of corporate policies and practices, the analysis yields some interesting observations of corporate reporting on the SDGs and decent work. The first two stages of the analysis provided a descriptive overview of the quantitative use, both in absolute and relative terms, of keywords in both types of corporate reports at two points in time. The analysis shows the increasing—at least quantitative—importance of the SDGs in corporate reporting during the observation period. And this applies equally to both word frequency analysis and the topical text-mining analysis.

There has also been an increase in corporate reports referring to SDG 8 (decent work and economic growth) with respect to the word frequency analysis. However, from the text-mining analysis it emerges that while the quantity of SDG 8 reporting increased for all companies publishing a sustainability report in 2010 and 2020, it decreased in the annual reports for 10 out of 33 companies. While this may indicate that over time annual reports have become less relevant for SDG 8 reporting, this finding should be scrutinised in further research. When looking at the analysis for both types of reports combined, in 2020 29 out of the 22 corporations in the sample referred to SDG 8 in either of the two reports, but four companies reduced the overall quantity of SDG 8 coverage in their reporting.

While the analysis yields some interesting results, one should not omit several methodological limitations of the chosen approach. To begin with, findings indicate that purely quantitative keyword frequency count-based analysis of corporate disclosure information should be treated with caution, especially analysis that focuses on total count data. In the reported analysis, moving from total count data to relative count data provided a more nuanced and differentiated picture of the reporting structures.

The chosen approach allows to compare and contrast the findings with the analysis of corporate disclosure information of accounting and consulting companies and other organisations, especially with respect to the reliability and validity of the results. As it is based on publicly available information and transparent in terms of the analytical process, the analysis can be easily replicated with data for different sets of companies and time periods.

Concerning research methods, the text mining analysis used a dictionary which was developed to measure SDG 8, which covers both decent work and economic growth. Future analysis could further specify the dictionary so that the analysis could distinguish between different aspects and dimensions of economic growth and decent work.

There are various implications of these findings, which should be addressed and explored in future research. To begin with, there seems to be considerable variation across companies with respect to cross-sectional data for both 2010 and 2020. Analysis could focus on identifying the drivers of cross-sectional (i.e., cross-company variation). Can this variation be explained by the usual control variables, such as company size or industry affiliation? Or are there other factors involved, such as company-specific events, NGO pressure, media reports, changes in corporate strategy, management composition, or formal and informal institutions? At a more general level, replicating the analysis with other company datasets or for different time periods may yield interesting insights on whether the findings are generalizable.

Furthermore, looking at changes over time, additional information on company-specific trajectories would be useful to identify industry-specific or company-specific factors. Adding data points for the years between 2010 and 2020 could produce a more nuanced and detailed picture of change processes. Does the sustainability and/or decent works-related intensity of corporate reporting change for all companies at the same time, or are there industry- or company-specific trajectories? What explains cross-company variation over time? While the reporting intensity seems to generally increase with respect to SDG reporting, there are several companies reducing decent work reporting. How can this be explained?

Ultimately, from the perspective of business ethics and responsible international business, this research raises several questions to be addressed in future research. Do these changes between 2010 and 2020 follow a linear trend? What are the drivers of the respective developments? The present analysis does not consider the qualitative content of the analysed documents. Further research should analyse the qualitative content of the respective reports, and analyse the link between corporate commitment, corporate behaviour and sustainability-related as well as decent work-related outcomes.

References

Aggarwal, C. C., & Zhai, C. (2018). *An introduction to text mining*. Sage.

Deegan, C. (2002). The legitimising effect of social and environmental disclosures—A theoretical foundation. *Accounting, Auditing & Accountability Journal, 15*(3), 282–311.

Deegan, C. (2014). Organizational legitimacy as a motive for sustainability reporting. In J. Unerman, J. Bebbington, & B. O'Dwyer (Eds.), *Sustainability accounting and accountability* (2nd ed., pp. 248–272). Routledge.

Drover, W., Wood, M. S., & Corbett, A. C. (2018). Toward a cognitive view of signalling theory: Individual attention and signal set interpretation. *Journal of Management Studies, 55*(2), 209–231.

Fields, G. S. (2003). Decent work and development policies. *International Labour Review, 142*(2), 239–262.

Global Reporting Initiative, UN Global Compact, & WSCSD. (2015). *SDG compass: The guide for business action on the SDGs.*

Hahn, R., & Kühnen, M. (2013). Determinants of sustainability reporting: A review of results, trends, theory, and opportunities in an expanding field of research. *Journal of Cleaner Production, 59*, 5–21.

ILO. (1999). *Report of the Director-General: Decent work*. International Labour Office.

ILO. (2007). *Toolkit for mainstreaming employment and decent work*. International Labour Office.

ILO. (2017). *Decent work and the 2030 agenda for sustainable development*. International Labour Office.
KPMG. (2016). *How to report on the SDGs—What good looks like and why it matters*.
Kwartler, T. (2017). *Text mining in practice with R*. Wiley.
Maniora, J. (2017). Is integrated reporting really the superior mechanism for the integration of ethics into the core business model? An empirical analysis. *Journal of Business Ethics, 140*(4), 755–786.
Michelon, G., Trojanowski, G., & Sealy, R. (2022). Narrative reporting: State of the art and future challenges. *Accounting in Europe, 19*(1), 7–47.
Patrick, K., & Bernd, B. (2012). Corporate sustainability management: Evidence from Germany. *Journal of Global Responsibility, 3*(2), 8–8.
Pogge, T., & Sengupta, M. (2016). Assessing the sustainable development goals from a human rights perspective. *Journal of International and Comparative Social Policy, 32*(2), 83–97.
PWC. (2017). *SDG reporting challenge 2017 exploring business communication on the global goals*.
PWC. (2018). *From promise to reality: Does business really care about the SDGs?*
PWC. (2019). *Creating a strategy for a better world*.
Rantanen, J., Muchiri, F., & Lehtinen, S. (2020). Decent work, ILO's response to the globalization of working life: Basic concepts and global implementation with special reference to occupational health. *International Journal of Environmental Research and Public Health, 17*(10), 3351.
Renwick, N. (2011). Millennium development goal 1: Poverty, hunger and decent work in Southeast Asia. *Third World Quarterly, 32*(1), 65–89.
Shoaf, V., Jermakowicz, E. K., & Epstein, B. J. (2018). Toward sustainability and integrated reporting. *Review of Business, 38*(1), 1–15.
Sinkovics, N., Vieira, L. M., & van Tulder, R. (2022). Working toward the sustainable development goals in earnest—Critical international business perspectives on designing and implementing better interventions. *Critical Perspectives on International Business, 18*(4), 445–456.
Spence, M. (1974). *Market signaling: Informational transfer in hiring and related screening processes*. Harvard University Press.
Tan, A., Benni, D., & Liani, W. (2016). Determinants of corporate social responsibility disclosure and investor reaction. *International Journal of Economics and Financial Issues, 6*(4), 11–17.
Thorne, L., Mahoney, L. S., & Manetti, G. (2014). Motivations for issuing standalone CSR reports: A survey of Canadian firms. *Accounting, Auditing & Accountability Journal, 27*(4), 686–714.

Trebilcock, A. (2018). Challenges in Germany's implementation of the ILO decent work for domestic workers convention. *International Journal of Comparative Labour Law and Industrial Relations, 34*(2), 149–176.

United Nations. (2000). Resolution adopted by the General Assembly [without reference to a Main Committee (A/55/L.2)]—55/2.

United Nations. (2015a). *Transforming our world: The 2030 agenda for sustainable development*. Resolution adopted by the General Assembly on 25 September 2015 [without reference to a Main Committee (A/70/L.1)] 70/1.

United Nations. (2015b). *Transforming our world: The 2030 agenda for sustainable development*. United Nations Development Group.

Van Tulder, R., Rodrigues, S. B., Mirza, H., & Sexsmith, K. (2021). The UN's Sustainable Development Goals: Can multinational enterprises lead the Decade of Action? *Journal of International Business Policy, 4*(1), 1–21.

Velte, P. (2021). Archival research on integrated reporting: A systematic review of main drivers and the impact of integrated reporting on firm value. *Journal of Management and Governance, 26*(3), 997–1061.

Wang, W., Kang, W., & Mu, J. (2023). Mapping research to the Sustainable Development Goals (SDGs). https://doi.org/10.21203/rs.3.rs-2544385/v2

World Commission on the Social Dimension of Globalization. (2004). *A fair globalization: Creating opportunities for all*. International Labour Office.

World Economic Forum. (2014). *White paper on business sustainability: What it is and why it matters*.

Zagelmeyer, S. (2019). Human rights reporting of BRIC and non-BRIC MNEs: An exploratory comparative analysis. In A. Chidlow, P. N. Ghauri, T. Buckley, E. C. Gardner, A. Qamar, & E. Pickerimg (Eds.), *The Changing strategies of international business* (pp. 157–174). Palgrave Macmillan.

5

MNE Intercession, Antitrust, and Supply Chain Slavery: A New Regulatory Strategy to Realise SDG 8.7

Brent Malcolm Burmester

1 Introduction

The United Nations (UN) has made clear that realisation of the Sustainable Development Goals (SDGs) depends on aligned efforts from states, civil society, and the business community's most influential members. This is no truer than in respect of Target 7 of SDG 8, (hereafter SDG 8.7) which sets out the priority to end child labour by 2025, and modern slavery, forced labour, and human trafficking by 2030.

Although MNEs domiciled in developed countries will not be caught subjecting their own employees to abuses and loudly condemn labour exploitation in their supply chains, their role in sustaining modern slavery remains significant. The practice of relocating production activities through international outsourcing and transferring economic risk and legal liability away from themselves through an elaborated chain of

B. M. Burmester (✉)
Centre for Research on Modern Slavery, University of Auckland Business School, Auckland, New Zealand
e-mail: b.burmester@auckland.ac.nz

N. Sinkovics et al. (eds.), *International Business and SDG 8*, The Academy of International Business, https://doi.org/10.1007/978-3-031-46802-5_5

suppliers and distributors, results in subcontractors resorting to labour super-exploitation in order to retain their place in global production networks (Crane, 2013).

Some MNEs, especially consumer-facing, issue assurances that they understand the problem of modern slavery and are making the necessary private governance reforms to eliminate it from their supply chains. They voluntarily take positive steps towards ending labour rights violations, revising supply contracts and purchasing practices, engaging the services of independent social auditors, and forming anti-slavery alliances with competitors and non-governmental organisations. However, there remains deep antipathy towards the idea that shareholders should make sacrifices in the cause of foreign labour, and many companies pay mere lip service to anti-slavery campaigning.

Consumer and investor activism has so far proved inadequate to stimulate sincere commitment to eradicating labour exploitation from supply chains, and they are likely to weaken as the global economy slips into recession and thereafter into a succession of climate-induced crises. There are strong indicators that the majority of MNEs will only play their part subject to command. Accordingly, ground-breaking legislative responses are being trialled in several countries (Ford & Nolan, 2020). New and forthcoming legislation is either aimed directly at modern slavery, as in Australia, New South Wales, and the United Kingdom, or more broadly at human rights violations implicating business, as in France, Germany, and Norway.

With the advent of these national laws, a new relationship is forming between the law and corporate power. Legislation now seeks to compel MNEs to harness their market power and intercede on behalf of workers in rights-violating firms in their supply chains. Historically, the law ensuring proper market conduct, known as competition law or, in the United States, antitrust, has deterred coercion of independent firms by powerful corporations. This is an area of law with deep historical roots, more than a century of judicial rulings and legislative action, augmented by a vast and energetic academic literature. Modern slavery law, compelling MNEs to make greater use of their influence over supply chain participants, appears to hold a mirror to antitrust, which is intent on stemming the abuse of power by companies in possession of dominant market positions, such as those occupied by MNE lead firms, suggesting potential complementarities if brought together conceptually and in practice. This chapter considers whether antitrust might offer a means to reinforce MNE liability for supply chain slavery, and thus help realise SDG 8.7.

2 SDG 8.7, Supply Chain Slavery, and Modern Slavery Law

2.1 SDG 8.7

In 2015, the UN promulgated seventeen SDGs, among them SDG 8, to promote sustained, inclusive and sustainable economic growth, full and productive employment, and decent work for all. Targets 1–6 of SDG 8 relate to economic growth, productivity, development, efficiency, and full employment in decent work, especially for youth. SDG 8.9 concerns jobs in sustainable tourism and 8.10 aims to create greater public access to banking and finance. Targets 8.7 and 8.8 stand apart in their call to end labour rights abuses. SDG 8.8 promotes the need to uphold the rights of all who labour, emphasising the particular disrespect shown to migrants. SDG 8.7 concentrates on the labouring minority who experience human rights violations in the course of their employment, and declares the international community's intention to:

> Take immediate and effective measures to eradicate forced labour, end modern slavery and human trafficking and secure the prohibition and elimination of the worst forms of child labour, including recruitment and use of child soldiers, and by 2025 end child labour in all its forms.

This is an ambitious target. Between 2016 and 2021, the number of people in modern slavery *increased* by 10 million to an estimated 50 million people, according to the International Labour Organization, Walk Free Foundation, and the International Organization for Migration (ILO et al., 2022). This, admittedly approximate, figure includes prison labour, women in forced marriages who do not constitute the primary subjects of concern here. This leaves around a third of the total victims of forced labour in the private sector, the majority trafficked into the sex industry. However, an unmeasured proportion of the remainder is bound within multi-tiered global supply chains subject to the private governance of MNEs. Our inability to accurately count the victims is ultimately far less important than the relationship between their suffering and MNE profitability.

2.2 Supply Chain Slavery

Modern slavery occurs everywhere, even in the most developed countries, and in industries ranging from agriculture, construction, horticulture, and mining, to automobiles, cell phones, electronics, and high fashion (Chantavanich et al., 2016; Crane et al., 2022). Those subjects to modern slavery are seldom caged or chained, but they endure working conditions for which there can be no contractual compensation —one may not contract out of one's fundamental freedoms—and for which none is forthcoming. Skrivankova (2014, p. 1) observes that "the use of forced labour makes 'business sense', even if illegal, because the risks of discovery and prosecution are low, and [there is] weak enforcement of labour standards".

The connection between modern slavery and the flagship institutions of capitalism is coming under increased scrutiny (see, for example, Boersma & Nolan, 2022; Crane et al., 2019; LeBaron, 2021; New, 2015). MNEs supply chains are multi-tiered, highly fragmented, and often entwined with international labour supply chains. The complexities of MNEs' subcontracting networks allow the practice of modern slavery to remain hidden, and it is reasonable to assume this is not wholly unintended. Although IB scholarship on modern slavery is comparatively rare, a few examples are beginning to come to light (cf. Burmester et al., 2019; Caruana et al., 2021; Michailova et al., 2020; Stringer & Michailova, 2018; Stringer et al., 2021b). Nevertheless, this phenomenon demands far greater attention.

2.3 Modern Slavery Law

Following California's Transparency in Supply Chains Act of 2010, a small number of governments have enacted legislation designed to enlist corporations in the eradication of modern slavery. These laws encourage transparency, requiring organisations above a certain scale to publish reports on the risks of labour rights abuse in their supply chains. It transpires, however, that transparency legislation alone cannot move the dial, as corporate compliance is often perfunctory, if it is forthcoming at all (Islam & Van Staden, 2021; Pinnington et al., 2022; Rogerson et al., 2020; Schaper & Pollach, 2021; Stringer et al., 2021a).

In the wake of failed disclosure regimes comes a new generation of laws to tackle modern slavery and other abuses, in the form of mandatory human rights due diligence (mHRDD) legislation. These laws command companies to identify and remedy adverse human rights impacts associated with their supply chains, including abuses associated with modern slavery. As noted above, where abuses are detected or anticipated, mHRDD includes the duty to intercede to the extent that the corporation can. If corporations are found wanting in the commission of their due diligence, independent commissioners can perform investigations, levy fines, and initiate judicial procedures that might conclude with more serious penalties. These would be, for the most part, civil in nature, but criminal sanctions could be applied in cases of wilful neglect or where a particularly strong causal link is found between the dictates of the lead firm and the resort to rights abuses by the third party.

This latest generation of mHRDD and modern slavery laws began in 2017 with the French Duty of Vigilance Act, followed by the Netherlands' Child Labour Due Diligence Act 2019, Germany's Act on Corporate Due Diligence Obligations in Supply Chains 2021, the Swiss Code of Obligations 2022, and Norway's Transparency Act of 2022. These ultimately take their inspiration from the *Guiding Principles on Business and Human Rights* (UNGPs), endorsed by the United Nations Human Rights Council in 2011. Particularly relevant is Principle 19, which states that a business should, in response to the identification of adverse human rights impacts linked to it through a business relationship, take appropriate action according to its "leverage in addressing the adverse impact”. The commentary accompanying Principle 19 makes clear that the reference to leverage is with respect to entities directly responsible for human rights infringement (United Nations Office of the High Commissioner on Human Rights, 2011).

3 Intercession and Market Power

3.1 MNEs' Duty to Intercede

The performance of mHRDD does not require special competencies from companies. That is, due diligence expects the obligated entity to do only what is reasonable, and that is a matter ultimately left to the courts to determine the facts. SMEs, for example, possess limited means of confirming working conditions in enterprises to which they are vertically connected and may have very little corrective influence even over first-tier members of their supply chains. It is unreasonable to expect them to direct investigations across national and organisational boundaries in search of malfeasance, then demand its cessation and supervise restitution for those suffering harm. However, one advantage of this standard of care is that what is deemed reasonable will change as technologies and societal expectations evolve.

The duty to intercede becomes interesting when it must be performed by companies whose strategic decisions shape and reshape activity over multiple nodes of their internationally configured supply chains. These are lead firms, with significant strategic freedom. Gereffi distinguishes between “producer-driven” and “buyer-driven” chains, where lead firms' power derives from control over essential technologies, or their influence over consumption through the control over brands (Gereffi, 1994). These are invariably MNEs, either in the strict sense of being firms engaged in foreign direct investment (FDI) or in that they control externalised international production and distribution almost as comprehensively as they might through FDI. The MNE, then, is distinguished by its international market power, its relative autonomy in the supply chain, and its strategic freedom with respect to one or more global markets.

3.2 Deriving the Intercession Duty in a Human Rights Frame

Commentary around mHRDD characterises the intercession duty as the legal formalisation of the moral imperative to utilise a capacity to act in service of human rights. The UNGPs make clear that states are bound to protect human rights and businesses must respect them. In this analysis, the intercession duty, imposed upon corporations through national legislation, emanates first from the duty of the MNE's state of domicile to protect human rights, even extraterritorial. Thus, the MNE serves as an instrument of the state, and this use is legitimised by the corporation's duty to respect. Moreover, the MNE is sufficiently proximate, strategically speaking, to the site of violation to incur a 'bystander's duty' to step in to avert harm. Seen this way, mHRDD law is an expression of the state's obligation in international law and the MNE's obligation as an emergent personality in international law.

The human rights justification for mHRDD is complemented by the distinctively European legal tradition of punishing 'bad Samaritans' (McIntyre, 1994). Notably, European jurisdictions, where a failure to render assistance may attract criminal sanction, have advanced further in respect of imposing mHRDD than common law countries where such failures are deemed only morally problematic (McIntyre, 1994). For example, in the United States, persons, individual and corporate, are not subject to a general obligation to engage in 'rescue' when they have made no formal undertaking to play that role (Abraham & Kendrick, 2018). Thus, key jurisdictions in the global economy will struggle to enact and enforce full mHRDD. Perhaps not coincidentally, Canada's Bill S-211, addressing child and forced labour in supply chains, makes no material advance on the disclosure regimes of first-generation modern slavery laws, despite being passed in May 2023.

3.3 Market Power, Intercession, and Liability

An alternative explanation of the supply chain intercession duty derives from the abuse of market power. In this reading, an MNE must be compelled to intercede where rights violations occur in their supply chains where it has not exerted its, potentially unlawful, market power to prevent them. The duty rests on an assumption that the MNE is not newly possessed of sufficient market power to coerce subcontractors into compliance with international labour norms, rather, that power existed prior to the risk of violation and was not relied upon to attenuate that risk.

This is entirely consistent with how IB construes MNEs' adaptation to, and propulsion of, globalisation through outsourcing labour-intensive or high compliance-cost activities to developing countries, retreating from direct control over subsidiary production and thus insulating themselves from liability for ensuing harms (Contractor et al., 2010). The withdrawal from equity-sourced control over production was emphatically advanced by the ability of MNEs to leverage international control over essential intellectual properties, thanks to the 1995 implementation of the Trade-Related Aspects of Intellectual Property Rights (TRIPS), a global IP regime installed by and for MNEs (Sell, 2002). Also relevant in the sphere of international law is the *absence* of a global antitrust regime, which would have crippled MNE efforts to exert extraterritorial control over third-party firms.

Modern slavery and business and human rights law treat the MNE community as jointly morally accountable and severally legally liable—although weakly so—for the persistence of labour super-exploitation in MNE-dominated supply chains. The conventional IB account of MNE reconfigurations since the 1980s supports this stance. MNE power to prevent forced labour has been deliberately or, at best, negligently withheld, opening the employment field to entities that know little of, and care little for, international labour standards. This reading finds MNEs culpable for failing to place demands for adherence to labour standards on foreign employers that would be otherwise responsive. The finding of liability for an omission to act is not in itself a legal novelty, but the nature of the omission in this scenario is extraordinary, because it is a failure to coerce a third party into behaviour the law itself cannot or will not command.

4 Market Power and Economic Coordination

4.1 Antitrust vs mHRDD

The concerns of antitrust seem somewhat removed from the defence of labour rights, especially those of offshore third-party employees. Antitrust addresses market dominance or monopolisation within a nationally defined product market; restrictive trade practices, which are an abuse of the power associated with monopoly; and mergers and acquisitions, which serve to increase industrial concentration and the potential for monopolisation. The point of these various bodies of law is to prevent the abuse of power afforded by monopoly. Competition lawyers, law scholars, and judges are not entirely in accord about why it is important to keep markets free from monopolisation, or how that should be achieved (Paul, 2020). However, the working consensus in the antitrust community is that monopoly should be challenged when it diminishes consumer welfare.

The regulation of competition remains almost exclusively national in scope, leaving MNEs free to establish dominance in an extensive range of product markets with which most consumers are familiar, from sunglasses to petroleum. Also working in the favour of MNEs is that states tolerate monopolistic positions on the grounds of efficiency and rivalry or contestation. Generally, competition law adheres tightly to microeconomic orthodoxy, insofar that it regards competition as a guarantor of allocative efficiency and the maximisation of consumer welfare. But courts remain ready to be convinced that fierce rivalry in a duopoly, or the credible threat of entry to a monopolised market by one or more powerful economic agents, such as a state-owned enterprise or a foreign MNE, might provide a sufficient disincentive to manipulate prices or quantities contrary to the consumer's interest. Courts are also prepared to hear arguments extolling the efficiency enhancing virtues of scale and scope, which large MNEs boast in abundance, and thus allow the acquisition or maintenance of a dominant position. These exceptions depend very much on the fact that the putative interests of consumers have been allowed to eclipse those of other actors.

The call to restore the defence of labour as a cause for antitrust intervention is growing in response to the fissuring of the workplace described in Weil (2014), leading to the emergence of the 'gig economy' and its associated precarity. Critics of the consumer welfare fixation draw on a longstanding association between labour rights and antitrust. The statutory suppression of monopolies began in response to the alarming power accumulated by US railway businesses structured as trusts (hence 'antitrust'). This was considered a threat not only to other economic actors, but to democracy itself. The giant firm, not yet structured in the form of the contemporary corporation, simply possessed too much influence over outcomes in and around markets that it threatened to undermine government in the general interest. Further, it was perceived monopolists not only had the power to set prices above competitive rates, they had the power to set wages below them. Gradually, courts and legislatures accepted that one way to constrain the power of dominant firms was to allow the cartelisation of labour, in the form of unions. This is known as the labour exemption, in that what is not allowed for sellers of commodities is allowed for sellers of their own labour (Paul, 2020). The right to organise for the purposes of collective bargaining is recognised in the International Labour Organization's Convention 98.

What happens when labour is deprived of this right in countries that do little else to protect labour rights or deter monopoly? Ultimately, predictably, modern slavery emerges.

4.2 Antitrust and Economic Coordination

An emerging theme in the previous sections has been the relationship between the duty of intercession to relieve modern slaves in supply chains, and the extent of the firm. That is, the duty flows from the potential for the locus of abuse to be internal to the MNE; the potential for the employees at risk to be employed by the MNE itself, and thereby made safe. Within the realm of competition law scholarship, the extent of the firm, indeed, the very fact of its existence, has become the subject of intensifying interest. At this point, our examination of the duty to intercede intersects with new thinking in law and economics.

An emergent body of antitrust policy advocacy builds upon critical reconsideration of the historical roots of antitrust in common law, social sanction, and economic theory (Paul, 2020; Steinbaum, 2021). In essence, it argues that the principles and purposes of contemporary competition law are narrow, illogical, and ideologically biased (Paul, 2019, 2020). The resultant structuring of economic activity, particularly the concentration of economic power in corporations—MNEs especially—and the disenfranchisement of organised labour, is exposed as unnecessary and unjust (Steinbaum, 2019). Sanjukta Paul, an influential contributor in this vein, insists that the proper function of antitrust is to ensure economic coordination rights are allocated in the interests of social justice. This entails the enforcement of contextually appropriate trade-offs between efficiency and equity, competition and cooperation.

IB is very familiar with the transaction cost explanation of firm limits, but for firms to coalesce so that transaction costs are minimised, it must first be possible for that coalescence to be permissible in law. The existence of the firm is obviously not illegal, but it is not entirely clear why. The problem resides in the lack of clarity regarding economic coordination rights. As Paul (2020) argues, antitrust is ultimately about delimiting the population of persons with whom a given economic actor is entitled to coordinate. Coordination, in this sense, relates to the setting of transacting terms offered to parties *external* to the coordinated dyad, including with whom else coordinating actors may transact or engage in further coordination. Firms competing in a product market, for example, have no right to coordinate on such matters, and this seems intuitively correct. Similarly, a seller may not impose vertical restraints on a buyer, dictating resale price or restricting to whom the buyer may resell (IB works differently here because of the absence of transnational antitrust).

Firms are awash with coordination disallowed between market participants. Because this coordination minimises transaction costs, potentially to the consumer's benefit, antitrust grants what has been dubbed the "firm exemption" (Paul, 2019). However, to curtail market power competition authorities may seek to modify firm limits through forced divestment, or *externalisation.* In contrast, the intercession duty pushes in the opposite direction, nudging the MNE towards *internalisation.* Legislation cannot insist that MNEs acquire third parties in their supply chains where modern slavery risk is high, but the requirement that MNEs directly engage with abusive employees to restore compliance with international labour standards incentivises reconsideration of firm boundaries. The level of supervision mandated by the duty to intercede raises transaction costs potentially to the point that it might be easier for MNEs to make rather than buy. Although that could be achieved through reshoring or friend-shoring production activities, this would entail the severance of contractual relations with the non-compliant company, which leaves the victims of labour rights violation in a worse position. Perceiving that this remedy might be favoured by lead firms, the guidance around the observance of HRDD explicitly advises that contract termination should be a last resort.

For present purposes, the most interesting aspect of the reformulation of antitrust as an allocator of economic coordination rights, is that these rights pertain not only to classical hierarchic coordination within firms, but also to the right to exert coordination across markets. Antitrust, as we have seen, generally withholds that right, but the intercession duty depends on it. Just as the economic coordination framework challenges the 'obviousness' of the firm, it also puts back into issue the 'evil' of vertical restraints. Are they necessarily wrong? The intercession duty suggests otherwise.

4.3 Modern Slavery as Dysfunctional Eonomic Coordination

We may reconceive modern slavery in MNE supply chains as part of the broad range of legal challenges falling under the rubric of economic coordination. The recognition of the firm exception in antitrust is particularly interesting in the context of intercession.

By externalising labour-intensive production to employers unrestrained by international labour norms, MNEs have achieved on an international basis, what they have done in their home countries and developed host countries through a process described as workplace fissuring (Weil, 2014). This involves relinquishing employment relations to low-profile third parties, either contract labour suppliers or employees-in-all-but-name who are legally designated as independent contractors who are forbidden to collude, who then run the gauntlet of labour law violations. Thus, coordination between workers and small producers in developing and developed country contexts is suppressed by law: anti-union law in developing countries, antitrust in the developed.

The reconceptualisation of competition law as the law of economic coordination is potentially very important to the realisation of SDG 8.7 and to international business practice and scholarship. Challenges to the paradigm of economic regulation signal increasing policy relevance for leading topics of interest within international business (IB) and strategy, in particular the boundaries and organisation of the firm and the governance of internationalised production systems. Since the mid-1980s, IB has been fascinated by the advent of the increasingly 'fabless' firm, as MNEs began to shed their manufacturing capacity in favour of outsourcing (Contractor, 1990; Kotabe, 1989; Miles & Snow, 1986). This phenomenon soon became entangled in the offshoring surge that began in the 1990s. IB and adjacent fields of study, especially in the GVC domain, (e.g. Gereffi, 2019) have closely followed the organisational implications of these trends, analysing the changing shape and permanence of firm boundaries and interactions across state borders. This research is already beginning to make a positive difference in the sphere of public policy by informing the design of modern slavery and business and human rights legislation (eg Barrientos et al., 2010), and can go further if allied to the regulation of economic coordination.

5 The Prospects for Transnational Regulation

5.1 Paths to Globalising Modern Slavery Governance

The preceding exploration of the entwining of mHRDD and antitrust suggests alternative avenues to transnational regulation of employer conduct that have yet to be tested. At present, the following approaches to international governance may be discerned.

5.1.1 National Implementation

The first is underway in the form of complementary national legislations that, if sufficiently ubiquitous, consistent, and effective, creates genuinely transnational obligations on corporations, capturing the greater part of the world's MNE population and, literally by extension, millions of lesser enterprises situated extraterritorially. Should too few countries opt to introduce this legislation, or if many more do, but without effective penalties, MNEs will be able to evade burdensome obligations through selection of legal domicile.

5.1.2 Supranational Implementation

The second approach is to replicate or advance upon second-generation national legislative innovations through supranational legal texts. The EU offers the only extant example of the former, in the guise of its Corporate Sustainable Reporting Directive, which came into effect in January 2023. It will not be effective across the entire EU territory until mid-2025, by which time all EU member states should have passed legislation embodying the principles laid out in the Directive.

5.1.3 Global Implementation

The third approach takes the form of the United Nations' Binding Instrument on Business and Human Rights. The Binding Instrument would set a new benchmark in terms of the imposition of duties on MNEs and would range much further than labour super-exploitation. The duty to intervene is expected to play an important role therein. Negotiations of the text of the Binding Instrument are ongoing, and it is not clear that it will gather the necessary support in the UN General Assembly to come into force. The technical and political challenges in making MNEs subject to international law are considerable, and, for now, the prospects for this initiative remain uncertain.

5.2 A New Hope: Allying Modern Slavery Law with Antitrust

Encouraging MNEs to take their human rights due diligence seriously is the key challenge to the realisation of SDG 8.7. As noted in the introduction, some form of compulsion is needed. The preceding discussion reveals that this compulsion could come from the enforcement of competition law, most especially if it is administered on an international basis.

The promise of antitrust as a lever to enforce mHRDD rests in the relationship between market power and the duty to intercede. The goal of antitrust is to constrain the employment of market power to coordinate with parties that should be free to make independent strategic decisions, and on the other, the goal of mHRDD is to compel the use of that power to coordinate with supply chain partners to expunge employment practices that violate human rights. Where antitrust would seek to diminish market power, mHRDD law would see it preserved to effect pro-social change. There, then, is the boost modern slavery law so badly needs.

Where? In the potential for an MNE to retain its power, or at least not be stripped of it altogether, by demonstrating its proactivity in the sphere of human rights due diligence, especially in its execution of the intercession duty. The pro-social deployment of monopoly power thus presents as a defence against the application of antitrust penalties, especially where antitrust is reactive to the detection of power, as opposed to its misuse. Paradoxically, the internalisation of a production site where the risk of labour rights violations is high, increasing the power of the MNE over the supply chain, would be the most cogent demonstration of the MNE's preparedness to utilise its power responsibly. This would then dampen the fire of a global antitrust authority to order divestiture.

Here, too, is a solution to a seemingly intractable problem in the mHRDD domain. The simplest solution for an MNE confronted by a serious labour abuse in its supply chain is to simply sever its link with the offending participant. This is all but guaranteed to make the lives of modern slaves worse, so it is crucial that the duty to intercede is honoured. That is far more likely if an MNE can use its good faith engagement with supply chain participants as a means of protecting its hard-won market positions from zealous enforcement of antitrust standards.

Nationally administered antitrust cannot contend with the power wielded by the MNE over and through global supply chains, limiting its instrumentality in the modern slavery context. That is, national market power, the purview of national antitrust, does not necessarily grant a company an advantage in the protection of human rights extraterritorial. The corporate power that matters accrues from positions in markets spanning national territories, product categories, technologies, and production factors. Effective antitrust at the international level would clearly pose a significant threat to MNEs, but would consist of more than a plurality of national regimes aligned in content, intent, and extent. A web of national competition law systems, however well integrated, remains hamstrung by the narrow national competence of antitrust authorities. A transnational antitrust regime would instead be equipped to comprehend market power wielded on a global scale and therefore would be capable of striking at the way MNEs uniquely acquire and abuse their dominance. It would require an authority operating beyond the national level, with the means to discern and contend with the accumulation of market power that flows from the integration of a globally integrated system of production, distribution, and marketing.

In the absence of a global antitrust regime to complement the UN's nascent Binding Instrument on Business and Human Rights, we look to the EU as a model for what might become a reality on a larger scale. Within the EU there now exists, side by side, a supranational competition regime together with a supranational mHRDD regime. These have been designed and implemented in isolation from one another, but there now exists an opportunity for their natural complementarity to surface. It might not be long before an MNE anticipating antitrust intervention in the European market perceives it might reduce its liability through engagement in mHRDD and rely defensively on its efforts to eliminate modern slavery. The limiting factor here is that the most egregious violations of human rights in the workplace are not within the EU, but outside even that extensive community of nations. Only a truly global antitrust regime can incentivise the minimum level of anti-slavery engagement from MNEs necessary to make abolition possible.

6 Concluding Remarks

New thinking in the sphere of business and human rights may be complemented and augmented new thinking in antitrust. Reconceiving the legal challenge of modern slavery in terms of economic coordination carries major advantages. It situates the regulatory problem of labour exploitation in global supply chains within an issue area with well over a century of theory, policy, jurisprudence, and social engagement. The remapping promises new tools for analysis and solution design. Moreover, while it has proved notoriously difficult to elevate labour standards to the same normative priority as international rules governing trade and investment, competition rules are rising to a new prominence in international law (Noonan, 2008). Advances in the legal theory of economic coordination not only offer the chance to expand the effective domain of international competition law, but also grant a new creating an opportunity to exert legal pressure from an entirely new direction on MNEs practising irresponsible supply chain coordination.

References

Abraham, K. S., & Kendrick, L. (2018). There's no such thing as affirmative duty. *Iowa Law Review, 104*, 1649–1698.

Barrientos, S., Gereffi, G., & Rossi, A. (2010). Economic and social upgrading in global production networks: Developing a framework for analysis. *International Labor Review, 150*(3/4), 319–340.

Boersma, M., & Nolan, J. (2022). Modern slavery and the employment relationship: Exploring the continuum of exploitation. *Journal of Industrial Relations, 64*(2), 165–176.

Burmester, B., Michailova, S., & Stringer, C. (2019). Modern slavery and international business scholarship: The governance nexus. *Critical Perspectives on International Business, 15*(2/3), 139–157.

Caruana, R., Crane, A., Gold, S., & LeBaron, G. (2021). Modern slavery in business: The sad and sorry state of a non-field. *Business & Society, 60*(2), 251–287.

Chantavanich, S., Laodumrongchai, S., & Stringer, C. (2016). Under the shadow: Forced labour among sea fishers in Thailand. *Marine Policy, 68*, 1–7.

Contractor, F. J. (1990). Contractual and cooperative forms of international business: Towards a unified theory of modal choice. *Management International Review, 30*, 31–54.

Contractor, F. J., Kumar, V., Kundu, S. K., & Pedersen, T. (2010). Reconceptualizing the firm in a world of outsourcing and offshoring: The organizational and geographical relocation of high-value company functions. *Journal of Management Studies, 47*(8), 1417–1433.

Crane, A. (2013). Modern slavery as a management practice: Exploring the conditions and capabilities for human exploitation. *Academy of Management Review, 38*(1), 49–69.

Crane, A., LeBaron, G., Allain, J., & Behbahani, L. (2019). Governance gaps in eradicating forced labor: From global to domestic supply chains. *Regulation and Governance, 13*(1), 86–106.

Crane, A., LeBaron, G., Phung, K., Behbahani, L., & Allain, J. (2022). Confronting the business models of modern slavery. *Journal of Management Inquiry, 31*(3), 264–285. https://doi.org/10.1177/1056492621994904

Ford, J., & Nolan, J. (2020). Regulating transparency on human rights and modern slavery in corporate supply chains: The discrepancy between human

rights due diligence and the social audit. *Australian Journal of Human Rights, 26*(1), 27–45.
Gereffi, G. (1994). The organization of buyer-driven global commodity chains: How US retailers shape overseas production networks. In G. Gereffi & M. Korzeniewicz (Eds.), *Commodity chains and global capitalism* (pp. 95–122). Praeger.
Gereffi, G. (2019). Global value chains and international development policy: Bringing firms, networks and policy-engaged scholarship back in. *Journal of International Business Policy, 2*(3), 195–210.
International Labour Organization, Walk Free Foundation & International Organization for Migration. (2022). *Global estimates of modern slavery*. International Labour Organization.
Islam, M. A., & Van Staden, C. J. (2021). Modern slavery disclosure regulation and global supply chains: Insights from stakeholder narratives on the UK Modern Slavery Act. *Journal of Business Ethics, 180*(2), 455–479.
LeBaron, G. (2021). *Combatting modern slavery*. Polity Press.
Kotabe, M. (1989). "Hollowing-out" of US multinationals and their global competitiveness: An intrafirm perspective. *Journal of Business Research, 19*(1), 1–15.
McIntyre, A. (1994). Guilty bystanders? On the legitimacy of duty to rescue statutes. *Philosophy & Public Affairs, 23*(2), 157–191.
Michailova, S., Stringer, C., & Mezias, J. (2020). Letter from the editors: Special issue on "Investigating modern slavery: How IB scholarship can contribute". *AIB Insights, 20*(2).
Miles, R. E., & Snow, C. C. (1986). Organizations: New concepts for new forms. *California Management Review, 28*(3), 62–73.
New, S. J. (2015). Modern slavery and the supply chain: The limits of corporate social responsibility? *Supply Chain Management, 20*(6), 697–707.
Noonan, C. (2008). *The emerging principles of international competition law*. Oxford University Press.
Paul, S. (2019). Fissuring and the firm exemption. *Law & Contemporary Problems, 82*, 65.
Paul, S. (2020). Antitrust as allocator of coordination rights. *UCLA Law Review, 67*, 378–431.
Pinnington, B., Benstead, A., & Meehan, J. (2022). Transparency in supply chains (TISC): Assessing and improving the quality of modern slavery statements. *Journal of Business Ethics*.
Rogerson, M., Crane, A., Soundararajan, V., Grosvold, J., & Cho, C. H. (2020). Organisational responses to mandatory modern slavery disclosure

legislation: A failure of experimentalist governance? *Accounting, Auditing and Accountability Journal, 33*(7), 1505–1534.
Schaper, S., & Pollach, I. (2021). Modern slavery statements: From regulation to substantive supply chain reporting. *Journal of Cleaner Production, 313*, 127872.
Sell, S. K. (2002). Industry strategies for intellectual property and trade: The quest for TRIPS, and post-TRIPS strategies. *Cardozo Journal of International & Comparative Law, 10*, 79–108.
Skrivankova, K. (2014). Forced labour in the United Kingdom. *Joseph Rowntree Foundation*, 1–16.
Steinbaum, M. (2019). Antitrust, the gig economy, and labor market power. *Law & Contemporary Problems, 82*, 45.
Steinbaum, M. (2021). Common ownership and the corporate governance channel for employer power in labor markets. *The Antitrust Bulletin, 66*(1), 123–139.
Stringer, C., & Michailova, S. (2018). Why modern slavery thrives in multinational corporations' global value chains. *Multinational Business Review, 26*(3), 197–206.
Stringer, C., Burmester, B., Michailova, S., & Harré, T. (2021). *Toward a modern slavery act in New Zealand—Legislative landscape and steps forward*. https://www.auckland.ac.nz/content/dam/uoa/business/about/our-research/research-institutes-andentres/CReMS/CRMS%20Toward%20a%20Modern%20Slavery%20Act%20v1.1%20WEB.pdf
Stringer, C., Kartikasari, A., & Michailova, S. (2021b). 'They make a business out of desperate people': The role of recruitment agents in cross-border labour chains. *Australian Journal of Management, 46*(4), 672–689.
United Nations Office of the High Commissioner for Human Rights. (2011). *Guiding principles on business and human rights: Implementing the United Nation's 'protect, respect, and remedy' framework*. U.N. HR/PUB/11/04.
Weil, D. (2014). *The fissured workplace*. Harvard University Press.

6

Hiding in Plain Sight: Transparency and Ethics in Fashion Industry Global Value Chains

Louise Curran and Khalid Nadvi

1 Introduction

The Rana Plaza building collapse in Dhaka, Bangladesh in April 2013, which killed over 1100 people, is considered *the* worst disaster in the global fashion industry. It was, however, not the first such tragedy to result in significant loss of life in garment production. Deaths arising from poor health and safety measures have been a long-standing feature of fashion supply chains and disasters have been key mobilising events to promote better working conditions and greater transparency. The Triangle shirtwaist factory fire in New York in 1911 which killed 150 led to a raft of health and safety regulations and a regime of labour and building inspections. Similarly, Rana Plaza fostered several private

L. Curran (✉)
TBS Business School, Toulouse, France
e-mail: l.curran@tbs-education.fr

K. Nadvi
University of Manchester, Manchester, UK
e-mail: khalid.nadvi@manchester.ac.uk

N. Sinkovics et al. (eds.), *International Business and SDG 8*, The Academy of International Business, https://doi.org/10.1007/978-3-031-46802-5_6

and public–private health and safety governance initiatives focusing on building safety and working conditions in Bangladesh (Bair et al., 2020; Oka et al., 2020). It has also encouraged extensive efforts to improve transparency across fashion's global value chains (GVCs), as well as regulation to force companies to undertake due diligence (CEC, 2022). The assumption behind such efforts is that transparency and traceability will improve working conditions and wages in the fashion sector, thus contributing to the achievement of SDG8. Yet the link between such efforts and sustainability and ethics of GVCs is not automatic.

In this chapter, we focus on transparency and ask whether the extensive efforts which have gone into making fashion supply chains more transparent contribute to more sustainable and ethical outcomes? Our work draws on recent conceptualisations of transparency and ethical trade to develop a framework based on the key features of transparency identified by Egels-Zandén et al. (2015) and the principles of ethical trade, as defined by the Ethical Trading Initiative (ETI).[1] We use this framework to explore the potential impact of the transparency data emerging from fashion GVCs on ethics and sustainability, supplementing our analysis with interviews with key actors in the transparency ecosystem.

Our preliminary findings indicate that, although significant progress has been made, large variations in transparency still exist across the fashion industry. In addition, although more detailed disclosures certainly contribute to better understanding of GVCs, they also obscure many of the key factors of importance to ethical sourcing.

Clearly transparency is one of a range of tools which contribute to securing better outcomes for workers in fashion GVCs. We do not doubt that supply chain transparency is a step forward. Transparency facilitates due diligence and enables Non Government Organisations (NGOs) to access workers, such that redress in cases of unethical conduct is easier. However, as currently operationalised, we find that it provides limited information on many key ethical issues within GVCs and thus seems unlikely to have significant impacts on their ethics and sustainability.

[1] https://www.ethicaltrade.org/resources/eti-base-code.

2 Role of 'Transparency' in Ethical Sourcing in Global Value Chains

What distinguished Rana Plaza from the Triangle disaster a century earlier was not just the greater loss of life, but the international nature of the impacts. The deaths in Dhaka affected not just local workers and the Bangladesh state, but global retailers and consumers. In today's fashion industry local suppliers connect to distant end markets through complex GVCs organised and governed by global 'lead' firms, usually brand retailers. Rana Plaza was home to production for several such brands, yet most were completely unaware of their links to the building, which housed their second and third-tier suppliers.

The GVC framework provides a heuristic mapping of the links between lead firms and their multiple and globally disparate suppliers, as well as an understanding of the power and governance that shape these links (Gereffi et al., 2005). The role of standards relating to labour, working conditions, ethical norms and environmental impacts have been critical to discussions on the organisation of GVCs and lead firms' governance of suppliers (Nadvi, 2008). As concerns have emerged on the efficacy of private, lead firm driven traceability audits, there has been growing recognition of the need to incorporate state regulation in order to improve ethical outcomes (Alford & Phillips, 2018; Bartley, 2018).

Extant research on the effectiveness of lead firm-led traceability certification systems in GVCs is often sceptical about their capacity to secure improved working conditions and labour rights (Barrientos & Smith, 2007; Bartley, 2018; Freeman, 2003; Locke et al., 2009; Nadvi, 2008). Partly because of this, state regulations to improve 'due diligence', traceability and transparency on key labour issues have emerged and the European Commission has tabled a proposal for a Directive on Due Diligence in supply chains (CEC, 2022). In parallel, following Rana Plaza novel and/or more extensive transparency measures have emerged for the global fashion sector which focus on several aspects of sustainability. Yet, there has been limited scrutiny of the extent to which such transparency measures can actually make fashion sourcing more responsible and improve ethical outcomes (Egels-Zandén et al., 2015).

Transparency by lead firms with regard to their suppliers has long been a contested agenda. Firms at the forefront of supplier transparency included Levis and Nike. Doorey (2011) has explored how they came to publish their suppliers' lists after years of resistance. He highlighted the importance of both NGO campaigns and internal company reorganisation. Once some companies began to divulge their supply chain partners, this led to calls for a level playing field across the sector (Doorey, 2011; Levy & Egan, 2003).

Most observers see greater openness as a positive evolution, yet there are those who question its value. Some consider that it could have negative effects if it replaces responsibility. Gold and Heikkurinen (2018, p. 325) have coined the term the 'transparency fallacy' which they define as '*…an erroneous belief that stakeholder claims for corporate transparency will lead to increased corporate responsibility in international supply chains*'.

Much depends on how transparency is conceptualised and the extent to which it goes beyond disclosure of suppliers. In their in-depth analysis of the transparency efforts of one fashion company, Egels-Zandén et al., (2015, p. 95) defined supply chain transparency as encompassing: '*…disclosure of information about supplier names, sustainability conditions at suppliers and buyers' purchasing practices…*'. They conceived transparency as going far beyond factory lists, to include access to audit reports on factory conditions (often also resisted by suppliers) and purchasing practices (which were not disclosed). Their findings indicate that, even a firm that was seeking to be highly transparent: '*…managed to define transparency to, at least partly, serve its own interests by not disclosing central but sensitive information about purchasing practices and markups…*' (op. cit.: 100).

Thus, transparency often obscures issues that are vital to understanding the link between lead firm behaviour and social and environmental outcomes. Fieldwork has consistently shown that purchasing practices like the use of buyer power to push risk further down the supply chain and increasingly short lead times imposed on suppliers, have negative worker impacts, including high levels of overtime, insecure contracts and vulnerability to sudden changes in working practices (Barrientos & Smith, 2007; Locke et al., 2009; Kollbrunner, 2021; Plank et al., 2012). Thus, any assessment of the *ethics* of a lead firm's interaction with its suppliers along the GVC needs to cover this aspect. As we will see below, such information is rarely publicly available.

In terms of the impact of existing public regulation, there are several analyses of the company disclosures required under the Californian, UK and Australian anti-slavery legislation (Birkey et al., 2018; Pinnington et al., 2022). These regulations, which require disclosure of due diligence in a 'command and control' approach (Dubbink et al., 2008), are generally found to be ineffective. Many companies do not fulfil the requirements and those that do often only provide minimal information.

The French due diligence legislation, which came into effect in 2017, was seen as an important advance in increasing corporate responsibility along their supply chains, including third parties with whom they had an 'established economic relationship'. Analysis of how the law has been integrated into companies' operations indicates that its impact has been limited, with companies taking a strongly 'managerial' approach and NGOs critical of reporting (Barraud de Lagerie et al., 2020). Thus, questions still remain about the effectiveness of regulatory efforts on 'due diligence' and its attendant traceability requirements. In this context understanding the effectiveness of transparency efforts is even more important.

3 The Fashion Transparency and Ethics Ecosystem

The ecosystem of activism and monitoring of the fashion sector is increasingly complex. As highlighted above, the ethics of fashion sourcing has been a concern for decades and most actors on this issue predate those focusing on transparency. The ETI was founded in the UK in 1998 as an international cross-sectoral multi-stakeholder initiative (MSI) including firms, trade unions and NGOs. It promotes more ethical GVCs through a base code of ethical trading practices for member companies (discussed below). Fair Wear is a Dutch MSI focused on improving labour conditions in the garment industry, set up in 1999 with the help of the Dutch government. Their code of labour practices is very similar to ETI. In 2021 ETI and Fairwear together set up another

NGO—The Industry We Want (TIWW)—which aims to support cooperation towards more sustainable fashion. To help this process they are developing metrics to measure progress across three core issues of wages, purchasing practices and greenhouse gas emissions.

The Sustainable Apparel Coalition (SAC) is a more business-oriented fashion MSI, set up in the US in 2011 by Walmart and Patagonia. They too recently joined TIWW. ACT or 'Action on a living wage' is another MSI including trade unions and 17 brands focused on wages. At the factory level, the International Labour Organisation's (ILO) Better Work programme undertakes regular audits of member facilities and provides summary data on findings on working conditions.[2]

Several key frameworks are also relevant, including the UN Guiding Principles on Business and Human Rights (UN, 2011), the ILO's labour standards, especially its core conventions,[3] and the OECD Due Diligence Guidelines for the fashion sector (OECD, 2018). These frameworks are often incorporated into the operation of MSIs. Finally, there are several fashion-specific NGOs in this ecosystem that are often involved in MSIs, as well as transparency initiatives discussed below. Many are part of the Clean Clothes Campaign (CCC) collective, founded in Holland in 1989 which now includes 237 associations active in 45 countries.

The transparency landscape is more recent, having developed markedly in the last decade to include extensive data provision. The most far-reaching, in terms of coverage, is the Fashion Transparency Index (FTI), published annually by Fashion Revolution, an NGO, established after Rana Plaza, with the vision of: '*A global fashion industry that conserves and restores the environment and values people over growth and profit*'. In parallel, the Open Apparel Registry (OAR) was established to provide a user-friendly database to centralise supplier data provided by firms in reaction to civil society activism. Know The Chain (KTC) is a collaboration between several NGOs focusing specifically on forced

[2] https://portal.betterwork.org/transparency/compliance#.

[3] https://www.ilo.org/global/standards/introduction-to-international-labourstandards/conventions-and-recommendations/lang--en/index.htm.

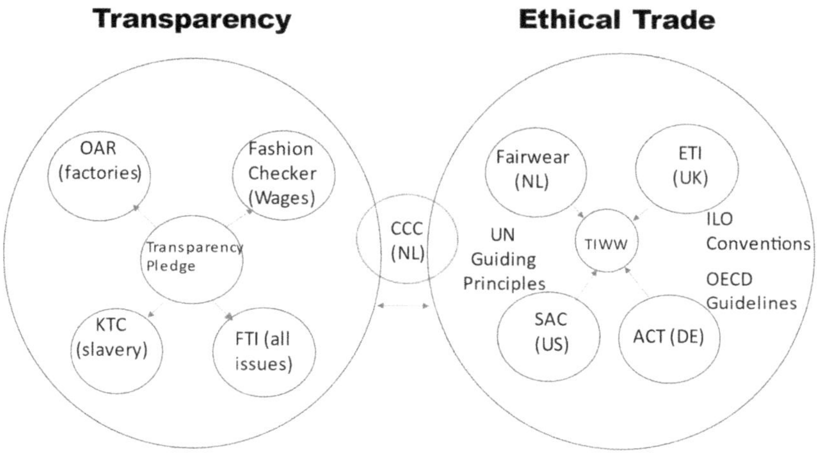

Fig. 1 Key initiatives in transparency and ethical trade in the fashion sector

labour, working with companies and investors. Fashion Checker, developed by the Clean Clothes Campaign (CCC) focuses on wages. Finally, the Transparency Pledge is a joint initiative by NGOs like CCC and Human Rights Watch and Trade Unions pressuring fashion brands to commit to a minimum level of transparency in their supply chains, including by providing data to the OAR.

An overview of the different initiatives and their focus are presented in Fig. 1, while the key transparency databases which they provide are detailed in Table 1.

4 Analytical Framework—Conceptualising Transparency and Ethical Trade

In Fig. 2 we build on existing work to propose an analytical framework to explore the links between transparency and the extent to which GVCs respect ethical standards. Based on Egels-Zandén et al.'s (2015) definition, we conceptualise GVC transparency (in the left-hand box) as incorporating (i) names of suppliers (ii) information on sustainability conditions of production and (iii) purchasing practices. In terms of the

Table 1 Transparency initiatives, coverage and funding

Name	Coordinator	Coverage	Source	Number of fashion brands covered (2021)	Number of indicators	Funding
Open Apparel Registry (OAR)	OAR	Factory lists	Company websites, MSIs	400+	8 (although generally only the address is provided)	Laudes Foundation; Partnership for Sustainable Textiles; Humanity United (The Omidyar Group)
Fashion Transparency Index (FTI)	Fashion Revolution	Company disclosure	Questionnaire	250	240	British Council; European Union Laudes Foundation
Fashion Checker	CCC	Living wage	Questionnaire, fieldwork	108	5	EU
Know the Chain (KTC)	KTC	Forced labour	Company websites, questionnaire	37	74	Partnership between the Business & Human Rights Resource Centre, Humanity United, Sustainalytics, and Verité
Better Work	ILO	Factory performance on FoA, H&S, wages, etc.	Factory Audits	Not linked explicitly to brands	33	ILO and International Finance Corporation (IFC)

Source Own elaboration on the basis of website information key characteristics of ethical trade (in the right-hand box), there is a widespread consensus on its core aspects, based on the ILO Declaration on Fundamental Principles and Rights at Work (ILO, 1998) and the UN Declaration of Human Rights. The base codes of the Fairwear Foundation and the ETI are based on these principles and cover the same issues, although the ETI adds a requirement on ensuring no inhumane treatment.

We leverage this framework to analyse how the data in the key transparency databases could help to inform our understanding about the actual sustainability conditions in fashion supply chains. In this short chapter we cannot explore the data in detail. Our objective is simply to draw attention to the potential of transparency efforts to contribute to more ethical and sustainable outcomes for GVC actors and highlight some key omissions in the current data. We draw on the different aspects of GVC transparency on the left of Fig. 2 to inform the extent to which the nine core aspects of ethical trade set out on the right could be seen to be respected within the fashion sector.

Fig. 2 A framework for connecting transparency and ethical trade

5 Methodology

Although all the key available databases detailed in Table 1 address transparency, they seek to illuminate different aspects. In terms of factories, the Open Apparel Registry (OAR) details supplier lists disclosed by companies themselves, as well as organisations of which they are members, especially MSIs like Fairwear and the Dutch AGT.[4] In terms of conditions and policies, the most extensive database is the Fashion Transparency Index (FTI),[5] which provides data on 250 companies across issues including the freedom to organise, child and slave labour. This is the database that provides the most extensive data. Other databases are more specific: Know the Chain (KTC) is focused on modern slavery,[6] covering 37 key fashion brands and retailers. CCC's Fashion Checker[7] is focused on wages, providing ratings between A and E (although no brand gets better than C). Unless otherwise stated, we reference data from the 2021 version of these databases or data provided in June 2022 from websites.

Another key initiative of relevance is the ILO Better Work programme, which publishes summary data on their factory audits, including key issues related to working conditions, pay, health and safety and freedom to organise. The ILO does not provide summary data on these audits, so to get an overview of the extent to which these results help inform the key issues of interest, we analysed 370 recent results, including all audits in 2021 and 2022 (to the end of April). Most of the audits were in Vietnam (216 audits) or Jordan (85 audits), although they also audited factories in Haiti (26), Indonesia (27) and Nicaragua (16).

In order to obtain more contextual data about the history, use and objectives of the different databases and ensure that we were properly interpreting them, we contacted all of the organisations included in Table 1. Representatives of Fashion Revolution, the OAR, the CCC,

---

[4] https://openapparel.org/.

[5] https://www.fashionrevolution.org/about/transparency/.

[6] https://knowthechain.org/benchmark/.

[7] https://fashionchecker.org/.

FairWear/TIWW, ETI and the ILO Better Work agreed to be interviewed, as did a representative of the clothing due diligence team in the OECD. Details of interviews are provided in Table 2 in annex. In the following sections, we explore the extent to which these different databases inform the bases of ethical trade.

6 What Can Be Divined from Factory Lists?

A key aspect of transparency is the provision of factory lists. This was a core demand of early campaigners and is seen as vital to action to improve working conditions and responsible business practices. To get an overview of what can be divined from these lists, we analysed those from the top 10 global fashion companies by sales[8] included in OAR, as well as the best performing brand in FTI—OVS—for comparison. The main sources of supply are presented in Fig. 3. As China, Bangladesh, Vietnam, Turkey, India and the EU were common sources, we highlight these. However, some companies relied on less traditional locations. Sri Lanka is a key source for L Brands, which owns Victoria's Secret (26% of suppliers), while Brazil is the most important source for C&A (47% of suppliers).

Although these details are interesting, they are of limited usefulness for understanding working conditions. Firstly, a given percentage of suppliers does not necessarily represent a similar percentage of goods. Some facilities are far larger than others and are likely to provide more goods. In addition, the number of suppliers declared per lead firm varies hugely, from 1671 for C&A to 115 for L Brands. Secondly, supplier location only informs us about ethics in as much as there is an assumption that sourcing from developed or European countries is less likely to result in infringements of ethical trading principles than sourcing in developing countries, where regulations are less stringent and/or weakly

[8] To develop this list we started from BizVibes list of top fashion retailers and excluded American Eagle and Abercrombie and Fitch, neither of whom disclose factory lists. We added Primark and C&A, both of whom had higher revenues than Next—the lowest revenue company in the list.

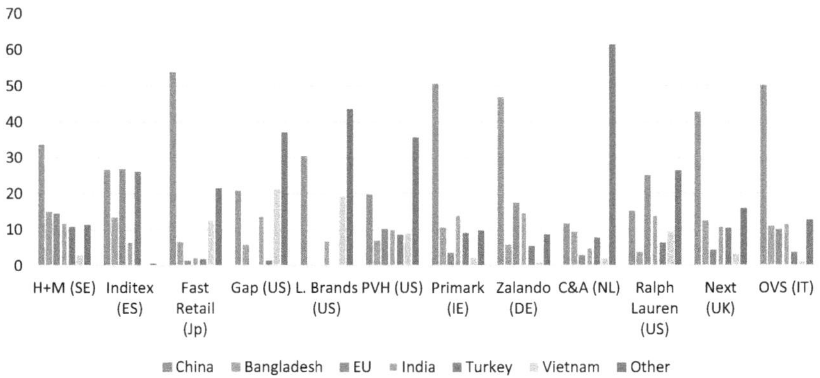

Fig. 3 Key sources for top 10 global fashion companies (*Source* Own calculations based on OAR data May–June 2022)

enforced. The OECD 'risk-based' approach is partly based on the principle that certain countries and sectors represent a higher risk of abuses than others (OECD, 2018).

However, there is plenty of evidence that abuses occur in developed countries (see Hammer et al., 2015 on the UK). CCC has highlighted that the legal minimum garment production wage in Eastern European EU members is between 36% (Czechia) and 19% (Bulgaria) of the living wage, while in non-EU countries in the region the situation is often worse.[9] TIWW data on the gap between the living and minimum wage in key apparel sourcing countries indicates it is 45% globally, ranging from 2% in Honduras to 71% in Indonesia.[10] Cross-referencing this with company sourcing data can to some extent illuminate whether decent wages are likely to be paid within their GVCs.

OAR does not include the possibility to disclose data on other issues of importance to ethical trade, like migrant labour and union membership. According to FTI, only a small number of companies disclose the percentage of migrant labour in their factories (18 for tier 1, 14 for processing facilities and 4 for raw material suppliers). Thus, the extent to which these lists can inform our understanding of the likelihood of

[9] https://cleanclothes.org/campaigns/europe-floor-wage.

[10] https://www.theindustrywewant.com/wages.

labour abuses along GVCs, is mainly linked to the extent to which a given geography has existing legislation that is effectively implemented. It is interesting to note that the company that scores best in the FTI—the Italian brand OVS—does not have a supplier profile that is hugely different from the other brands. Thus, ethical and transparent GVCs can be secured across different geographies.

7 What Can Be Divined on the Sustainability Conditions of Production

In terms of what existing data from the transparency initiatives can tell us about how clothing GVCs conform to the principles of ethical trade highlighted in Fig. 2, the usefulness of the data varies depending on the issue at hand. We briefly explore the relevance of the data to these principles below.

7.1 Employment Is Freely Chosen

Modern slavery is a key concern in fashion value chains and most companies have a commitment to address the issue. For example, only 31 companies in the FTI database have not committed to ensuring that there is no slavery in their supply chains, although 84 do not report on how they are putting commitments on eliminating slavery into practice. However, there are no outcome indicators on actual levels of slavery in supply chains in the FTI database and few companies report on this indicator.

KTC is specifically focused on modern slavery, but they only monitor 37 brands. The best performing was Lululemon from Canada, whose score was 84/100, while the worst performing were Shenzhou International Group from Hong Kong, which scored 3 and Prada (Italy) and Anta Sports (China) which scored 5. KTC also assesses the company's remedy programmes and responses to allegations, where they look in detail at the number of allegations of forced labour in supply chains and how companies reacted. The company with the highest number of allegations (4) was Primark, which got a score of 16/100 on this indicator.

Migrant labour is sometimes linked to practices which amount to 'unfree' labour, both because of the fact that workers sometimes have to pay fees to secure a job and the fact that they often live in company accommodation and may need to surrender their travel documents (Crane et al., 2022). Exactly half of the companies in FTI have commitments to monitoring migrant and contract labour in their supply chains and most provide details of how they monitor. Slightly more (155) report they are monitoring living conditions, primarily in dormitories, although only 44 disclose how.

7.2 Freedom of Association/Collective Bargaining

FTI provides quite extensive details on the commitments of fashion retailers to freedom of association (FoA) in their supply chains, as well as how they monitor and interact with trade unions and workers. In terms of commitments to FoA, 72 fashion companies included all those which were monitored, while 105 included all but one. However, the level of monitoring and implication of trade unions and worker representatives was considerably lower. FTI reports that only 18 companies monitor unions in their first-tier factories, with 15 indicating whether they have a worker's representative. The figures for second-tier factories are 11 and 9, although 23 and 24 companies report the aggregate percentage of facilities covered by unions and collective bargaining agreements, respectively. The results were better in terms of the number of companies that disclose how workers are involved in due diligence (52) and remediation (53).

Better Work audits reported few problems in relation to FoA (1 factory), punishment of trade unionists (1 factory) or termination of employment for joining a union (1 factory), however 19 factories in Vietnam, almost 9% of those audited, were found to have issues with employer involvement in trade union decisions and in 2 factories workers were obliged to join a union, raising questions on unions' independence. Finally, there were many problems in Jordan with non-respect for collective agreements (82% of factories).

7.3 Discrimination in Employment

The majority of companies assessed by FTI commit to diversity and inclusion, as well as equal pay and indicate that they seek to ensure that their supply chains are free of discrimination. Many disclose details of their policy to achieve these aims. Overall, close to half of the companies in the FTI index got at least 2 out of a potential 2.75 points on these three objectives. However, monitoring outcomes are poor, with only 53 companies reporting the gender breakdown of workers in their Tier 1 factories, 28 in Tier 2, and 8 in raw materials. As fashion is quite a female-dominated industry, these figures are not, on their own, very insightful, as details of the gender breakdown by activity are rarely provided.

The 2021 version of the FTI also included a special set of indicators on gender and racial equality, covering the extent to which companies publish data on gender-related violence in their suppliers, as well as the gender and race-based wage gap and distribution of work roles. Performance was poor, with only 37 companies getting more than 3 out of a potential 7 points. 100 companies got zero ratings for this section. Companies provide little detail of the situation in their suppliers.

7.4 No Child Labour

Child labour has historically been a key issue of concern in the fashion sector (Kolk & Tulder, 2002) and so it is unsurprising that most companies have a policy of ensuring that there is none in their supply chain. In the FTI database, only 27 don't have such a policy. However, these commitments are not always backed up by action, as only 119 companies actually include the objective in their supplier policies (through codes of conduct, etc.).

7.5 Safe Working Conditions

The FTI provides indicators on the extent to which companies have publicly committed to safe working conditions in their supply chains, but there are no concrete outcome indicators in this issue. Given that many of the efforts to increase transparency in the supply chain have emerged because of the Rana Plaza disaster, it is concerning that company commitments are not better monitored. In general companies rely on factory audits to highlight health and safety (H&S) breaches. In terms of brand transparency, most do not report on H&S issues in any depth.

An indication of the extent to which key safety protocols are applied at factory level can be gleaned from Better Work's audits, where many H&S failures were noted. Only 41% of factories passed the audit with no problems, with particularly high pass levels in Vietnam (56%), Nicaragua (50%) and Indonesia (48%). The main safety issues highlighted were ineffective fire detection systems (19%), blocked emergency exits (18%) and lack of cooperation on H&S between management and workers (16%). Jordan had particularly extensive failings in worker accommodation with lack of preparation for emergencies (50%) and lack of fire protection (17%). Haitian factories had very high levels of inaccessible emergency exits (73% of factories) and inadequate emergency drills (39% of factories). Most of these factories have been in the programme for some time and so should, in theory, be amongst the best in their sector. Yet still safety issues persisted.

7.6 No Harsh or Inhuman Treatment

In terms of the objective to ensure that workers are not subject to harsh or inhuman treatment and that mental health and wellbeing are promoted, in FTI 101 companies report that they have such objectives both at company level and for their supply chains, while 81 disclosed how they intended to fulfil these objectives. Again, there are no output indicators in the database. As a recent NGO report underlined, gender-based violence and harassment continue to be an issue in fashion supply chains, including those of many high-profile brands (Bhattacharjee & Khambay, 2022). The same report found that this behaviour was linked to purchasing practices of brands, especially unstable and unpredictable ordering procedures.

7.7 Living Wage

FTI provides details of the extent to which companies declare commitments to achieving a living wage in their supply chain, as well as reporting on whether this is achieved. There is a huge difference between declared commitments, where 128 companies out of the 250 studied scored more than 50% of the theoretical maximum and the provision of details on wage levels—where only 7 companies scored more than 50% and none received the maximum score. The CCC's Fashion Checker rates brands specifically on the extent to which they assure that workers are paid the living wage. Three companies—Kings of Indigo (NL), Patagonia (US) and Zeeman (NL) passed the requirement to have an action plan, public commitment and separate labour costs, although none got over an 'E' in payment of living wages.

Thus, even the most transparent fashion companies on wages did not provide details beyond the % earning a living wage, with no details of how far below the threshold some suppliers may be. In addition, there is no detailed data provided to back up such claims. Thus, their transparency, although undoubtedly better than their peers, remains at a very general level.

7.8 Reasonable Working Hours

In terms of ensuring reasonable working hours in the company and its supply chain, 70 companies in the FTI database disclosed this objective, as well as their procedures for securing it, while 105 reported having such procedures. Thus, there is awareness in the industry of the need to monitor and address excessive working hours. Yet, there are no outcome indicators disclosed in FTI. Factory audits are probably the most pertinent source of information. However, Better Work factory audits did not report any findings on unreasonable working hours.

7.9 Legal Employment Contracts

In terms of the objective to ensure that workers in supply chains have legal contracts of employment, FTI reports the extent to which companies disclose having such policies and whether they integrate this objective into their monitoring systems. Although over half of the companies had a commitment to ensure workers in their supply chains had legal employment contracts, only 60 companies reported monitoring procedures.

The reduction, or monitoring, of homeworking is also relevant to this objective, as it is rare for homeworkers to have formal employment contracts. This practice, which remains widespread in the fashion sector in many countries, also poses difficulties for monitoring several other criteria for ethical trade, most obviously child labour, working hours, safety and capacity to organise (Freeman, 2003). Almost a third of companies have no policy on homeworking and no procedures in place to prevent it. Only 22 companies, 19 of which are in Europe, have both.

There are no outcome indicators on the extent to which workers have legal contracts or work from home. Factory audits are the most likely source of information on the former, although they do little to illuminate the conditions of workers operating outside the factory. In the Better Work audit reports analysed, the absence of valid employment contracts was only reported in two factories, both in Indonesia. The audits also reported on whether the factories were making efforts to avoid the use of short-term contracts and only reported one factory, in Vietnam, as not doing so.

8 What Can Be Divined from Transparency in Buying Practices?

Although FTI has some ratings on disclosures on purchasing, most companies are not very transparent, and it is difficult to obtain brand-level data on purchasing practices. Better Buying[11] does an annual survey enabling suppliers to rate buyers. However, results are only shared with subscriber companies and trends are aggregated and anonymised in the public version. TIWW uses this data to provide an aggregate rating of the purchasing practices of members of the ETI and Fairwear, who scored 8 points and 28 points above the industry average, respectively, in the 2021 survey.[12] Both organisations noted that their different scores reflected their varied memberships (large international retailers for the former and smaller niche operators for the latter). No company-specific data is provided, so this transparency feature cannot be analysed in detail on the basis of existing data.

FTI data on purchasing practices are very limited. The section on links to human rights and environmental performance in GVCs has three data points on disclosure of whether employees other than the CSR team are incentivised to improve human rights in the supply chain; whether executive pay is linked to such objectives and how supplies are incentivised to improve their performance through longer-term contracts or price premiums. 57% of companies got zero for this section and only 12 got the maximum points. The section on payment terms and conditions has 4 data points, including disclosure of average length of payment terms and the % of the order paid upfront. 88% of companies got zero or 1/5 for their disclosures in this section.

In terms of the 9 principles of ethical trade in Fig. 2, data limitations mean that we cannot analyse the impact of purchasing pratices on each, but they are undoubtedly a key factor in wage rates and working hours. On wage rates, ring-fencing labour costs in negotiations is a key NGO objective. FTI reports that 23 companies disclose how they ring-fence, but only two (H&M and C&A) disclose the percentage of

[11] https://betterbuying.org/.

[12] https://www.theindustrywewant.com/purchasingpractices.

orders covered. Although ACT members are supposed to commit to ring-fencing wages, the FTI finds that only 13 of the 27 member brands that they monitor disclose how they do so. For working hours, where overtime is strongly linked to urgent orders, the FTI provides no data points on the extent to which companies ensure that they provide visibility to their suppliers on future orders, such that they can stagger their production and avoid sudden peaks.

9 Conclusion

The key objective of this chapter is to interrogate how transparency initiatives can illuminate the sustainability of fashion GVCs and their capacity to deliver the SDG8 objective of decent work. Overall, our findings indicate that, despite major advances, much of the information provided by brands is unlikely to illuminate the core aspects of ethical GVCs, as defined by ILO and mirrored by ETI and Fairwear. The greatest progress has undoubtedly been in relation to factory disclosure. The more widespread provision of supplier listings enables better understanding of the geography of GVCs and supports action on worker voice and working conditions.

In terms of the basic principles of ethical trade highlighted in Fig. 2, many disclosures provide little insight. The detail provided is often very 'shallow', focusing on names and addresses of suppliers, and in most cases only covers first-tier suppliers. Few factory lists provide 'deeper' details, such as the presence of a trade union, the percentage of women employed and the recourse to migrant labour. Data on the other core ETI principles related to the absence of slave labour, working conditions, wages, working hours, discrimination or the regularity of employment is very limited and tends to focus on commitments, rather than outcomes. In addition, very few companies provide information to illuminate the final key aspect of transparency—purchasing practices. Whether in detailing how and to what extent they ring-fence labour costs or ensure 'reasonable' working hours and legal employment contracts, transparency initiatives largely obscure these core issues vital to achieving SDG8.

This finding, which mirrors the work of Egels-Zandén et al. (2015), highlights the limitations of transparency, as currently framed, as a tool for securing progress on decent work. Lack of transparency on purchasing practices is particularly concerning. Research confirms that the capacity of factories to provide sustainable working conditions for their employees is highly dependent on the nature of their relationship with the lead firm and the contractual conditions which the latter propose (Plank et al., 2012). The failure to illuminate these, or to acknowledge the extent to which sustainable production systems are predicated on appropriate contractual relationships, certainly limits the impact of the extensive progress on transparency.

Our work highlights how the different aspects of transparency identified by Egels-Zandén et al. (2015) can inform different elements of worker outcomes. Figure 4 identifies some tentative linkages which emerge from our work. Factory lists, the provision of which has expanded rapidly, provide data on country of origin, which helps to identify potential risks linked to lack of labour rights, or low wages, as well as informing facility level issues, like worker voice and modern slavery. On the other hand, working hours and contracts (as well as wages) are strongly linked to purchasing practices, as lead firms have the capacity to specify wage conditions through their contracts, particularly by 'ring-fencing' labour costs.

The question of the living wage is also illuminated by factory lists, as they indicate the country of production and wages are highly dependent

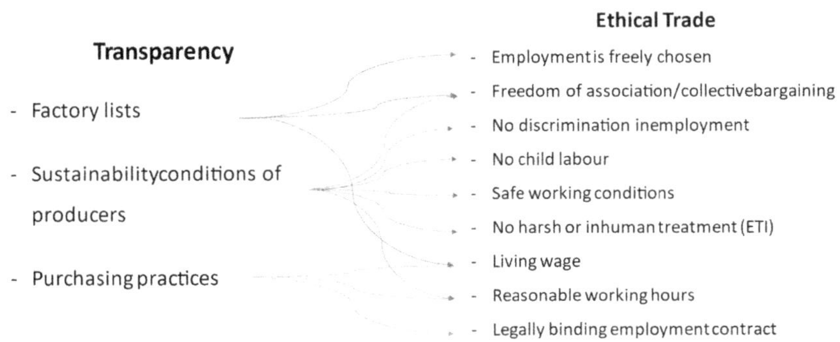

Fig. 4 Linking supply chain transparency and ethical trade

on geography. The other aspects of ethical trade, like child labour and safe working conditions, are strongly related to the sustainability conditions of production. Greater transparency through listing of factories enables such issues to be controlled, but only factory audits can illuminate conditions at the facility level, and transparency on auditing is very limited. Overall, like Egels-Zandén et al. (2015), we find that transparency is often defined in a way that excludes certain inconvenient parts of the story. Transparency thus risks serving lead firm interests rather than those of workers or ethics.

Clearly transparency is one of a range of tools which contribute to the objective of ethical fashion. We do not doubt that huge advances have been made in supply chain transparency in the last two decades. Our interviewees were unanimous in concurring that this progress was significant and greatly facilitates the capacity of civil society organisations to have informed dialogue with lead firms and militate for real change. However, they also agreed that even that basic level of transparency was not universal and that regulation is necessary to force those who still refuse to provide factory lists.

There is potential both for increased efforts to secure more transparency and further research exploring this emerging ecosystem. Companies could leverage existing audits and reports to provide more public data on their suppliers. In this context, the Better Work programme is instructive. The summary data from Better Work audits illuminates the extent to which core ethical principles are respected in GVCs and whether facilities and countries are progressing on decent work, yet the cost and labour-intensive nature of the process is a barrier. In our interview the ILO acknowledged this: '*It's a very expensive intervention at the workplace. Its not scalable*' (Author interview, October 2022).

Finally, an emerging issue which further complicates both public and private efforts to secure ethical fashion is the growth of new e-commerce actors, headquartered in countries with limited public oversight. These 'ultra-fast fashion' brands have also been criticised for working conditions and pose major challenges to efforts to secure transparency (Kollbrunner, 2021). Civil society actors recognised that there was a risk that progress secured by Western brands to make supply chains more transparent and address ethical concerns could be wiped out if these more 'ethical' brands cease to be the key global actors. More research on the impacts of these market shifts on the ethics of fashion will be vital to informing emerging private and public efforts in this rapidly changing context.

Glossary of Terms

CCC Clean Clothes Campaign
ETI Ethical Trading Initiative
FoA Freedom of Association
FTI Fashion Transparency Index
GVC Global Value Chain
H&S Health and Safety
ILO International Labour Organisation
KTC Know The Chain
MSI Multi-stakeholder Initiative
OAR Open Apparel Registry
OECD Organisation for Economic Cooperation and Development
SAC Sustainable Apparel Coalition
TIWW The Industry We Want

Appendix: Table

See Table 2.

Table 2 Interviews conducted for the project

Organisation	Job title	Date of interview
OECD	Responsible for Due Diligence in fashion sector	1/4/22
Fashion Revolution	French representative	16/5/22
Clean Clothes Campaign	Responsible transparency	26/5/22
Fashion Revolution	Responsible for the Fashion Transparency Index	24/06/22
Ethical Trading Initiative	Textile and clothing lead	5/10/22 and 24/10/22
Fairwear and TIWW	Responsible for TIWW	5/10/22
ILO	Responsible for Better Work	5/10/22

References

Alford, M., & Phillips, N. (2018). The political economy of state governance in global production networks: Change, crisis and contestation in the South African fruit sector. *Review of International Political Economy, 25*(1), 98–121.

Bair, J., Anner, M., & Blasi, J. (2020). The political economy of private and public regulation in post-Rana Plaza Bangladesh. *ILR Review, 73*(4), 969–994.

Barraud de Lagerie, P., Béthoux, E., Mias, A., & Penalva Icher, E. (2020). La mise en œuvre du devoir de vigilance: une managérialisation de la loi? *Droit et société, 106*(3), 699–714.

Barrientos, S., & Smith, S. (2007). Do workers benefit from ethical trade? Assessing codes of labour practice in global production systems. *Third World Quarterly, 28*(4), 713–729.

Bartley, T. (2018). *Rules without rights: Land, labor and private authority in the global economy*. Oxford University Press.

Bhattacharjee, S. S., & Khambay, A. (2022). *Unbearable harassment*. Business and Human Rights Centre.

Birkey, R. N., Guidry, R. P., Azizul Islam, M., & Patten, D. M. (2018). Mandated social disclosure: An analysis of the response to the California transparency in supply chains act of 2010. *Journal of Business Ethics, 152*, 827–841.

CEC. (2022). *Proposal for a directive on corporate sustainability due diligence and amending Directive (EU) 2019/1937*. Commission of the European Communities.

Crane, A., Soundararajan, V., Bloomfield, M. J., LeBaron, G., & Spence, L. J. (2022). Hybrid (un)freedom in worker hostels in garment supply chains. *Human Relations, 75*(10), 1928–1960.

Doorey, D. J. (2011). The transparent supply chain: From resistance to implementation at Nike and Levi-Strauss. *Journal of Business Ethics, 103*, 587–603.

Dubbink, W., Graafland, J., & van Liedekerke, L. (2008). CSR, Transparency and the role of intermediate organisations. *Journal of Business Ethics, 82*, 391–406.

Egels-Zandén, N., Hulthén, K., & Wulff, G. (2015). Trade-offs in supply chain transparency: The case of Nudie Jeans Co. *Journal of Cleaner Production, 107*, 95–104.

Freeman, D. (2003). Homeworkers in global supply chains. *Greener Management International, 43*, 107–118.

Gereffi, G., Humphrey, J., & Sturgeon, T. (2005). The governance of global value chains. *Review of International Political Economy, 12*(1), 78–104.

Gold, S., & Heikkurinen, P. (2018). Transparency fallacy: Unintended consequences of stakeholder claims on responsibility in supply chains. *Accounting, Auditing and Accountability Journal, 31*(1), 318–337.

Hammer, N., Plugor, R., Nolan, P., & Clark, I. (2015). *New industry on a skewed playing field: Supply chain relations and working conditions in UK garment manufacturing*. University of Leicester. Centre for Sustainable Work and Employment Futures.

ILO. (1998). *ILO declaration on fundamental principles and rights at work.* International Labour Organisation.

Kolk, A., & Tulder, R. (2002). Child labor and multinational conduct: A comparison of international business and stakeholder codes. *Journal of Business Ethics, 36*(3), 291–301.

Kollbrunner, T. (2021). *Toiling away for Shein.* Public Eye. https://stories.publiceye.ch/en/shein/. 28 April 2022.

Levy, D., & Egan, D. (2003). A neo-gramscian approach to corporate political strategy: Conflict and accommodation in the climate change negotiations. *Journal of Management Studies, 40*(4), 803–829.

Locke, R. M., Amengual, M., & Mangla, A. (2009). Virtue out of necessity? Compliance commitment and the improvement of labor conditions in global supply chains. *Politics and Society, 37*(3), 319–351.

Nadvi, K. (2008). Global standards, global governance and the organization of global value chains. *Journal of Economic Geography, 8*(3), 323–343.

OECD. (2018). *OECD due diligence guidance for responsible supply chains in the garment and footwear sector*. OECD Publishing.

Oka, C., Egels-Zanden, N., & Alexander, R. (2020). Buyer engagement and labour conditions in global supply chains: The Bangladesh Accord and beyond. *Development and Change, 51*(5), 1306–1330.

Pinnington, B., Benstead, A., & Meehan, J. (2022). Transparency in Supply Chains (TISC): Assessing and Improving the Quality of Modern Slavery Statements. *Journal of Business Ethics, 182*, 619–636.

Plank, L., Rossi, A., & Staritz, C. (2012). *Workers and social upgrading in "fast fashion": The case of the apparel industry in Morocco and Romania* [ÖFSE Working Paper, No. 33]. Austrian Foundation for Development Research (ÖFSE).

UN. (2011). *Guiding principles on business and human rights: Implementing the United Nations 'Protect, Respect and Remedy' Framework*. United Nations.

7

MNEs and Disadvantaged Communities in Emerging Markets: Paths to SDG8

Renan Oliveira, Jayne Cathcart, Axèle Giroud, Jorge Carneiro, and Pervez N. Ghauri

1 Introduction

The thematic review presented in this chapter aims to investigate "How MNEs interact with disadvantaged communities in emerging markets" and explores how such interactions may facilitate decent work and economic development (SDG8). Understanding how MNEs and communities interact is important since MNEs can help achieve several SDGs pertinent to disadvantaged communities, such as SDG8 and those related to alleviating poverty (SDG 1) and inequality (SDG 10). The

R. Oliveira · J. Carneiro
São Paulo School of Business Administration (FGV EAESP), São Paulo, Brazil
e-mail: renan.oliveira@fgv.edu.br

J. Carneiro
e-mail: jorge.carneiro@fgv.br

J. Cathcart (✉) · P. N. Ghauri
University of Birmingham, Birmingham, UK
e-mail: c.j.cathcart@bham.ac.uk

N. Sinkovics et al. (eds.), *International Business and SDG 8*, The Academy of International Business, https://doi.org/10.1007/978-3-031-46802-5_7

SDG framework offers a positive and inclusive way forward to integrate social and environmental with economic aspects in the field of international business (IB) (Sinkovics et al., 2022).

MNEs play a central role in addressing SDG8 for several reasons. First, MNEs can link wealthy economies together (and, importantly, wealthy economies with poorer ones) and facilitate access to capital knowledge and value systems across borders on a large scale (Meyer, 2004; Sachs, 2012). In this way, MNEs are viewed as a channel that facilitates access to capital, markets and technology to help propagate new small businesses and create employment opportunities. Indeed, there is a growing expectation that MNEs should find solutions that will empower people experiencing poverty and include them in the social and economic ecosystem, improving their living standards (Wood et al., 2008).

Engaging with SDGs enables private sector firms to demonstrate their willingness to respond to stakeholder pressure and to comply with industry trends. In doing so, firms can not only mitigate competitive or regulatory risk but also develop new capabilities that will redefine the private sector in society, enabling firms to rebuild legitimacy and trust (Lashitew, 2021; Rosati & Faria, 2019; van Tulder et al., 2021). Therefore, involvement with the SDG agenda enables MNEs to satisfy their quest for economic performance and contribute towards sustainable development.

The current IB literature is criticised for insufficient focus on the potential role of MNEs in attaining the SDGs (Sinkovics et al., 2022; van Zanten & van Tulder, 2018) and the deleterious impact that the activities of many MNEs during colonial and neocolonial periods such as socio-economic exclusion and unfair working conditions of indigenous populations (Boussebaa, 2023; Gammelgaard et al., 2020). Existing definitions of "development", which is a central component of SDG8,

P. N. Ghauri
e-mail: p.ghauri@bham.ac.uk

A. Giroud
The University of Manchester, Manchester, UK
e-mail: axele.giroud@mancheser.ac.uk

have been criticised for not taking "negative externalities" (relating to the production of goods and services) into account, nor the [negative] spill-over effects thereof across borders (Van Tulder & van Mil, 2022, p. 85). In particular, IB scholars concentrate on CSR activities conducted within or across borders (Kolk, 2016), how FDI contributes to host countries' economic and social development (Buckley et al., 2017), and how MNEs can integrate poorer segments of society into its strategies (e.g., the Bottom of Pyramid literature, Prahalad & Hart, 2009). More recent literature, however, points to the critical need to better understand how MNEs influence inequality in home and host countries (van der Straaten et al., 2023). The complex mechanisms underpinning MNE-community interactions remain unexplored in IB and broader management literature due to current fragmented conceptual approaches to understanding MNEs and disadvantaged communities, an issue that is particularly pertinent in the context of emerging markets.

In this chapter, we address the following research question: How do MNEs help contribute to the achievement of SDG8 through interaction with disadvantaged communities? To uncover the extent of existing knowledge on MNE-community interactions in the IB, management and closely related fields—economics and development studies—we first searched for relevant literature using three well-known databases: Web of Science, Scopus and ABI/INFORM. We searched for articles containing keywords such as "multinationals" or "global firms" AND "disadvantaged communities" or "poor communities" or "poverty" or "Base of the Pyramid" in the title, abstract and keywords sections. After removing duplicate articles and checking abstracts to ensure they collectively refer to (1) multinationals, (2) poverty alleviation and/or poor communities and (3) developing/emerging markets as the host context, a total of 41 articles were identified. We then conducted a thematic review of these papers, paying attention to the main objectives of SDG8 with regard to economic growth and employment generation. This chapter provides novel knowledge with new insights into how MNEs contribute to SDG8 through their interactions with disadvantaged communities and guiding future research.

2 Strategies Adopted by MNEs to Interact With Disadvantaged Communities

MNEs face several challenges when seeking to interact with disadvantaged communities. MNEs' ability to interact effectively with disadvantaged communities requires building relationships based on trust, commitment and legitimacy. Accessing "hard to reach" communities can be facilitated by collaborating with third parties such as Non-Governmental Organisations (NGOs) who are embedded in the community, can provide the MNE with information on the institutional environment and can influence the interaction between businesses and other entities (Mbalyohere & Lawton, 2022; Tasavori et al., 2014). When MNEs seek to engage with underprivileged communities in this way, they demonstrate commitment to a shared goal in the initial phase, which is imperative to the development of a more inclusive business model (Halme et al., 2012).

Particularly in stigmatised settings, where there is a need to gain legitimacy to operate, participatory engagement and transparent communication with communities are required to understand their needs and interests and to promote trust (Egbon et al., 2018; Newenham-Kahindi, 2011). MNEs can also foster interactions with impoverished communities by implementing Corporate Social Responsibility (CSR) initiatives. CSR is "the continuing commitment by business to behave ethically and contribute to economic development while improving the quality of life of the workforce and their families as well as of the local community and society at large" (World Business Council for Sustainable Development, 1999, p. 3).

The contemporary IB literature continues to shift towards a more inclusive approach to understanding how MNEs can interact with societal actors such as communities. Concepts derived from literature streams outside of IB are adopted to advance this literature area. Notably, value co-creation—originally proposed in the marketing literature—reflects on the potential for innovative, collaborative interactions and mutual value creation between MNEs and stakeholders (Agrawal & Rahman, 2015; Galvagno & Dalli, 2014). Another concept discussed in various social sciences disciplines and adopted in the IB literature is "capability development", which is crucial to tackling inequalities and can be developed through entrepreneurial activity and cooperation among various actors (Ghauri et al., 2022).

3 Existing Knowledge on MNEs' Interactions With Disadvantaged Communities

Reviewing articles selected on MNEs and disadvantaged communities in emerging markets enables us to frame existing knowledge on the approach adopted to define the term communities, identify existing interactions between MNEs and disadvantaged communities and theories used by scholars to date.

3.1 Various Types of "Disadvantaged" Communities

A myriad of terms relating to "disadvantaged communities"' are discussed in the literature. However, most studies evaluating MNE-community interactions refer to "local communities", whereas few studies adopt specific terms such as indigenous, host, poor, vulnerable, rural, fence-line or malnourished.

The definition of community also remains disputed in management and related literature areas. This, in part, may be due to the varying and sometimes diverging theoretical approaches applied to understanding the community concept. For example, stakeholder theory underpins Newenham-Kahindi's (2011, p. 255) definition of "community of place", which includes "community stakeholders who are directly or indirectly affected by foreign-owned business activities". Others have adopted an institutional perspective. For example, Brandl et al., (2022, p. 1134) assert that rural communities rely on informal community institutions, such as "longstanding traditions, norms, and customs that regulate rural areas, and the sustainable management of natural resources" by the local communities.

Definitions and related terms may also differ, given the socially constructed nature of communities. Individuals belonging to communities can hold multiple identities that are fluid across time and geographic regions or cultures (Brandl et al., 2022). Indeed, several authors argue that informal institutions such as culture underpin communities since they comprise individuals who identify and bond with each other through shared values, norms, ideology and beliefs or shared interests, resources and social issues (Kepe, 1999). Social identity processes are also emphasised in certain definitions. Where individuals share similar identities, this can lead to "collective action", which can act as a source of cohesion and identity among community members (Wilkinson, 1991).

3.2 Context Explored and Types of MNE-Interactions With Disadvantaged Communities

Most research focus on Africa's extractive sectors, including mining, oil and gas. Generally, extractive industries are considered "stigmatised", that is, "industries in which firms' products or production processes contribute negatively to an issue of societal concern" (Austin & Gaither, 2019, p. 10). In this setting, companies often engage in CSR initiatives to moderate stakeholders' concerns, thus offering a valuable context to study MNEs' engagement with societal issues. The stigmatised context also offers rich insights to understand MNE-community interactions since stakeholder response can be unpredictable (Austin & Gaither, 2019). Since many studies in our sample contribute to the CSR and ethics domain, it is unsurprising that they tend to examine Africa, a region with the lowest GDP per capita globally and where many extractive MNEs operate. Other studies examine manufacturing industries—including pharmaceutical and beauty—primarily in Asia—and services industries in Europe. It is evident from this analysis that there remains a gap for research not only in alternative industry sectors but also in regions beyond Africa.

3.3 Key Useful Theories to Study MNEs and Disadvantaged Communities

Our review establishes that stakeholder theory is the most commonly applied theory to evaluate MNE-community interactions (See Table 1). This finding is unsurprising since CSR is a key concept discussed in most articles and is one of the most popular theories in the CSR literature. The next most widely applied theory is Institutional theory. Under this premise, MNEs seek to engage in activities to help disadvantaged communities so that the firm can conform to different institutional contexts. While stakeholder and institutional theories infer that external factors drive MNE-community interactions, the type of actors influencing these actions differ. From an institutional perspective, MNEs seek to interact with communities for political reasons and primarily to meet societal expectations. In contrast, stakeholder theory suggests that specific external actors drive MNEs to interact with communities, and these actions can create value for the MNE and the community (Frynas & Yamahaki, 2016). Studies also refer to legitimacy theory—which is closely related to institutional theory—in terms of the assumption that firms seek to interact with communities to gain legitimacy. Other theories adopted are social contract theory (Ho et al., 2022) and network theory (Hadjikhani et al., 2016).

3.4 MNEs' Interactions with Disadvantaged Communities and Their Contribution to SDG8

Our analysis shows that decent work and economic growth (SDG8) is a key issue of societal concern in South America. By integrating stakeholder and legitimacy theories, Reimann et al. (2012) demonstrate that in the South American context employees and local governments influence firms towards engaging with SDG8- related issues and that micro-entrepreneurs are important intermediaries to advancing this agenda. While the potential to integrate micro-entrepreneurs from communities into MNE value chains has been recognised in the IB literature for some

Table 1 Main theories used by scholars investigating MNE interactions with disadvantaged communities

Core Theory	Perspective
Stakeholder theory	Organisations' have obligations to many individuals and groups who "affect or are affected by the organisation's mission" (Freeman, 1984, p. 54)
Institutional theory	Firms' survival and growth depend on acquiring legitimacy within institutional environments (Scott, 1995)
Legitimacy theory	Firms operate based on a social contract with society and firms' survival and growth depend on their legitimacy within society (Frynas & Yamahaki, 2016)
Business network theory	Unlike business relationships that are built on a recognised dyadic business actor structure, relationships in CSR are erected on a wider social network structure. Thus, the relationship elements that are pivotal for holding these actors together in a network are: knowledge, commitment, trust and legitimacy
Social Contract theory	A social contract exists between business and society. A social license to operate may exist which is "the acceptance or approval by local communities and stakeholders of a business enterprise's operations or projects in a certain area" (Demuijnck & Fasterling, 2016, p. 675)

time (e.g., Prahalad, 2006) the mechanisms underpinning integration and the role of other stakeholders are unclear.

Since research on MNEs' contribution to SDGs remains in the exploratory stages, key insights can be gained from related fields beyond management. For example, the possibility that MNEs can consider social upgrading and contribute to SDG8 is offered in the Salience and Institutional Analysis and Design (SIAD) framework—developed from the Economics and Development studies fields. By integrating elements from stakeholder and institutional theories, the framework is used to explain strategic factors driving cooperation between MNEs and informal rivals for natural resource use and how these aspects can lead to sustainable development for local communities (Yakovleva & Vazquez-Brust, 2018).

Further examples of insights from the literature linking MNE-community interactions and actions relating to SDG8 are outlined in Tables 2 and 3.

Table 8 provides a structure to identify ways in which MNEs can help achieve SDG8 through their activities and interactions with communities, notably through their contribution to economic activities in host (developing) countries, including supply chain activities with suppliers and/or customers and schemes and programmes they set up with and for disadvantaged communities. Several studies (see Table 3) focus on employment generation for members of disadvantaged communities by MNEs or companies along their value chain activities, and some identify the potential challenges of modern slavery. As daunting as it might sound, "the world officially declared an end to slavery in 1981 when Mauritania was the last country to ban the legal recognition of the ownership of individuals" (UNDP, 2021, p. 8). However, more than 40 million people remain trapped in the contemporary form of slavery, and even more alarmingly, one in four victims of a modern form of slavery are children and 71% of victims are women and girls (UNDP, 2021). For example, in 2023, over 200 workers in Brazil were found to be working in slavery conditions. Workers were kept in captivity, suffered physical violence such as electric shocks and pepper spray, and low payment was delayed (Nemitz, 2023) and deducted to cover expenses for lodging and food (Alvez, 2023). In April 2023, the Ministry of Work and Social Security released a list of over 280 employers that subjected their workers to conditions analogous to slavery (Bond, 2023).

With regard to the specific types of employment, several studies uncover the important role of MNEs in creating the right type of employment, notably contributing (positively or negatively) to income and/or gender inequality. Gender equality" (SDG5) is an important issue that overlaps with the objectives of SDG8 (Rai et al., 2019, p. 368). Unless SDG8 considers unpaid work (mainly housework performed by women), it cannot address SDG8 in its full potential. MNEs can create programmes to support these women. Frey (2017) critically questions whether SDG8 protects full employment and decent work as human rights obligations of states or merely as benefits of economic growth. Existing research suggests MNEs have a moral and ethical obligation to

Table 2 Illustrations of literature linking MNE-community interactions to SDG8

Authors	Main topic	Relevance to SDG8
Reimann et al. (2012)	Possible influence of local stakeholders on MNEs' CSR in emerging economy subsidiaries, and local legitimacy	Local employees and local governments drive firms to push for high standards in their working conditions and to engage in developing the local community
Prahalad (2006)	BOP as an opportunity	MNEs can improve work conditions for BOP by collaborating with NGOs and local government to provide jobs
Alvez (2023); Nemitz (2023)	Slavery work conditions and forced labour in the Brazilian wine industry	Developing legislation at national and coordination at international levels to mitigate forced labour
Bond (2023)	Government actions	Whistleblowing on companies who use any type of modern slavery
Yakovleva and Vazquez-Brust (2018)	Use the Salience and Institutional Analysis and Design framework to analyse the MNE strategies used to address informal miners across different governance levels in the gold mining sector of Ghana	MNEs can take an active role in assisting artisanal small-scale mining (ASM) workers in social up-grading and up-skilling, providing technical expertise and improving ASM health and safety and environmental practices

(continued)

Table 2 (continued)

Authors	Main topic	Relevance to SDG8
UNDP (2021)	Assess change in Human Development index globally	MNEs can implement policies that focus on investment and innovation to build capacities to respond to global challenges relating to human development

Table 3 SDG8 targets and MNE-community interactions

	Potential MNE-community examples	References
Target 8.1 Sustain per capita economic growth	MNEs contribute to increased growth, which in turn benefits (or not) all segments of society. MNEs can provide direct investment in communities: schools and infrastructure. Indirectly enhance the range of consumer goods available and employ migrant workers	Garvin et al. (2009); Hadjikhani et al. (2016)
Target 8.2 Higher levels of economic productivity through technological upgrading and innovation	FDI increases growth by introducing new technologies, such as new production processes and techniques, managerial skills, ideas and new types of capital goods MNEs can contribute by partnering with local institutions to promote technical and vocational training, which will increase the quality of jobs (Montiel et al., 2021) and the productivity thereof (van Tulder & van Mil, 2022)	Bardy et al. (2012); Montiel et al. (2021); van Tulder and van Mil (2022)

(continued)

Table 3 (continued)

	Potential MNE-community examples	References
Target 8.3 Development-oriented policies that support productive activities, decent job creation, entrepreneurship, creativity and innovation	Innovative knowledge generation and development of innovative human capital through increasing the experience and skills of employees, who undertake more complex tasks, and of local businesses who gain new knowledge MNEs may need to adapt their human resources management practices and their vendor contracting policies to reconceptualised views of what constitutes "decent work" in "flex societ[ies] with the majority of the population working on short-term contracts" (van Tulder & van Mil, 2022, p. 84) or as free-lancers, as is the case of the Brazilian legal "enterprise" form named "individual micro-entrepreneur (MEI)", which may be particularly relevant for (young) mothers who cannot afford to leave their small children at a nursery or a daycare centre and need to work from home and may contribute to reducing informal employment and the gender gap MNEs shall warrant that "the needs of workers *indirectly employed* in the company's supply chains" (van Tulder & van Mil, 2022, p. 711, emphasis in the original) are fairly met	Peerally et al. (2019); van Tulder and van Mil (2022)

(continued)

Table 3 (continued)

	Potential MNE-community examples	References
Target 8.4 Decouple economic growth from environmental degradation	Recycling can reduce the need to source new inputs to retain the same level of production. Recycling and reusing raw materials also offer the MNE a way to reduce costs and enhance brand value, quality, and price control within supply chains	Dauvergne and LeBaron (2013)
Target 8.5 Full employment and decent work for all women and men, young people and people with disabilities	Work with institutional actors such as trade associations and NGOs to promote gender equality in work. In doing so the MNE can gain support and legitimacy to operate from the state and institutional actors	Beddewela and Fairbrass (2016)
Target 8.6 Provide education and training to reduce the proportion of youth not in employment	Work with institutional actors such as trade associations and NGOs to promote universal education. In doing so the MNE can gain support and legitimacy to operate Develop education initiatives such as the provision of scholarships, technical and vocational training schools and teachers	Beddewela and Fairbrass (2016); Eweje (2006)
Target 8.7. Eradicate forced labour, end modern slavery and human trafficking	Multinationals play an important role here. They can and should have control of their value chain	N/A

(continued)

Table 3 (continued)

	Potential MNE-community examples	References
Target 8.8 Protect labour rights for all workers, including migrant workers and those in precarious employment	IKEA form cooperative third-party partnerships with organisations including UNICEF to address issues of corporate responsibility including child labour	Strand (2009)
Target 8.9 Policies to promote sustainable tourism to create jobs and promote the local culture and products	Hotel MNEs can use local business networks to source and promote sustainable products. They can form local partnerships to develop CSR initiatives that are aligned with local employee causes such as training and educating the local workforce	Ertuna et al. (2022)
Target 8.10 Strengthen capacity of domestic financial institutions to foster access to banking and financial services	Provision of micro-credit to micro-entrepreneurs from disadvantaged communities. Provision of banking services to the poor	N/A
Target 8.a Increase Aid for Trade support for developing countries	MNEs offer micro-credit schemes, skill acquisition centres, investment in small and medium enterprises and business development programmes	Eweje (2006); Idemudia (2009)
Target 8.b Global strategy for youth employment	MNEs can develop education initiatives that enhance employment opportunities for youth	Eweje (2006)

promote the right type of employment (e.g., part of SDG8), especially because the conduct of business across borders can create and perpetuate precarious work conditions (Butler, 2004; Prasad & Durepos, 2016).

Another theme that is emphasised in numerous studies is that of MNEs' GVCs or value chain within countries where they operate and the multiple ways in which value chain activities affect local communities. To contribute, MNEs need to take responsibility for their full value chain, even if they do not own their suppliers in developing countries

(Ghauri, 2022, p. 2). By doing so, MNEs can invest in training and demand local partners comply with work conditions across their entire supply chain. Yet, according to Ghauri et al. (2021), MNEs can implement local hiring programs that promote a diverse workforce in terms of gender and ethnicity which contributes to social advancement.

4 Conclusions: Paving the Way for Future Research

Despite the limited time remaining to achieve the UN SDGs and increasing recognition of the integral role MNEs can play in this endeavour, to date, research on the role of MNEs in addressing SDGs remains in its infancy. In particular limited research has been conducted on SDGs that are highly pertinent to disadvantaged communities, most importantly SDG8 (decent work and economic growth) which is the focus of this chapter, but also to related goals such as SDG1 (no poverty), SDG2 (no hunger), or SDG10 (reduced inequalities). Given that many emerging markets have limited resources to act upon all SDGs, some emerging countries may need to prioritise action, for instance, focusing on "economic and social SDG target over ecological ones" (van Tulder & van Mil, 2022, p. 93), and/or foster collaboration with various key stakeholders, especially MNEs as a key source of finance and economic activity. Though MNEs strategically invest in host countries to increase returns, their activities result in significant externalities that can help the host country achieve its SDGs (Montiel et al., 2021). In this chapter, we have demonstrated that, to date, too few studies examine the impact of MNEs on disadvantaged communities and fewer still uncover the complex mechanisms through which MNEs contribute to SDG8 when interacting with these communities.

By extending our review to explore not only IB research but also broader management and closely related literature areas (Economics and Development studies), we can structure existing knowledge to better address the wide-ranging nature of SDG8 objectives. While IB studies on MNEs and communities tend to adopt a macro analysis and/or conceptualise communities merely as economic actors at the BOP, other fields of study offer various different explanations and perspectives. We showed that stakeholder, institutional and legitimacy theories are applied most frequently, but inconsistently across studies on the nature of interactions between MNEs and communities. For the purpose of SDG8, partnerships and the unique role of institutional actors such as NGOs and local government to facilitate MNE-community interactions appear crucial, whereas other studies highlight the importance of primary stakeholders to pinpoint how MNEs' interactions with communities contribute to SDG8. As a conclusion to this chapter, we call for future research to consolidate existing knowledge, to integrate the varying theoretical approaches to advance a more comprehensive understanding of the complex nature of interactions between MNEs and communities and to focus more carefully on SDG objectives per se.

A more integrative approach is needed to take this vital research area forward, incorporating stakeholder, legitimacy and institutional theories to advance a more comprehensive conceptual framework than existing studies. In doing so, we call for future research to better capture the multiplicity of actions, strategies and mechanisms that MNEs can employ to facilitate interactions with and possibly form relationships with "hard to reach" communities. Section 3 in this chapter points to several themes of importance, spanning direct and indirect impact MNEs have, notably through their value chain activities, on potential employment for members of disadvantaged communities, including examining risks of human rights infringements and modern slavery, but also numerous other actions adopted by MNEs that affect local communities. Since most studies in our sample tend to evaluate extractive industries located in Africa, there is a need to extend the analysis to alternative industry and cultural contexts, always keeping SDG8 targets in mind. In particular, understanding how MNEs in "less stigmatised" industries—or services industries—located in other emerging regions (e.g., Latin America or Asia) can interact with local communities is an avenue for future research.

Adopting a more inclusive and integrative approach, will facilitate a broader analysis that accounts for the possibility that MNEs and communities co-create value through engaging with multiple stakeholders. This approach is consistent with studies conducted in the broader management literature—and the ethics and CSR domain—which emphasise the importance of various external stakeholders (such as NGOs, trade associations and local government) in facilitating MNE-community interactions. Indeed, MNEs' face pressures to go beyond philanthropic donations and instead find inclusive solutions to empower people experiencing poverty and integrate them into economic and social systems. MNEs can directly contribute to SDG8 through investment in schools and infrastructure to encourage individuals from disadvantaged communities to enter the workforce. By collaborating with local institutional stakeholders such as NGOs and local governments, MNEs can develop and implement educational initiatives and training programmes tailored to the needs of disadvantaged communities. In this way, MNEs are vital in facilitating decent work and economic growth (SDG8).

From a critical perspective, it is still "unclear how IB research can contribute to the SDGs, as they are designed as country-level goals for governments to achieve, not as firm-level goals" (Montiel et al., 2021, p. 1000). The extensive scope and complexity of the 17 SDGs, 169 targets and 232 unique indicators, plus the lack of shared understanding of how to operationalise the SDGs create obstacles to MNEs from acting. Moreover, since businesses still tend to focus on short-term profits, particularly in uncertain times, SDGs are often adopted in an ad hoc manner rather than selecting and implementing SDGs that are aligned with MNEs' long-term goals (Lashitew, 2021). This approach can continue to propagate scepticism in society of MNEs' actions. Future research targeting these critical points is welcomed.

References

Agrawal, A. K., & Rahman, Z. (2015). Roles and resource contributions of customers in value co-creation. *International Strategic Management Review, 3*(1–2), 144–160. https://doi.org/10.1016/j.ism.2015.03.001

Alvez, T. (2023). *Brazil: Well-known wineries involved in alleged modern slavery scandal*. Business & Human Rights Resource Centre; Business & Human Rights Resource Centre. https://www.business-humanrights.org/en/latest-news/brazil-well-known-wineries-involved-in-slave-labor-scandal/.

Austin, L., & Gaither, B. M. (2019). Redefining fit: Examining CSR company-issue fit in stigmatized industries. *Journal of Brand Management, 26*(1), 9–20. https://doi.org/10.1057/s41262-018-0107-3

Bardy, R., Drew, S., & Kennedy, T. F. (2012). Foreign investment and ethics: How to contribute to social responsibility by doing business in less-developed countries. *Journal of Business Ethics, 106*(3), 267–282. https://doi.org/10.1007/s10551-011-0994-7

Beddewela, E., & Fairbrass, J. (2016). Seeking legitimacy through CSR: Institutional pressures and corporate responses of multinationals in Sri Lanka. *Journal of Business Ethics, 136*(3), 503–522. https://doi.org/10.1007/s10551-014-2478-z

Bond, L. (2023). *In Brazil, 289 employers flagged on slave labor list*. Agência-Brasil; EBC.

Boussebaa, M. (2023). Decolonizing international business. *Critical Perspectives on International Business, 19*(4), 2023. https://doi.org/10.1108/cpoib-12-2022-0121

Brandl, K., Moore, E., Meyer, C., & Doh, J. (2022). The impact of multinational enterprises on community informal institutions and rural poverty. *Journal Of International Business Studies, 53*(6, SI), 1133–1152. https://doi.org/10.1057/s41267-020-00400-3

Buckley, P. J., Doh, J. P., & Benischke, M. H. (2017). Towards a renaissance in international business research? Big questions, grand challenges, and the future of IB scholarship. *Journal of International Business Studies, 48*(9), 1045–1064. https://doi.org/10.1057/S41267-017-0102-Z/TABLES/2

Butler, J. (2004). *Precarious life: The powers of mourning and violence*. verso.

Dauvergne, P., & LeBaron, G. (2013). The social cost of environmental solutions. *New Political Economy, 18*(3), 410–430. https://doi.org/10.1080/13563467.2012.740818

Demuijnck, G., & Fasterling, B. (2016). The social license to operate. *Source: Journal of Business Ethics, 136*(4), 675–685. https://doi.org/10.1007/s10551-015-2976-7

Egbon, O., Idemudia, U., & Amaeshi, K. (2018). Shell Nigeria's global memorandum of understanding and corporate-community accountability relations: A critical appraisal. *Accounting, Auditing and Accountability Journal, 31*(1), 51–74. https://doi.org/10.1108/AAAJ-04-2016-2531

Ertuna, B., Gu, H., & Yu, L. (2022). "A thread connects all beads{"}: Aligning global CSR strategy by hotel MNCs. *Tourism Management, 91*. https://doi.org/10.1016/j.tourman.2022.104520

Eweje, G. (2006). Environmental costs and responsibilities resulting from oil exploitation in developing countries: The case of the Niger Delta of Nigeria. *JoOURNAL OF BUSINESS ETHICS, 69*(1), 27–56. https://doi.org/10.1007/s10551-006-9067-8

Freeman, R. E. (1984). *Strategic management: A stakeholder approach*. Cambridge university Press.

Frey, D. F. (2017). *Economic growth, full employment and decent work: The means and ends in SDG 8, 21*(8), 1164–1184. https://doi.org/10.1080/13642987.2017.1348709

Frynas, J. G., & Yamahaki, C. (2016). Corporate social responsibility: Review and roadmap of theoretical perspectives. *Business Ethics, 25*(3), 258–285. https://doi.org/10.1111/beer.12115

Galvagno, M., & Dalli, D. (2014). Theory of value co-creation: A systematic literature review. *Managing Service Quality, 24*(6), 643–683.

Gammelgaard, J., Haakonsson, S., & Just, S. N. (2020). Corporate scramble for Africa? Towards a postcolonial framework for transglocal development governance. *Organization Studies, 41*(9), 1213–1233.

Garvin, T., McGee, T. K., Smoyer-Tomic, K. E., & Aubynn, E. A. (2009). Community-company relations in gold mining in Ghana. *Journal of Environmental Management, 90*(1), 571–586. https://doi.org/10.1016/j.jenvman.2007.12.014

Ghauri, P. (2022). The role of multinational enterprises in achieving sustainable development goals. *AIB Insights*, *22*(1), 1–5. https://doi.org/10.46697/001c.31077

Ghauri, P., Fu, X., & Minayora, A. (2022). Digital technology-based entrepreneurial pursuit of the marginalised communities. *Journal of International Management, 28*(2), 100948. https://doi.org/10.1016/J.INTMAN.2022.100948

Ghauri, Strange, R., & Cooke, F. L. (2021). Research on international business: The new realities. *International Business Review, 30*, 1–11. https://www.sciencedirect.com/science/article/pii/S0969593121000019

Hadjikhani, A., Lee, J. W., & Park, S. (2016). Corporate social responsibility as a marketing strategy in foreign markets The case of Korean MNCs in the Chinese electronics market. *International Marketing Review, 33*(4), 530–554. https://doi.org/10.1108/IMR-03-2014-0104

Halme, M., Lindeman, S., & Linna, P. (2012). Innovation for inclusive business: Intrapreneurial bricolage in multinational corporations. *Journal of Management Studies, 49*(4), 743–784. https://doi.org/10.1111/J.1467-6486.2012.01045.X

Ho, S. S. H., Oh, C. H., & Shapiro, D. (2022). Can corporate social responsibility lead to social license? A sentiment and emotion analysis. *Journal of Management Studies.*

Idemudia, U. (2009). Oil extraction and poverty reduction in the Niger Delta: A critical examination of partnership initiatives. *Journal of Business Ethics, 90*(SUPPL. 1), 91–116. https://doi.org/10.1007/s10551-008-9916-8

Kepe, T. (1999). The problem of defining "community": Challenges for the land reform programme in rural South Africa. *Development Southern Africa, 16*(3), 415–433. https://doi.org/10.1080/03768359908440089

Kolk, A. (2016). The social responsibility of international business: From ethics and the environment to CSR and sustainable development. *Journal of World Business, 51*(1), 23–34. https://doi.org/10.1016/J.JWB.2015.08.010

Lashitew, A. A. (2021). Corporate uptake of the sustainable development goals: Mere greenwashing or an advent of institutional change? *Journal of International Business Policy, 4*, 184–200. https://doi.org/10.1057/s42214-020-00092-4

Mbalyohere, C., & Lawton, T. C. (2022). Engaging informal institutions through corporate political activity: Capabilities for subnational embeddedness in emerging economies. *International Business Review, 31*(2). https://doi.org/10.1016/j.ibusrev.2021.101927

Meyer, K. E. (2004). Perspectives on multinational enterprises in emerging economies. *Journal of International Business Studies, 35*(4), 259–276. https://doi.org/10.1057/PALGRAVE.JIBS.8400084

Montiel, I., Cuervo-Cazurra, A., Park, J., Antolín-López, R., & Husted, B. W. (2021). Implementing the United Nations' Sustainable Development Goals in international business. *Journal of International Business Studies, 52*(5), 999–1030. https://doi.org/10.1057/S41267-021-00445-Y/TABLES/1

Nemitz, E. (2023). *Forced labour vineyards in Brazil expose modern slavery*. Fair Planet; Fair Planet. https://www.fairplanet.org/editors-pick/brazil-forced-labour-modern-slavery/

Newenham-Kahindi, A. M. (2011). A global mining corporation and local communities in the lake Victoria Zone: The Case of Barrick Gold Multinational in Tanzania. *Journal Of Business Ethics, 99*(2), 253–282. https://doi.org/10.1007/s10551-010-0653-4

Peerally, J. A., De Fuentes, C., & Figueiredo, P. N. (2019). Inclusive innovation and the role of technological capability-building: The social business Grameen Danone Foods Limited in Bangladesh. *Long Range Planning, 52*(6). https://doi.org/10.1016/j.lrp.2018.04.005

Prahalad. (2006). *The fortune at the bottom of the Pyramid*. Pearson Prentice Hall.

Prahalad, C. K., & Hart, S. (2009). *The fortune at the bottom of the Pyramid: Eradicating poverty through profits, revised and updated 5th Anniversary Edition.* Wharton School Publishing.

Prasad, A., & Durepos, G. (2016). From margin to center: listening to silenced subjectivities in international business. *Critical Perspectives on International Business, 12*(3), 218–221.

Rai, S. M., Brown, B. D., & Ruwanpura, K. N. (2019). SDG 8: Decent work and economic growth—A gendered analysis. *World Development, 113*, 368–380. https://doi.org/10.1016/J.WORLDDEV.2018.09.006

Reimann, F., Ehrgott, M., Kaufmann, L., & Carter, C. R. (2012). Local stakeholders and local legitimacy: MNEs' social strategies in emerging economies. *Journal of International Management, 18*(1), 1–17. https://doi.org/10.1016/j.intman.2011.06.002

Rosati, F., & Faria, L. G. D. (2019). Business contribution to the sustainable development agenda: Organizational factors related to early adoption of SDG reporting. *Corporate Social Responsibility and Environmental Management, 26*(3), 588–597. https://doi.org/10.1002/CSR.1705

Sachs, J. D. (2012). From millennium development goals to sustainable development goals. *The Lancet, 379*(9832), 2206–2211. https://doi.org/10.1016/S0140-6736(12)60685-0

Scott. (1995). *Institutions and organizations*. Sage.

Sinkovics, N., Vieira, L. M., & van Tulder, R. (2022). Working toward the sustainable development goals in earnest–critical international business perspectives on designing and implementing better interventions. *Critical Perspectives on International Business, 18*(4), 445–456.

Strand, R. (2009). Corporate responsibility in scandinavian supply chains. *Journal Of Business Ethics, 85*, 179–185. https://doi.org/10.1007/s10551-008-9937-3

Tasavori, M., Ghauri, P., & Zaefarian, R. (2014). The entry of multinational companies to the base of the Pyramid: A network perspective. In *International Business and Institutions after the Financial Crisis* (pp. 39–52). Palgrave Macmillan, London. https://doi.org/10.1057/9781137367204_4

UNDP. (2021). *Corruption and Contemporary forms of slavery: Examining relationships and addressing policy gaps*. UNDP. file:///C:/Users/rholi/OneDrive/OneDrive/FGV-Postdoc/Postdoc/Book_chapter/UNDP-Corruption-and-Contemporary-Forms-of-Slavery-Relationships-and-Addressing-Policy-Gaps.pdf van der Straaten, K., Narula, R., & Giuliani, E. (2023). The multinational enterprise, development, and the inequality of opportunities: A research agenda. *Journal of International Business Studies, 1–18*,. https://doi.org/10.1057/S41267-023-00625-Y/FIGURES/2

van Tulder, R., Rodrigues, S. B., Mirza, H., & Sexsmith, K. (2021). The UN's sustainable development goals: Can multinational enterprises lead the Decade of Action? *Journal of International Business Policy, 4*(1), 1–21. https://doi.org/10.1057/s42214-020-00095-1

Van Tulder, R., & van Mil, E. (2022). *Principles of sustainable business: Frameworks for Corporate Action on the SDGs*. Taylor & Francis.

van Zanten, J. A., & van Tulder, R. (2018). Multinational enterprises and the sustainable development goals: An institutional approach to corporate engagement. *Journal of International Business Policy, 1*(3–4), 208–233. https://doi.org/10.1057/s42214-018-0008-x

Wilkinson, K. (1991). *The community in Rural America*. Greenwood Press.

Wood, V. R., Pitta, D. A., & Franzak, F. J. (2008). Successful marketing by multinational firms to the bottom of the pyramid: Connecting share of heart, global "umbrella brands", and responsible marketing. *Journal of Consumer Marketing, 25*(7), 419–429. https://doi.org/10.1108/07363760810915635/FULL/HTML

World Business Council for Sustainable Development. (1999). *Corporate social responsibility: Meeting changing expectations*. World Business Council for Sustainable Development.

Yakovleva, N., & Vazquez-Brust, D. A. (2018). Multinational mining enterprises and artisanal small-scale miners: From confrontation to cooperation. *Journal of World Business, 53*(1), 52–62. https://doi.org/10.1016/J.JWB.2017.08.004

8

The Role of Foreign Multinational Corporations in Innovation Capability Upgrading of Subnational Peripheries

Shasha Zhao

1 The Core-Periphery Inequality

The core assumption underpinning the global innovation strategies of MNEs is that countries in the global South (emerging economies) are mainly recipients of MNE knowledge developed in the global North (advanced economies) (Coe et al., 1997; Dunning, 1993). This was driven by the significantly more advanced innovation capabilities in the North and limited opportunities in the South caused by weak national institutions including the absence of effective innovation systems and government policies (Archibugi & Iammarino, 2002).

However, recent findings offered by global innovation studies seem to challenge this traditional paradigm (Haakonsson & Ujjual, 2015; Haour & Jolly, 2014; Jha et al., 2015; Zhang et al., 2022; Zhao et al., 2022). For instance, Jha et al. (2015) find the global innovation scene reflects a rather different empirical development through the increasing

S. Zhao (✉)
University of Surrey, Guildford, UK
e-mail: shasha.zhao@surrey.ac.uk

N. Sinkovics et al. (eds.), *International Business and SDG 8*, The Academy of International Business, https://doi.org/10.1007/978-3-031-46802-5_8

sourcing of innovation from dissimilar and less-advanced South. What makes this phenomenon remarkable is MNE subsidiaries in the South are departing from technology adaptation roles (i.e., production), instead developing into new knowledge generators (i.e., new product development) (Awate et al., 2014; Dodourova et al., 2021; Zhao et al., 2020, 2021).

Within existing study of MNE innovation, for International Business scholars, the traditional assumption of the spatial dimension in FDI research has remained at the country level as the location unit of analysis—a tradition that has come under some serious scrutiny recently (including Beugelsdijk & Mudambi, 2013; Castellani & Santangelo, 2016; Chidlow et al., 2015; Goerzen et al., 2013; Luo et al., 2019; Stallkamp et al., 2017). Instead, a renewed perspective accounting for '*both international and subnational spatial heterogeneity*' is called for to act as the more appropriate basis for FDI location research (Beugelsdijk & Mudambi, 2013, p. 413). Subnational variation can be more notable in certain economies due to, for example, pro-market reforms not proceeding at the same pace across all regions, which has led to significant heterogeneity in subnational institutions (Luo et al., 2019). Thus, subnational FDI locational choice is also likely to vary (Ma et al., 2013). In contrast, *subnationalism* has traditionally been rooted in economic geography research where regional variation is well-recognized and documented. This literature frequently distinguishes between 'core' regions with high global and local *connectivity* (resource availability) and *performance* (economic, legal, and social development), and 'peripheral' regions which are comparatively lagging behind.

Given that regional differences are seen by MNEs as important drivers of FDI (Goerzen et al., 2013; Zhao, 2019), core regions are by far the largest recipients of innovation FDI (Castellani & Santangelo, 2016; fDi Markets, 2017; Zhao et al., 2020). This further strengthens the capability of these regions and reinforces the core-periphery regional development gap (Asheim et al., 2011). Thus, less attractive peripheral regions are potentially deprived of the much-needed innovation capability upgrading—otherwise achievable through knowledge exchange with locally embedded innovative subsidiaries (Mudambi & Santangelo, 2016). Whilst core regions in both advanced and emerging economies continue to prosper in terms of innovation capability development, this study argues it is imperative to develop an in-depth understanding of whether and how subsidiary innovation contributes to capability upgrading of the peripheral regions. Furthermore, it puts forward important policy considerations regarding necessary interventions to achieving a more balanced innovation capacity development across regions. Fundamentally, this chapter aims to answer two related questions: (1) What is the role of MNE subsidiaries in the upgrading of innovation capability of peripheral regions? (2) What are the regional policy considerations for attracting and benefitting from inward innovation FDI.

Answers to these two questions also highlight the usefulness of this line of inquiry for examining the role of MNEs in emerging economies' progress in achieving SDG 8. Particularly, the role of MNEs in innovation capability upgrading can contribute to Target 8.2 on 'achieve[ing] higher levels of economic productivity through diversification, technological upgrading and innovation, including through a focus on high value added and labour-intensive sectors' and Target 8.3 on 'promote[ing] development-oriented policies that support productive activities, decent job creation, entrepreneurship, creativity and innovation, and encourage the formalization and growth of micro-, small- and medium-sized enterprises, including through access to financial services' (United Nations, n.d.)

2 Current State of Knowledge

2.1 Two Major Drivers of North–South Innovation Connectivity: MNE and Location

The recent international business and management literature concerning the wider geographical spread of innovation FDI across both advanced and emerging economies can be grouped by two angles of analysis: MNE and location. Taking the *MNE* as the starting and focal point of discussion, it is argued that the historical and recent (re)organization of MNE global value chains has largely contributed to the advancing of innovation capabilities across both advanced and emerging economies (Lema et al., 2015; Zhao et al., 2020, 2021).

Specifically, an earlier disaggregation of value chain activities saw many MNEs locate low (predominantly in the South) and high (predominantly in the North) value-adding activities in geographically dispersed locations that were the most appropriate at that time (Gereffi et al., 2005). This required them to implement continuous processes for codifying and systematizing tacit knowledge (created in the North) in order to turn new and creative ideas into standardized and repetitive activities (Cano-Kollman et al., 2016). Codified knowledge was then constantly transferred to the MNE subsidiaries in lower-cost locations to carry out various 'finely sliced' production and assembly-related activities. These continuous processes from North to South have promoted faster learning and upgrading of capabilities in emerging economies (Kumaraswamy et al., 2012; Lema et al., 2015). These subsidiaries located focused on fairly narrow activities, 'fitting' into the MNE's global value chain but working in a complementary fashion with the subsidiaries located in the North. This eventually allowed these subsidiaries to move up the chain. Lema et al. (2015) found support for this notion in the case of Bosch's Brazilian subsidiary, which over time has been able to move up the chain by first improving current products and processes and then developing new products and processes related to its main activity, i.e., production. Similarly, Mudambi and Santangelo (2016) argue that in cutting-edge industries (e.g. biotechnology) many MNEs have set up knowledge-intensive subsidiaries in India. What is behind this investment decision is '*their [the subsidiaries] connectivity with and integration into global value chains, so that they typically undertake the 'standardized' activities fine sliced out of even high-knowledge processes like R&D*' (p. 3). This continuous 'spillover' of higher value-adding activities is likely to promote fast learning and upgrading in the country. Despite this recognition that these subsidiaries have been upgrading, whether and how the local region (e.g. suppliers, alliances or joint venture partners, and research institutions and universities) can benefit from the upgrade remains largely unknown.

Conversely taking *location* as the focal point of discussion, emerging economies have been identified to initiate extensive endogenous efforts in the building up of national innovation capabilities (exemplars are China, India, and Brazil) (Liu et al., 2011; Mabey & Zhao, 2017; Woetzel et al., 2015). Specifically, emerging economies' governments have led a nationwide 'catch-up' process by developing a number of pro-innovation conditions, including investment in higher education and the retention of (highly) skilled native and foreign researchers and managers, the development of clusters (encompassing local firms and support systems), and the availability of large financial resources—all contributing to the creation of a more attractive innovation FDI destination (Liu et al., 2011; Zhao & Zhang, 2007). Whilst innovation capability building is a top priority for national governments, it is important to learn from past economic geography studies that the specific policy-making and implementation process is predominately formulated and undertaken at the regional level (Crescenzi & Iammarino, 2017; Zhao, 2016; Zhao & Zhang, 2007). Subsequently, regions with ineffective policies and systems, as well as resource limitations are prone to a lack of inward FDI. However, this important component in regional variation has been largely neglected in international business and innovation research (with the exception of Mudambi & Santangelo, 2016), highlighting the importance of this chapter.

A thorough review of the two areas of literature across International Business, Innovation, and Economic Development leads to the conclusion that to date there is very little in the way of conceptually and empirically linking the role of MNE innovation FDI, the effects on the technological upgrading of the peripheral, subnational regions in both advanced and emerging economies, and the reverse effects on the MNEs. That is, there lacks a wider conceptualization of the nexus. In the next section, I will provide some early evidence on the nexus by way of reviewing and evaluating some of the exemplar studies and the evidence they provided.

3 Unfolding the Nexus of MNE FDI, Subnational Peripheries, and Local Capability Upgrading

A review of the IB literature on MNE, peripheries, and effects has unfolded evidence along two main dimensions. The first dimension—with exemplar evidence from five IB studies—concerns internal (MNE) and external (location) factors as the catalyst for MNE FDI in peripheries (Lee et al., 2016; McDonald et al., 2018; Prashantham & Bhattacharyya, 2020; Stallkamp et al., 2017; Santangelo, 2004). The second dimension—with exemplar evidence from two IB studies—concerns MNE FDI as a key mechanism of technological upgrading in subnational peripheries (Mudambi & Santangelo, 2016; Santangelo, 2009). I consider these two dimensions to be equally important when understanding the nexus. This is because the first set of evidence offers a useful explication of the antecedents to MNE FDI in subnational peripheries, which acts as a theoretical steppingstone for understanding the consequences. Next, I first examine the two sets of evidence in greater details, which leads me to derive at a summary table (Table 1) highlighting all key variables identified in the seven studies. Building on it, I propose a conceptual framework (Fig. 1) that offers several overarching constructs and their relationships or effects. The purpose of the framework is not only to provide a new, holistic way of conceptualising the nexus of MNE FDI, subnational peripheries, and the impact on host countries but for IB scholars to consider it as a basis for their future research that extends this line of inquiry.

3.1 Some Early Evidence

In terms of the first dimension, the focus has been on investigating possible internal (MNE) and external (location) factors as the catalyst for MNE FDI in peripheries. More specifically, Santangelo (2004) analysed the locational preferences of MNEs across provinces (i.e., e.g., sub-regional political and economic territorial units) of Sicily in Italy in

Table 1 Main variables studied by each of the seven articles

No	Author and year	Antecedent	Mechanism	Consequence	Moderator
1	Santangelo (2004)	Local resources (skilled labour, trade openness, proximity to universities, information costs)		Agglomeration in specific tech clusters	Development policies at the subnational level
2	Santangelo (2009)		Creation of linkages between subsidiary and local counterparts	MNE knowledge spillovers to local counterparts	MNE subsidiary local market strategy and organizational structure
3	Lee et al. (2016)	Local supply and demand resources		FDI location choice between core and neighbouring peripheries	MNE location-boundedness, technological intensity, sector difference
4	Mudambi and Santangelo (2016)	MNE subsidiary attributes (entry timing, entry mode, and mandate)	Integration of local resources and international connectivity (through MNEs) over time	Emerging technological cluster	
5	Stallkamp et al. (2017)	Subnational entry locations (core vs. periphery)		Location choice and pace in within-country expansion	

(continued)

Table 1 (continued)

No	Author and year	Antecedent	Mechanism	Consequence	Moderator
6	McDonald et al. (2018)	Locational disadvantages		Lack of inward FDI	Proximity of subnational peripheries to core cities
7	Prashantham and Bhattacharyya (2020)		Co-innovations between MNEs and SMEs		Polices for promoting co-innovations at the subnational level

Articles are in chronological order

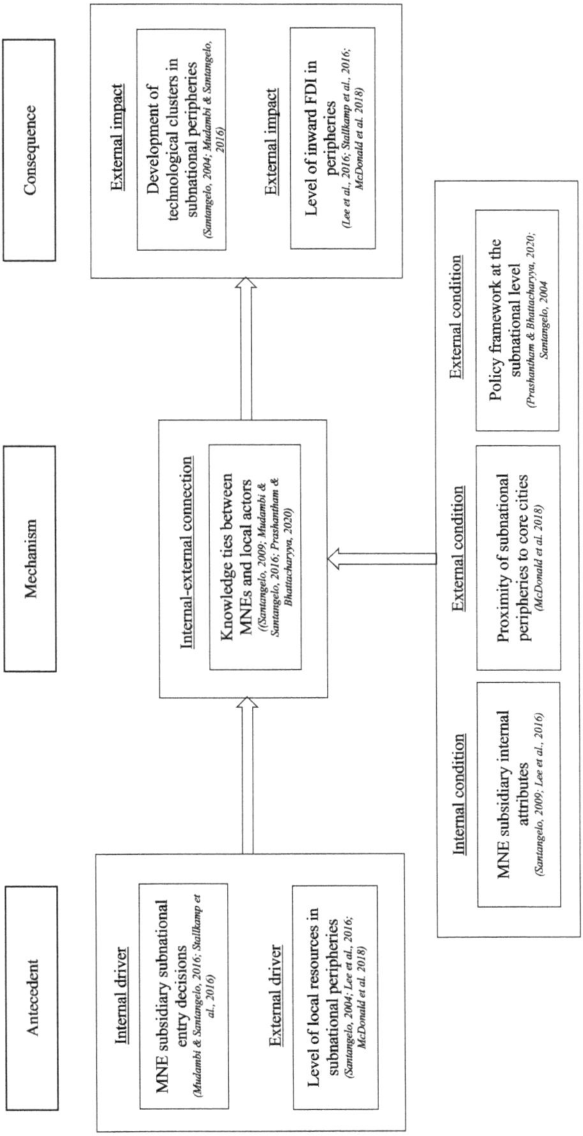

Fig. 1 Conceptualization of the relationship between MNEs and host subnational peripheries

the light of an incentives programme granted under a new regional development policy. She noted that whilst IB scholars were paying increasing attention to subnational units, they had focused mostly on core regions, neglecting the peripheral ones. Her article, based on a unique set of data, evidenced that unlike what was predicted by the literature, the locational preferences of MNEs in Sicily were driven by local high-skilled competences (including high wages), high degrees of trade openness, proximity to universities, and low information costs. The findings also showed that an agglomeration of foreign affiliates in electronics, and chemicals and pharmaceuticals in a cluster known as the 'Etna Valley' was forming. Similarly, locational characteristics were also found to be crucial in the work by McDonald et al. (2018). More specifically, they found that peripheries' close proximity to core regions was a key driver for inward FDI to the peripheries. The authors drew on relevant perspectives from the economic geography literature to investigate the locational determinants of MNE FDI into peripheral cities within an emerging economy. It was argued that peripheral cities in emerging economies were attracting a growing proportion of global FDI flows, but the IB literature lacks a framework for understanding subnational determinants of FDI, particularly into non-core locations. Drawing on the core-periphery model, they found that whilst peripheral cities tended to have a negative effect on FDI, this effect is positively moderated by proximity to core cities. The study highlighted the importance of considering interactions between place and space when investigating locational issues in IB. The work by Prashantham and Bhattacharyya (2020) also took an exclusive view of the external, locational drivers of MNE FDI in subnational peripheries. It was found that local innovation policy helps to promote MNE-SME co-innovation in peripheries. More specifically, the authors drew on the division of entrepreneurial labour literature to explore policy-induced efforts that facilitate MNE–SME collaboration for innovation in peripheral subnational regions in China and the UK. Their inductive study found that boundary work (i.e., the process of connecting actors in systems of social, economic, or political relations to facilitate access to valued resources (Stovel & Shaw, 2012, p. 141) manifested differently in advanced and emerging economies. That is, bottom-up opportunity discovery in the UK and top-down opportunity creation in China, with the former involving a bespoke policy measure and the latter a 'bricolage' approach of making do with an existing generic policy that was creatively utilised. It highlighted the importance of integrative and innovative regional policies for promoting mutually beneficial MNE–SME collaboration.

Taking a slightly different approach of a dual perspective of the internal (MNE) and external (location) conditions, Lee et al. (2016) examined the two-dimensional effects on MNEs' decisions to invest in core versus peripheral subnational locations. More specifically, building on the differences between the services and manufacturing sectors, the findings showed that MNEs from the two sectors showed different responsiveness to their final FDI location choices in the subnational regions of a host country. Using the case of Korea, the location decisions made by service MNEs were more likely to be driven by demand-side considerations, whereas those made by manufacturing MNEs were more likely to be influenced by supply-side characteristics of subnational regions. Further, subnational location decisions made by both high-tech and low-tech manufacturing MNEs considered the availability of local skill and technology resources within a core region more importantly than that from its neighbouring, non-core regions. Subnational location decisions made by location-bound service MNEs exhibited the same intra-regional effects for local market potential; however, those by non-location-bound service MNEs considered the local market potential from non-core regions more importantly than that within a core region. Along the same, internal conditions, Stallkamp et al. (2017)'s study focused on the question of how the initial subnational entry location of foreign MNEs in China influenced their subsequent within-country location choices and expansion speed. They distinguished between MNEs that establish their first subsidiary in co-ethnic cores-dense agglomerations of other firms from the same country of origin and MNEs that locate their first subsidiary in the periphery, i.e., outside of these co-ethnic cores. By employing a geo-visualisation methodology, the authors were able to identify co-ethnic cores in the country. The findings provided evidence of path dependency, in that (a) entry through subnational locations with strong co-ethnic communities is followed by expansion into other locations where co-ethnic communities are present and that (b) entry through co-ethnic communities accelerates the pace at which MNEs establish additional subsidiaries.

For the second dimension, the focus has been on MNE FDI as a key mechanism of technological upgrading in subnational peripheries. More specifically, the study by Santangelo (2009) highlighted that MNEs' knowledge spillovers in the local region occurred through linkages creation between the subsidiary and local actors. What had been less known in the literature is the factors that affected the creation of the linkages. Using a peripheral subnational sub-regional area, the author identified the important roles of subsidiaries' local market strategy and organisational structure played in local linkages creation. Further, it was emphasised that the creation of MNE-local actor linkages is more likely to develop when market rival relationships existed among subsidiaries which had a competence-creating scope within the corporate organisational structure instead of competence-exploiting scope. Similarly, Mudambi and Santangelo (2016)'s work also suggested strong evidence of MNE knowledge spillovers taking place in subnational peripheries *albeit* the focus is more dynamic and extensive. More specifically, the authors focused on a period of five decades and applied a dynamic model to highlight the critical role of MNE subsidiary entry timing, entry mode, and mandate in transforming a peripheral area of a European economy into an 'emerging' technological cluster. Such a cluster facilitated further internal (local) resources and external (international) connectivity to be established.

In Table 1, a summary of all the identifiable key variables from the seven studies is provided.

3.2 A Conceptual Framework for the Nexus

Building on my evaluation of the early evidence (see Table 1), a framework (Fig. 1) is developed to provide more clarity and possibility in conceptualising the nexus. For example, the works by Mudambi and Santangelo (2016) and Stallkamp et al. (2017) identified internal drivers of MNE FDI in subnational peripheries, whilst works from Santangelo (2004), Lee et al. (2016), and McDonald et al. (2018) unfolded external drivers. I term these drivers as antecedents in the framework. Next, the works by Santangelo (2009), Mudambi and Santangelo (2016), and Prashantham and Bhattacharyya (2020) all highlighted the importance of internal (MNE)–external (local actor) connectivity. That is, strong knowledge ties between MNEs and local actors in the subnational peripheries need to be established to derive more knowledge spillovers. I thus consider this as a crucial mechanism. Last, the works by Lee et al. (2016), Stallkamp et al. (2017), and McDonald et al. (2018) found internal and external factors to affect the level of inward FDI into the subnational peripheries. On the other hand, Santangelo (2004) and Mudambi and Santangelo (2016) identified these factors to contribute to the emergence of new technological clusters in subnational peripheries. These are considered consequences in the framework.

4 Implications on Sustainability Research in International Business

This chapter contributes to a novel area of study that integrates international business research with economic geography. Instead of core regions, this chapter draws scholarly attention to subnational peripheral regions within countries and is one of the first studies to scrutinise research on MNE FDI in this context. Whilst innovation in the North and South has received increasing attention, research largely focuses on locational characteristics as determinants of FDI decisions (e.g. Castellani & Santangelo, 2016; Chidlow et al., 2015). This study argues for a different analytical perspective: one where (innovation) FDI decision can be a critical determinant of its host location's development trajectory through regional innovation capability upgrade. Hence, it simultaneously investigates strategic (firm-level) and policy (location-based) considerations and the relationships between them.

Core-peripheral inequality is significant in the case of not only emerging economies but advanced, what is little known is the distinctive interaction between subsidiary innovation and subnational peripheries—whether and how benefits can be created for the latter to deal with the inequality problem. Previous theories and literature based on core regions cannot account for the idiosyncrasies of the peripheries. This chapter is thus likely to help promote scholarly thinking in this new and under-explored area. The conceptual framework contributes to new theory development, through the identification of mechanisms upgrading regional innovation capability. For example, the role of MNEs in sustainability has been under increasing scrutiny and negative publicities. The need for these firms to prove themselves as global citizens and sustainability partners becomes imperative. The main management challenge is therefore the emerging prerequisite to balance both financial performance (shareholder driven) and sustainable development (society driven). There have been ad hoc cases of successful management approaches to address this complex, though little systematic evidence remains available in International Business research. Future research could undertake primary, inductive, or case studies to seek new empirical insights that can act as a useful basis for new conceptualization of the role of MNEs in technological upgrading in subnational peripheries.

4.1 Implications on Corporate Practices

The potential role MNEs can play in the upgrading of innovation capability of peripheral regions is likely to bring reverse effects (location-to-firm) to the locally embedded subsidiaries. It is expected that as local innovation capability is being upgraded (through intensive stakeholder learning), subsidiaries are likely to experience innovation-related benefits, such as increased reverse knowledge transfer and localized innovation opportunities. Therefore, it is in the interest of subsidiary managers to consider what strategy and organizational practices should be in place to best capture emerging benefits.

4.2 Implications on Sustainable Development Policies

The introduction of a new policy-making framework is likely to be useful in the promotion of peripheral regions as an attractive innovation-FDI location. A more even national capability development framework can act as a counterbalance to tendencies towards widening regional inequalities. The development of the policy-making framework is likely to be well-informed by findings from inductive studies. Empirical data can potentially help to establish the quality and strength of knowledge exchange links with local stakeholders. Moreover, this data will enable identification of facilitating and limiting factors in the formation and maintenance of knowledge exchange links. Subsequently, a new policy-making framework more effective in addressing local limitations and promoting local opportunities can be extremely valuable (Sinkovics et al., 2022). More broadly, the literature presented also highlights a novel angle for understanding the role of MNEs in emerging economies' progress on achieving SDG 8, particularly Targets 8.2 and 8.3.

5 Conclusion

Given that innovation FDI takes place at the regional level, core regions (high global and local connectedness and performance) have been the main recipients compared to peripheral regions. This uneven distribution extends the inequality gap between core and peripheral regions within a nation state and has significant implications for peripheral regional development. This chapter uses insightful evidence found in exemplar studies to unfold the relationship between MNEs and innovation capability upgrade of peripheral regions. By scrutinising seven key sets of findings, three contributions are made: First, it scrutinises early evidence concerning MNEs and host subnational peripheries and unfolds the current state of knowledge; Second, it introduces a conceptual framework that maps out the nexus of MNE FDI, subnational peripheries, and local innovation upgrading. These contributions speak to the IB, Innovation, and Economic Development scholarships, providing a useful conceptual basis for future research examining the nexus of MNE innovation, FDI, and the upgrading of peripheral regions. Third, it highlights how this line of scholarly inquiry can be useful for evaluating the current progress on achieving UN's Sustainable Development Goal 8, particularly Targets 8.2 and 8.3.

References

Asheim, B. T., Smith, H. L., & Oughton, C. (2011). Regional innovation systems: Theory, empirics and policy. *Regional Studies, 45*(7), 875–891.

Archibugi, D., & Iammarino, S. (2002). The globalization of technological innovation: Definition and evidence. *Review of International Political Economy, 9*(1), 98–122.

Awate, S., Larsen, M. M., & Mudambi, R. (2014). Accessing vs sourcing knowledge: A comparative study of R&D internationalization between emerging and advanced economy firms. *Journal of International Business Studies, 46*(1), 63–86.

Beugelsdijk, S., & Mudambi, R. (2013). MNEs as border-crossing multi-location enterprises: The role of discontinuities in geographic space. *Journal of International Business Studies, 44*(5), 413–426.

Cano-Kollmann, M., Cantwell, J., Hannigan, T. J., Mudambi, R., & Song, J. (2016). Knowledge connectivity: An agenda for innovation research in international business. *Journal of International Business Studies, 47*(3), 255–262.

Castellani, D., & Santangelo, G. (2016, December 2–4). Quo vadis? Cities and the location of cross-border activities. In *European International Business Academy Conference Proceedings*. Vienna University of Economics and Business, Vienna.

Chidlow, A., Holmström-Lind, C., Holm, U., & Tallman, S. (2015). Do I stay or do I go? Sub-national drivers for post-entry subsidiary development. *International Business Review, 24*(2), 266–275.

China Institute of City Competitiveness and Advanced Institute for Contemporary China Studies of Hong Kong Baptist University. (2000–2016). *Yearbook of China city competitiveness*. Enrich Professional Publishing.

Coe, D. T., Helpman, E., & Hoffmaister, A. W. (1997). North-South R&D spillovers. *The Economic Journal, 107*(440), 134–149.

Crescenzi, R., & Iammarino, S. (2017). Global investments and regional development trajectories: The missing links. *Regional Studies, 51*(1), 97–115.

Dodourova, M., Zhao, S., & Harzing, A. W. (2021). Ambidexterity in MNC knowledge sourcing in emerging economies: A microfoundational perspective. *International Business Review, 32*, 101854.

Dunning, J. H. (1993). *Multinational enterprises and the global economy*. Addison Wesley.

fDi Intelligence. (2003–2016). *fDi markets*. Financial Times Press.

Gereffi, G., Humphrey, J., & Sturgeon, T. (2005). The governance of global value chains. *Review of International Political Economy, 12*(1), 78–104.

Goerzen, A., Asmussen, C. G., & Nielsen, B. B. (2013). Global cities and multinational enterprise location strategy. *Journal of International Business Studies, 44*(SI), 427–450.

Haakonsson, S. J., & Ujjual, V. (2015). Internationalisation of R&D: New insights into multinational enterprises' R&D strategies in emerging markets. *Management Revue, 26*(2), 101–122.

Haour, G., & Jolly, D. (2014). China: The next innovation hot spot for the world. *Journal of Business Strategy, 35*(1), 2–8.

Jha, S., Dhanaraj, C., & Krishnan, R. (2015). *How does multinational R&D evolve in emerging markets?* (Working Paper). International Institute for Management Development, 2015-02.

Kumaraswamy, A., Mudambi, R., Saranga, H., & Tripathy, A. (2012). Catch-up strategies in the Indian auto components industry: Domestic firms' responses to market liberalization. *Journal of International Business Studies, 43*(4), 368–395.

Lee, I. H., Hong, E., & Makino, S. (2016). Location decisions of inward FDI in sub-national regions of a host country: Service versus manufacturing industries. *Asia Pacific Journal of Management, 33*, 343–370.

Lema, R., Quadros, R., & Schmitz, H. (2015). Reorganising global value chains and building innovation capabilities in Brazil and India. *Research Policy, 44*(7), 1376–1386.

Liu, F. C., Simon, D. F., Sun, Y. T., & Cao, C. (2011). China's innovation policies: Evolution, institutional structure, and trajectory. *Research Policy, 40*(7), 917–931.

Luo, Y., Zhang, H., & Bu, J. (2019). Developed country MNEs investing in developing economies: Progress and prospect. *Journal of International Business Studies, 50*, 633–667.

Ma, X., Tong, T. W., & Fitza, M. (2013). How much does subnational region matter to foreign subsidiary performance? Evidence from Fortune Global 500 Corporations' investment in China. *Journal of International Business Studies, 44*(1), 66–87.

Mabey, C., & Zhao, S. (2017). Managing five paradoxes of knowledge exchange in networked organizations: New priorities for HRM? *Human Resource Management Journal, 27*(1), 39–57.

McDonald, C., Buckley, P. J., Voss, H., Cross, A. R., & Chen, L. (2018). Place, space, and foreign direct investment into peripheral cities. *International Business Review, 27*(4), 803–813.

Mudambi, R., & Santangelo, G. D. (2016). From shallow resource pools to emerging clusters: The role of multinational enterprise subsidiaries in peripheral areas. *Regional Studies, 50*(12), 1965–1979.
National Bureau of Statistics of China. (2000–2016). *Statistical yearbook*. China Statistical Press.
Prashantham, S., & Bhattacharyya, S. (2020). MNE–SME co-innovation in peripheral regions. *Journal of International Business Policy, 3*, 134–153.
Santangelo, G. D. (2004). FDI and local capabilities in peripheral regions: The Etna Valley case. *Transnational Corporations, 13*, 73–108.
Santangelo, G. D. (2009). MNCs and linkages creation: Evidence from a peripheral area. *Journal of World Business, 44*(2), 192–205.
Sinkovics, N., Vieira, L. M., & van Tulder, R. (2022). Working toward the sustainable development goals in earnest—Critical international business perspectives on designing and implementing better interventions. *Critical Perspectives on International Business, 18*(4), 445–456.
Stallkamp, M., Pinkham, B. C., Schotter, A. P., & Buchel, O. (2017). Core or periphery? The effects of country-of-origin agglomerations on the within-country expansion of MNEs. *Journal of International Business Studies, 49*, 1–25.
Stovel, K., & Shaw, L. (2012). Brokerage. *Annual Review of Sociology, 38*, 139–158.
United Nations. (n.d.). *Sustainable development goal 8*. United Nations. https://sdgs.un.org/goals/goal8. Accessed 20 Aug 2023.
Woetzel, J., Chen, Y., Manyika, J., Roth, E., Seong, J., & Lee, J. (2015). *The China effect on global innovation*. McKinsey Global Institute of McKinsey & Company.
Zhang, L. E., Zhao, S., Kern, P., Edwards, T., & Zhang, Z. X. (2022). The pursuit of indigenous innovation amid the Tech Cold War: The case of a Chinese high-tech firm. *International Business Review*, 102079.
Zhao, S. (2016). Co-evolution of innovative subsidiaries and global cities of emerging economies: The case of Beijing and Shanghai. In *Regional Studies Association Winter Conference Proceedings*, 24–25 November, London.
Zhao, S. (2019). Healthy cities and sustainable innovation. In W. Leal Filho, A. M. Azul, L. Brandli, P. G. Ozuyar, & T. Wall (Eds.), *Sustainable cities and communities*. Encyclopedia of UN sustainable development goals. Springer.
Zhao, S., Liu, X., Andersson, U., & Shenkar, O. (2022). Knowledge management of emerging economy multinationals. *Journal of World Business, 57*(1), 101255.

Zhao, S., Tan, H., Papanastassiou, M., & Harzing, A. W. (2020). The internationalization of innovation towards the South: A historical case study of a global pharmaceutical corporation in China (1993–2017). *Asia Pacific Journal of Management, 37*, 553–585.

Zhao, S., Papanastassiou, M., Pearce, R. D., & Iguchi, C. (2021). MNE R&D internationalization in developing Asia. *Asia Pacific Journal of Management, 38*, 1–25.

Zhao, S. X., & Zhang, L. (2007). Foreign direct investment and the formation of global city-regions in China. *Regional Studies, 41*(7), 979–994.

9

Blockchain Technology Adoption for Economic and Social Upgrading

Umair Shafi Choksy, Muhammad Ayaz, and James Francis

1 Introduction

Global value chains (GVCs) have become increasingly complex due to the growing volumes of global trade, leading to concerns about disruptions, workers' rights, and environmental damage, among other aspects (De Marchi & Gereffi, 2023; Gereffi et al., 2022). Many businesses are turning to traceability to enhance trust in GVCs (Ponte et al., 2019; Chen et al., 2022). Traceability is important in GVCs as it helps firms track whether quality standards are met and identify potential bottlenecks to minimize any disruptions (Azevedo et al., 2023). As a

U. S. Choksy (✉)
University of Stirling Management School, Scotland, UK
e-mail: umair.choksy@stir.ac.uk

M. Ayaz
Institute of Business Administration Karachi, Karachi, Pakistan
e-mail: muhammadayaz@iba.edu.pk

J. Francis
Kent Business School, University of Kent, Kent, UK

N. Sinkovics et al. (eds.), *International Business and SDG 8*, The Academy of International Business, https://doi.org/10.1007/978-3-031-46802-5_9

result, there has been a significant rise in research on the application of blockchain technology in GVCs (Ferrantino & Koten, 2019; Alves et al., 2022; Singh et al., 2022). Blockchain technology is a sophisticated method of data recording that makes use of distributed ledger technology to keep track of information in a distributed online database (Sarode et al., 2021). It provides new ways of recording, updating, validating, and sharing digital transparent records with participants in a decentralized manner to enhance trust based on consensus mechanisms (Chen et al., 2022). According to Zion Market Research (2022), the market for blockchain technology in supply chain management (SCM) was worth over $262.9 million in 2021 and is projected to increase to $3.153 billion by 2028. Companies such as Walmart, Kroger, Cargill, Coca-Cola, Carrefour, COFCO International Ltd, and Starbucks are embracing blockchain technology in their value chains to track and trace their products, materials, and services to gain efficiency, save costs, and capture more value in their value chains.

Similarly, blockchain technology can also help businesses meet the increasing demand for improving sustainability performance as regulators, community, civil society, and consumers are demanding greater transparency from global companies in monitoring and reporting their sustainability performance and progress related to the sustainable development goals (SDGs) (Saberi et al., 2019). For example, Tambe and Tambay (2020) propose an artificial intelligence (AI)—and blockchain-based due diligence process that could enable organizations to monitor modern slavery practices in their value chains. Di Vaio et al. (2023) argue that organizations can embed blockchain technology in corporate governance models to achieve gender equality and inclusion. For reporting purposes, blockchain provides a transparent and verifiable digital certificate to prove companies' social and environmental performance which is crucial for meeting the challenges associated with reporting progress on SDGs (de Villiers et al., 2021). Therefore, the growth of blockchain technology and its promise to impact economic, social, and environmental outcomes have prompted a demand for greater research into its effects (Chang et al., 2020). To date, much research on blockchain has focused on its economic impact and its potential for social impact is generally under-emphasized in the literature (Di Vaio et al., 2023).

In the GVC literature, one important concept is upgrading, i.e., understanding how participation in GVCs could lead to improvements in firm-level (economic upgrading), worker-level (social upgrading), and/or environmental (environmental upgrading) outcomes for suppliers in a developing economy (DE). The concept of upgrading is regarded by various international development organizations as a pathway to achieve economic and social development in developing countries. Participation in GVCs puts developing countries 'firms and economies on potentially dynamic learning curves' which provides an opportunity to develop their skills and competencies to move into more value-adding activities (Gereffi, 1999, p. 39). Correspondingly, this creates more employment opportunities and leads to better employment opportunities for workers (Milberg & Winkler, 2011). Therefore, the achievement of economic and social upgrading in GVCs is considered a means to achieve SDG 8: decent work and economic growth.

The current literature on blockchain technology in SCM is relatively established. It predominantly focuses on unpacking the benefits of blockchain technology in facilitating transparency, traceability, and visibility across supply chains (Gurtu & Johny, 2019). However, there is a need to understand the winners and losers among supply chain actors when supply chain activities stretch across different geographical and institutional boundaries. Therefore, the GVC lens can help in understanding to what extent blockchain technology adoption can benefit DE suppliers (Golini et al., 2016). This is because the GVC literature brings into focus the power asymmetries between global firms and developing country suppliers. Upgrading in GVCs does not always lead to positive outcomes for all firms and may lead to downgrading for many (Ayaz et al., 2019; Khan et al., 2020). It is important that the trade-offs are identified so that we can understand the ways in which positive outcomes can be ensured for all actors in GVCs. This is an important aspect of achieving inclusive growth and decent work through GVCs. As a result, this conceptual paper aims to address the following question:

> How can the adoption of blockchain technology in GVCs shape (facilitate/discourage) economic and social upgrading in a DE context?

Drawing upon the GVC governance and blockchain technology literature in regard to SCM, we look at the linkages between lead firms and DE suppliers and identify how the adoption of blockchain technology might have differential outcomes for each of these actors. As a result, we attempt to move the discussion from a supply chain perspective to specific firms in the periphery regions that may face distinct consequences of the adoption of blockchain technology in GVCs. Furthermore, we highlight the trade-offs between economic and social upgrading for DE suppliers and the conditions under which this trade-off can be minimized when GVCs adopt blockchain technology. We develop a conceptual framework and propositions to explain the relationship between blockchain technology adoption and its implications for economic and social upgrading in GVCs. Figure 1 presents a visual representation of the framework.

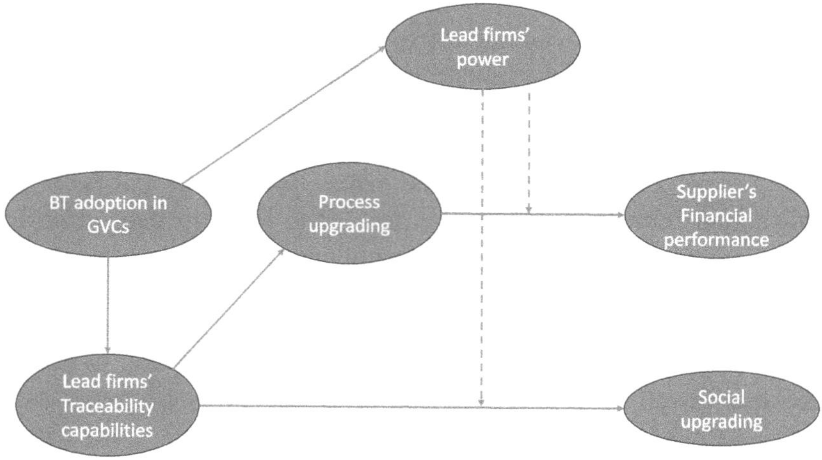

Fig. 1 Conceptual framework

2 Blockchain Technology Adoption, Traceability, and Process Upgrading

Blockchain technology is an intricate approach to keeping track of information online. It uses a special method called distributed ledger technology, where data are stored in blocks. Each block is connected to the one before it, creating a chain of blocks in a particular order. This design ensures that the integrity of the chain is preserved, preventing any unauthorized alterations or tampering (Sarode et al., 2021).

With blockchain technology, the business and transaction logic for every type of commerce could potentially change to enable digital assets to be managed or transacted securely and privately (Chen et al., 2022). Blockchain technology enables secure information sharing and governance throughout the value chain and helps address supply chain traceability[1] and credibility concerns (Guo et al., 2020).

Bager et al. (2022) have found support for this in the coffee supply chain. The implemented blockchain model successfully established a chain of custody, connecting coffee to specific lots and farmers, thus increasing supply chain actors' knowledge about product origin. It demonstrated the successful transfer of information on quality, sustainability practices, and certification standards from individual farmers to downstream actors, including consumers. Furthermore, the integration of blockchain and AI technologies can enable the development of an all-encompassing predictive system to manage pandemics and preserve the environment (Charles et al., 2023). Blockchain technology can assist in the early detection of outbreaks, securing the medical supply chain, and expediting drug delivery. AI-based techniques enable real-time epidemic outbreak monitoring, pandemic trend forecasting, and coronavirus symptom identification for the purposes of treatment. Furthermore, Chen et al. (2022) also report that blockchain technology adoption has enabled GVCs to have a single line of sight across all supply chain activities and be more reliable in getting goods to market, more

[1] We take Schwägele's (2005) definition of traceability as both tracing and tracking, whereby tracing includes the origin of the item from upstream activities of supply chain and tracking involves monitoring the flow of downstream activities.

agile in responding to customer demand changes, and more collaborative in cross-organizational automation. Based on the above arguments, we propose that:

> *P1: Blockchain technology adoption will improve lead firms' traceability capabilities.*

We further postulate that lead firms' traceability capabilities will mediate between blockchain technology adoption and a DE supplier's process upgrading. In the GVC literature, economic upgrading is used as a pathway to move up the value chain (Gereffi, 1999) or deepen firm-level capabilities to increase the economic margins from GVC activities (Morrison & Pietrobelli, 2007). One type of economic upgrading that applies to our paper is process upgrading. The process upgrading of firms in GVCs is defined as a process of transforming inputs into outputs in a more efficient manner. Process upgrading occurs through the adoption of technology or better organization of the production process. While the process upgrading of a DE supplier depends on a host of factors including absorptive capacity, mutual trust, and regulatory support, among others (Nath et al., 2022), we argue that the most important driver for process upgrading in the context of blockchain technology adoption will be the traceability capabilities of lead firms.

The literature on blockchain technology has yet to explicitly include GVC concepts, such as process upgrading, in the discussion. The most widely discussed outcome of blockchain technology-led traceability is improvement in the overall efficiency of supply chain activities. We consider this a form of process upgrading at the supply chain level. Using blockchain technology to utilize smart contracts is one of the biggest drivers of increased efficiency. 'Smart contracts facilitate, verify and enforce the agreement (transaction) between supply chain participants automatically' (Manupati et al., 2019, p. 2225). For example, Nanayakkara et al. (2021) have found that smart contracts can be employed in the construction sector to better track budgets and spending, as well as to mitigate payment and financial difficulties including payment security (Nanayakkara et al., 2021). Similarly, in the context of the dairy industry, blockchain technology increases the overall quality and safety of the products/services and improves process control for managing product recalls (Casino et al., 2021). This is because the improvement in lead firms' traceability capabilities due to blockchain technology adoption enables them to have more insight into the activities of the suppliers and whether these suppliers meet quality requirements. As a result, these suppliers are indirectly pressured to engage in process upgrading. Therefore, we argue that the traceability capabilities of lead firms improve the overall efficiency of the supply chain which is achieved through process upgrading at the firm level. Therefore, in the context of global value chains, we argue that:

P2: Lead firms' traceability capabilities will lead to DE suppliers' process upgrading.

Since the purpose of process upgrading is for DE suppliers to improve their economic margins, we argue that process upgrading should, in principle, lead to an improvement in suppliers' financial performance. The majority of the literature assumes that economic upgrading automatically leads to an improvement in suppliers' financial performance. However, Choksy et al. (2017) demonstrate that this may not necessarily be the case. They argue that it depends on the contextual contingencies involved in the upgrading process including GVC governance, supplier strategies, managerial agencies, and the GVC position of suppliers, in addition to their absorptive capacity (Morrison & Pietrobelli, 2007), as well as regulatory support, mutual trust between lead firm and supplier (Nath et al., 2022) and the institutional environment (Sinkovics et al., 2019), among others.

Recent studies provide some evidence that blockchain technology can improve profits for supply chain members by enhancing their efficiency and reducing repetitive tasks (e.g., of process upgrading; Benstead et al., 2022; Islam & Polonsky, 2020). Similarly, Choksy et al. (2022) have also found a positive link between all aspects of economic upgrading and financial performance. Based on these findings, we argue that, without any negative contextual conditions, blockchain adoption will have a positive impact on traceability, which in turn will facilitate process upgrading. Similarly, without any negative contextual condition, our proposition is that process upgrading will lead to an improvement in suppliers' financial performance.

P3: The process upgrading of DE suppliers will lead to an improvement in their financial performance.

3 Blockchain Technology Adoption, Traceability, and Social Upgrading

There are several different ways in which blockchain technology can improve traceability and outcomes for workers in the DE context. The GVC literature uses the term 'social upgrading' to explain the improvement in the decent work conditions and entitlements of workers. Barrientos et al. (2011) divide social upgrading into two components: (a) measurable standards and (b) rights and entitlements. Measurable standards are aspects of worker improvement that can be quantifiable and observed tangibly, including worker pay, social protection, and working hours. In contrast, rights and entitlements are qualitative changes in worker well-being, including freedom of expression and collective bargaining power. In this paper, we focus on the component involving measurable standards of social upgrading.

There is empirical evidence that using blockchain technology to track workers' travel and identification and linking it to visas and employment contracts can prevent cases of forced labour (Christ & Helliar, 2021, p. 117). To ensure that GVCs are free from slavery, workers need to register themselves by providing information for biometric digital IDs to their employers (Stuit et al., 2022, p. 17). The use of blockchain technology can thus enhance the social outcomes for workers by improving the methods involved in employee documentation and identification, which can help reduce unethical employment practices.

Furthermore, wages can be immutably recorded with blockchain technology, preventing disparities in payment and ensuring that workers receive what they are due. Businesses that fail are held accountable (Chandan, 2019, p. 956). As a result, workers are not exploited and are compensated appropriately. Therefore, when blockchain technology is integrated into worker documentation and payment systems, it can be a driving force in improving social outcomes for workers.

Blockchain technology 'has the capacity and potential to provide an alternative means through which auditing and human rights groups can verify that an agency is operating in full compliance with laws and regulations regarding these types of behaviours' (Berdik et al., 2021, p. 11). For example, Benstead et al. (2022) report that blockchain technology provides verified information that reduces the risk of exploitation. As a result, the working conditions of employees will be better regulated, leading to fair work and safety practices (Kshetri, 2021). Benstead et al. (2022) have also found similar evidence in their study of the clothing industry. Based on this evidence, we propose that:

P4: Lead firms' traceability capabilities will lead to the improvement of DE suppliers' social upgrading (according to measurable standards).

4 The Role of Lead Firms' Power

Lead firms can use their power in GVCs to influence how the adoption of blockchain technology may shape upgrading and performance outcomes for actors across GVCs. They can do so in several ways including governance and coordination, as well as setting standards for blockchain adoption and collaborating with diverse stakeholders (Gereffi et al., 2005; Sinkovics et al., 2019). We argue that the adoption of blockchain technology by lead firms further strengthens their power (Dauvergne, 2022). Dicken et al. (2001) view power as both structural (power possessed in resources) and relational (power exercised through actions). Drawing on Dicken et al. (2001), we posit that the structural power of lead firms will be their control over the blockchain technology in GVCs and the relational type will be their willingness or unwillingness to share data derived through blockchain technology from all or some actors in GVCs. In GVCs where lead firms are orchestrating the adoption of blockchain technology, its use is serving their business interests, not sustainability concerns. The efficiency and productivity gains are doing more to accelerate the concentration of wealth and power of lead firms than advance decent work conditions.

Bager et al. (2022) argue that blockchain technologies have the potential to increase the power of the owners of the data. It is important that all actors in the value chain share data and have equal access to information. Otherwise, it will lead to information asymmetry and will advantage actors that have preferential access to the system. In their study of the agro-food industry, they note that blockchain implementation may benefit some GVC actors more than others, and lead actors such as importers and roasters hold more power than smaller producers and farmers. Similarly, in the context of forestry value chains, Gallemore et al. (2022) discuss two types of digital technologies—open and closed technologies. Whereas open-source technologies redistribute power to an array of actors in GVCs, closed technologies like blockchain encourage the concentration of power among a few large actors. When adopting closed technologies, lead firms set new standards for others to follow. The authors cite the case of Nestlé, which used closed technologies to strengthen its bargaining power and protect its reputation. Through collaboration with Earthworm Foundation, as well as other partners present on the ground, Nestlé conducted supplier assessments and maintained a transparency dashboard. These measures aimed to provide Nestlé with more direct leverage over its supply. In this case, Nestlé's approach to blockchain adoption allowed them to closely monitor and exert control over their suppliers. Therefore, Gallemore et al. (2022) conclude that closed technologies like blockchain technology could be costly and inaccessible to all but well-resourced actors, thus enhancing the capacity of lead firms to extract value from sustainability demands.

Finally, Bernards et al. (2022) argue that since the majority of blockchain initiatives in local and GVCs are permissioned rather than permissionless, blockchain technology adoption further empowers lead firms, expanding the influence of for-profit consultancies and audit agencies, and promoting quantitative metrics as a form of remote governance. The development and operation of blockchain projects are primarily led by large firms and major consultancies, limiting the involvement of specialized sustainability audit firms. This undermines socio-political transparency and perpetuates the marginalization of those affected by unsustainable practices or labour abuses (Bernards et al., 2022). Based on this, we propose that:

P5: Blockchain technology adoption will increase lead firms' power in GVCs.

There is a wide range of literature on GVCs that unpacks how lead firms use their power to create an audit culture and hold DE suppliers accountable for complying with sustainability standards. However, these DE suppliers often do not have the financial and strategic resources to meet these standards. As a result, the existence of traceability will help lead firms understand whether suppliers are meeting sustainability standards. However, the power of lead firms means that they can implement these sustainability standards in a way that will mainly benefit their own commercial goals instead of leading to actual changes in working conditions (LeBaron & Lister, 2021).

P6: The extent of lead firms' power will negatively moderate the link between lead firms' traceability capabilities and DE suppliers' social upgrading (measurable standards).

Building on the moderating role of the extent of lead firms' power between traceability and working conditions, we similarly postulate that the extent of a lead firm's power in a value chain will limit the positive impact of process upgrading on suppliers' financial performance. Based on Choksy et al. (2017), we argue that lead firms' power adds contextual contingency whereby process upgrading is shaped by the pressure exerted by lead firms. These pressures shape suppliers' efforts to improve their efficiency, management processes, and speed, which will improve the efficiency of the overall supply. These in turn benefit lead firms but do not necessarily lead to increased financial performance for suppliers. In fact, the investment suppliers will have to make in technology and people to engage in process upgrading will squeeze their margins and reduce their financial performance. Similarly, Nath et al. (2022) report that a trading partner's influence plays a critical role in assisting supply chain partners to benefit from blockchain technology adoption. Trading partners can use their power against DE suppliers to leverage favourable deals in negotiations. This leads to the unequal distribution of economic rents in favour of the lead firms (trading partners in this case). Based on the above reasoning, we propose that:

P7: The extent of lead firms' power will negatively moderate the relationship between process upgrading and suppliers' financial performance.

5 Conclusion

This chapter developed a conceptual framework that explains how blockchain technology adoption in GVCs could lead to economic and social upgrading (see Fig. 1). The framework provides directions for future research on upgrading GVCs. First, researchers need to document the impact of blockchain technology adoption on the economic upgrading of DE suppliers. Although blockchain technology adoption has the potential for improving the performance of developing country suppliers participating in GVCs, it poses serious risks for value appropriation in GVCs. This is because blockchain technology adoption has the capability to enlarge the power of lead firms which could further increase the power imbalance and thus the distribution of economic rents in favour of lead firms. Second, researchers need to investigate the ways in which blockchain technology adoption can impact social upgrading. Blockchain technology offers the ability to improve transparency, which could enhance the social upgrading prospects in GVCs. However, with an increase in lead firms' power, the outcomes for workers and communities might not be positive. The proposed framework and propositions provide guidelines for researchers interested in conducting empirical research on blockchain technology adoption in GVCs and its consequences for DE suppliers and workers with the aim of critically investigating the pathways to meet SDG 8: decent work and economic growth. Finally, we recommend future studies explore the role of institutional conditions and the regulatory environment in (a) facilitating/

hindering a supplier's capacity to benefit from blockchain technology adoption and (b) mitigating the power imbalances in GVCs, as well as (c) promoting more open technologies in GVCs.

References

Alves, L., Ferreira Cruz, E., Lopes, S. I., Faria, P. M., & Rosado da Cruz, A. M. (2022). Towards circular economy in the textiles and clothing value chain through blockchain technology and IoT: A review. *Waste Management & Research, 40*(1), 3–23.

Ayaz, M., Ashraf, M. J., & Hopper, T. (2019). Precariousness, gender, resistance and consent in the face of global production network's 'reforms' of Pakistan's garment manufacturing industry. *Work, Employment and Society, 33*(6), 895–912.

Azevedo, P., Gomes, J., & Romão, M. (2023). Supply chain traceability using blockchain. *Operations Management Research*. https://doi.org/10.1007/s12063-023-00359-y

Bager, S. L., Singh, C., & Persson, U. M. (2022). Blockchain is not a silver bullet for agro-food supply chain sustainability: Insights from a coffee case study. *Current Research in Environmental Sustainability, 4*, Article 100163.

Barrientos, S., Gereffi, G., & Rossi, A. (2011). Economic and social upgrading in global production networks: A new paradigm for a changing world. *International Labour Review, 150*(3–4), 319–340.

Benstead, A. V., Mwesiumo, D., Moradlou, H., & Boffelli, A. (2022). Entering the world behind the clothes that we wear: Practical applications of blockchain technology. *Production Planning & Control*, 1–18.

Berdik, D., Otoum, S., Schmidt, N., Porter, D., & Jararweh, Y. (2021). A survey on blockchain for information systems management and security. *Information Processing & Management, 58*(1), 102397.

Bernards, N., Campbell-Verduyn, M., & Rodima-Taylor, D. (2022). The veil of transparency: Blockchain and sustainability governance in global supply chains. *Environment and Planning C: Politics and Space, 5*, 89–95.

Casino, F., Kanakaris, V., Dasaklis, T. K., Moschuris, S., Stachtiaris, S., Pagoni, M., & Rachaniotis, N. P. (2021). Blockchain-based food supply chain traceability: A case study in the dairy sector. *International Journal of Production Research, 59*(19), 5758–5770.

Chandan, A. (2019). How blockchain can help in supply chain sustainability, 2019 Chandan. In *Association for Information Systems* (pp. 953–960).
Chang, Y., Iakovou, E., & Shi, W. (2020). Blockchain in global supply chains and cross border trade: A critical synthesis of the state-of-the-art, challenges and opportunities. *International Journal of Production Research, 58*(7), 2082–2099.
Charles, V., Emrouznejad, A., & Gherman, T. (2023). A critical analysis of the integration of blockchain and artificial intelligence for supply chain. *Annals of Operations Research*, 1–41.
Chen, W., Botchie, D., Braganza, A., & Han, H. (2022). A transaction cost perspective on blockchain governance in global value chains. *Strategic Change, 31*(1), 75–87.
Choksy, U. S., Ayaz, M., Al-Tabbaa, O., & Parast, M. (2022). Supplier resilience under the COVID-19 crisis in apparel global value chain (GVC): The role of GVC governance and supplier's upgrading. *Journal of Business Research, 150*, 249–267.
Choksy, U. S., Sinkovics, N., & Sinkovics, R. R. (2017). Exploring the relationship between upgrading and capturing profits from GVC participation for disadvantaged suppliers in developing countries. *Canadian Journal of Administrative Sciences/revue Canadienne des Sciences de l'Administration, 34*(4), 356–386.
Christ, K. L., & Helliar, C. V. (2021). Blockchain technology and modern slavery: Reducing deceptive recruitment in migrant worker populations. *Journal of Business Research, 131*, 112–120.
Dauvergne, P. (2022). Is artificial intelligence greening global supply chains? Exposing the political economy of environmental costs. *Review of International Political Economy, 29*(3), 696–718.
De Marchi, V., & Gereffi, G. (2023). Using the global value chain framework to analyse and tackle global environmental crises. *Journal of Industrial and Business Economics, 50*(1), 149–159.
de Villiers, C., Kuruppu, S., & Dissanayake, D. (2021). A (new) role for business—Promoting the United Nations' Sustainable Development Goals through the internet-of-things and blockchain technology. *Journal of Business Research, 131*, 598–609.
Dicken, P., Kelly, P. F., Olds, K., & Wai-Chung Yeung, H. (2001). Chains and networks, territories and scales: Towards a relational framework for analysing the global economy. *Global Networks, 1*(2), 89–112.

Di Vaio, A., Hassan, R., & Palladino, R. (2023). Blockchain technology and gender equality: A systematic literature review. *International Journal of Information Management, 68*, 102517.

Ferrantino, M. J., & Koten, E. E. (2019). Understanding Supply Chain 4.0 and its potential impact on global value chains. In *Global value chain development report*. World Trade Organization, Geneva.

Gallemore, C., Delabre, I., Jespersen, K., & Liu, T. (2022). To see and be seen: Technological change and power in deforestation driving global value chains. *Global Networks, 22*(4), 615–630.

Gereffi, G. (1999). International trade and industrial upgrading in the apparel commodity chain. *Journal of International Economics, 48*(1), 37–70.

Gereffi, G., Humphrey, J., & Sturgeon, T. (2005). The governance of global value chains. *Review of International Political Economy, 12*(1), 78–104.

Gereffi, G., Pananond, P., & Pedersen, T. (2022). Resilience decoded: The role of firms, global value chains, and the state in COVID-19 medical supplies. *California Management Review, 64*(2), 46–70.

Golini, R., Caniato, F., & Kalchschmidt, M. (2016). Linking global value chains and supply chain management: Evidence from the electric motors industry. *Production Planning & Control, 27*(11), 934–951.

Guo, S., Sun, X., & Lam, H. K. (2020). Applications of blockchain technology in sustainable fashion supply chains: Operational transparency and environmental efforts. *IEEE Transactions on Engineering Management*.

Gurtu, A., & Johny, J. (2019). Potential of blockchain technology in supply chain management: A literature review. *International Journal of Physical Distribution & Logistics Management, 49*(9), 881–900.

Islam, M. T., & Polonsky, M. J. (2020). Validating scales for economic upgrading in global value chains and assessing the impact of upgrading on supplier firms' performance. *Journal of Business Research, 110*, 144–159.

Kshetri, N. (2021). Blockchain and sustainable supply chain management in developing countries. *International Journal of Information Management, 60*, 1–16.

Khan, M. J., Ponte, S., & Lund-Thomsen, P. (2020). The 'factory manager dilemma': Purchasing practices and environmental upgrading in apparel global value chains. *Environment and Planning A: Economy and Space, 52*(4), 766–789.

LeBaron, G., & Lister, J. (2021). The hidden costs of global supply chain solutions. *Review of International Political Economy, 29*(3), 669–695.

Manupati, V. K., et al. (2019). A blockchain-based approach for a multi-echelon sustainable supply chain. *International Journal of Production Research, 58*(7), 2222–2241.

Milberg, W., & Winkler, D. (2011). Economic and social upgrading in global production networks: Problems of theory and measurement. *International Labour Review, 150*(3–4), 341–365.

Morrison, A., & Pietrobelli, C. (2007). Global value chains and technological capabilities: a framework to study industrial innovation in developing countries. In *Dynamic Capabilities Between Firm Organisation and Local Systems of Production* (pp. 175–198). Routledge.

Nanayakkara, S., et al. (2021). Blockchain and smart contracts: A solution for payment issues in construction supply chains. *Informatics, 8*(2), 1–16.

Nath, S. D., Khayer, A., Majumder, J., & Barua, S. (2022). Factors affecting blockchain adoption in apparel supply chains: Does sustainability-oriented supplier development play a moderating role? *Industrial Management & Data Systems, 122*(5), 1183–1214.

Ponte, S., Gereffi, G., & Raj-Reichert, G. (2019). Introduction to the handbook on global value chains. In *Handbook on global value chains* (pp. 1–27).

Saberi, S., Kouhizadeh, M., Sarkis, J., & Shen, L. (2019). Blockchain technology and its relationships to sustainable supply chain management. *International Journal of Production Research, 57*(7), 2117–2135.

Sarode, R. P., Poudel, M., Shrestha, S., & Bhalla, S. (2021). Blockchain for committing peer-to-peer transactions using distributed ledger technologies. *International Journal of Computational Science and Engineering, 24*(3), 215–227.

Schwägele, F. (2005). Traceability from a European perspective. *Meat Science, 71*(1), 164–173.

Singh, C., Wojewska, A. N., Persson, U. M., & Bager, S. L. (2022). Coffee producers' perspectives of blockchain technology in the context of sustainable global value chains. *Frontiers in Blockchain, 5*, 955463.

Sinkovics, N., Choksy, U. S., Sinkovics, R. R., & Mudambi, R. (2019). Knowledge connectivity in an adverse context: Global value chains and Pakistani offshore service providers. *Management International Review, 59*(1), 131–170.

Stuit, A., Brockington, D., & Corbera, E. (2022). Smart, commodified and encoded: Blockchain technology for environmental sustainability and nature conservation. *Conservation and Society, 20*(1), 12–23.

Tambe, P., & Tambay, P. (2020). Reducing modern slavery using AI and blockchain. In *2020 IEEE/ITU International Conference on Artificial Intelligence for Good (AI4G)* (pp. 22–27). IEEE.

Zion Market Research. (2022). The blockchain technology in supply chain management market—Global industry analysis. In *Blockchain Technology in Supply Chain Management Market Size 2022*. https://www.zionmarketresearch.com/report/blockchain-technology-in-supply-chain-management-market. Accessed 29 Aug 2022.

10

Circular Economy and Social Upgrading in Global Value Chains: An Analytical Perspective on Social Upgrading in the Global South

Omar Al-Tabbaa, Zaheer Khan, and Gary Knight

1 Introduction

The circular economy (CE) is an economic model that departs from the traditional linear production model, which follows a "take-make-dispose" approach, and instead, promotes the continuous circulation of materials and resources through recycling, reusing, and remanufacturing (Moreau et al., 2017). Therefore, this paradigm is in harmony with the

O. Al-Tabbaa
University of Leeds, Leeds, UK
e-mail: O.F.O.AlTabbaa@leeds.ac.uk

Z. Khan (✉)
University of Aberdeen, Aberdeen, UK
e-mail: zaheer.khan@abdn.ac.uk

Innolab, University of Vaasa, Vaasa, Finland

G. Knight
Willamette University, Salem, OR, USA
e-mail: gknight@willamette.edu

N. Sinkovics et al. (eds.), *International Business and SDG 8*, The Academy of International Business, https://doi.org/10.1007/978-3-031-46802-5_10

UN Sustainable Development Goals (SDGs), as it can contribute to achieving SDGs 3 (ensuring health and well-being for all), 9 (fostering industry, innovation, and infrastructure), and 12 (promoting responsible production and consumption).

Accordingly, the potential of the CE to mitigate the negative environmental impacts, particularly those related to various manufacturing processes within global value chains (GVCs), has been widely recognized (de Lima et al., 2022). Importantly, these studies highlight how the CE can play a pivotal role in addressing the environmental challenges associated with resource depletion, waste generation, and pollution across different stages of production and consumption within GVCs and making them sustainable. Although these studies offer valuable evidence regarding the potential impact of implementing the CE and provide insights into the value-added mechanisms in terms of environmental benefits, there are still two critical gaps that need to be addressed.

First, it remains unclear whether and to what extent the adoption of CE model can contribute to social upgrading[1] (Rossi, 2019) within the participating countries and firms involved in the upstream supply chains (Barford & Ahmad, 2021, ILO, 2023a). This raises concerns about the social effect of the CE, especially when applied in the global South, where countries typically suffer from institutional voids[2] (Amankwah-Amoah et al., 2023; Donbesuur et al., 2023), and lack support from the formal institutions to improve the working conditions within the GVCs that are coordinated and controlled by the lead firms from developed markets (cf., Soundararajan et al., 2018). In this regard, questions arise regarding the effects of CE practices on the achievement of the SDG8[3]

[1] Refers to the process of improving working conditions, wages, labor rights, and overall social well-being within a given context. It involves advancements in employment opportunities, skills development, and social protection, leading to a higher standard of living and improved quality of life for individuals and communities.

[2] Refer to the absence or inadequacy of formal institutions, such as laws, regulations, and organizational structures, that are necessary for the functioning of an efficient and effective economic system. These voids can include gaps in legal frameworks, weak governance structures, lack of regulatory enforcement, and limited access to essential services. Institutional voids often create challenges and opportunities for businesses operating in environments with weak institutional support.

[3] SDG 8, or Sustainable Development Goal 8, is one of the 17 global goals established by the United Nations in 2015 as part of the 2030 Agenda for Sustainable Development. The

including, job creation, job quality, workers' rights, and the redistribution of benefits (Luthin et al., 2023), as the transition processes (i.e., from linear to circular) are often prone to social injustices (Vanhuyse et al., 2022). Accordingly, there is a need to explore the broader societal impact of CE adoption, such as community well-being and local economic resilience of participating countries, which all are connected with the fulfillment of SDG8. *Second*, we know relatively little about the "workers as agents in social upgrading processes" in GVCs (p. 828) (Marslev et al., 2022), especially when practicing business model innovation aiming to deliver environmental gains (Vazquez-Brust & de Souza Campos, 2023). In effect, the literature on GVCs has been criticized due to its predominant emphasis on economic upgrading (i.e., improving the economic conditions of the participating suppliers) (Dindial et al., 2020), which has been deemed to pay less attention to the concerns of labor and neglect to consider the effects on workers' social well-being at work and their overall working conditions.

Recognizing these critical gaps, it becomes evident that we need to pay more attention to the overlapping area between CE and GVCs domains (i.e., the application of the CE paradigm in GVC in order to make the GVCs sustainable and transparent given the widespread incidents of modern slavery practices within the GVCs reported in the popular media outlets) (Guardian, 2023).

Accordingly, this study investigates the interplay between the application of the CE paradigm, and social upgrading in GVCs, within the context of the global South. We developed a novel analytical framework that systematically discusses the potential role of CE strategies in promoting social upgrading within GVCs primarily situated in the global South, but it has the potential to inform best practices for the global North GVCs. The framework is conceptually grounded in the affordance perspective, offering a fresh lens to understand how the CE paradigm can facilitate social improvements, alongside environmental ones, in GVCs based in the global South where most of the suppliers are based.

---

goal of SDG 8 is to "Promote sustained, inclusive, and sustainable economic growth, full and productive employment, and decent work for all."

More specifically, we propose that firms need to consider the *affordances* of the CE model that need adaptation (i.e., actualization) which can adapt the CE strategies into practices that take into account the social aspects within the GVCs and their extended environment in order to address the grand challenges. To this end, in our analysis, we connect the CE affordances, which are based on the 9R CE framework (Potting et al., 2017) that provides a comprehensive view of CE strategies (Liu et al., 2022), with the recently identified five key themes for the issue of decent work conditions in the global South set by the International Labour Organization (ILO) (ILO, 2023a). In addition, and given the sensitivity of context in the global South (Ciulli & Kolk, 2023), we incorporated the effect of institutional enablers and barriers which typically affect the effectiveness of the adaptation process of the CE process (Vanhuyse et al., 2022). We support our propositions using several illustrative examples.

2 Social Upgrading in the CE: Toward an Analytical Framework Using the Affordance Perspective

The primary objective of this chapter is to develop an analytical framework that elucidates the potential contribution of the CE paradigm to social upgrading in GVCs primarily located in the global South. By doing so, our focus lies on the intersection between the CE and GVC, or the utilization of the CE paradigm within the GVC context in order to examine social upgrading.

2.1 The Affordance Perspective

According to the affordance perspective, individuals do not passively observe their environment but actively engage with it based on the affordances they perceive (Shin, 2017), thus affordances represent the actionable possibilities that objects offer to individuals, guiding their behavior and interactions (Grgecic et al., 2015). These affordances are not inherent properties of the objects themselves but are perceived in relation to the capabilities and intentions of the perceiver. By considering affordances, individuals can quickly assess how objects can be utilized or manipulated to achieve their goals.

The perception of these affordances enables individuals to directly couple their perception with action, without the need for explicit decision-making processes (Kaaronen, 2017). Importantly, the concept of affordance extends beyond the physical realm and applies to the interaction between individuals and technology as well. Within the technology domain, a digital technology like Artificial Intelligence (AI), according to the affordance perspective, possesses a set of fundamental material properties or characteristics (such as the ability to summarize a text or generate a picture). However, these properties should be regarded as necessary prerequisites for affordances rather than the affordances themselves (Markus & Silver, 2008). Instead, affordances are observed to arise from the interaction between the technology and a particular actor to achieve a specific target (Tim et al., 2020), whereby affordances can be regarded as a "relational concept" (Tim et al., 2020) that signifies the potential for goal-oriented actions that an organization can undertake through the utilization of a specific technology (Markus & Silver, 2008).

Due to its relevance, this perspective has been applied effectively in many fields, for example, to explore the possibilities of technologies in helping companies achieve their specific goals (Volkoff & Strong, 2013), to enable policy makers to promote policies that translate sustainable thinking into sustainable behavior (Kaaronen, 2017), and to understand how the new digital technologies, as adopted by international firms, can contribute to sustainable development (Ciulli & Kolk, 2023).

By embracing the affordance perspective, we propose that implementing the CE paradigm (along with its associated principles including waste reduction, product circularity, and nature regeneration), can provide opportunities (i.e., affordances) for companies to integrate the social dimension and contribute to the social upgrading process within their GVCs, in addition to the environmental gains. However, it is crucial to bear in mind that affordances represent potential or opportunities for action (Anderson & Robey, 2017). That is, although the object (e.g., the EC model) may provide multiple affordances, it is up to the actor utilizing the technology to determine whether they will take advantage of all available opportunities or not (Leonardi, 2011). In other words, the presence of affordances does not guarantee their complete utilization by the actor. The actor's choices, capabilities, and intentions play a significant role in determining which affordances are actually realized and acted upon. Hence, the realization of affordances depends not only on the object properties but also on the strategic decisions and actions of the actor involved.

2.2 CE Affordances for Social Upgrading in GVC

The affordance perspective emphasizes the interaction between individuals or entities and their environment, focusing on the potential actions and possibilities that the environment offers. In the context of the CE paradigm, this perspective recognizes that adopting circular practices creates opportunities for firms to engage in social upgrading (i.e., improving the social conditions for workers and communities involved in the production process) within their GVCs. We illustrate the connection between CE affordance for social upgrading in Fig. 1.

Our framework suggests that integrating the CE paradigm into GVCs has the potential to improve working conditions for firms in the global South that act as suppliers to lead firms originating from the global North. However, it is important to note that the adoption of the CE does not guarantee an impact on the working environments of participating firms, as the CE often prioritizes environmental goals and tends to focus more on technocratic strategies for industry and products (ILO, 2023a).

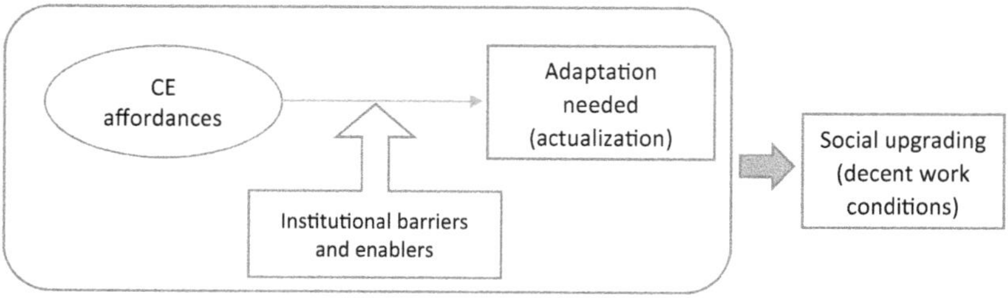

Fig. 1 CE affordance for social upgrading in global South GVCs

Additionally, implementing the CE model typically requires substantial financial investment and commitment from lead firms and their associated entities, such as suppliers. Consequently, these organizations may become overly focused on the environmental aspects of the CE, potentially overlooking the inclusion of social considerations within its scope.

The proposed framework integrates two essential aspects. The first focuses on the key concerns identified in the realm of decent working conditions, derived from an extensive review of hundreds of empirical articles on the CE, environmental factors, and related conditions (ILO, 2023a), as summarized in Table 1. The second aspect relates to the CE principles, including resource efficiency, waste reduction, and product lifecycle management, which the lead firms in GVCs can adapt and leverage to foster social upgrading within their chain, thereby promoting better working conditions for the firms involved in the globalized manufacturing arrangements in the global South. We establish the conceptual integration/connection by adopting the affordance lens.

The framework starts by highlighting that the adoption of the CE paradigm in a GVC can offer avenues for addressing the social issues in the value chain. We discuss these avenues (the affordances) as CE strategies, then these strategies with the key aspects of decent work conditions (ILO, 2023a).

The CE, as a concept, aims to promote sustainable resource management by minimizing waste and maximizing the value of resources (Di Vaio et al., 2023). It has evolved overtime through three distinct phases (with specific focus): dealing with waste (emphasizing the need to effectively deal with waste and reduce environmental impact), then developed to connecting input and output in strategies for eco-efficiency and maximizing value retention. These phases have yielded different strategies to address the focus of each phase (Blomsma et al., 2023). Implementing effective strategies is crucial for the successful transition to a CE (Blomsma et al., 2019). However, existing research on CE strategies lacks a commonly agreed-upon categorization (Liu et al., 2022). For instance, several studies (e.g., Cagno et al., 2021, Lopes de Sousa Jabbour et al., 2018) have built upon the three principles of the CE proposed by the Ellen MacArthur Foundation (2015). These principles include *preserving*

Table 1 Analyzing the work-related key aspects[a] in the CE model applied in the global South

Work-related issue	Focus	Key insights
Labor market and sectoral transformation	The application of the CE can create jobs, and induce changes in existing employability content and structures	• The CE has the potential to create new jobs at all skill levels and support resilient growth, particularly when combined with policies addressing material consumption and tax reform. For example, in Latin America and the Caribbean (over 10 million jobs) and Europe (around 0.5 million jobs) are expected mainly in the recycling and reprocessing sectors • Among these regions, the European Union (EU) is anticipated to experience the most substantial employment gains, benefiting from its early adoption of CE principles as a "first mover." Yet, studies on the net employment effects of the circular transition still vary in their estimates due to different methodologies and assumptions

Work-related issue	Focus	Key insights
The informal economy	The informal economy plays a significant role in the CE, especially in low-income countries where informal sectors like reuse, repair, waste collection, and recycling provide employment opportunities. However, the informal economy is often overlooked in the CE agenda	• CE discussions and policy approaches often focus on the formal economy, overlooking the significant presence of circular interventions in the informal economy of the global South • The informal economy, which comprises a diverse range of economic activities and employs a large portion of the global population, plays a crucial role in the CE transition but is not adequately included in the CE agenda • CE activities within the informal economy, such as waste picking, provide economic opportunities to individuals with low formal skills and education, but poor working conditions and environmental hazards can be prevalent, particularly in the Global South • Transboundary movement of waste and second-hand goods from the Global North to countries with inadequate waste management infrastructure exacerbates the challenges associated with informality

(continued)

Table 1 (continued)

Work-related issue	Focus	Key insights
Work reallocation and skills development	Transitioning to circular sectors requires appropriate training and policy support for workers. Acquiring the necessary "deep skills" for circular interventions relies on employers and educational institutions understanding circular business models	• The successful reallocation of workers from linear to circular sectors depends on access to training and related policy measures. Yet, the CE is estimated to disrupt only 2% of existing jobs globally, with the potential to create over 100 million new jobs depending on training and skills interventions • Reskilling and upskilling will be crucial for workers in current linear sectors, such as construction, transport, and certain areas of energy, to tap into new job opportunities in the EC. This implies that ongoing training across occupations will be more important than acquiring entirely new sets of skills • Circular jobs require significant work experience and training, especially for specific activities like sorting, repair, and redesign. Educational pathways in the circular economy will require practical and vocational modes of learning, higher education, and lifelong learning across all fields • Developing the deep skills required for CE interventions can be challenging, particularly in lower-income countries with less investment in tertiary education and limited vocational training offerings

Work-related issue	Focus	Key insights
		• The specific digital skills and technological capabilities required for circular economy interventions in the global South are understudied
Working conditions and social protection	Occupational health and safety issues are prevalent in circular activities, particularly in the global waste trade and second-hand goods flow from the global North to the global South. Workers in these sectors often face exposure to toxic waste, highlighting the need for improved working conditions, health protections, and social safeguards in the CE	• The CE has been proposed as a solution to address poverty. Can alleviate poverty through better wages, working conditions, and economic benefits for vulnerable communities, particularly in the global South • Occupational health and safety concerns in the CE are associated with global waste trade and second-hand goods flow from global North to global South countries. Loopholes in waste and second-hand goods legislation, along with weak regulatory frameworks, contribute to illegal circular activities. The most disadvantaged groups in the Global South, often in the informal sector, face negative health and safety risks • The growth of new enterprises and sectors within the CE raises concerns about workers' ability to improve their conditions. As circular business models emphasize shared ownership and collaborative consumption, workers in the service sector may face challenges in conducting collective bargaining and receiving support from traditional trade unions or employer associations. Typical workers, including temporary, self-employed, and platform workers, often lack legal protections and face inequality

(continued)

Table 1 (continued)

Work-related issue	Focus	Key insights
		• Work in waste management, a significant component of the circular economy, often provides a meager livelihood for marginalized groups. Workers in excluded segments of the labor market, such as the elderly, homeless, refugees, migrants, and marginalized groups, engage in informal and sub-standard working conditions without social protection. Poor-quality circular jobs, even if they contribute to sustainability, can reinforce and recreate existing injustices and inequalities
Gender discrimination and social equity	The transition to a CE is expected to increase female employment globally, offering opportunities for gender equity. However, there is a lack of in-depth research on the social impacts of circular economy interventions among underrepresented groups such as migrant workers and youth. Addressing gender discrimination and social equity issues in the circular economy requires more comprehensive and inclusive studies	• CE interventions have been identified as a potential social equity solution for at-risk youth and as a strategy for entrepreneurship in low-income contexts • Without strong policies and programs addressing gendered aspects of labor market participation and access, prevailing gender inequalities are unlikely to be offset • Barriers hindering women's participation in green jobs within the CE include skill mismatches, limited access to financial resources and information technologies, and discriminatory social norms

Work-related issue	Focus	Key insights
		• The current CE movement shows low social ambition in terms of gender, often perpetuating feminization of poverty and precarious working conditions • There is a need to address social and climate justice concerns, such as the distribution of benefits and meaningful participation, in CE policies. Current policy instruments and proposals for the CE are considered narrow and fall short of providing a holistic and legal framework for a just transition

[a]Complied and adapted from ILO (2023a), OECD (2022), Mies and Gold (2021), and Padilla-Rivera et al. (2021)

and enhancing natural capital (by managing finite stocks and balancing renewable resource flows), *optimizing resource yields* (by circulating products, components, and materials for maximum utility in both technical and biological cycles), and *fostering system effectiveness* (by identifying and eliminating negative externalities like pollution, climate change, toxins, congestion, and health impacts associated with resource use) (Foundation, 2015). Others developed the Circular Strategies Scanner as a tool for evaluating and implementing CE strategies, where it helps to analyze and categorize different approaches to achieve sustainable resource management (Blomsma et al., 2019). Moreover, Barnabè and Nazir (2022) regarded the CE as a circular economic model that builds upon a number of core guiding principles including Reduce, Reuse, Recycle, Reproduce/Remanufacture, Redesign/Repurpose, and Recover (MacArthur, 2013). While these studies adopted different strategies for the CE, it can be realized that these strategies are built upon a number of principles that are summarized by (Potting et al., 2017). Therefore, in this study, we adopt the 9R CE framework developed by Potting et al. (2017) as it provides a comprehensive view of CE strategies, see Fig. 2. Together, the application of these strategies (or any combination of them) offers the environmental gains (affordances) that add value to society.

Next, we discuss the affordances of these strategies in the domain of social upgrading and decent work conditions in the GVCs of global South.

Decent work, as a concept, refers to work that meets certain criteria to ensure the well-being and dignity of workers (Gereffi, 2019; ILO, 2023b). As such, decent work is characterized by fair income, providing a secure employment relationship with safe working conditions (Montiel et al., 2021). It emphasizes equal opportunities and treatment for all individuals, including social protection for workers and their families. Decent work also promotes personal development and social integration, allowing workers the freedom to express their concerns and engage in collective bargaining or organizing activities (Nasr & Al-Tabbaa, 2023). Recently, the International Labour Organization (ILO) identified five key themes for the issue of decent work in the global South (ILO, 2023a). These five themes capture the work-related opportunities and challenges, as identified and discussed in the empirical literature, for

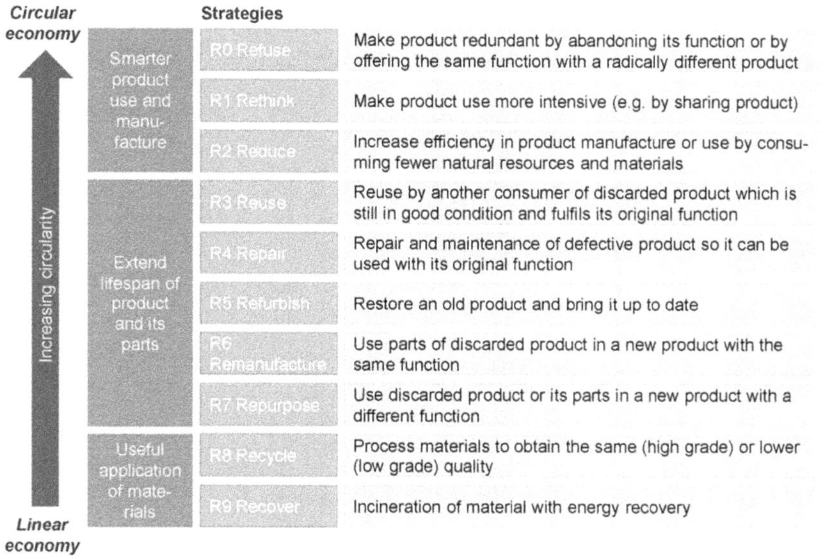

Fig. 2 A framework for the CE Strategies: from linear to circular (*Source* Potting et al., 2017)

the CE model when applied in the global South. Table 1 analyzes these themes and provides reflections on their focus and key insights.

As discussed earlier, and presented in Fig. 1, the fundamental proposition in this study is that the affordance perspective can be used to understand how the application of the CE model, with necessary adaption (i.e., the actualization), which in turn can yield advancement in the working conditions in global South, and thus promoting the social upgrading dimension in GVCs. By combing the affordance of CE Strategies (as in Fig. 2) with the decent work themes (as in Table 1), we discuss our conceptual framework and explicate how the application of the CE strategies can offer advancement for the working environment and contribute toward social upgrading in the GVCs. We present the affordance of the CE to address the work-related issues in Table 2.

First, labor market and sectoral transformation. As the adoption of the CE paradigm entails the devolvement of several CE strategies (Potting et al., 2017), these new strategies are expected to contribute toward

Table 2 Integrating the social dimension in the CE model in GVCs

Work-related issue[a]	CE affordances (What to offer?)[b]	Actualization (how?)	Institutional need
Labor Market and Sectoral Transformation: *Improve employability and contribute to job creation*	• Adoption of the CE model *offers* new tasks and processes, which can create new job opportunities (e.g., eco-design) and the development of new sectors (at various stages of the value chain) such as renewable energy, waste management, repair and maintenance, and recycling in the global South • Adoption of the CE model *offers* the opportunity to develop local and decentralized systems within the CE which support the establishment of SMEs and contribute to job creation in regions where traditional industries may have declined. These enterprises will create more "layers" in the GVC supply system	• This shift requires a skilled workforce to carry out the new activities (e.g., repair and refurbishment tasks). This demands the widespread implementation of skills training programs delivered by both firms and the government • The leading firms need to rethink the structure of their suppliers' network to involve the smaller emerging suppliers (as a new level of supply) • The leading firms (in the GVCs) can develop specialized training programs along their value chain	• To establish an effective training scheme, adequate initial support is needed at the national and regional levels • Individuals losing their current jobs may not necessarily be the same ones benefiting from the new job opportunities. This underscores the need for comprehensive public support and strategies to address the potential impact on workers in specific sectors

Work-related issue[a]	CE affordances (What to offer?)[b]	Actualization (how?)	Institutional need
Informality and the CE: *Integrate and recognize entities comprising the informal economy*	• Adopting the CE approach demands changes in the business model (i.e., the working paradigm) of the GVC to become more circular. This *offers* an opportunity to develop new business models that better integrate and recognize the suppliers in the informal economy (e.g., waste collectors)	• Business model co-design (between the lead and suppliers) • Social interactions and collaborations collaboration between formal and informal actors to identify and leverage hidden resources and capabilities in the informal economy	• Government can recognize the informal activities which entail granting legal rights, protections, and access to resources for informal actors participating in GVC • Government can extend its capacity-building programs for informal workers. In this regard, NGOs and private sectors can play a key role in facilitating the programs
	• Adopting circular practices, such as recycling and upcycling, *offers* formal value chains the potential to tap into the skills, knowledge, and resources present in the informal economy. This repurposing of resources can create opportunities for informal actors to participate more in the GVC	• By recognizing the value and contributions of the informal economy, formal actors can engage in inclusive partnerships, providing support, training, and access to markets for informal actors	• Institutional support in terms of microfinance schemes, credit facilities, and market linkages can help informal actors to integrate in the CE activities • Strong labor regulations and enforcement mechanisms can provide a safety net and promote inclusive participation • Developing robust information systems can help policymakers and stakeholders understand the contributions and challenges faced by the informal economy

(continued)

Table 2 (continued)

Work-related issue[a]	CE affordances (What to offer?)[b]	Actualization (how?)	Institutional need
Work Reallocation and Skills Development	• The adoption of CE practices requires a different set of skills compared to conventional linear models (e.g., smart design and production that enable resource recovery and extend products and parts lifecycle). This offers the opportunity for skills development and capacity building o#in new areas (e.g., resource recovery, product design for circularity, and green technologies). The affordances offered by the CE create avenues for developing a skilled workforce that can contribute to circular value chains and drive innovation	• Knowledge exchange platforms, networks, and partnerships can be established to facilitate CE-related learning and information sharing among stakeholders. These platforms provide a space for the dissemination of best practices, case studies, and success stories, enabling individuals and firms to learn from each other and stay updated on the latest advancements in CE practices	• The state needs to provide an environment where collaboration between educational institutions, industry, and government entities can facilitate the identification of skill gaps and the design of targeted training initiatives. This collaboration ensures that the skills development programs align with the specific needs of the CE, fostering a skilled workforce capable of driving innovation and sustainable practices
	• The CE encourages experimentation, collaboration, and learning among various stakeholders. Thus, it offers affordances for knowledge sharing, best practices, and innovation in sustainable business models and processes. Continuous learning and innovation contribute to skills development by fostering creativity, adaptability, and entrepreneurial mindsets		• Developing comprehensive skill mapping and reskilling programs for the wide-ranging scope of circular sectors and activities is challenging, and there is a need for national level understanding of the skills required for remanufacturing and related sectors in low-income countries

Work-related issue[a]	CE affordances (What to offer?)[b]	Actualization (how?)	Institutional need
Working Conditions and Social Protection	• Extending the CE model, lead firms have the opportunity to co-develop with their suppliers and implement transparent monitoring and tracing systems specifically designed to track and ensure better working conditions • These monitoring arrangements can be integrated into the CE practices, allowing for enhanced transparency and accountability in the supply chain • By traceability and transparency, lead firms can encourage suppliers to adopt responsible labor practices and improve working conditions throughout the GVC	• The affordance lens emphasizes the role of technology, data sharing, and collaboration in achieving these improvements. Through the use of advanced digital systems and real-time monitoring, the CE can provide the necessary affordances for lead firms to ensure social protection and foster better working conditions within the GVC	• Collaboration and coordination among various stakeholders, including governments, lead firms, suppliers, and labor unions, are essential to establish and maintain institutional arrangements that support improved working conditions. This can involve the development of industry-wide standards, certification schemes, and codes of conduct • Strong governance mechanisms are necessary to monitor and enforce compliance with these institutional conditions. This includes effective inspection and auditing processes, as well as mechanisms for addressing grievances and ensuring accountability for violations

(continued)

Table 2 (continued)

Work-related issue[a]	CE affordances (What to offer?)[b]	Actualization (how?)	Institutional need
Gender discrimination and social equity	• The transition to a CE model requires a diverse set of skills, *offering* the potential for skills development and training programs that specifically target women. This can help overcome existing gender disparities in access to training and qualifications, enabling women to participate in new job roles and contribute to the circular value chain • The CE's emphasis on transparency and traceability *offers* affordances for addressing gender discrimination. It enables the identification and elimination of gender biases, discrimination, and unfair labor practices throughout the value chain. By implementing monitoring systems and standards, the CE can ensure that gender equity is upheld, and social accountability is promoted	• Establishing collaboration among diverse stakeholders, including governments, businesses, civil society, and women's rights organizations can leverage their collective expertise and resources to advocate for gender-responsive policies, promote social equity, and ensure that the benefits of the CE are accessible to all	• There is a need for an institutional environment that supports the development and implementation of gender-responsive policies that promote gender equality and social equity • This involves establishing laws and regulations that protect women's rights, ensure equal access to resources and opportunities, and address gender-based discrimination in the workplace

[a]Informed by Table 1
[b]Informed by Fig. 2

job creation across the value chain. For instance, the useful application of materials, as illustrated see Fig. 2, will yield significant growth in recycling and reprocessing.

In this regard, the CE is expected to create a new million jobs at all levels that would support resilient growth in the global South. For instance, in recent years, the forestry-cellulose-paper sector has significantly enhanced its circularity, driven by multiple trends. The rising demand for sustainable products and the growing emphasis on resource-intensive sectors complying with stricter intentional requirements and standards serve as strong incentives for adopting circular processes within the industry. This transition opens up diverse employment opportunities, such as jobs in sustainable forest management, efficient waste management, and innovative recycling and repurposing practices within the involved global supply chains in the Latin America and the Caribbean (ECLAC, 2021). However, the job creation resulting from the application of the CE model within the GVC would demand specialized training. The unique requirements of circular jobs call for a skilled workforce equipped with the necessary knowledge and expertise. Consequently, there is a need for institutional support at the national level to establish effective training programs, where governments take an active role in providing the resources, infrastructure, and policies required to facilitate comprehensive training initiatives. Such setting can empower workforce in the global South to meet the demands of the adoption of the CE paradigm (Moreno-Mondejar et al., 2021).

Second, Informality and the CE. The CE offers affordances for addressing informality in two key ways. Integration of informal Suppliers who are mostly operating in the lower tiers, where the shift to a circular business model necessitates changes in the GVC's working paradigm. This provides an opportunity to develop new business models that better incorporate and acknowledge suppliers operating within the informal economy, such as waste collectors (Dewick et al., 2022). By recognizing their contributions, the CE can help integrate informal actors into formal value chains through the transfer of best practices and key know-how related to sustainability. On the other hand, utilizing informal resources and skills, as circular practices like recycling and upcycling enable formal value chains to leverage the skills, knowledge, and resources available in the informal economy. By repurposing these resources, the CE creates opportunities for informal actors to actively participate in the GVC. This integration can enhance their livelihoods and provide them with more sustainable economic prospects. For example, Troschinetz and Mihelcic (2009) found that frugal household economics and the presence of local markets for used materials play significant roles in promoting sustainable recycling of municipal waste. These informal markets, along with the expertise of informal actors in waste recovery and their ability to find customers for recycled materials, are crucial components of necessity-driven CE practices in low-income settings. The practices of informal actors offer opportunites of adding value to recyclable materials at every stage of the value chain, leading to the emergence of viable businesses centered around recycling (Jaligot et al., 2016). These findings highlight the potential for leveraging existing informal systems and local markets to drive circularity and promote sustainable waste management practices in resource-constrained environments (Korsunova et al., 2022).

Third, work reallocation and skills development. Transitioning to circular business models often requires new skills and knowledge. By investing in skill development initiatives, information-sharing platforms, and collaborations companies can empower their workforce and societies, enhancing their employability and promoting social mobility. This can contribute to social upgrading by providing workers with opportunities for personal and professional growth. For example, the collaboration and sharing of knowledge have benefited waste picker cooperative Reciclando Sueños in the context of the CE (Gutberlet et al., 2017). Waste pickers possess invaluable knowledge about material composition and recyclability, enabling them to identify materials that may not be accepted by the traditional recycling industry. The expertise and experience of waste pickers can significantly enhance the effectiveness of the CE, saving industries money and reducing the amount of waste destined for landfills. On the other hand, collaborations between waste picker organizations and companies, such as Limpex (a global corporate chemistry industry), have resulted in workshops and training sessions for employees, leading to a 50% increase in the efficiency of waste sorting systems in offices and production areas (Gutberlet & Carenzo, 2020). In addition, by utilizing digital technologies the CE can make the GVCs more transparent in terms of promoting workers' well-being.

Fourth, Working Conditions and Social Protection. The affordances of the CE model offer promising opportunities to address working conditions and enhance social protection within the GVC. The CE model enables lead firms to collaborate with their suppliers and jointly develop transparent monitoring and tracing systems through the integration of digital technololgies focused on improving working conditions. By actively involving suppliers in the design and implementation process, these arrangements can effectively address labor issues. Moreover, The CE practices provide a framework for integrating monitoring arrangements into the supply chain. This integration enhances transparency and accountability, allowing for better tracking and assessment of working conditions throughout the GVC. Through traceability and transparency, lead firms can incentivize their suppliers to adopt responsible labor practices. As an example, in a recent study (García-Muiña et al., 2021), the Social Organizational Life Cycle Assessment (SO-LCA) methodology was applied to a ceramic tile manufacturing industry to monitor the social dimension of firms adopting the CE. In this trial, real-time data collection and analysis were facilitated through a Business Intelligence interface. By involving a panel of experts from the organization, specific social metrics were developed, aggregated into social indices, and correlated to stakeholders and social impact categories. This approach allowed for the identification of essential social metrics and quantifying the organization's contribution to the social dimension of the CE. The results confirmed the feasibility of using monitoring techniques, including Industry 4.0 digital technologies, to assess the social impact of firms and their alignment with CE objectives.

Finally, gender discrimination and social equity can be addressed through the adoption of CE practices in two key ways. Firstly, the CE creates opportunities for targeted skills development and training programs aimed at women, enabling them to access training and qualifications and close the gender gap in employment. This empowers women to participate in new job roles within the circular value chain. Secondly, the CE's emphasis on transparency and traceability in the production process provides a means to tackle gender discrimination. By implementing customized monitoring systems and standards, the CE can identify and mitigate gender biases, discrimination, and unfair labor practices at all stages of the value chain (ILO, 2023a). This commitment ensures that gender equity is upheld and social accountability is promoted. Through these measures, the CE contributes to a more inclusive and equitable society by actively addressing gender discrimination and promoting social justice.

3 Conclusion

This chapter addresses the intersection between the CE and GVCs while focusing on the social dimension (decent work) within the global South. By developing an analytical framework grounded in the affordance perspective, we explore how CE strategies can be adapted to promote social upgrading alongside environmental improvements in GVCs, which contributes to the fulfillment of the SDG8. The framework incorporates the 9R CE framework and the International Labour Organization's key themes for decent work conditions, while considering the influence of institutional enablers and barriers in the global South context. We contribute to the existing literature by offering a fresh perspective on the intersection of the CE and GVCs, highlighting the potential for social gains through CE strategies. It emphasizes the need to consider social aspects alongside environmental goals and identifies the importance of adaptation to address the social dimension effectively. Moreover, the study recognizes the influence of institutional context, particularly in areas with institutional voids, on the outcomes of social upgrading initiatives in the CE. By shedding light on these complexities and nuances, the chapter provides valuable insights for policymakers, businesses, and stakeholders involved in promoting sustainable development and inclusive growth through circular practices. The framework and examples presented in this chapter serve as practical tools for understanding and leveraging the potential of the CE to realize social benefits within GVCs. Overall, this research contributes to advancing knowledge and guiding efforts toward a more holistic and socially responsible implementation of the CE in the global South.

References

Amankwah-Amoah, J., Nyuur, R. B., Hinson, R., Kosiba, J. P., Al-Tabbaa, O., & Cunningham, J. A. (2023). Entrepreneurial strategic posture and new technology ventures in an emerging economy. *International Journal of Entrepreneurial Behavior & Research, 29*, 385–407.

Anderson, C., & Robey, D. (2017). Affordance potency: Explaining the actualization of technology affordances. *Information and Organization, 27*, 100–115.

Barford, A., & Ahmad, S. R. (2021). A call for a socially restorative circular economy: Waste pickers in the recycled plastics supply chain. *Circular Economy and Sustainability, 1*, 761–782.

Barnabè, F., & Nazir, S. (2022). Conceptualizing and enabling circular economy through integrated thinking. *Corporate Social Responsibility and Environmental Management, 29*, 448–468.

Blomsma, F., Pieroni, M., Kravchenko, M., Pigosso, D. C. A., Hildenbrand, J., Kristinsdottir, A. R., Kristoffersen, E., Shahbazi, S., Nielsen, K. D., & Jönbrink, A.-K. (2019). Developing a circular strategies framework for manufacturing companies to support circular economy-oriented innovation. *Journal of Cleaner Production, 241*, 118271.

Blomsma, F., Tennant, M., & Ozaki, R. (2023). Making sense of circular economy: Understanding the progression from idea to action. *Business Strategy and the Environment, 32*, 1059–1084.

Cagno, E., Neri, A., Negri, M., Bassani, C. A., & Lampertico, T. (2021). The role of digital technologies in operationalizing the circular economy transition: A systematic literature review. *Applied Sciences, 11*, 3328.

Ciulli, F., & Kolk, A. (2023). International business, digital technologies and sustainable development: Connecting the dots. *Journal of World Business, 58*, 101445.

de Lima, F. A., Seuring, S., & Sauer, P. C. (2022). A systematic literature review exploring uncertainty management and sustainability outcomes in circular supply chains. *International Journal of Production Research, 60*, 6013–6046.

Dewick, P., de Mello, A. M., Sarkis, J., & Donkor, F. K. (2022). The puzzle of the informal economy and the circular economy. *Resources, Conservation and Recycling, 187*, 106602.

Di Vaio, A., Hasan, S., Palladino, R., & Hassan, R. (2023). The transition towards circular economy and waste within accounting and accountability models: A systematic literature review and conceptual framework. *Environment, Development and Sustainability, 25*, 734–810.

Dindial, M., Clegg, J., & Voss, H. (2020). Between a rock and a hard place: A critique of economic upgrading in global value chains. *Global Strategy Journal, 10*, 473–495.

Donbesuur, F., Zahoor, N., Al-Tabbaa, O., Adomako, S., & Tarba, S. Y. (2023). On the performance of platform-based international new ventures: The roles of non-market strategies and managerial competencies. *Journal of International Management, 29*, 101002.

ECLAC. (2021). *International trade outlook for Latin America and the Caribbean: Pursuing a resilient and sustainable recovery*. ECLAC.

Foundation, E. M. (2015). *Growthwithin: A circular economy vision for a competitive Europe*.

García-Muiña, F., Medina-Salgado, M. S., González-Sánchez, R., Huertas-Valdivia, I., Ferrari, A. M., & Settembre-Blundo, D. (2021). Industry 4.0-based dynamic social organizational life cycle assessment to target the social circular economy in manufacturing. *Journal of Cleaner Production, 327,* 129439.

Gereffi, G. (2019). Global value chains and international development policy: Bringing firms, networks and policy-engaged scholarship back in. *Journal of International Business Policy, 2*, 195–210.

Grgecic, D., Holten, R., & Rosenkranz, C. (2015). The impact of functional affordances and symbolic expressions on the formation of beliefs. *Journal of the Association for Information Systems, 16*, 2.

Guardian. (2023). *UK efforts to tackle modern slavery are waning, analysis finds.*

Gutberlet, J., & Carenzo, S. (2020). *Waste pickers at the heart of the circular economy: A perspective of inclusive recycling from the Global South.*

Gutberlet, J., Carenzo, S., Kain, J.-H., & Mantovani Martiniano de Azevedo, A. (2017). Waste picker organizations and their contribution to the circular economy: Two case studies from a Global South perspective. *Resources.*

ILO. (2023a). *Decent work in the circular economy: An overview of the existing evidence base.*

ILO. (2023b). *International labour organization.* Decent Work.

Jaligot, R., Wilson, D. C., Cheeseman, C. R., Shaker, B., & Stretz, J. (2016). Applying value chain analysis to informal sector recycling: A case study of the Zabaleen. *Resources, Conservation and Recycling, 114*, 80–91.

Kaaronen, R. O. (2017). Affording sustainability: Adopting a theory of affordances as a guiding heuristic for environmental policy. *Frontiers in Psychology, 8*, 1974.

Korsunova, A., Halme, M., Kourula, A., Levänen, J., & Lima-Toivanen, M. (2022). Necessity-driven circular economy in low-income contexts: How informal sector practices retain value for circularity. *Global Environmental Change, 76*, 102573.

Leonardi, P. M. (2011). When flexible routines meet flexible technologies: Affordance, constraint, and the imbrication of human and material agencies. *MIS Quarterly*, 147–167.

Liu, Q., Trevisan, A. H., Yang, M., & Mascarenhas, J. (2022). A framework of digital technologies for the circular economy: Digital functions and mechanisms. *Business Strategy and the Environment, 31*, 2171–2192.

Lopes de Sousa Jabbour, A. B., Jabbour, C. J. C., Godinho Filho, M., & Roubaud, D. (2018). Industry 4.0 and the circular economy: A proposed research agenda and original roadmap for sustainable operations. *Annals of Operations Research, 270*, 273–286.

Luthin, A., Traverso, M., & Crawford, R. H. (2023). Assessing the social life cycle impacts of circular economy. *Journal of Cleaner Production, 386*, 135725.

MacArthur, E. (2013). Towards the circular economy, economic and business rationale for an accelerated transition. *Ellen MacArthur Foundation: Cowes, UK*, 21–34.

Markus, M. L., & Silver, M. S. (2008). A foundation for the study of IT effects: A new look at DeSanctis and Poole's concepts of structural features and spirit. *Journal of the Association for Information Systems, 9*, 5.

Marslev, K., Staritz, C., & Raj-Reichert, G. (2022). Rethinking social upgrading in global value chains: Worker power, state-labour relations and intersectionality. *Development and Change, 53*, 827–859.

Mies, A., & Gold, S. (2021). Mapping the social dimension of the circular economy. *Journal of Cleaner Production, 321*, 128960.

Montiel, I., Cuervo-Cazurra, A., Park, J., Antolín-López, R., & Husted, B. W. (2021). Implementing the United Nations' sustainable development goals in international business. *Journal of International Business Studies, 52*, 999–1030.

Moreau, V., Sahakian, M., Van Griethuysen, P., & Vuille, F. (2017). Coming full circle: Why social and institutional dimensions matter for the circular economy. *Journal of Industrial Ecology, 21*, 497–506.
Moreno-Mondejar, L., Triguero, Á., & Cuerva, M. C. (2021). Exploring the association between circular economy strategies and green jobs in European companies. *Journal of Environmental Management, 297*, 113437.
Nasr, A., & Al-Tabbaa, O. (2023). On the role and nature of alliance management capability in family business: Empirical evidence from a developing market. *Thunderbird International Business Review, 65*, 237–252.
OECD. (2022). *The OECD re-circle project—Policy perspectives*. OECD Publishing.
Padilla-Rivera, A., do Carmo, B. B. T., Arcese, G., & Merveille, N. (2021). Social circular economy indicators: Selection through fuzzy delphi method. *Sustainable Production and Consumption, 26*, 101–110.
Potting, J., Hekkert, M. P., Worrell, E., & Hanemaaijer, A. (2017). *Circular economy: Measuring innovation in the product chain*. Planbureau voor de Leefomgeving.
Rossi, A. (2019). Social upgrading. In S. Ponte, G. Gereffi, & G. Raj-Reichert (Eds.), *Handbook on global value chains* (p. 272). Edward Elgar Publishing.
Shin, D.-H. (2017). The role of affordance in the experience of virtual reality learning: Technological and affective affordances in virtual reality. *Telematics and Informatics, 34*, 1826–1836.
Soundararajan, V., Khan, Z., & Tarba, S. Y. (2018). Beyond brokering: Sourcing agents, boundary work and working conditions in global supply chains. *Human Relations, 71*, 481–509.
Tim, Y., Ouyang, T., & Zeng, D. (2020). Back to the future: Actualizing technology affordances to transform Emperor Qin's terracotta warriors Museum. *Information & Management, 57*, 103271.
Troschinetz, A. M., & Mihelcic, J. R. (2009). Sustainable recycling of municipal solid waste in developing countries. *Waste Management, 29*, 915–923.
Vanhuyse, F., Rezaie, S., Englund, M., Jokiaho, J., Henrysson, M., & André, K. (2022). Including the social in the circular: A mapping of the consequences of a circular economy transition in the city of Umeå, Sweden. *Journal of Cleaner Production, 380*, 134893.
Vazquez-Brust, D., & de Souza Campos, L. M. (2023). Wrap-up: Equitable circular economy, nesting the social dimension in the circular economy. In *The social dimensions of the circular economy* (pp. 309–317). Springer.

Volkoff, O., & Strong, D. M. (2013). Critical realism and affordances: Theorizing IT-associated organizational change processes. *MIS Quarterly, 37*, 819–834.

11

Sustainability in Entrepreneurial Ecosystems Going Global

David Audretsch and Antje Fiedler

1 Introduction

The United Nations' Sustainable Development Goals set an ambitious agenda for the future development of nations (Sinkovics et al., 2021). It consists of 17 goals aimed at improving socioeconomic well-being and environmental sustainability, resulting in a fairer and more inclusive society. Entrepreneurship will be critical for achieving the SDGs, particularly Goal 8 (SDG8), which aims to foster "Decent work and economic growth." Through entrepreneurship, society can realize "full and productive employment, and decent work, for all women and men",

D. Audretsch
Indiana University, Bloomington, IN, USA
e-mail: daudrets@indiana.edu

A. Fiedler (✉)
University of Auckland, Auckland, New Zealand
e-mail: a.fiedler@auckland.ac.nz

N. Sinkovics et al. (eds.), *International Business and SDG 8*, The Academy of International Business, https://doi.org/10.1007/978-3-031-46802-5_11

by 2030 (UN, 2015). Ultimately, through entrepreneurship, the ambition is to eliminate forced labor and human trafficking and improve societal equality (UN, 2015).

Scholars have highlighted the critical role of entrepreneurial ecosystems in fostering entrepreneurial opportunities (Theodoraki et al., 2020). Entrepreneurial ecosystems comprise various interconnected elements, including institutions and culture, organizations, actors, and processes that govern a certain entrepreneurial context (Isenberg, 2010; Mason & Brown, 2014; Stam & Spigel, 2016). It is argued that within the entrepreneurial ecosystem, knowledge between different actors flows more freely (Qian, 2018), resulting in collaboration between different actors that supports the economic and social development of a region (Wurth et al., 2022). Importantly, an attribute of a vibrant entrepreneurial ecosystem is that they host a diverse set of actors and may also include socially oriented actors such as impact investors who explicitly address environmental and social issues prevalent within the region. Social networks within ecosystems provide support and knowledge for various firms, including micro-businesses (Roundy, 2020), and young entrepreneurs, including students (Miller & Acs, 2017). Thus, they can provide the potential for promoting more inclusive and diverse enterprise, by providing access to knowledge and financial services to under-resourced people—which are key issues to address to provide more equal opportunities and advance ambitions of SDG8 (see Rai et al., 2019 for a more detailed discussion on various targets and indicators of SDG8, in the context of gender and labor rights). Taken together, entrepreneurial ecosystems may be critical to advance regional inclusive growth and support the achievement of SDG8.

In the context of an entrepreneurial ecosystem, it is important to also recognize the pivotal roles of entrepreneurs for achieving 'inclusive growth' by creating opportunities for decent work and fostering positive societal change (Baskaran et al., 2019). The understanding how entrepreneurs contribute to economic growth and the transformation of society has evolved over time. During the second industrial era, with its focus on large-scale manufacturing as the underlying force driving economic performance, there was little concern, either in the scholarly literature or among thought leaders in business and policy, for entrepreneurship. Rather, the key to the mainstay economic goals of jobs, growth, and competitiveness involved large-scale global manufacturing companies. However, with the advent of the third industrial era, with its focus on knowledge and innovation as the key to strong economic performance, entrepreneurship emerged as a policy priority. What motivates, inspires, drives, or inversely inhibits or suppresses entrepreneurship has become a focus of both academic research and public policy (Thurik et al., 2023). The early thinking, which was reflected in subsequent policies, focused on the entrepreneur and their firm in isolation. Such thinking and policies proved to be limited, if not inherently flawed.

In his vastly influential book, Lerner (2009) concluded that public policy to stimulate entrepreneurship would result in a *Boulevard of Broken Dreams: Why Public Efforts to Boost Entrepreneurship and Venture Capital Have Failed–and What to Do about It.* As Lerner (2009) concluded, public policy to ignite entrepreneurship resulted in uneven and, in some cases, uninspiring results. The limitation was neither public policy nor entrepreneurship, per se. Rather, it was the policy approach, forged by academic thinking, that viewed entrepreneurship as existing in a silo, cut off from community and societal influences. It took new research, thinking, and ideas to clarify that the problem was neither public policy nor entrepreneurship. It was the myopic view that entrepreneurs and their ventures can be viewed, analyzed, and assisted in isolation, as if they were economic silos. New research fuelled a new view placing entrepreneurs at the center of a community shaping entrepreneurial prospects. The constellation of organizations, institutions, individuals, and firms comprising this community became characterized as constituting an entrepreneurial ecosystem.

The new research and emerging view of entrepreneurship as being shaped by an entrepreneurial ecosystem has resulted in a new public policy approach to stimulating entrepreneurship. Rather than instruments that directly engage entrepreneurs and their firms, this new policy approach prioritizes instruments that directly engage the various elements of the entrepreneurial ecosystem, which in turn indirectly enhance entrepreneurship. Thus, the view that entrepreneurship is a key force in attaining societal goals is not new. What is new, however, is the priorities of social goals. In the contemporary world, a new set of priorities has replaced, or at least supplemented, the traditional economic goals—environmental protection, inclusion of all groups in society, and an equitable distribution of income and wealth, or what can be characterized as a sustainable society.

While research and policy have identified how and why entrepreneurship can contribute to attaining traditional economic values, little is known about the links between entrepreneurship and the societal values of sustainability. However, sustainable entrepreneurship is expected to play a pivotal role in the transitional phase of ecosystems for achieving transformative growth, and creating a sustainable society. Sustainable entrepreneurship balances economic, social, and environmental objectives (Dacin et al., 2010), therein promoting more inclusive and responsible enterprise. Sustainable entrepreneurship brings forth the inherent trade-offs among these goals (Vedula et al., 2022). Schumpeter's conceptualization of entrepreneurship acknowledges the existence of varied goals and associated trade-offs, and while this might be necessary it is insufficient on its own to achieve more inclusive economic growth. Entrepreneurship also requires innovation (Audretsch et al., 2016). This means that sustainable entrepreneurship is concerned with the processes that create a new capacity for society to promote prosperity.

Building on the idea that entrepreneurs are key actors for transformative change, the knowledge spillover theory of entrepreneurship has revealed that a portion of the knowledge required for entrepreneurial pursuits resides with other actors such as larger firms, private research institutes, or universities. These other actors might not fully grasp the value of knowledge, leaving room for entrepreneurs to pursue new opportunities. Through their action, entrepreneurs augment how society uses knowledge for enterprise (Audretsch, 2009). The same might also be said about new or changing societal values. Therefore, from the perspective of the knowledge spillover theory, sustainable entrepreneurship is about the role of the entrepreneur in the dissemination of knowledge and values that promote more inclusive and responsible business practices among various actors.

Aligning existing entrepreneurial ecosystems toward the SDG agenda requires transformative change, as priorities shift from focusing on economic growth toward multiple, and sometimes competing, goals, involving a wider range of actors. We still lack an understanding of how entrepreneurial ecosystems contribute to sustainable entrepreneurship, which is aligned with the SDG agenda (Volkmann et al., 2021), and the role of different actors in re-shaping and transforming entrepreneurial ecosystems toward more inclusive growth. Transformative change is typically carried out by entrepreneurial agents who challenge the status quo and offer alternative strategies and processes for value creation.

The aim of this chapter is to explore mechanism that connect local ecosystems to international networks, thereby enhancing the capacity of entrepreneurial ecosystems for more inclusive growth opportunities, supporting SDG8. The chapter responds to calls for a better understanding how the field of international business can contribute toward promoting the SDG Agenda (Rygh et al., 2022). We posit that agents and ideas critical for transformation toward sustainability are often related to a global context. Overall, this chapter identifies salient global institutions and agents that may contribute to the transformation of entrepreneurial ecosystems toward sustainability.

2 Increased Connectivity of Entrepreneurial Ecosystems and Sustainable Opportunities

There is evidence that entrepreneurial ecosystems evolve to support sustainable entrepreneurship by learning from other ecosystems. In this evolution, knowledge about how to better promote and scale sustainable business ideas flows across borders. Participants in entrepreneurial ecosystems either observe players in other, often overseas, entrepreneurial ecosystems or are directly connected to them. This leads to a convergence about how to better support sustainable business ideas. In the following, we use incubators, accelerators, and NGOs as examples to demonstrate that international connectivity can be a key mechanism for shaping entrepreneurial ecosystems to better support sustainable opportunities.

Incubators engage with entrepreneurial ventures during the early stages of their formation (Baskaran et al., 2019) and thus might be in a better position to shape entrepreneurial values. Often, they host a diverse set of entrepreneurial actors, including rural entrepreneurs, minorities, and socially disadvantaged groups (Baskaran et al., 2019). It can be expected that globally oriented incubators will advance inclusive growth compared to local ones. The associations with international networks of incubators can facilitate knowledge sharing and collaborations, often explicitly in relation to cultural and environmental activities (Franco et al., 2018). To illustrate, the governments of the Republic of Korea and the Republic of Indonesia founded the Green Business Center (GBC) in 2011 as an incubator to assist green Korean and Indonesian start-ups. It is based in Jarkarta, Indonesia, and hosts entrepreneurial ventures focused on eco-innovation and sustainable development. Sharing eco-information and green policies relevant to enterprise development is part of their objective (GreenBusinessCenter, 2023). Such cross-national knowledge sharing of green policies is expected to accelerate the transformation of ecosystems toward sustainability, as it provides opportunities to learn from each other's mistakes and share best practices. Here it is important to note that policy approaches explicitly aim to foster transnational knowledge spillovers to advance social and environmental goals.

Accelerators also have a global orientation, thereby creating a wider set of opportunities for their members. For example, SparkLabs Global Ventures is a network of 7 accelerators and 6 VC funds that collectively invested in over 450 entrepreneurial start-ups across 6 countries. The SparkLabs are run by teams of entrepreneurs with international experience. The goal of SparkLabs is to "*build leading startup ecosytems around the world and help all entrepreneurs at the earliest stages of growth*" (Sparkslabgroup, 2023a). Their members have access to international investors and mentors. While they support a range of start-ups with high growth potential, they also have events related to green start-ups, such as impact investing, or opportunities related to sectors critical for sustainable transformation, such as clean energy, including a dedicated SparkLabs Clean Energy accelerator based in Singapore (Sparkslabgroup, 2023b).

It can be expected that accelerators with a greater depth and breadth of investors can better support responsible entrepreneurs contributing to inclusive growth. Impact investment—or social finance—provides funding for ventures that aim to create economic, social, and environmental value (Agrawal & Hockerts, 2021). While impact investors support entrepreneurs across a wide range of geographies and industries (Ormiston et al., 2015), access will be mediated by matchmakers. Thus, the international connectivity of the network of accelerators is expected to enable or limit specific opportunities, and those with a wider international network are more likely to attract impact investment which is critical to provide new opportunities to under-resourced entrepreneurs for establishing sustainable venture.

Finally, early research suggests that international NGOs can enable the formation of local entrepreneurial ecosystems in emerging markets and that entrepreneurial ecosystems coevolve (Juma et al., 2023). International organizations and NGOs are important in enhancing international connectivity among entrepreneurs by shaping and supporting local ecosystems. The largest global multistakeholder coalition is the Global Alliance for Social Entrepreneurship, hosted by the Schwab Foundation for Social Entrepreneurship. They currently have 106 members, such as corporations, accelerators, impact finance, governments, and researchers aiming to enhance social entrepreneurship by addressing topics related to inequality, diversity and inclusion, entrepreneurship, and social justice (Global Alliance for Social Entrepreneurship, 2023). Thus, through these international organizations and NGOs, knowledge related to inclusive growth becomes more widely disseminated, creating opportunities for transformative change in local ecosystems. These transnational international NGOs and coalitions dedicated to support social entrepreneurship directly target the advancement of the SDG8 agenda to promote more inclusive and diverse enterprise and provide access to resources and knowledge to under-resourced communities.

3 Entrepreneurs and International Knowledge Flows About Sustainable Opportunities

A key force to convey sustainable practices are also entrepreneurs themselves, as they challenge the status quo, and can provide new job opportunities. Past studies have consistently shown the importance of entrepreneurial human capital in how entrepreneurs challenge their existing competitors (Dimov, 2010) as well as how they develop networks in response (Fath et al., 2021). Building on these insights, we posit that three types of international experience of entrepreneurs, namely, that of returnee entrepreneurs, global argonauts, and immigrant entrepreneurs with sustainable values, can affect the shift of ecosystems toward more inclusive growth.

While local sustainable entrepreneurs might serve as role models for others, their impact on the ecosystem might be relatively limited when their business models fail to achieve scale (Wisdom et al., 2022). A key challenge for sustainable entrepreneurs is to challenge established power structures within their ecosystem. Legacy players are expected to defend their past investments and stifle sustainable entrepreneurial activities that challenge the status quo (Audretsch & Fiedler, 2023). However, entrepreneurs with an international background and respective networks might be in a better position to challenge well-established norms and routines in a local context and thus introduce more transformative change. They can also use alternative templates to adjust structural factors and processes within the local entrepreneurial ecosystem, and be a central force for the creation of new job opportunities.

First, returnee entrepreneurs are an important cross-country mechanism expected to foster sustainable opportunities in their home countries (Audretsch & Fiedler, 2022) and advance the local knowledge base. Returnee entrepreneurs may pursue different goals. Some may explicitly focus on helping local communities, and provide financial resources to enable entrepreneurship. These returnee entrepreneurs often have a desire to bring about positive change. They have empathy for the struggles of their nascent community, helping them to recontextualize knowledge in their home country (Tran & Truong, 2022). Their international experience enables them to better recognize opportunities for their home country to enable more decent work opportunities (Kenney et al., 2013). Others might create new and often advanced opportunities that provide employment opportunities and fuel economic growth. For example, the founder of the Taiwanese company Gogoro established a battery swap network for e-scooters. His innovation supports the Taiwanese government's goal to Net-Zero Emission by 2040 by electrifying scooters in the region through technology (Chien et al., 2023).

While the positive impact of returnee entrepreneurs on economic growth, particularly in emerging economies, has been recognized (Dai & Liu, 2009; Kenney et al., 2013), their social orientation also has a capacity for transformative change and indeed for becoming a central player in the advancement of local ecosystems. To illustrate, Vietnamese returnee have been a critical force in the creation of an entrepreneurial ecosystem in Vietnam, emulating certain factors of the Silicon Valley—a context in which many of them have experience (Audretsch & Fiedler, 2022). An example of the potential wide-reaching impact of an individual entrepreneur is the Vietnamese venture MindX, which was co-founded by Thu Hà. Today, the venture has the aspiration to become a key pillar of the Vietnamese education and entrepreneurial ecosystem. Hà grew up in a relatively poor village that provided limited work opportunities for her generation, typically limited to farming and labor, and young people sometimes even pursued illegal activities. After participating in the Google Ambassador Program for Southeast Asia, she realized how technology and education could lift a nation's prospects. MindX started as a nonprofit organization offering free coding classes and later transitioned to a private business model in the ed-tech sector, which has already supported approximately 40,000 students (Nguyen, 2023; Vn Economy, 2023). Thus, the experience of living in a different context can help entrepreneurs gain both a vision and knowledge relevant to advance SDG8.

Secondly and similarly, immigrant entrepreneurs can facilitate more inclusive growth opportunities for their host countries. Their ability to better connect to and leverage international networks widens opportunities and can contribute to deepening trade relationships with other countries, ultimately creating local work opportunities (Åkesson, 2016; Sui et al., 2015). Several governments, particularly in developing markets, have launched programs to attract immigrant entrepreneurs aiming to achieve their SDG goals toward more inclusive economic growth (Duan, 2023). While there is some agreement that immigrant entrepreneurs can have a positive impact on economic growth, they might also be a critical mechanism for transforming entrepreneurial ecosystems toward sustainability. Greater cultural diversity within an entrepreneurial ecosystem can contribute to knowledge spillovers (Audretsch & Belitski, 2017; Ratten, 2021). In this vein, Kautto (2019) argues that the unique characteristics and backgrounds of migrant entrepreneurs, such as language and cultural knowledge and unconventional attitudes toward innovation, have the capacity to change the attitudes and behavior of other actors within an ecosystem in the host country, who may emulate these entrepreneurs. Overall, immigrant entrepreneurs can contribute to the transformation of entrepreneurial ecosystem development, as they offer unique networks and knowledge.

Finally, global argonauts might be critical to empowering other entrepreneurs, such as minority entrepreneurs and socially disadvantaged groups in rural areas. Global argonauts have the capacity to better take advantage of various global opportunities, as they may have unique knowledge with regard to various cultures, values, and practices (Goxe et al., 2022). They are typically highly U.S.-educated immigrants who also benefit from their global networks when exploiting opportunities (Saxenian, 2006). Global argonauts may display characteristics of returnee entrepreneurs or migrant entrepreneurs but they are distinct in that they maintain a global orientation. The important characteristic is that global argonauts do not embed themselves in a single context but remain flexible and travel back and forth between multiple countries (Saxenian, 2006). They may remain, for instance, in the US, but develop business across different regions. Thus, they tend to establish two-way (Welch et al., 2016), or multi-way, permanent exchange networks.

Existing research has focused on how argonauts explore opportunities for economic growth, but they may also play a critical role in achieving inclusive growth by connecting rural, underprivileged communities to global markets. Thus, global argonauts might be critical boundary spanners to enable decent work for impoverished communities by connecting them to distant business opportunities. They can better identify and connect to a context more conducive to value work created by impoverished communities in which resource constraints have been persistent.

4 Discussion and Conclusions

In this chapter, we have argued that the SDG8 can be promoted via international connectivity of ecosystems and entrepreneurial mobility. Flow of ideas and people enables knowledge spillovers of sustainable values and practices across borders. We have outlined two main mechanisms critical for the transition toward more inclusive growth. First, international organizations and networks, such as global incubators, accelerators, and NGOs promote the transition of entrepreneurial ecosystems toward more sustainable opportunities. Sustainable goals and practices flow across borders between these actors. Second, and subsequently, we have identified three types of actors as a subset of the broader 'global pipelines' (Bathelt et al., 2004) that can convey sustainable practices, and also create new job opportunities. Such flows of individual entrepreneurs can in turn provide new impulses in the entrepreneurial ecosystem, lifting sustainability. Together, these flows are likely to accelerate the transition of local entrepreneurial ecosystems toward sustainability.

Our chapter points toward new research opportunities at the intersection between international business and the entrepreneurial ecosystems literature, which we will elaborate below. First, future research could focus on the role of globally connected entrepreneurs in driving entrepreneurial ecosystems toward more sustainability. Currently, the entrepreneurial ecosystem literature mainly focuses on how knowledge flows within the systems, but investigating the role that entrepreneurs with global networks may play in the transition of the ecosystem toward more inclusive growth will provide fruitful avenues for research. Research could also investigate how such international flows of knowledge and ideas, via people, compete against homegrown ideas and firms, as well as what types of power struggles emerge (Audretsch & Fiedler, 2023). Countries differ in regard to history, culture, language, and stage of economic development. Context will impact how practices and ideas travel between ecosystems and will be embraced. In this vein, the research could also focus on the impact of ideas that spill over to a particular local context. In particular, in emerging markets, the benefits of better access to ecosystems might not benefit all participants equally (Kenney et al., 2013), creating a risk of even increasing inequalities within society (Rai et al., 2019).

Second, our contribution also draws attention to how some of the structural elements of the shift toward more sustainable-oriented entrepreneurial ecosystems are affected by international organizations, such as NGOs, transnational institutions such as the SDG, and the spread of knowledge about how sustainable entrepreneurship can be supported in an ecosystem through incubators or impact investing. Here, our chapter draws attention to the structural aspects of knowledge flow across borders. Future research could investigate such knowledge flows more directly to see to what extent ecosystems converge with regard to sustainable goals (Cloitre et al., 2022).

In closing, this chapter focuses on two distinct areas of how entrepreneurial ecosystems will likely benefit from international knowledge flows in their transformation toward more sustainability, either through entrepreneurs or structurally. The topics we have canvassed are likely to gain salience. Our brief outline should be seen as an invitation to appreciate more the increasingly global nature of the role of entrepreneurs and the entrepreneurial ecosystem they are embedded in, as their immediate support structure, in accelerating the transformation of precisely these entrepreneurial ecosystems toward more inclusive growth and SDG8.

References

Agrawal, A., & Hockerts, K. (2021). Impact investing: Review and research agenda. *Journal of Small Business & Entrepreneurship, 33*(2), 153–181.

Åkesson, L. (2016). Multi-sited accumulation of capital: Cape Verdean returnees and small-scale business. *Global Networks, 16*(1), 112–129.

Audretsch, D. B. (2009). The entrepreneurial society. *The Journal of Technology Transfer, 34*, 245–254.

Audretsch, D. B., & Belitski, M. (2017). Entrepreneurial ecosystems in cities: Establishing the framework conditions. *The Journal of Technology Transfer, 42*, 1030–1051.

Audretsch, D. B., & Fiedler, A. (2022).The Vietnamese entrepreneurship paradox: How can entrepreneurs thrive without political and economic freedom? *The Journal of Technology Transfer, 47*, 1179–1197.

Audretsch, D. B., & Fiedler, A. (2023). Power and entrepreneurship. *Small Business Economics, 60*(4), 1573–1592.

Audretsch, D. B., Kuratko, D. F., & Link, A. N. (2016). Dynamic entrepreneurship and technology-based innovation. *Journal of Evolutionary Economics, 26*, 603–620.

Baskaran, A., Chandran, V. G. R., & Ng, B. K. (2019). Inclusive entrepreneurship, innovation and sustainable growth: Role of business incubators, academia and social enterprises in Asia. *Science, Technology and Society, 24*(3), 385–400.

Bathelt, H., Malmberg, A., & Maskell, P. (2004). Clusters and knowledge: Local buzz, global pipelines and the process of knowledge creation. *Progress in Human Geography, 28*(1), 31–56.

Chien, Y. H., Hsieh, I. Y. L., & Chang, T. H. (2023). Beyond personal vehicles: How electrifying scooters will help achieve climate mitigation goals in Taiwan. *Energy Strategy Reviews, 45*, 101056.

Cloitre, A., Dos Santos Paulino, V., & Theodoraki, C. (2022). The quadruple/quintuple helix model in entrepreneurial ecosystems: an institutional perspective on the space case study. *R&D Management*. https://doi.org/10.1111/radm.12547

Dacin, P. A., Dacin, M. T., & Matear, M. (2010). Social entrepreneurship: Why we don't need a new theory and how we move forward from here. *Academy of Management Perspectives, 24*(3), 37–57.

Dai, O., & Liu, X. (2009). Returnee entrepreneurs and firm performance in Chinese high-technology industries. *International Business Review, 18*(4), 373–386.

Dimov, D. (2010). Nascent entrepreneurs and venture emergence: Opportunity confidence, human capital, and early planning. *Journal of Management Studies, 47*(6), 1123–1153.

Duan, C. (2023). Theory selection and applications for immigrant enterprises, entrepreneurs and entrepreneurship (IEEE) research. *Entrepreneurship Education, 6*(1), 69–89.

Fath, B., Whittaker, H., & Fiedler, A. (2021). Developing venture opportunities amidst rivalry: Entrepreneurs' backgrounds and the governing role of maintaining confidence. *Entrepreneurship & Regional Development, 33*(7–8), 641–667.

Franco, M., Haase, H., & Correia, S. (2018). Exploring factors in the success of creative incubators: A cultural entrepreneurship perspective. *Journal of the Knowledge Economy, 9*(1), 239–262.

GreenBusinessCenter. (2023). Vision & Mission. https://greenbusinesscenter.org/vision-mission

Global Alliance for Social Entrepreneurship. (2023). Map of alliance member activities. https://initiatives.weforum.org/global-alliance-for-social-entrepreneurship/map

Goxe, F., Mayrhofer, U., & Kuivalainen, O. (2022). Argonauts and Icaruses: Social networks and dynamics of nascent international entrepreneurs. *International Business Review, 31*(1), 101892.

Isenberg, D. J. (2010). How to start an entrepreneurial revolution. *Harvard Business Review, 88*(6), 40–50.

Juma, N., Olabisi, J., & Griffin-EL, E. (2023). External enablers and entrepreneurial ecosystems: The brokering role of the anchor tenant in capacitating grassroots ecopreneurs. *Strategic Entrepreneurship Journal*.https://doi.org/10.1002/sej.1462

Kautto, D. (2019). Social influences in cross-border entrepreneurial migration policy. *Journal of International Business Policy, 2*, 397–412.

Kenney, M., Breznitz, D., & Murphree, M. (2013). Coming back home after the sun rises: Returnee entrepreneurs and growth of high tech industries. *Research Policy, 42*(2), 391–407.

Lerner, J. (2009). *Boulevard of broken dreams: Why public efforts to boost entrepreneurship and venture capital have failed–and what to do about it*. Princeton University Press.

Mason, C., & Brown, R. (2014). Final report for OECD LEED programme. Entrepreneurial ecosystems and growth oriented entrepreneurship. https://www.oecd.org/cfe/leed/Entrepreneurial-ecosystems.pdf

Miller, D. J., & Acs, Z. J. (2017). The campus as entrepreneurial ecosystem: The University of Chicago. *Small Business Economics, 49*, 75–95.

Nguyen. (2023). EdTech in Vietnam: Understanding foreign investment trends in 2023. https://www.vietnam-briefing.com/news/key-foreign-investments-in-edtech-in-vietnam-this-year-and-why.html

Ormiston, J., Charlton, K., Donald, M. S., & Seymour, R. G. (2015). Overcoming the challenges of impact investing: Insights from leading investors. *Journal of Social Entrepreneurship, 6*(3), 352–378.

Qian, H. (2018). Knowledge-based regional economic development: A synthetic review of knowledge spillovers, entrepreneurship, and entrepreneurial ecosystems. *Economic Development Quarterly, 32*(2), 163–176.

Rai, S. M., Brown, B. D., & Ruwanpura, K. N. (2019). SDG 8: Decent work and economic growth–A gendered analysis. *World Development, 113*, 368–380.

Ratten, V. (2021). Sport entrepreneurial ecosystems and knowledge spillovers. *Knowledge Management Research & Practice, 19*(1), 43–52.

Roundy, P. T. (2020). Regional differences in impact investment: A theory of impact investing ecosystems. *Social Responsibility Journal, 16*(4), 467–485.

Rygh, A., Chiarapini, E., & Segovia, M. V. (2022). How can international business research contribute towards the sustainable development goals? *Critical Perspectives on International Business., 18*(4), 457–487.

Saxenian, A. (2006). *The new argonauts: Regional advantage in a global economy*. Harvard University Press.

Sinkovics, N., Sinkovics, R. R., & Archie-Acheampong, J. (2021). Small- and medium-sized enterprises and sustainable development: In the shadows of large lead firms in global value chains. *Journal of International Business Policy, 4*(1), 80–101.

Sparkslabsgroup. (2023a). Founded by entrepreneurs for entrepreneurs. https://www.sparklabsgroup.com

Sparkslabsgroup. (2023b). Sparkslabs clean energy. https://www.sparklabsgroup.com/accelerator-cleanenergy.php

Stam, F., & Spigel, B. (2016). Entrepreneurial ecosystems. *USE Discussion Paper Series, 16*(13), 1–15.

Sui, S., Morgan, H. M., & Baum, M. (2015). Internationalization of immigrant-owned SMEs: The role of language. *Journal of World Business, 50*(4), 804–814.

Theodoraki, C., Messeghem, K., & Audretsch, D. B. (2020). The effectiveness of incubators' co-opetition strategy in the entrepreneurial ecosystem: Empirical evidence from France. *IEEE Transactions on Engineering Management, 69*(4), 1781–1794.

Thurik, A. R., Audretsch, D. B., Block, J. H., Burke, A., Carree, M. A., Dejardin, M., Rietveld, C. A., Sanders, M., Stephan, U., & Wiklund, J. (2023). The impact of entrepreneurship research on other academic fields. Small Business Economics, 1–25.

Tran, Y., & Truong, A. T. T. (2022). Knowledge recontextualization by returnee entrepreneurs: The dynamic learning perspective. *Journal of International Management, 28*(3), 100922.

UN. (2015). Sustainable development goals. Transforming our world: The SDGs 2030. https://sdgs.un.org/2030agenda

Vedula, S., Doblinger, C., Pacheco, D., York, J. G., Bacq, S., Russo, M. V., & Dean, T. J. (2022). Entrepreneurship for the public good: A review, critique, and path forward for social and environmental entrepreneurship research. *Academy of Management Annals, 16*(1), 391–425.

Vn Economy. (2023). Nếu không lì lợm, chúng tôi đã bỏ cuộc t`ư 3-4 năm trư´ơc. https://vneconomy.vn/co-founder-mindx-neu-khong-li-lom-chung-toi-da-bo-cuoc-tu-3-4-nam-truoc.htm

Volkmann, C., Fichter, K., Klofsten, M., & Audretsch, D. B. (2021). Sustainable entrepreneurial ecosystems: An emerging field of research. *Small Business Economics, 56*(3), 1047–1055.

Welch, A., & Hao, J. (2016). Global argonauts: Returnees and diaspora as sources of innovation in China and Israel. *Globalisation, Societies and Education, 14*(2), 272–297.

Wisdom, K., Bienkowska, M., Klofsten, H., & Mavin, H. (2022). *Challenges of start-ups developing circular business models*. IDEAS 2022: Interdisciplinary Conference on Innovation, Design, Entrepreneurship, and Sustainable Systems, São Paulo, Brazil, 28–30 Nov, 2022.

Wurth, B., Stam, E., & Spigel, B. (2022). Toward an entrepreneurial ecosystem research program. *Entrepreneurship Theory and Practice, 46*(3), 729–778.

12

Towards a Typology of Governance Mechanisms in Cross-sector Partnerships Based on Multiple Agency Theory

Jihye Kim, Ji-Won Song, and Dhruba Borah

1 Introduction

The United Nations recognises cross-sector partnerships as important to achieving the seventeen sustainable development goals (SDGs) (UN, 2015). These partnerships involve business, government, and civil society organisations (CSOs) which form the three sectors of society. CSOs, often called the "third (powerful) sector", include households, trade

J. Kim (✉)
University of Dundee, Dundee, UK
e-mail: jkim001@dundee.ac.uk

J.-W. Song
University of Edinburg, Edinburg, UK
e-mail: jiwon.song@ed.ac.uk

D. Borah
University of Liverpool, Liverpool, UK
e-mail: dhruba.borah@liverpool.ac.uk

N. Sinkovics et al. (eds.), *International Business and SDG 8*, The Academy of International Business, https://doi.org/10.1007/978-3-031-46802-5_12

unions, voluntary associations, hospitals, churches, markets, and capitalist enterprises (Wood, 1990); these can all pressurise or collaborate with the other two sectors to address societal issues (Teegen et al., 2004).

Addressing global challenges in management requires solutions beyond individual actors' efforts by governments, businesses, or CSOs in isolation (Laasonen et al., 2012; Sakarya et al., 2012). Cross-sector partnerships can offer possible solutions to multifaceted societal problems (Shrivastava & Guimarães-Costa, 2017). For example, Arslaan et al. (2020) present three cases from Nigeria, Pakistan, and Turkey concerning how cross-sector partnerships involving all three sectors proved to be vital in fighting against the COVID-19 pandemic. In the context of SDG8, such cross-sector partnerships have been found to be particularly useful. For instance, in the context of India, studies (Borah et al., 2019, 2023) find cross-sector partnerships for developing fresh engineering graduates with adequate industrial and societal competencies and achieving SGD8. On the other hand, Dahan et al. (2010) document how Nestlé has been collaborating with local NGOs and governments in West Africa through the Nestlé cocoa initiative to ameliorate labour conditions, and worker competencies, and encourage sustainable agriculture in the region.

Despite these potential benefits, successful collaborations are difficult to achieve due to variations in underlying partnership motives (Quélin et al., 2017). Business-CSO partnerships, for instance, face conflicts due to distinct goals: market-driven for firms and public-good-oriented for CSOs (Mars & Lounsbury, 2009). Differences in expectations may hinder building a common agenda for such collaboration (Ashman, 2001).

Dahan et al. (2010), Rivera-Santos and Rufín (2010), and Jamali and Keshishian (2009) describe the collaborations between CSOs and firms as non-traditional partnerships, odd couples, and uneasy alliances respectively, that are "not inherently successful arrangements and that a number of foundational underpinnings have to be carefully designed and crafted to promote the success of collaborative venture" (Jamali & Keshishian, 2009, p. 282). Therefore, a growing interest can be seen in investigating the dynamics of cross-sector partnerships to identify the challenges and how to mitigate them (Arenas et al., 2013; Tencati and Zsolnai, 2010; Waddell, 2017).

However, we argue that several gaps exist in this literature providing limited insights into the cross-sector collaboration issues. First, the literature seems to be focused on two-sector collaborations between businesses and CSOs (e.g., Dahan et al., 2010; den Hond et al., 2015; Jamali & Keshishian, 2009; Rivera-Santos & Rufín, 2010; van Huijstee & Glasbergen, 2010) with little attention given to examining the dynamics of other types of cross-sector partnerships such as business-government, government-CSO partnerships, and/or partnerships involving all three sectors. Second, the institutional logic perspective, while explaining the macro-level differences between organisations embedded in different sectors and the complications created by such differences, cannot fully cover all the challenges experienced in cross-sector collaborations, particularly those arising at the micro level, i.e., at the level of the employees involved in the collaboration. Complications may arise due to parallel commitments. For example, firms have to perform tasks related to their partnership with the government while their employees need to also complete responsibilities allocated by their original employer. Such governance challenges cannot be explained using the institutional logics perspective which, thus, calls for the application of a theory that can help examine more agency issues, such as the agency theory (Quélin et al., 2017).

In this chapter, we use the "multiple agency theory" (Hoskisson et al., 2012) to explain the governance issues in cross-sector partnerships. In doing so, we identify five typologies of cross-sector partnerships with distinct governance structures and highlight three problems: institutional logic differences, temporal disparities, and free-riding behaviour. This study makes significant contributions to the literature. First, to the best of our knowledge, this is one of the few studies (e.g., Borah & Ellwood, 2022; Rivera-Santos et al., 2017) to use multiple agency theory to investigate cross-sector collaborations and the typologies identified have hardly been discussed before. While the three agency problems mentioned above were initially identified by Rivera-Santos et al. (2017) in the context of business-CSO collaboration, our study argues their presence in other types of cross-sector partnerships as well. However, our study underscores that these issues affect each partnership type differently, leading us to offer more nuanced implications for researchers and practitioners.

2 Cross-sector Partnership

A cross-sector partnership can be defined as relatively "intensive, long-term interactions between organisations from at least two sectors (business, government, and/or civil society) aimed at addressing a social or environmental problem" (Clarke & Crane, 2018, p. 303). Such partnerships require involved actors to undertake resource-sharing and make strong commitments aimed at generating positive values for the wider community (Sullivan & Skelcher, 2002).

The partnerships aim to benefit an external beneficiary who is not directly involved in resource supply (Seitanidi & Crane, 2013; Waddock, 1988). For instance, Pfizer, a multinational pharmaceutical giant, partnered with local CSOs in Uganda in order to combat HIV and AIDS. The CSOs assisted Pfizer to distribute the drugs to affected people across the country. In this case, the HIV/AIDS-affected people are the external beneficiaries of the Pfizer and local CSOs' partnership.

Establishing cross-sector partnerships may lead to benefits for all parties involved. For example, collaborating with CSOs provides firms and governments access to societal needs, social capital, and networks with local community leaders, politicians, and regulators (Marano & Tashman, 2012). Such collaborations can also offer CSOs access to funding from governments and firms, which is a key to achieving their social objectives through long-term and large-scale projects (Ashman, 2001).

3 Governance Mechanisms in Cross-sector Partnerships

Scholarly attention has recently turned to the governance mechanisms in cross-sector partnerships and the difficulties in monitoring such processes (Liu & Wilkinson, 2014; Van den Hurk & Verhoest, 2015). Achieving success in such partnerships is challenging due to variations in participants' expectations regarding timelines, costs, and outcomes (Van Marrewijk et al., 2008). Furthermore, different leadership styles, decision-making arrangements, and routines among participants create obstacles to collaboration (Quélin et al., 2017). In addition, partners have distinct goals from one another: governments pursue the public good, firms embrace profit-oriented market logic (Mars & Lounsbury, 2009), and CSOs are shaped by independent voluntary efforts based on common interests and needs (Teegen et al., 2004) termed "collective action" (Olson, 1982).

The governance mechanisms in cross-sector partnerships can be explained by agency theory known as the "agency relationship" (Gomez-Mejia & Balkin, 1992). The agency relationship consists of the principal and the agent, where the principal designates an agent to represent their interests (Hoskisson et al., 2012). The most used example is the relationship between shareholders as principals, and company executives as agents. An agency problem is a conflict of interest inherent in any relationship where agents are expected to act in the principal's best interests (Arthurs et al., 2008).

Rivera-Santos et al. (2017) use the principal–agent relationship to explain the governance mechanisms of NGO and firm collaborations (see Fig. 1). They suggest that within a collaborative project involving a firm and an NGO, both entities can engage their employees or external hires (referred to as Business-to-NGO or B2N alliance employees). In line with agency theory, these employees are the agents of the NGO (principal) and the company managers (principal). One obvious principal–agent relationship occurs between the donors of the NGO and the NGO's managers; meanwhile, shareholders of the concerned firm and the firm's managers share the second obvious principal–agent relationship. The alliance reveals two additional principal–agent relationships:

between the NGO and the B2N alliance employees, and between the firm and the B2N alliance employees. This, thus, suggests that the B2N alliance employees have dual identities or principals: B2N employees as the agents of NGO managers, who might prioritise societal goals; and, contrastingly, as the agents of firm managers, the B2N alliance employees also need to fulfil the firm's profitability objectives.

Rivera-Santos et al. (2017) also indicate the existence of two additional principal–agent relationships: between the NGO's external beneficiary and the NGO managers, and beneficiary of NGO and the B2N employees. Each NGO represents a section of society or the environment. For instance, NGOs such as People Ethical Treatment for Animals (PETA) work for animal rights. While animals are the external beneficiary of PETA's activities, PETA's representation of animal rights is not decided by any legal contract between the animals and the NGO. Rivera-Santos et al. (2017) call such NGOs "the claimed agents of external beneficiaries". For NGOs dealing with community concerns, the community will constitute the external beneficiary and the NGO's decision-making might be driven by concerns that the communities face. On the other hand, if the external beneficiary is active, the B2N employees might also be affected by these beneficiaries as the B2N employees work towards solving issues that the external beneficiaries may

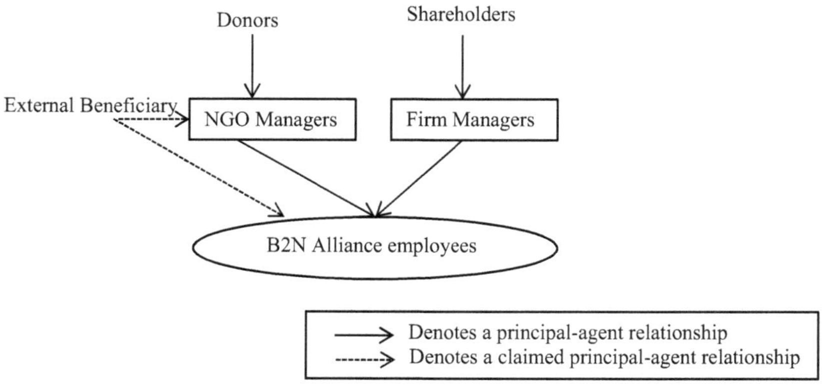

Fig. 1 Principal–agent relationship in NGO-firm collaboration (Rivera-Santos et al., 2017)

face. Rivera-Santos et al. (2017) term such a relationship as a "claimed principal-agent relationship" as CSOs claim to represent the views/needs of their principals (communities).

However, the challenge in using Rivera-Santos et al.'s (2017) framework to investigate cross-sector partnerships lies in its limited scope, excluding complex partners such as government organisations. According to Selsky and Parker (2005), cross-sector partnerships for addressing social and environmental issues occur in four ways: firms-nonprofit, business-government, government-nonprofit, and trisector. Such partnerships could bring communal contributions by addressing "meta-problems" (Selsky & Parker, 2005) which often exceed the single-sector capabilities and boundaries. Such contributions may include "addressing institutional voids where governments are not able to fully provide public resources, governments in these situations can take a leadership role in defining priority issues" (Peloza & Falkenberg, 2009, p. 107).

Based on Rivera-Santos et al.'s (2017) framework, we include three different types of cross-partnerships: firms, CSOs, and government, while proposing five governance mechanisms. This contribution is in line with Selsky and Parker (2005), who argue that researchers usually "do not distinguish between bisector and trisector partnerships, so it is sometimes difficult to separate studies into the appropriate categories" (p. 863).

4 Type of Cross-sector Partnership and Governance Problems Caused by Multiple Agencies

4.1 Type 1 Cross-sector Partnership: Government-Firm(s) with No CSO Involvement

Extensive research (Albareda et al., 2007; Van Huijstee & Glasbergen, 2008; Wright, 2016) explores government-firm partnerships. Governments and firms bring two necessary capabilities. Governments provide legitimacy and knowledge of social issues while firms bring industry-specific expertise. Employees in the collaborations, termed business-to-government (B2G) alliance employees act as agents of both government executives and firm managers.

Collaborating with government can help international businesses gain political legitimacy in new markets (Arenas et al., 2013). Legitimacy theory suggests that organisations define legitimacy as "a generalised perception or assumption that the actions of an entity are desirable, proper, or appropriate with some socially constructed system of norms, beliefs, and definitions" (Suchman, 1995, p. 574). Legitimate firms benefit from "more trustful and committed stakeholder relationships with fewer transaction costs, receive more support for their operations from communities, and are more likely to access useful knowledge and resources for stakeholder networks" (Marano & Tashman, 2012, p. 1127).

When a firm collaborates with a government with no CSO involvement, the firm's main interest lies in value creation and business-oriented goods provision. A government, however, prioritises addressing local social needs (Jay, 2013; Pache & Santos, 2010). Thus, the firm's institutional logic follows market logic, whereas the government's institutional logic focuses on public service provision. The innately considerable difference in institutional logics between them could be mitigated by the firm's activities such as frequent reporting of the progress of collaboration to satisfy government officials. Also, temporal horizon differences between the principals linked to institutional logics could also lead to agency problems. Governments, as public goods providers, are likely to have long-term goals to achieve, whereas firms as commercial logic followers, seek short-term gains (Rivera-Santos et al., 2017). However, in Type 1, government officials prefer setting specific project implementation timelines when collaborating with firms to achieve social and economic objectives.

Regarding free-riding and opportunistic behaviour, we can expect a low level of such behaviour in this type since firms and governments both favour formal control governance in collaboration partnerships. Regular progress reports may be required, and the government may not release funds if these are not completed or are unsatisfactory. Hence, firms may be obliged to fulfil the expectations of the collaborative project.

4.2 Type 2 Cross-sector Partnership: Government-Firm(s) Alliance with CSOs as the "Claimed Principal of Government"

Several studies (Hartman et al., 2007; Laasonen et al., 2012) explore how CSOs pressure governments and firms for collaborations. When CSOs pressurise governments to develop collaborative projects, a principal–agent relationship emerges between the CSO managers and government executive. CSOs are the claimed principals of the government influencing the decision-making of the government which indirectly influence the decision-making of B2G employees, though there might not be any legal contract binding the government and B2G alliance employees to adhere to the suggestions or demands of the CSOs.

In Type 2, CSOs may also lead in outlining the priority areas for collaborative projects and connecting firms with the relevant government authorities. Meanwhile, the CSOs may also directly influence the B2G alliance employees to ensure the social projects meet the necessary requirements set or demanded by the CSOs. In such alliances, apart from principal–agent relationships existing between government executives and B2G alliance employees (one relationship), and between firm managers and B2G alliance employees, there may also exist two claimed principal–agent relationships between CSO managers and the government agent, and between the CSO managers and B2G alliance employees. In this type of collaboration, as the CSO serves as the claimed principal of the government, the CSO tends to have specific demands and their voice could be intensified. While the CSO could be seen as the leader who takes the initiative and sets the agenda, the government participates in communication with firms to ensure the achievement of a collaborative outcome. In this case, firms actively engage with government agents to understand CSO requirements, aiming to reduce criticism and proactively address future concerns through CSR strategies (Torugsa et al., 2013).

When a firm collaborates with a government and with CSOs as the "claimed principal of government", the collaboration begins under constant pressure from the CSOs. The CSOs as advisers provide guidelines to the government while the government acts as the translator of the CSOs' intentions and plays an important role in mediating the principals' (CSOs and firms) potential tensions. Despite the claimed principal–agent relation, CSOs and the government share aligned goals and institutional logic (public goods provision or social welfare). This would prevail over the private goods provision logic that firms have in this type of collaboration. In addition, we claim that Type 2 shows a low level of temporal differences and opportunistic behaviour due to the formal control mechanism of a strong government, the specific timeline of projects, and high trust (Min, 2022).

4.3 Type 3 Cross-sector Partnership: CSO(s)-Firm(s) with No Government Involvement

Scholars argue that the initiation of social projects may be the result of a bottom-up approach, with minimal government involvement in their development (e.g., Fraser et al., 2006). Rather, firms collaborate with CSOs to understand the needs of a social project and then develop the necessary process. This collaboration can be a response to increasing pressure from CSOs or a proactive measure to prevent potential disruptions caused by CSO protests. In such partnerships, CSOs can form two principal–agent relationships—one with the CSO's managers and B2C (business to CSO) alliance employees and another between the firm managers and B2C alliance employees.

A similar partnership model could be observed within supply chains. If a large industrial customer holds more influence over its suppliers (e.g., in cases, where there are many companies in the market who could supply raw materials to the organisation), it can pressurise its suppliers, or potential suppliers, to follow specific standards making their collaboration contingent on compliance (Lenox & Nash, 2003). Therefore, suppliers are increasingly encouraged to partner with CSOs to acquire certifications endorsing their sustainable production process (Darnall et al., 2018).

In CSOs-firms collaboration without government involvement, both principals with different institutional logics (market-based vs. public good-based) will face conflicts of interests and goals (Rivera-Santos et al., 2017). Institutional logic discrepancies are even noticeable within the same principal groups (CSOs and firms). Although they share similar social and economic goals, multiple actors within the same groups may have different capabilities and interests. Such in-group differences may cause an elevated level of challenge from institutional logic differences. Divergent decision-making processes and goal orientations hinder seamless collaboration, causing disagreements over timelines for implementing social objectives and revealing significant temporal differences. Compared to firm-firm collaboration, which is based on equity partnerships, firm-CSO collaboration does not enforce formal contracts and strong control mechanisms. The absence of government agents results in a higher likelihood of free-riding and opportunistic behaviour due to weak governance structures.

4.4 Type 4 Cross-sector Partnership: CSO(s)-Firm(s) Alliance with CSOs as the "Claimed Agent of Government"

When firms form a collaboration with CSOs as the "claimed agents of government", CSOs often act as government-hired entities to design and implement social projects (Barr et al., 2005). The government's coercive and hierarchical characteristics can influence CSOs' decision-making, as they operate as sub-government entities (Chen & Graddy, 2010; Cho & Gillespie, 2006; Etzioni, 1961; Najam, 1996). Hence, these could be seen as government-centred partnerships where CSOs perform sub-government functions and engage in firms to deliver the government's power (Kramer, 2000). These alliances also include a claimed principal–agent relationship between the government executives and CSOs and between the government executives and B2C alliance employees.

The government's role in such partnerships could be initially as the adviser or sponsor, while the role could be extended from advising on CSOs to being engaged in monitoring the progress of collaboration. As government officials are held accountable for the outcomes of the collaboration, the role of the government is not limited to just adviser, it could also serve as administrator between the conflicts arising from firms and CSOs through soft and hard contracts (Borah et al., 2023), and as watchmen. The government may also create a separate infrastructure to offer easy access to grants for CSOs and firms.

When a firm forms a collaboration with CSOs as the "claimed agent of government", we can expect a high level of government involvement as a principal in the partnership. Min (2022) argues that the logic of government will be dominant in government-CSO collabora-tions due to the top-down approach, bolstering regulatory, hierarchical, and coercive institutional logic. Although the goals of CSOs and governments will become aligned, innate institutional logic differences between CSOs and firms will persist.

Furthermore, we claim that Type 4 has a low level of temporal differences and free-riding and opportunistic behaviour. The government tends to monitor collaboration progress regularly and sets up specific timelines for projects. Also, due to the government's role as a project principal, CSOs may be less reluctant to demonstrate opportunistic behaviour. For instance, government contracts and funding hold CSOs accountable, incentivising meeting deadlines and targets. Akurugoda et al. (2017) offer an example of the government in Sri Lanka, where CSOs assist the government in engaging local communities for policymaking.

4.5 Type 5 Cross-sector Partnership: Government-Firm(s)-CSO(s) Alliance

While the literature points out that cross-sector partnerships require complex interactions among partners, there might be instances where all three actors could work in parallel to develop collaborative projects. In Type 5, governments become direct collaborators rather than mere administrators, influencing the decision-making of B2C2G (business to CSOs to government) alliance employees. These alliance employees also include representatives from the government and, therefore, the government does not share a principal status in the relationship with the B2C2G alliance employees.

One of the most distinctive characteristics of such partnerships is the frequent presence of partners to complement each sector (Selsky & Parker, 2005). Governments could present the coercive and regulatory power that companies and CSOs lack; CSOs could provide knowledge of the local market to help the marketing/R&D department to create opportunities; and firms could bring their hands-on experience and skills to improve the social issues. However, multiple principals having different expectations could also lead to tensions and conflict in agents (Cook et al., 2003). Therefore, while some researchers view such partnerships positively, reframing social issues from diverse viewpoints (Boguslaw, 2002; Huxham & Vangen, 2000; Otiso, 2003; Waddell & Brown, 1997), others consider them unachievable due to conflicting goals and interdependencies (Boguslaw, 2002).

Although the difficulties of managing trisector partnerships are well recognised (Idemudia, 2007; Jamali & Keshishian, 2009), tangible outcomes could be frequently seen in the context of development of industry certification standards and policymaking (Selsky & Parker, 2005). Those are "designed to address issues such as workers' and human rights, environmental degradation, and transnational industrial standards", and are aimed at creating "solutions to problems that increasingly evade competent resolution through nation-state regulations or multilateral agreements" (Moog et al., 2015, p. 472). Such multi-stakeholder initiatives offer a democratic environment for discussion where the economic interests (i.e., opinions of the firms) are balanced by social interests (Moog et al., 2015). The government's role in such multi-stakeholder initiatives could be as lawmaker, adviser, or sponsor. Global public policy networks (GPPN) are the most widely discussed forms of multi-stakeholder initiative, usually formed to develop standards for sustainable business operations. The most visible GPPN, notably the United Nations Global Compact (UNGC) establishes standards for sustainable business practices, promoting ethical values (Detomasi, 2006; Rasche, 2012).

Government, firm, CSO partnerships are formed for pragmatic and ideological reasons such as constraints in the state's resources, strategic goal alignments, and the belief that a single actor cannot solve all the societal problems (McQuaid, 2000). However, in Type 5, challenges stemming from differing institutional logics are expected due to all actors sharing principal status. While partners' institutional logics differ, broadly categorised as market or non-market logic, the discrepancy between CSOs and firms is likely greater than that between CSOs and the government. However, when looking at the relationship between the government and CSOs more closely, it is important to note that their approaches to achieving goals are different. Although CSOs and the government may have the same institutional logic—public service—CSOs adopt a bottom-up approach, while the government leans towards top-down methods (Min, 2022). Thus, in this type, all partners may be sceptical of the motivations of their collaboration partners and fear damage to their organisations if the collaboration fails (Selsky & Parker, 2005). Temporal differences among partners are minimal, as government officials often set specific timelines, similar to other types. The challenges from free-riding and opportunistic behaviour will be low in this type due to high project visibility to stakeholders and built-in checks and balances. Since all the actors work on the same project, stakeholders surrounding them will be keenly interested. The principal status shared by partners fosters mutual accountability, restraining opportunistic behaviour. In Fig. 2, we summarise each type of cross-sector partnerships and visualise the governance mechanisms.

5 Discussion and Conclusion

5.1 Implications for Theory and Literature

This chapter makes several novel contributions to the literature on cross-sector partnerships. First, it employs agency theory to examine the governance structures and challenges, diverging from the previous

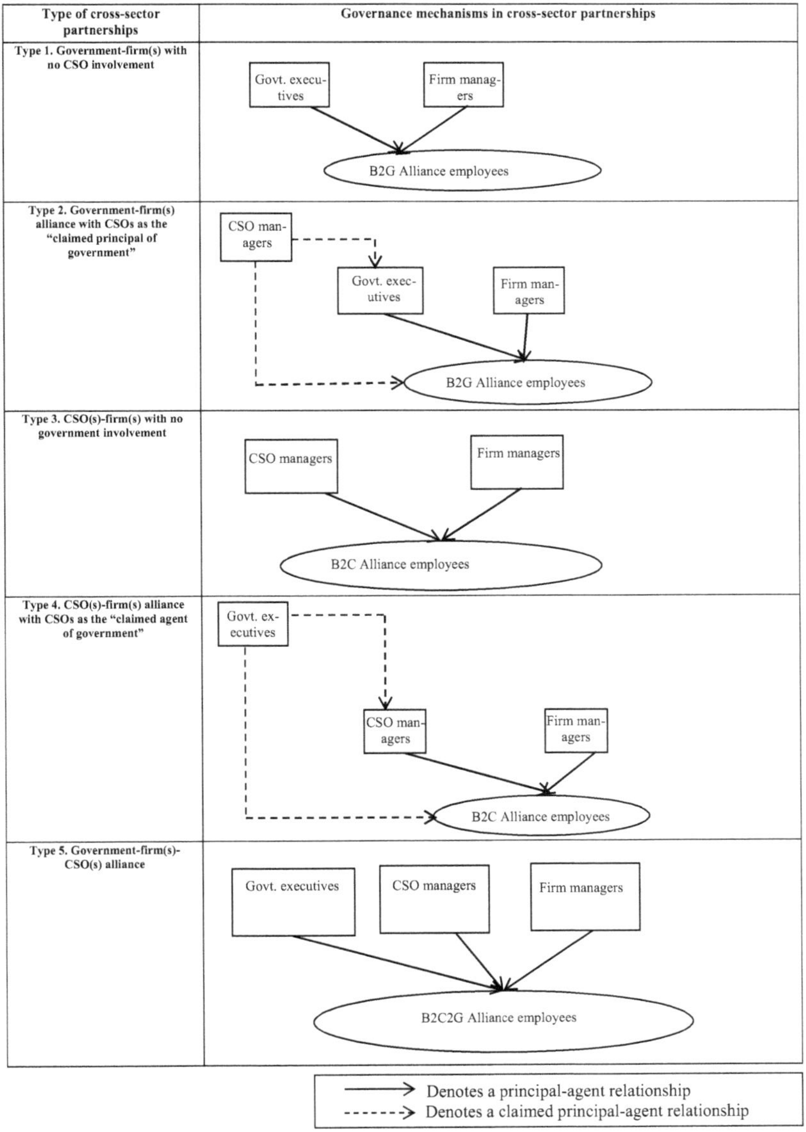

Fig. 2 Type and governance mechanisms of cross-sector partnerships

institutional logic perspectives (Kolk & Lenfant, 2012; Quélin et al., 2017; Savarese et al., 2021). While existing research mostly addresses partnership challenges at the organisational level, this study adopts multiple agency theory to highlight agency-related issues at the micro level involving employees/agents and principals.

Although Rivera-Santos et al. (2017) have also employed agency theory, this chapter extends their work in a distinct way. Rivera-Santos et al. (2017) focus on business-CSO collaborations, overlooking intricate cross-sector engagements involving governments. Addressing this gap, this chapter presents four additional cross-sector collaboration types, in line with Rivera-Santos et al.'s (2017) call to "extend this theory (agency theory) to such types of cross-sector collaborations (NGO-government) and possibly even to tri-sector (firm-NGO-government) collaborations" (p. 872).

Furthermore, this chapter identifies three variants of business-CSO-government partnerships, which are: business-CSO-government partnerships, CSO-firm partnership with CSO as the claimed agent of the government, and government-firm partnership with the government as the claimed agent of CSO. These three variants differ from one another in terms of governance structures. In the first variant, all three organisations share the same principal–agent relationship with the partnership employees. However, in the latter two variants, the government administrator becomes the principal of the CSO manager and the CSO manager becomes the principal of the government administrator, respectively. Previous literature overlooks these variants, potentially undermining the validity of discussions on challenges and mitigation strategies related to such partnerships.

5.2 Implications for Practice

Our discussion on cross-sector partnership typology and the inherent agency issues aims to guide firm managers, CSO managers, and government administrators in effectively managing such collaborations. Below, we offer recommendations on how agency problems can be reduced in these partnerships. Policymakers should engage in partnerships with businesses and CSOs leveraging government administrators' ability to ease conflicts between these entities when taking on a principal role. We argue that government administrators can use both hard and soft contracting to manage tensions between businesses and CSOs. CSOs and governments can also think about partnering with those firms that employ a hybrid institutional logic, that is, firms that embody a combination of market logic and public good logic, e.g., social enterprises. Such partnerships minimise conflicts of interest between the firm managers and other principals. Furthermore, CSO managers should also accept that, although social value creation is at the heart of any cross-sector partnerships, these partnerships should also be generating economic gains. This dual focus is important for attracting profit-oriented firms and enhancing CSOs' financial and resource management skills. Collaborating on profitable social projects can empower CSOs to refine reporting, communication, and strategic planning capabilities. As CSOs evolve into complex multinational organisations, adapting a market logic approach will reduce agency issues in cross-sector partnerships.

5.3 Limitations and Future Research Directions

This study has several limitations that offer avenues for future research. First, the conceptual nature of this study necessitates empirical work to confirm the arguments presented. Conducting an exploratory case study could offer real-world evidence on how the various types of cross-sector partnerships, proposed in this study, are implemented and what routines and cultural elements are adopted to facilitate such distinct types of governance structures. That said, some studies (Fransen & Kolk, 2007; Soundararajan et al., 2019) have previously examined governance structures in multi-stakeholder initiatives in the context of standard setting and global supply chains; however, none of these studies use agency theory and, therefore, empirical evidence on agency problems in such partnerships is almost non-existent. While a large-scale survey could help explain the most and less severe agency problems in different types of partnerships, in-depth case studies are vital for understanding how each problem can be effectively addressed. In addition, more research is needed at the micro level of cross-sector partnerships. We believe that the capabilities, career aspirations, and identity of individual agents could play a part in intensifying or reducing agency problems in various types of cross-sector partnerships. For example, even if all principals agree that a cross-sector partnership should generate both economic and social outcomes, the final implementation of the partnership still falls in the hands of the individual agents. Moreover, researchers should explore the governance structures in cross-sector partnerships that involve multinational enterprises (MNEs) and multinational CSOs. These partnerships introduce complexities stemming from additional agency relationships between MNE headquarters and subsidiaries, as well as CSOs. Finally, scholarly attention must extend to examining how cross-sector partnerships can actually address grand social and environmental challenges and SDGs. A potential avenue is to leverage George et al.'s (2016) framework to assess the extent and manner in which cross-sector partnerships contribute to addressing grand challenges and achieving SDGs, facilitating multi-level coordination and participation.

References

Albareda, L., Lozano, J. M., & Ysa, T. (2007). Public policies on corporate social responsibility: The role of governments in Europe. *Journal of Business Ethics, 74*(4), 391–407. https://doi.org/10.1007/s10551-007-9514-1

Akurugoda, I. R., Barrett, P., & Simpson, A. (2017). Different levels of NGO engagement and reactions of the government: Assessing the Sri Lankan experience. *Journal of Asian Development, 3*(2), 103–119. https://doi.org/10.5296/jad.v3i2.11143

Arenas, D., Sanchez, P., & Murphy, M. (2013). Different paths to collaboration between businesses and civil society and the role of third parties. *Journal of Business Ethics, 115*(4), 723–739. https://doi.org/10.1007/s10551-013-1829-5

Arslaan, M., Karim, N., Kadri, W. B., & Asghar, S. (2020). Local drug delivery to treat chronic periodontitis. *Journal of Bahria University Medical and Dental College, 10*(2), 158–162.

Arthurs, J. D., Hoskisson, R. E., Busenitz, L. W., & Johnson, R. A. (2008). Managerial agents watching other agents: Multiple agency conflicts regarding underpricing in IPO firms. *Academy of Management Journal, 51*(2), 277–294. https://doi.org/10.5465/amj.2008.31767256

Ashman, D. (2001). Civil society collaboration with business: Bringing empowerment back in. *World Development, 29*(7), 1097–1113. https://doi.org/10.1016/S0305-750X(01)00027-4

Barr, A., Fafchamps, M., & Owens, T. (2005). The governance of non-governmental organizations in Uganda. *World Development, 33*(4), 657–679. https://doi.org/10.1016/j.worlddev.2004.09.010

Boguslaw, J. (2002). Have We Arrived? Only When the Integration of Stakeholder Interests Becomes 'Business as Usual.' *Accountability Quarterly, 19*, 52–58.

Borah, D., & Ellwood, P. (2022). The micro-foundations of conflicts in joint university-industry laboratories. *Technological Forecasting and Social Change, 175*, 121377. https://doi.org/10.1016/j.techfore.2021.121377

Borah, D., Malik, K., & Massini, S. (2019). Are engineering graduates ready for R&D jobs in emerging countries? *Teaching-Focused Industry-Academia Collaboration Strategies. Research Policy, 48*(9), 103837. https://doi.org/10.1016/j.respol.2019.103837

Borah, D., Massini, S., & Malik, K. (2023). Teaching benefits of multi-helix university-industry research collaborations: Towards a holistic framework. *Research Policy, 52*(8), 104843. https://doi.org/10.1016/j.respol.2023.104843

Chen, B., & Graddy, E. A. (2010). The effectiveness of nonprofit lead-organization networks for social service delivery. *Nonprofit Management and Leadership, 20*(4), 405–422. https://doi.org/10.1002/nml.20002

Cho, S., & Gillespie, D. F. (2006). A conceptual model exploring the dynamics of government–nonprofit service delivery. *Nonprofit and Voluntary Sector Quarterly, 35*(3), 493–509. https://doi.org/10.1177/0899764006289327

Clarke, A., & Crane, A. (2018). Cross-sector partnerships for systemic change: Systematized literature review and agenda for further research. *Journal of Business Ethics, 150*(2), 303–313. https://doi.org/10.1007/s10551-018-3922-2

Cook, B., Dodds, C., & Mitchell, W. (2003). Social entrepreneurship—False premises and dangerous forebodings. *Australian Journal of Social Issues, 38*(1), 57–72. https://doi.org/10.1002/j.1839-4655.2003.tb01135.x

Dahan, N. M., Doh, J. P., Oetzel, J., & Yaziji, M. (2010). Corporate-NGO collaboration: Co-creating new business models for developing markets.

Long Range Planning, 43(2–3), 326–342. https://doi.org/10.1016/j.lrp.2009.11.003

Darnall, N., Ji, H., & Vázquez-Brust, D. A. (2018). Third-party certification, sponsorship, and consumers' ecolabel use. *Journal of Business Ethics, 150*, 953–969. https://doi.org/10.1007/s10551-016-3138-2

den Hond, F., de Bakker, F. G., & Doh, J. (2015). What prompts companies to collaboration with NGOs? Recent evidence from the Netherlands. *Business & Society, 54*(2), 187–228. https://doi.org/10.1177/0007650312439549

Detomasi, D. A. (2006). International regimes: The case of western corporate governance. *International Studies Review, 8*(2), 225–251. https://doi.org/10.1111/j.1468-2486.2006.00572.x

Etzioni, A. (1961). *Complex organizations: A sociological reader*. Holt, Rinehart and Winston.

Fransen, L. W., & Kolk, A. (2007). Global rule-setting for business: A critical analysis of multi-stakeholder standards. *Organization, 14*(5), 667–684. https://doi.org/10.1177/1350508407080305

Fraser, E. D., Dougill, A. J., Mabee, W. E., Reed, M., & McAlpine, P. (2006). Bottom up and top down: Analysis of participatory processes for sustainability indicator identification as a pathway to community empowerment and sustainable environmental management. *Journal of Environmental Management, 78*(2), 114–127. https://doi.org/10.1016/j.jenvman.2005.04.009

George, G., Howard-Grenville, J., Joshi, A., & Tihanyi, L. (2016). Understanding and tackling societal grand challenges through management research. *Academy of Management Journal, 59*(6), 1880–1895. https://doi.org/10.5465/amj.2016.4007

Gomez-Mejia, L. R., & Balkin, D. B. (1992). Determinants of faculty pay: An agency theory perspective. *Academy of Management Journal, 35*(5), 921–955. https://doi.org/10.5465/256535

Hartman, L. P., Rubin, R. S., & Dhanda, K. K. (2007). The communication of corporate social responsibility: United States and European Union multinational corporations. *Journal of Business Ethics, 74*(4), 373–389. https://doi.org/10.1007/s10551-007-9513-2

Hoskisson, R. E., Hitt, M. A., Ireland, R. D., & Harrison, J. S. (2012). *Competing for advantage*. Cengage Learning.

Huxham, C., & Vangen, S. (2000). Ambiguity, complexity and dynamics in the membership of collaboration. *Human Relations, 53*(6), 771–806. https://doi.org/10.1177/0018726700536002

Idemudia, U. (2007). Community perceptions and expectations: Reinventing the wheels of corporate social responsibility practices in the Nigerian oil industry. *Business and Society Review, 112*(3), 369–405. https://doi.org/10.1111/j.1467-8594.2007.00301.x

Jamali, D., & Keshishian, T. (2009). Uneasy alliances: Lessons learned from partnerships between businesses and NGOs in the context of CSR. *Journal of Business Ethics, 84*(2), 277–295. https://doi.org/10.1007/s10551-008-9708-1

Jay, J. (2013). Navigating paradox as a mechanism of change and innovation in hybrid organizations. *Academy of Management Journal, 56*(1), 137–159. https://doi.org/10.5465/amj.2010.0772

Kolk, A., & Lenfant, F. (2012). Business–NGO collaboration in a conflict setting: Partnership activities in the Democratic Republic of Congo. *Business & Society, 51*(3), 478–511. https://doi.org/10.1177/0007650312446474

Kramer, R. M. (2000). A third sector in the third millennium?. *Voluntas: International Journal of Voluntary and Nonprofit Organizations, 11*(1), 1–23. https://doi.org/10.1023/A:1008914531485

Laasonen, S., Fougère, M., & Kourula, A. (2012). Dominant articulations in academic business and society discourse on NGO–business relations: A critical assessment. *Journal of Business Ethics, 109*(4), 521–545. https://doi.org/10.1007/s10551-011-1143-z

Lenox, M. J., & Nash, J. (2003). Industry self-regulation and adverse selection: A comparison across four trade association programs. *Business Strategy and the Environment, 12*(6), 343–356. https://doi.org/10.1002/bse.380

Liu, T., & Wilkinson, S. (2014). Large-scale public venue development and the application of Public-Private Partnerships (PPPs). *International Journal of Project Management, 32*(1), 88–100. https://doi.org/10.1016/j.ijproman.2013.01.003

Marano, V., & Tashman, P. (2012). MNE/NGO partnerships and the legitimacy of the firm. *International Business Review, 21*(6), 1122–1130. https://doi.org/10.1016/j.ibusrev.2011.12.005

Mars, M. M., & Lounsbury, M. (2009). Raging against or with the private marketplace? Logic hybridity and eco-entrepreneurship. *Journal of Management Inquiry, 18*(1), 4–13. https://doi.org/10.1177/1056492608328234

McQuaid, R. W. (2000). The theory of partnership: Why have partnerships?. In *Public-private partnerships* (pp. 27–53). Routledge.

Min, B. H. (2022). Hybridization in government–civil society organization relationships: An institutional logic perspective. *Nonprofit Management and Leadership, 32*(3), 409–428. https://doi.org/10.1002/nml.21484

Moog, S., Spicer, A., & Böhm, S. (2015). The politics of multi-stakeholder initiatives: The crisis of the Forest Stewardship Council. *Journal of Business Ethics, 128*(3), 469–493. https://doi.org/10.1007/s10551-013-2033-3

Najam, A. (1996). Understanding the third sector: Revisiting the prince, the merchant, and the citizen. *Nonprofit Management and Leadership, 7*(2), 203–219.

Olson, M. (1982). *The rise and decline of nations: Economic growth, stagflation, and social rigidities*. Yale University Press.

Otiso, K. M. (2003). State, voluntary and private sector partnerships for slum upgrading and basic service delivery in Nairobi City Kenya. *Cities, 20*(4), 221–229. https://doi.org/10.1016/S0264-2751(03)00035-0

Pache, A. C., & Santos, F. (2010). When worlds collide: The internal dynamics of organizational responses to conflicting institutional demands. *Academy of Management Review, 35*(3), 455–476. https://doi.org/10.5465/amr.35.3.zok455

Peloza, J., & Falkenberg, L. (2009). The role of collaboration in achieving corporate social responsibility objectives. *California Management Review, 51*(3), 95–113.

Quélin, B. V., Kivleniece, I., & Lazzarini, S. (2017). Public-private collaboration, hybridity and social value: Towards new theoretical perspectives. *Journal of Management Studies, 54*(6), 763–792. https://doi.org/10.1111/joms.12274

Rasche, A. (2012). Global policies and local practice: Loose and tight couplings in multi-stakeholder initiatives. *Business Ethics Quarterly, 22*(4), 679–708. https://doi.org/10.5840/beq201222444

Rivera-Santos, M., Rufin, C., & Wassmer, U. (2017). Alliances between firms and non-profits: A multiple and behavioural agency approach. *Journal of Management Studies, 54*(6), 854–875. https://doi.org/10.1111/joms.12271

Rivera-Santos, M., & Rufín, C. (2010). Global village vs. small town: Understanding networks at the Base of the Pyramid. *International Business Review, 19*(2), 126–139. https://doi.org/10.1016/j.ibusrev.2009.07.001

Sakarya, S., Bodur, M., Yildirim-Öktem, Ö., & Selekler-Göksen, N. (2012). Social alliances: Business and social enterprise collaboration for social transformation. *Journal of Business Research, 65*(12), 1710–1720. https://doi.org/10.1016/j.jbusres.2012.02.012

Savarese, C., Huybrechts, B., & Hudon, M. (2021). The influence of interorganizational collaboration on logic conciliation and tensions within hybrid organizations: Insights from social enterprise–corporate collaborations. *Journal of Business Ethics, 173*, 709–721. https://doi.org/10.1007/s10551-020-04557-7

Seitanidi, M. M., & Crane, A. (2013). Conclusion: Re-imagining the future of social partnerships and responsible business. In *Social partnerships and responsible business* (pp. 416–435). Routledge.

Selsky, J. W., & Parker, B. (2005). Cross-sector partnerships to address social issues: Challenges to theory and practice. *Journal of Management, 31*(6), 849–873. https://doi.org/10.1177/0149206305279601

Shrivastava, P., & Guimarães-Costa, N. (2017). Achieving environmental sustainability: The case for multi-layered collaboration across disciplines and players. *Technological Forecasting and Social Change, 116*, 340–346. https://doi.org/10.1016/j.techfore.2016.11.019

Soundararajan, V., Brown, J. A., & Wicks, A. C. (2019). Can multi-stakeholder initiatives improve global supply chains? Improving deliberative capacity with a stakeholder orientation. *Business Ethics Quarterly, 29*(3), 385–412. https://doi.org/10.1017/beq.2018.38

Suchman, M. C. (1995). Managing legitimacy: Strategic and institutional approaches. *Academy of Management Review, 20*(3), 571–610. https://doi.org/10.5465/amr.1995.9508080331

Sullivan, H., & Skelcher, C. (2002). *Working across boundaries: Collaboration in public services*. Palgrave Macmillan.

Teegen, H., Doh, J. P., & Vachani, S. (2004). The importance of nongovernmental organizations (NGOs) in global governance and value creation: An international business research agenda. *Journal of International Business Studies, 35*(6), 463–483. https://doi.org/10.1057/palgrave.jibs.8400112

Tencati, A., & Zsolnai, L. (Eds.). (2010). *The collaborative enterprise: Creating values for a sustainable world* (Vol. 9). Peter Lang.

Torugsa, N. A., O'Donohue, W., & Hecker, R. (2013). Proactive CSR: An empirical analysis of the role of its economic, social and environmental dimensions on the association between capabilities and performance. *Journal of Business Ethics, 115*(2), 383–402. https://doi.org/10.1007/s10551-012-1405-4

UN. (2015). *Transforming our world: The 2030 agenda for sustainable development*. General Assembley 70 session.

Van den Hurk, M., & Verhoest, K. (2015). The governance of public–private partnerships in sports infrastructure: Interfering complexities in Belgium.

International Journal of Project Management, 33(1), 201–211. https://doi.org/10.1016/j.ijproman.2014.05.005

Van Huijstee, M., & Glasbergen, P. (2008). The practice of stakeholder dialogue between multinationals and NGOs. *Corporate Social Responsibility and Environmental Management, 15*(5), 298–310. https://doi.org/10.1002/csr.171

Van Huijstee, M., & Glasbergen, P. (2010). NGOs moving business: An analysis of contrasting strategies. *Business & Society, 49*(4), 591–618. https://doi.org/10.1177/0007650310365516

Van Marrewijk, A., Clegg, S. R., Pitsis, T. S., & Veenswijk, M. (2008). Managing public–private megaprojects: Paradoxes, complexity, and project design. *International Journal of Project Management, 26*(6), 591–600. https://doi.org/10.1016/j.ijproman.2007.09.007

Waddock, S. A. (1988). Building successful social partnerships. *MIT Sloan Management Review, 29*(4), 17.

Waddell, S. (2017). *Societal learning and change: How governments, business and civil society are creating solutions to complex multi-stakeholder problems*. Routledge.

Waddell, S., & Brown, L. D. (1997). Fostering intersectoral partnering: A guide to promoting cooperation among government, business, and civil society actors. *IDR Reports, 13*(3), 1–26.

Wood, E. M. (1990). The uses and abuses of 'civil society'. *Socialist Register*, 26.

Wright, C. F. (2016). Leveraging reputational risk: Sustainable sourcing campaigns for improving labour standards in production networks. *Journal of Business Ethics, 137*(1), 195–210. https://doi.org/10.1007/s10551-015-2552-1

13

A Microfoundational Framework of Institutions: Knowledge Transfer in Traditional Crafts for Sustainable Economic Growth

Krishna Kumar Balaraman and Elizabeth L. Rose

1 Introduction

Institutions, which are critical for knowledge transfer, are influenced by societal and behavioural norms as well as by trade and business. Institutions can constrain human interactions (Hodgson, 2006; North, 1991), while providing a framework for efficient social and economic interactions. While previous research has studied aspects of institutional voids (e.g., Gao et al., 2017; Luiz et al., 2017) and institutional microprocesses (Gray et al., 2015), understanding the situation in emerging economies can benefit from a consideration of institutional players at the micro, meso, and macro levels. This is especially important in the context of

K. K. Balaraman
Indian Institute of Technology Jodhpur, Jodhpur, Rajasthan, India
e-mail: krishna@iitj.ac.in

E. L. Rose (✉)
Indian Institute of Management Udaipur, Udaipur, Rajasthan, India
e-mail: elizabeth.rose@iimu.ac.in

N. Sinkovics et al. (eds.), *International Business and SDG 8*, The Academy of International Business, https://doi.org/10.1007/978-3-031-46802-5_13

culturally embedded industries, particularly the intergenerational knowledge transfer that is critical to the long-term viability and survival of traditional arts, as envisaged in the SDG 8.2 (https://unric.org/en/sdg-8/) target of focusing on 'high-value added and labour-intensive sectors'. Each of the institutional levels can contribute to addressing the various goals of SDG 8, from promoting development-oriented policies to local culture and products.

In this chapter, we present a conceptual framework of the microfoundations of institutions for knowledge transfer, highlighting how multilevel institutions enable the preservation of traditional arts and crafts, despite past colonial rule that decimated handicraft industries in countries such as India and China (Jones, 2023, p. 101). Exploratory analysis based on inputs from field work in the Indian arts and craft sector is also presented. We highlight the multilevel nature of institutions, and the importance of the micro and macro levels in this traditional industry.

2 Theoretical Background

The path-dependent nature of knowledge challenges its transfer and integration. Individuals are critical to the storage and transfer of knowledge that is often tacit and implicit (Argote & Ingram, 2000). Knowledge repositories that exist in groups often rely on technological tools for capturing explicit technology, in interrelated task networks (Argote & Ingram, 2000). The capture of knowledge—and its transfer from individuals to groups, and then to a larger network of constituents—requires an understanding of institutional microfoundations. In the context of traditional industries in emerging economies, the nature of knowledge capture—and the associated economic implications—differ at each level. Connecting the cultural basis of traditional knowledge transfer to modern methods of institutionalised economic methods is important for the long-term sustainability of dependent communities, such as entrepreneurs involved in the production of culturally embedded crafts. This also involves co-opting communities into traditional knowledge-driven industries for both economic impact and the maintenance and transfer of knowledge. This view leads to the need to expand our understanding of institutions as a multilevel construct, in the context of preserving traditional craft and knowledge and the associated economic sustenance, consistent with the SDG 8 agenda.

2.1 Institutions

Institutions have been described as 'systems of established and prevalent social rules that structure social interactions' (Hodgson, 2006, p. 2). North (2016, p. 74) proposes that an 'institutional framework provides the incentives that dictate the kind of skills and knowledge perceived to have the maximum pay-off', thus connecting the economic impact of institutions with the economic well-being of individuals (North, 1991). In the context of traditional arts and crafts, especially in emerging economies, institution-enabled knowledge transfer has the potential to contribute to legitimacy, as 'traditional techniques and production methods [are] often essential to the perceived authenticity of a producer and its products' (Sasaki et al., 2021, p. 249). This view considers culturally embedded businesses (either individual or consisting of a small social structure) as micro-institutions that exist in the presence of larger (and evolving) institutional environments, which suggests a need to study the institutional microfoundations of knowledge transfer in multilevel settings. The role of institutions in knowledge transfer is also driven by the need to enable the transfer and preservation of traditional knowledge in societies where long-followed methods of knowledge sharing are being disrupted, often due to technological and economy-based shifts in professional choices, putting the survival of traditional knowledge at risk (Jones, 2023). The problem may also be viewed as the microfoundations of institutional mechanisms or institutions as multilevel entities—micro, meso, and macro (Gray et al., 2015)—that enable knowledge capture and transfer. Thus, SD8 goals, such as encouraging the formalisation and growth of small and medium enterprises (SDG 8.3), can be addressed by understanding multilevel institutions. Large institutions, such as UNESCO, acknowledge that 'heritage constitutes a source of identity and cohesion for communities disrupted by bewildering change and economic instability' (https://en.unesco.org/themes/protecting-our-heritage-and-fostering-creativity). This view is further supported by UN's SDG goals, particularly SDG 8's aim to 'promote inclusive and sustainable economic growth, employment and decent work for all'.

2.2 Traditional Industry—Crafts

Craft is characterised by the prioritisation of human engagement (Kroezen et al., 2021) and a broad range of economic activities (highlighted in SDG 8.1 and 8.2), with a combination of traditional and transformed skills embedded in local communities and traditions (Sasaki et al., 2021). Craft firms can be considered as traditional and entrepreneurial, connected with both informal and formal networks in which institutional actors, such as trade associations (e.g., SDG 8.A), may act as network hubs (Thevenard-Puthod & Picard, 2011). These networks include individuals or small, limited-access groups in which the traditional knowledge is embedded in particular members and the tasks that they perform (McGrath & Argote, 2001). The traditional crafts industry involves a deep cultural embeddedness in local traditions, and small units involved in crafts must navigate the pressures of cultural specificity in products and processes to maintain their relevance (Sasaki et al., 2021). Craft can be seen as both traditional and industrialised (Kroezen et al., 2021), subject to transformation and cultural transposition (Sasaki et al., 2021). This perspective on the phenomenon of craft as traditional-transformed-industrialised is illustrated in Fig. 1, using the Indian examples of textiles and the specialised craft of Thanjavur painting (https://en.wikipedia.org/wiki/Thanjavur_painting).

2.3 Institutional Roles in SDG Goals

The role of institutions in creating sustainable art and craft sectors in emerging economies is well-illustrated by SDG 8 goals (Frey, 2017, Table 4) of promoting inclusive and sustainable growth. Artisans' attachment (at the micro-institutional level) to their work has

Craft	Traditional	Transformed	Industrialised
Focus	Intent Look Material	Adaptation Re-purposed	Process Techniques Transformation
Market / buyer	Exclusive	Discerning	Mass
How knowledge is transferred	Master-apprentice	Formal teaching + apprentice	Formal industrialised training
Illustration 1: Textile industry	• Hand-printed • Veg. dye • Organic cotton	• Handprinted • Synthetic dyes	• Machine-printed • Synthetic dye • Look-alike
Illustration 2: Thanjavur paintings	• Individualised • Taught 1-1 • Unique • Democratising art	• Modern art materials • Both modern patterns and traditional motifs	• Made to order, e.g.: https://www.myangadi.com/ma7tpmis007-peacock-tanjore-painting

Fig. 1 Craft forms as traditional-transformed-industrialised

economic impact, as they make choices based on discerning vs non-discerning buyers (Ranganathan, 2018); tourists looking for souvenirs (e.g., SDG 8.9) represent a very different market to collectors of fine art. Artisans also create economic value, and labour-market institutions can protect the economic interests of craft workers, particularly in emerging economies (Ranganathan, 2018). Understanding the role of institutions in preserving knowledge in this industry may help to sustain the value of traditional craft and maintain these economic imperatives, facilitating SDG goals. Institutions influence the uncertainty faced by economic actors (Luiz et al., 2017), requiring us to understand the nature of institutions in the traditional crafts industry as a multilevel construct, including individuals and groups.

2.4 Knowledge Transfer

Even in the evolving knowledge-oriented economy, traditional industries such as local crafts are emerging as a critical resource for wealth creation and income generation, especially in base-of-the-pyramid communities (Wang et al., 2020). The continued value of such crafts depends on preserving the authenticity of tools, processes, and knowledge. This requires a legitimising mechanism to preserve and transform, as relevant, the knowhow of traditional crafts and the associated production imperatives.

Institutions have been important in preserving such knowledge, as evidenced by the revival of the handloom weaving industry in India (Khaire, 2011). Government policies (Wang et al., 2020) and government-promoted institutions (highlighted in SDG 8.3) such as *Kadhi Gramodyog Bhavan* (www.khadigramodyogbhavan.com) and the National Institute of Fashion Technology (https://www.nift.ac.in/theinstitute) have helped in the preservation, promotion, and transformation of cultural goods and traditional craft.

Traditional artisans and aggregators, such as trade associations, also play key roles in preserving knowledge and continuation pertaining to traditional arts and crafts. The survival of the art and artisans depends on human capital, in terms of specific knowledge (Gimeno et al., 1997). Hence, it is important to consider institutional mechanisms at multiple levels, to create a framework with attributes that can help in understanding knowledge capture, preservation, and transfer mechanisms for maintaining the cultural and economic imperatives of traditional crafts, supporting SDG 8 goals.

2.5 Microfoundations in Knowledge Transfer

Individuals are critical to tacit knowledge in environments that require skilled human capital (Rothaermel & Hess, 2007), such as traditional crafts. Knowledge accumulation and preservation is based on organisational memory that resides in the minds of individuals and the connections among them (Aggarwal et al., 2017). An individual lost is knowledge lost.

'Rational behaviour (from neoclassical economics) and collective reasonable behaviour (from jurisprudence)' provide a microfoundational basis for the development of institutional mechanisms (Van de Ven & Lifschitz, 2013, p. 156). The microfoundational view of labour also suggests that knowledge is encoded in structure, and 'establishing new organisational and institutional technologies' (Kogut, 2008, pp. 53–55) facilitates the within-group transfer of personal knowledge. Thus, knowledge transfer depends on individuals and on group-level routines and behaviours (Aggarwal et al., 2017). From the microfoundational support provided by goal-framing theory (Foss & Lindenberg, 2013), knowledge transfer may depend on the value creation associated with the specific goal. External intervention for knowledge transfer, such as that from institutions, may have positive or negative effects, based on the value that participants place on the goal (Osterloh & Frey, 2000). Formal institutions can assist the long-term succession planning that traditionally relies on artisan-apprentice relationships within a community, by providing knowledge transfer opportunities to new players who are talented but not embedded in the traditional system (supporting SDG 8.3 and 8.5). Knowledge can be preserved and transferred by opting-in new participants who possess the economic incentive to undertake a career in traditional crafts (e.g., SDG 8.2, 8.3, and 8.6). Thus, institutions may provide a positive *crowding-in* effect by facilitating both economic incentives and social recognition (Osterloh & Frey, 2000).

Hence, a value-based (cultural and economic) view of knowledge transfer, preservation, and transformation in traditional craft (Fig. 2) depends on understanding the microfoundations of institutions at the micro, meso, and macro levels (Gray et al, 2015; Kogut, 2008).

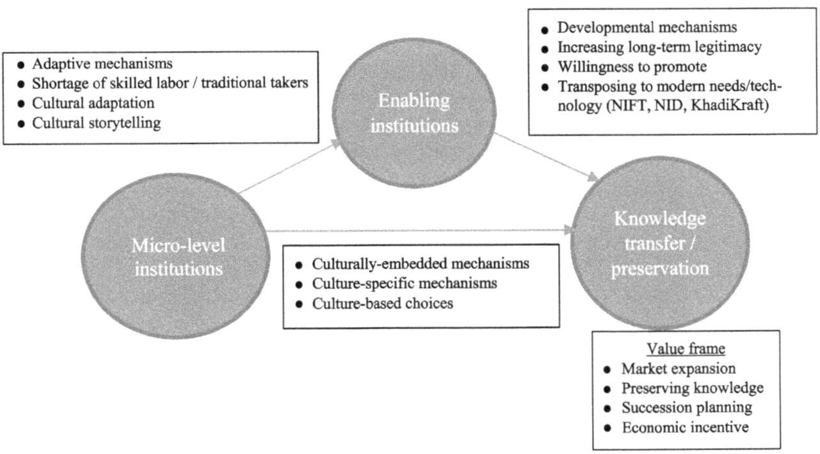

Fig. 2 Theoretical view of microfoundations of institutions for knowledge transfer

3 Framework

In the craft context, different levels of institutional mechanisms involve (a) individuals or small groups of traditional workers; (b) group-level associations such as trade guilds; and (c) larger entities such as educational institutions, government promotional councils, etc. The authenticity provided by traditional artisans' personal skills and processes, and the legitimacy provided by non-personalised structures and associations, combine to provide effective knowledge preservation and transfer. The conceptual structure of knowledge transfer is shown in Fig. 3; SDG 8 goals (Frey, 2017, Table 4) can be addressed by each institutional level.

At the micro level, many individual artisans continue to work alone or in age-old traditional settings, such as *durry* rug manufacturing (http://salawasdurry.com/) in India; these small groups aid in preserving knowledge and providing economic relevance to skilled participants. In such settings, skills, attitudes, and coordination mechanisms are embedded in the traditional craft (Kroezen et al., 2021), while transformation happens in the use of technology to approach markets. In the context of craft as

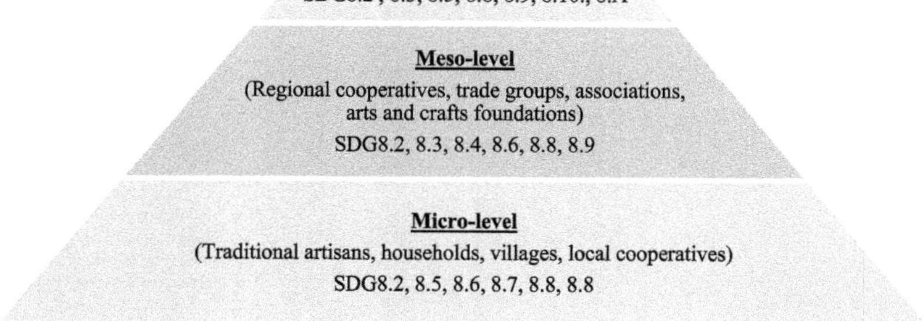

Fig. 3 Microfoundations of institutions in an emerging economy's traditional craft industry

traditional and industrial, this represents a transformed craft category (Fig. 1; Sasaki et al., 2021).

Meso-level institutions, such as voluntary and non-governmental organisations (http://www.handicrafts.nic.in/Page.aspx?MID=wwmkeKEl3ZxxDEv6idiu3Q==), play important roles in introducing new participants to the preservation of traditional knowledge, by connecting the knowledge to economic imperatives. For instance, Sangam (https://sangamproject.net/sangam-platform), a platform for craft-design partnerships, promotes linkages that offer long-term mutual benefit. Another example, Sadhna (https://sadhna.org/), builds a strong artisan base in handmade ethnic clothing by training non-traditional players, particularly tribal women, thus addressing both knowledge transfer and economic initiatives, consistent with SDG 8.8.

At the macro level, educational institutions such as India's National Institute of Fashion Technology contribute, as do governmental entities such as the Ministry of Textiles, which has schemes for handloom clusters and silk sectors that include provisions for technology upgradation funds (e.g., Comprehensive Handicrafts Cluster Development Scheme). This reflects the role of macro institutions in preserving knowledge and encouraging the transformation of traditional industries by including new players and the transposition of cultural products by technology adoption and market expansion.

We also need to consider the transformation and transposition of traditional craft for modern-day relevance, addressing new domestic and international markets (Sasaki et al., 2021). Considering recent models of craft configurations of skills and attitudes (Kroezen et al., 2021), we present a conceptual framework of the microfoundations of institutions for knowledge transfer in the traditional crafts industry in an emerging economy; see Fig. 4.

4 Exploratory Study

We report on some exploratory work undertaken in India's traditional arts and craft industry. We developed an initial guide for semi-structured interviews, and contacted a field researcher from a project studying this

Institutional level	Skills	Attitudes	Coordination mechanism for knowledge transfer
Micro	• Mastery • All-roundedness • Embodied expertise	• Dedication • Communality • Exploration	• Family • Apprentice • Person-to-person
Meso	• Transferable • Market awareness • Product adaptability / customisation • Inter-connectedness / networking	• Preservation • Exclusivity • Monetisation • Coordination	• Guilds • Industry grouping • Cooperatives • Positive *crowding-in*
Macro	• Commodity • Specificity • Abstract expertise	• Detachment / individuality • Planning • Exploitation	• Codified education • Knowledge capture mechanisms • Large institutions (including government)

Fig. 4 A conceptual framework of institutional microfoundations for knowledge transfer in an emerging economy's traditional crafts industry

industry, who provided input on the guide and shared some responses based on their interactions with artisans. We received written responses to some of our questions, from four artisans in the 'bone and horn' craft industry in the northwestern region of India.

4.1 Bone and Horn Craft

Traditionally, this craft utilised ivory. With the abolition of the ivory trade, driven by wildlife protection, artists shifted to carving bones and horns, producing items used primarily for decorative purposes (https://industries.rajasthan.gov.in/content/industries/handmadeinrajasthandepartment/artandcraft/hornandbonework/bonework.html). The ivory ban created transformation in the craft, with artisans experimenting with different material while retaining their traditional methods. The artists are conscious about using benign methods of raw material 'extraction', such as reuse and recycling of products, and using bones and horns from dead animals, rather than killing animals for the purpose of accessing material (http://www.rajasthancrafts.com/bone-horn.php). While the method used has not changed, differences in texture and quality have affected customers' perceptions regarding the value of the goods.

4.2 Analysis from Responses

Artisan 1 learned the art from their father, who originally worked with ivory. Shifting to new materials proved to be labour-intensive and time-consuming. The change of material also affected economic returns to the artisans; ivory items had yielded better returns. Previously strong export orders diminished with the change. Facing challenges from both increased input costs and lower returns, this artisan sells products predominantly through art galleries and exhibitions. They have local partnerships, but do not work with exporters. There is no nearby cluster of families engaging in the same craft.

While the artisan, as part of the micro-level institution, uses adaptive mechanisms with culturally embedded skills, the market and economic imperative creates stronger pressure on knowledge transfer/preservation (see Fig. 2), compared with earlier times. From the conceptual framework (Fig. 4), the coordination mechanism for knowledge transfer is between person-to-person and family, with attitudes of dedication and exploration. The artisan is surviving economically, but the survival of the art, in terms of knowledge transfer for the future, is yet to be addressed. Knowledge transfer happens through artisans at a micro-institutional level (Fig. 3).

Artisan 2 indicates that there is no cluster, but rather a group of people working for a master artist on various tasks. The group operates like a family. The artisan sells through exporters and has no local partnerships. The past was characterised by respect for the products and substantial export orders. However, the change of material lowered the perceived quality (probably an issue of value) and has affected the market. Interestingly, business flourished during Covid times, perhaps due to people staying at home and spending money on traditional local craft products to decorate their residences. Knowledge transfer occurs through artisans at a micro-institutional level, as well as through a meso-level arts and craft foundation (Fig. 3). The coordination mechanism for knowledge transfer in this setting is person-to-person and apprentice-based. Attitudes of communality, with the embodied expertise skills of critical artisans, facilitate the survival of the art and the artists.

Artisan 3 sells predominantly through art galleries and exhibitions, without local partners or exporter connections. The ivory phase was a flourishing period, in terms of economic returns and appreciation of the craft. However, the change of material resulted in degradation of both the perceived quality of the craft and the economic returns to traditional artisans. Moreover, competition from users of modern material and paints, through technology-facilitated reproduction of original products, is causing a downward spiral of the original craft. Recent developments, such as government-driven tax changes and demonetisation policies, along with Covid, have affected this artisan's financial well-being, putting both the survival of the craft and the related trade in peril. Intermediaries such as export houses and businesspersons are capturing most of the monetary value of the products, which has led to the degradation of the art and the artisan's quality of life.

This situation indicates that lack of economic incentive and erosion of culturally embedded mechanisms at the micro level (Fig. 2) can affect knowledge transfer and preservation. Both the art and the artisans must survive for future knowledge transfer and preservation. Further, it is generally micro-institutional players that primarily effect knowledge transfer and preservation.

Like Artisan 1, Artisan 4 was taught by their ivory-working father. Following the ivory ban, different materials made the process longer and more tedious. Market rates also reduced. Earlier, artisans felt respected, and the craft had good potential. Now, the change of material and falling income create challenges. Noting that the choice of raw material rests with the artisan, Artisan 4 sells through exporters and local buyers. While this artisan is not part of a cluster or group, they have associations with art and craft foundations. Thus, knowledge preservation is primarily through artisan-level contact.

Information from the four bone and horn artisans suggests that knowledge transfer occurs predominantly at the micro level, through person-to-person or group contact. The economic imperative is met primarily through local exhibitions or exporters; these are largely commercial operations with little inclination toward facilitating the sharing and transfer of traditional knowledge. Even from this limited exploratory evidence, we gain insights into the challenges faced by artisans, associated with the changing environment related to the sharing and preservation of knowledge in India's traditional arts and craft industry.

Secondary research provides supportive evidence that individual artisans and families are responsible for knowledge preservation in the traditional art and craft area, reinforcing the importance of micro-level institutions. For instance, the centuries-old hand-block printing technique known as *bagru*, from northwestern India, has been maintained by within-family generational involvement (https://indianexpress.com/article/meta-stories-of-strength-2022/chip-off-an-ancient-block-how-a-bagru-artisan-family-stamped-out-covid-blues-7828976/). In this craft, long-standing methods and materials are still utilised, and collections of artisans perform various traditional roles, while addressing the economic imperative. However, challenges arise from technological developments and attempts by commercial players to use machines for enhanced productivity. In the above-referenced article, an artisan notes that the wealth of knowledge is one reason that they do not consider abandoning this craft:

> *Bagru is in no danger of dying out. But the more we rely on machines, the more we discontinue a certain practice, the more traditional wisdom we lose forever. Our methods and experiences are not stored in computer files, they are passed down generations. The only way to keep our craft alive is to keep practising it.... a craft needs practitioners to keep it thriving.*

While there is a strong need for macro-level institutions, such as governments, to introduce supportive policies, it is critical to involve more youth, create contemporary motifs with traditional methods, and involve meso-level institutions such as large design houses, to ensure the preservation of traditional knowledge and to maintain the economic viability of these employment-generating craft businesses.

5 Conclusions

Our limited exploratory analysis suggests that knowledge transfer in Indian traditional craft design and production happens predominantly at micro level, enabled by meso- and macro-level institutions (Fig. 3). Higher-level institutions are important in terms of economic and policy support (SDG 8.3), which can facilitate the survival of the art and the artisans. This ensures knowledge sharing and preservation. Knowledge can be viewed as inherited, in a broad sense, providing the craft with a survival edge (Agarwal et al., 2004). Previous research (Gao et al., 2017) also posits that reputation is an important driver of long-term survival; for traditional arts and craft, the sharing and preservation of knowledge is important for authenticity-based reputation and, by extension, the survival of both art and artisan. The ability of micro-level institutions to perform their roles in traditional knowledge transfer is enmeshed with, and dependent on, the other institutional levels' acting as effective economic and policy agents. This study highlights that different institutional levels contribute to SDG goals.

As the survival of both the art and the artisans is needed for future knowledge transfer and preservation, the theoretical view should include survival as a mediator, at the micro level, between knowledge transfer and preservation. Figure 5 this modified view.

Further, artisans' abilities to cope with the challenges and opportunities evolving from ever-advancing technology require support from enabling institutions, especially with respect to promoting and establishing the authenticity of craft-related products. This could come from meso-level institutions, such as trade groups, but the primary support needs to be from macro-level institutions, including regulating authorities, certification bodies, and specialised arts and craft associations. Preserving authenticity is critical to the art's reputation, and thus the long-term survival (Gao et al., 2017) of both the craft and the artisans. Retaining authenticity requires the sharing and preservation of traditional knowledge. Today, the non-economic aspect of knowledge transfer is based on the traditional involvement of artisans, consistent with SDG 8.9. Policy-level factors (SDG 8.3) for engaging new entrants into traditional art and craft practices (SDG 8.5, 8.6, and 8.8), not just

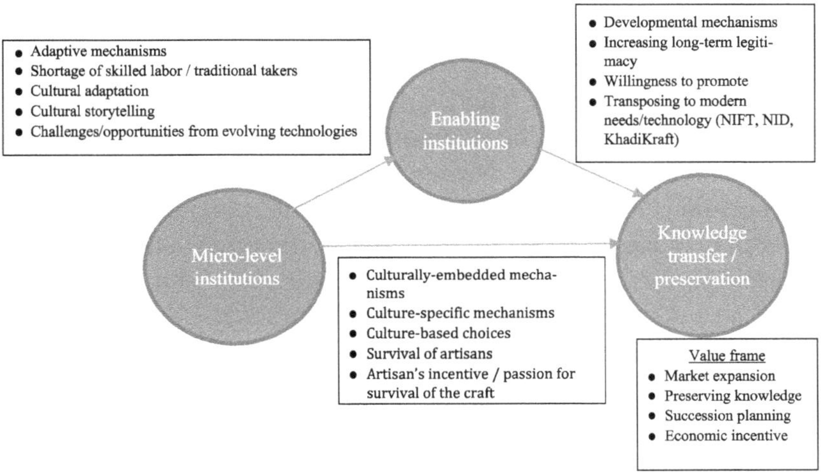

Fig. 5 Modified theoretical view of microfoundations of institution for knowledge transfer

as an economic imperative, must be explored, especially in the context of knowledge sharing and preservation. A modified conceptual framework including these points is presented in Fig. 6.

Institutional Level	Skills	Attitudes	Coordination Mechanism for Knowledge Transfer
Micro	• Mastery • All-roundedness • Embodied expertise	• Dedication • Communality • Exploration • Survival of the art	• Family • Apprentice • Person-to-person
Meso	• Transferable • Market awareness • Product adaptability / customisation • Inter-connectedness / networking	• Preservation • Exclusivity • Monetisation • Coordination • Survival of the artisan	• Guilds • Industry grouping • Cooperatives • Positive *crowding-in* • Channelising new entrants
Macro	• Commodity • Specificity • Abstract expertise	• Detachment individuality • Planning • Exploitation	• Codified education • Knowledge capture mechanisms • Large institutions (including government) • Protection mechanism for authenticity

Fig. 6 Modified conceptual framework of microfoundations of institutions for knowledge transfer in the traditional crafts industry in an emerging economy

The exploratory work also raises questions regarding product vs. process in the preservation and transfer of knowledge in the context of arts and crafts. How should traditional industries adapt to changes in product and processes (Fig. 7)? How should institutions at various levels interact to protect the traditional ways, and facilitate the survival of artisans and the art? In seeking to address such questions, research can contribute to socially relevant topics with real impact, including SDG 8. This chapter teases out some factors, indicated in the framework, that need further conceptualisation and testing. We aim to contribute toward an understanding of multilevel institutional effects and related policy in knowledge sharing and preservation, using the context of India's traditional arts and craft industry.

We propose a multilevel framework to investigate the role of institutions as intermediaries in the transfer of culturally embedded knowledge. The multilevel view of institutions can help to illuminate the micro-foundational interactions of institutional players in both preserving (and expanding) traditional knowledge bases, while maintaining economic incentives and development and providing decent work opportunities to more people. Succession planning can move from traditional, family-based approaches, to include a larger talent pool of artisans and creators, thus supporting the SDG 8 vision.

Craft	Traditional	Transformed	Industrialised
Focus	• Intent • Look • Material • Process • Product	• Adaptation • Re-purposed • Protect process with evolving technique • Material substitution	• Process • Techniques • Transformation • Material change
Market / Buyer	Exclusive	Discerning	Mass
How knowledge is transferred	Master-apprentice	Formal teaching + apprentice	Formal industrialised training
Illustration 1: Textile industry	• Hand-printed • Vegetable dye • Organic cotton	• Hand-printed • Synthetic dyes	• Machine-printed • Synthetic dye • Look-alike
Illustration 2: Thanjavur paintings	• Individualised • Taught 1-1 • Unique • Democratising art	• Modern art materials used • Both modern patterns and traditional motifs	• Made to order, e.g.: https://www.myangadi.com/ma7tpmis007-peacock-tanjore-painting

Fig. 7 Modified craft forms as traditional-transformed-industrialised

References

Agarwal, R., Echambadi, R., Franco, A. M., & Sarkar, M. B. (2004). Knowledge transfer through inheritance: Spin-out generation, development, and survival. *Academy of Management Journal, 47*(4), 501–522.

Aggarwal, V. A., Posen, H. E., & Workiewicz, M. (2017). Adaptive capacity to technological change: A microfoundational approach. *Strategic Management Journal, 38*(6), 1212–1231.

Argote, L., & Ingram, P. (2000). Knowledge transfer: A basis for competitive advantage in firms. *Organizational Behavior and Human Decision Processes, 82*(1), 150–169.

Comprehensive Handicrafts Cluster Development Scheme (CHCDS). Ministry of Textiles Schemes, Government of India. http://texmin.nic.in/sites/default/files/11d_Guidelines_of_development_of_mega_cluster_scheme_Handicrafts_nmcc_cs_20090312.pdf. Accessed 21 Feb 2022.

Foss, N. J., & Lindenberg, S. (2013). Microfoundations for strategy: A goal-framing perspective on the drivers of value creation. *Academy of Management Perspectives, 27*(2), 85–102.

Frey, D. F. (2017). Economic growth, full employment and decent work: The means and ends in SDG 8. *The International Journal of Human Rights, 21*(8), 1164–1184.

Gao, C., Zuzul, T., Jones, G., & Khanna, T. (2017). Overcoming institutional voids: A reputation-based view of long-run survival. *Strategic Management Journal, 38*(11), 2147–2167.

Gimeno, J., Folta, T. B., Cooper, A. C., & Woo, C. Y. (1997). Survival of the fittest? Entrepreneurial human capital and the persistence of underperforming firms. *Administrative Science Quarterly, 42*(4), 750–783.

Gray, B., Purdy, J. M., & Ansari, S. (2015). From interactions to institutions: Microprocesses of framing and mechanisms for the structuring of institutional fields. *Academy of Management Review, 40*(1), 115–143.

Hodgson, G. M. (2006). What are institutions? *Journal of Economic Issues, 40*(1), 1–25.

Jones, G. (2023). *Deeply responsible business: A global history of values-driven leadership*. Harvard University Press.

Khaire, M. (2011). The Indian fashion industry and traditional Indian crafts. *Business History Review, 85*(2), 345–366.

Kogut, B. (2008). *Knowledge, options, and institutions*. Oxford University Press.

Kroezen, J., Ravasi, D., Sasaki, I., Żebrowska, M., & Suddaby, R. (2021). Configurations of craft: Alternative models for organizing work. *Academy of Management Annals, 15*(2), 502–536.

Luiz, J., Stringfellow, D., & Jefthas, A. (2017). Institutional complementarity and substitution as an internationalization strategy: The emergence of an African multinational giant. *Global Strategy Journal, 7*(1), 83–103.

McGrath, J. E., & Argote, L. (2001). Group processes in organizational contexts. In M. A. Hogg & R. S. Tindale (Eds.), *Blackwell handbook of social psychology: Group processes* (pp. 603–627). Blackwell Publishing.

North, D. C. (1991). Institutions. *Journal of Economic Perspectives, 5*(1), 97–112.

North, D. C. (2016). Institutions and economic theory. *The American Economist, 61*(1), 72–76.

Osterloh, M., & Frey, B. S. (2000). Motivation, knowledge transfer, and organizational forms. *Organization Science, 11*(5), 538–550.

Ranganathan, A. (2018). The artisan and his audience: Identification with work and price setting in a handicraft cluster in Southern India. *Administrative Science Quarterly, 63*(3), 637–667.

Rothaermel, F. T., & Hess, A. M. (2007). Building dynamic capabilities: Innovation driven by individual-, firm-, and network-level effects. *Organization Science, 18*(6), 898–921.

Sasaki, I., Nummela, N., & Ravasi, D. (2021). Managing cultural specificity and cultural embeddedness when internationalizing: Cultural strategies of Japanese craft firms. *Journal of International Business Studies, 52*(2), 245–281.

Thevenard-Puthod, C., & Picard, C. (2011). Identity and very small firms networks: The case of craft firms. In *ICSB world conference proceedings* (p. 1). International Council for Small Business (ICSB).

Van de Ven, A. H., & Lifschitz, A. (2013). Rational and reasonable microfoundations of markets and institutions. *Academy of Management Perspectives, 27*(2), 156–172.

Wang, S. L., Gu, Q., Von Glinow, M. A., & Hirsch, P. (2020). Cultural industries in international business research: Progress and prospect. *Journal of International Business Studies, 51*(4), 665–692.

14

Reviewing Worker and Producer Cooperative Contributions Toward SDG8 in Developing and Developed Economies

Frank Siedlok, Lisa Callagher, and Stefan Korber

1 Introduction

The United Nations (UN) 17 Sustainable Development Goals (SDGs) represent one of the decade's most essential and challenging development agendas. Achieving the SDGs requires collaborative and transformative actions undertaken by multiple stakeholders, including businesses of all shapes and sizes (Sinkovics et al., 2020, 2021) and a better understanding of alternative organizational forms that successfully combine social and business logics (Callagher et al., 2022). Cooperatives are one such organizational form and significantly contribute to local and global economies

F. Siedlok (✉)
University of St. Andrews, St. Andrews, UK
e-mail: fsiedlok@dunelm.org.uk

L. Callagher · S. Korber
University of Auckland, Auckland, New Zealand
e-mail: l.callagher@auckland.ac.nz

S. Korber
e-mail: s.korber@auckland.ac.nz

N. Sinkovics et al. (eds.), *International Business and SDG 8*, The Academy of International Business, https://doi.org/10.1007/978-3-031-46802-5_14

(Ajates, 2020). Cooperative principles such as shared collective ownership, democratic decision-making, and member participation align well with calls for more sustainable and inclusive economic growth.

Beyond their economic contribution, cooperatives embody distinct sets of principles and practices that can potentiate collective action to address social and environmental challenges (Callagher et al., 2022; Liu & Guenther, 2022). These can subsequently diffuse across organizational and national boundaries (Errasti et al., 2023; Siedlok et al., 2021, 2023). In light of the increased focus on sustainable development, cooperatives have attracted renewed interest as a viable organizational form that can help to address a range of socio-economic and environmental issues in regions underserved by traditional organizational forms (Slade Shantz et al., 2020) or at a global scale (Novkovic, 2022; Siedlok et al., 2021). The literature suggests that producer and worker cooperatives can offer viable means to achieve sustainable and inclusive economic growth in both developing and developed economies (Bastida et al., 2022; Bibby, 2014; Kociatkiewicz et al., 2021).

In this chapter, we first introduce and review the cooperative model and principles. Then, we move to a focus on worker and producer cooperatives and establishing their relationship with international business and SDG8. To illustrate our arguments, we provide several examples of cooperative contributions toward employment and decent work from developed and developed contexts. We end the chapter with a more critical view of the limits of cooperatives vis-à-vis achieving SDG8 and outline avenues for future research.

2 Cooperatives, Cooperative Principles, and SDGs

Cooperatives are broadly defined as organizations that adhere to the principle of shared ownership, in which members have control over the use and benefits of the means of production (Slade Shantz et al., 2020, p. 505). With profit either reinvested in the enterprise or shared by the members, cooperatives' predominant existence is to serve their members to realize their everyday *economic, social, and cultural needs and aspirations* without necessarily aiming to maximize benefits for any individual group of shareholders (ICA, 2017). Such a broad definition captures a wide range of types and sizes of cooperatives, such as worker, producer, consumer, and financial cooperatives.[1] Due to more substantial coverage in organizational studies and their significant role in international business, we focus predominantly on worker and producer cooperatives.

Regardless of the type, size, or location, cooperative organizations are expressed through a set of generally agreed values of *self-help*, *self-responsibility*, *democracy*, *equality*, *equity*, and *solidarity*. In practice, those values are enacted through the seven cooperative principles outlined in Table 1. Those principles underpin the nature, structure, and behaviors of cooperatives, as well as their relation to their members, partners, communities, and local economies that cooperatives operate in. By embodying and enacting those principles, cooperatives also directly contribute to achieving SDGs.

Cooperatives are closely aligned with SDGs, and with SDG8 in particular, for a variety of reasons. Traditionally, cooperatives have been invoked in response to market failures and to empower and emancipate members (Boone & Özcan, 2014; Tadesse et al., 2020). Compared to traditional investor-owned businesses, cooperatives tend to care for a broader range of stakeholders (Callagher & Garnevska, 2023) and are portrayed as more resilient during crises (Jaumier, 2016a). The focus on maximizing benefits for multiple stakeholders, which is enshrined in four of the cooperative principles, is part of the reason cooperatives have been explicitly associated with the SDGs (ILO, 2016) and sustainability (ICA, 2017). The ICA states that, as enterprises based on values and principles, cooperatives put fairness and equality first allowing people to create sustainable enterprises that *generate long-term jobs and prosperity*.[2] Indeed, cooperatives play an essential role in addressing social ills and creating new opportunities in regions underserved by other organizational forms (Slade Shantz et al., 2020). In developed economies,

---

[1] Multiple classifications exist and most are based on functions served or activities performed by cooperatives. This can lead to overlaps and overly lengthy typologies. See https://corporatefinanceinstitute.com/resources/wealth-management/cooperatives/

[2] https://www.ica.coop/en.

Table 1 Cooperative principles

Cooperative principle	Meaning
Voluntary and open membership	Voluntary organizations, open to all persons able to use their services and willing to accept the responsibilities of membership
Democratic member control	Democratically controlled by their members, who actively participate in setting their policies and making decisions
Member economic participation	Members equitably contribute to and democratically control the cooperative's capital, part of which remains the common property of the cooperative and where surpluses are usually allocated to developing the Cooperative, while members usually receive limited compensation on capital subscribed as a condition of membership
Autonomy and independence	Autonomous and democratically controlled by the members
Education, training, and information	Education and training provision for members, elected representatives, managers, and employees so they can contribute effectively to the development of their cooperatives while educating the public about the nature of cooperatives
Cooperation among cooperatives	Cooperatives support each other
Concern for community	Cooperatives support the sustainable development of their communities

cooperatives can offer some balance to neoliberal capitalism by empowering employees and SMEs against large companies or global supply chains (Kociatkiewicz et al., 2021; Siedlok et al., 2023).

While adherence to and salience of the principles is contingent on the cooperative and its institutional and cultural context (Birchall, 2012; Novkovic, 2022), most cooperatives adhere to the principles of member ownership, democratic member control, and member economic participation (Principles #1, 2, and 3) where members have control over the use and benefits of their means of production. Shared ownership and collective decision-making are portrayed as the main reasons for ongoing tensions, inefficiencies, and a potential cause for cooperatives failure (Siedlok et al., 2023). Yet, somehow paradoxically, those same principles simultaneously create conditions for fairness, equality, and empowerment (c.f., Kociatkiewicz et al., 2021).

Consequently, the success of cooperatives, and their contribution to SDGs, results from achieving a dynamic balance between economic and social benefits (Siedlok et al., 2023): while profitability is necessary, profits are often seen to serve broader community needs directly through employment and indirectly through income and access to goods or services at reasonable costs (Kociatkiewicz et al., 2021). Growth, seen as at odds with sustainability and addressing global challenges (Rai et al., 2019), is more likely to be utilized in cooperatives for a range of social goals and to support local communities rather than satisfy distant investors (Bibby, 2014; Callagher & Garnevska, 2023). For all those reasons, cooperatives have been portrayed to perform more 'responsible capitalism' (Paranque & Willmott, 2014). Yet, despite being 'present to a much greater extent in market economies than has been suggested in the literature' (Novkovic, 2008, p. 2169) and being an essential thread in the fabric of international business (Ajates, 2020; Errasti et al., 2023), IB scholars paid relatively little attention to this organizational form (Siedlok et al., 2021).

3 Worker and Producer Cooperatives, International Business, and SDG8

Cooperatives have been at the forefront of improving work conditions, creating new employment opportunities, and empowering women and marginalized communities. Further, they offer protection to those in precarious work and, more recently, address maladies of (unsustainable) capitalist growth and self-interests (Berry & Bell, 2018; Ribeiro-Duthie, 2020). In this section, we outline the fundamental characteristics of worker and producer cooperatives and their contribution to SDGs in developing and developed contexts.

3.1 The Structure and Characteristics of Worker and Producer Cooperatives

Worker cooperatives are businesses that are owned and managed collectively by their employees, who share decision-making power and ownership rights. Each worker typically has an equal vote in major decisions and a stake in the company's profits, fostering a more democratic and equitable workplace environment. Worker cooperatives have been portrayed as an antidote to employee exploitation, increasing disparity in remuneration between managers and employees, dehumanization of work, a potential solution to principal-agent problems, and a pathway to more satisfying work and well-being (Burdín & Dean, 2009; Kociatkiewicz et al., 2021). Besides, worker cooperatives can empower local communities, mobilize local resources and protect employment and workers from economic shocks and crises, making them particularly valuable to local economic development efforts (Bastida et al., 2022).

Although most remain local, worker cooperatives are often embedded in global supply chains. Some of the largest and most emblematic worker cooperatives have embarked on internationalization strategies, transforming into multinational companies. For example, *Up Group* operates subsidiaries in 50 countries, *Mondragon Group* controls some 140 foreign subsidiaries across 37 countries, *Sacmi* operates in 13, and *Irizar* in 5 countries (Errasti et al., 2023). The degree to which worker cooperatives transmit core cooperative principles to their subsidies varies significantly, often following a gradual process (ibid.). Thus, the impact of worker cooperatives in some localities might be protracted.

Similarly, producer cooperatives are collectively owned and operated by their members who share decision-making and benefits that result from their efforts. Producer cooperatives undertake the processing, marketing, and sales of goods and services supplied by the members. Members of producer cooperatives can be individual producers and business entities supplying goods or services to the cooperative. A cooperative structure enables local producers to cope with market malfunctions or competitive pressures and enter markets and global value chains that would be beyond the capabilities of an individual member. There are over 40,000 producer cooperatives in the agricultural sector alone, accounting for 40–60% of global trade. Many are national or global brands (e.g., FrislandCampina, Zespri) others supply high-value offerings to global production systems (e.g., Livestock Improvement Corporation, Sacmi). The Food and Agriculture Organization (FAO) links producer cooperatives in the agricultural sector to promoting food security, agricultural productivity, access to the market, and providing income opportunities, thus directly contributing to SDG2 (Zero hunger) and SDG1 (No poverty).

3.2 Worker and Producer Cooperatives in Developing Economies

Producer and worker cooperatives offer employment to marginalized populations and maintain a presence in locations that are seen as unprofitable by investor-owned firms (Novkovic, 2008). Many women-led cooperatives emerged in patriarchal societies, tapping into crafts, agriculture, manufacturing, and marketing of local produce, tourism, housing, and other services. These allow women to participate in economic activities, gain independence (Khumalo, 2014), and improve their social standing within the community. Through working as a community network, cooperatives provide greater learning among members and access to external knowledge, often embedded in global value chains. Moreover, many cooperatives offer technical and business training for members (Tadesse et al., 2020) that enhances the development of entrepreneurial behaviors of members (Bastida et al., 2022) and further contributes to the strength of the local economy. This process of strengthening the local economy is further enhanced by cooperatives helping to circulate money locally and prevent capital leakage (Khumalo, 2014).

Many worker and producer cooperatives emerged as a means of organizational and business challenges to allow members to collectively achieve what they could not achieve individually (Khumalo, 2014). Examples frequently refer to economies of scale, pooling of resources, access to equipment, or increased bargaining power as the main factors behind the emergence of cooperatives in developing economies. For instance, Tadesse and colleagues (2020) link the establishment of seed cooperatives to the failure of the public sector and as an alternative strategy to improve seed quality and seed system efficiency that can increase the competitive advantage of smallholder farmers. In post-conflict or developing economies, cooperatives can help to transform societies by tackling power imbalances, improving workers' conditions (Lambru & Petrescu, 2014), and creating opportunities for the direct involvement of communities in tackling poverty or access to necessary production means. For instance, the origins of Mondragon, the largest worker-owned cooperative, are linked to an impoverished local economy in post-Civil War Spain where the founder, a priest, mobilized citizens to provide the community with education, healthcare, and better housing (Romeo, 2022). Those improvements soon led to the first industrial cooperative. Subsequently, Mondragon became the most significant contributor to the regional economy and community.

3.3 Worker and Producer Cooperatives in Developed Economies

Worker cooperatives in developed economies are associated with their ability to resist different forms of power stemming from neoliberal capitalist arrangements, including exploitation of the workforce (Wiksell, 2020). Kreinin and Aigner (2022) note that we live in a work-centered society where inequity and overconsumption intertwine with work that is increasingly detached from societal or individual welfare. In addition, neoliberal ideologies result in the exploitation of workers, in particular in precarious areas of employment that are often dominated by ethnic minorities, women, and immigrants. Precarious work is characterized by unpredictable schedules, physical hazards, more significant potential for abuse, psychological stress, and fewer worker benefits (Berry & Bell, 2018). Worker and producer cooperatives can enable resistance to such a potential for exploitation (Wiksell, 2020).

For instance, Paranque and Willmott (2014) contend that John Lewis, a UK premium worker cooperative retailer, exemplifies a viable and comparatively responsible enterprise that successfully, to an extent, manages to prioritize 'the happiness of all its members, through their worthwhile and satisfying employment in a successful business' (p. 607) over profit. Similarly, Kociatkiewicz et al. (2021) note that worker-owned cooperatives can counter the alienation of workplaces and offer a more meaningful and engaging workplace. Ownership and economic participation in worker cooperatives also translate to higher commitment and lower employee turnover and absenteeism (Jackall & Levin, 2021). More recently, the cooperative form has been considered as a possible means of business succession when the founders of a company retire and want to give back to those who contributed to its success (Jaumier, 2016b) or as a buy-out option when there is a risk of closure (Jaumier, 2016a).

Similarly, producer cooperatives in developed economies allow small producers to plug into global value chains while offering members increased bargaining power against buyers, processors, brokers, and marketers who hold a more dominant bargaining position (Jentoft & Davis, 1993, p. 356). Further, economies of scale enable producer cooperatives to conduct tailored scientific research and development that are beyond the reach of most members. Producer cooperatives facilitate knowledge sharing and co-creation that, in turn, can lead to faster rates of innovation, productivity gains, and adoption of more sustainable production practices (Fiore et al., 2020; Kyriakopoulos et al., 2004; Siedlok et al., 2023). Finally, producer cooperatives are seen as better equipped for action toward sustainable growth than investor-led companies (Bibby, 2014; see also Siedlok et al., 2023) and particularly apt for large-scale collective action (Callagher et al., 2022). However, research cautions that their contribution to solving environmental issues is not always uniformly adopted (Callagher & Garnevska, 2023).

As these examples show, producer and worker cooperatives offer a range of benefits that directly address SDGs in general, and specifically SDG8 in both developing and developed economies. This should not be surprising given the central role of People and Profit that stem from cooperative principles (Callagher & Garnevska, 2023). By relating to the responsibility matrix (see Sinkovics et al., 2020), cooperative principles and values, if adhered to, place most cooperatives in the area of enhanced to advanced depth and operational and embedded levels of responsibility. However, while the preceding examples suggest that cooperatives are the answer to global challenges and a means to achieving SDGs, a more critical assessment needs to be exercised.

4 Not a Panacea

Cooperatives, as an organizational arrangement, have received severe criticism. Much of that critique is associated with their alleged lack of long-term competitiveness that stems from challenges associated with conflicting economic and social demands (Boone & Özcan, 2014). In the long term, democratically owned and controlled organizations are assumed to only survive the pressure of global value chains if they abandon cooperative principles in favor of neoliberal ideals (Ajates, 2020). While this has been disproved (Bretos & Errasti, 2017), the integration of social and economic goals remains a challenging and ongoing organizational task that is prone to failure (Siedlok et al., 2023). Despite the ethos of people and profit, cooperatives have also been found to take advantage of the unequal treatment of non-member employees or suppliers. This issue is particularly relevant in the internationalization of cooperatives as many multinational cooperatives consist of a cooperative core at home and capitalist subsidies (Errasti et al., 2023). Paradoxically then, SDG8 might not materialise in those parts of the world that need better working conditions the most. It is also worth remembering that cooperatives do not respond well to government interventions or control (Khumalo, 2014; Lambru & Petrescu, 2014), and are therefore not necessarily an easy policy fix to meeting SDGs.

There are also some apparent issues with SDGs that need to be acknowledged and addressed. SDGs have been criticized, with SDG8 coming under the most extensive criticism due to the apparent internal inconsistencies to simultaneously call for economic growth and decent work (Kreinin & Aigner, 2022). Similarly, growth and environmental sustainability are often contradictory goals that are hard to recognize. However some, albeit few, examples highlight that growth, quality of work, and environmental issues can be combined. For example, in the last few years, Zespri, a kiwifruit marketing organization that is owned by orchardists has reinforced cooperative principles by strengthening member ownership and control, investing in members' upskilling, and, more recently, fully embracing a sustainability agenda (Siedlok et al., 2023). Similarly, but at a much smaller scale, Scopix, a French cooperative sheet-metal factory showed how workers, who refer to themselves as 'cooperators' developed practices to retain an emancipatory dimension to their work and constructed 'craft ethics' as a counterweight to rationalize work processes that dominate factory work (Jaumier & Daudigeos, 2021). While worthy of consideration, these examples remain outliers and there is a need for more work to understand how such paradoxical strategic goals can be integrated.

While SDGs and an increased appetite for the transformation of economic reality can give cooperatives a second chance, we should spend some more time and effort to conceptualize better, operationalize and understand the performative potential of cooperatives (Siedlok et al., 2023) toward SDG8, before we jump at the appealing promise of overturning capitalism. Such scholarship is needed to avoid mishaps and misappropriations of good intentions (e.g. see Bowden et al., 2021).

References

Ajates, R. (2020). Agricultural cooperatives remaining competitive in a globalised food system: At what cost to members, the cooperative movement and food sustainability? *Organization, 27*(2), 337–355. https://doi.org/10/ghk7tc

Bastida, M., Vaquero García, A., Pinto, L. H., & Olveira Blanco, A. (2022). Motivational drivers to choose worker cooperatives as an entrepreneurial alternative: Evidence from Spain. *Small Business Economics, 58*(3), 1609–1626. https://doi.org/10.1007/s11187-021-00459-8

Berry, D., & Bell, M. P. (2018). Worker cooperatives: Alternative governance for caring and precarious work. *Equality, Diversity and Inclusion: An International Journal, 37*(4), 376–391. https://doi.org/10.1108/EDI-02-2017-0027

Bibby, A. (2014, March 11). Co-operatives are an inherently more sustainable form of business. *The Guardian*. http://www.theguardian.com/social-enterprise-network/2014/mar/11/co-op-business-sustainability

Birchall, J. (2012). A 'member-owned business' approach to the classification of co-operatives and mutuals. In D. P. McDonnell & E. C. Macknight (Eds.), *The co-operative model in practice: International perspectives* (pp. 67–82). Co-operative Education Trust Scotland. http://www.ssrn.com/abstract=2163490

Boone, C., & Özcan, S. (2014). Why do cooperatives emerge in a world dominated by corporations? The diffusion of cooperatives in the U.S. bio-ethanol industry, 1978–2013. *Academy of Management Journal, 57*(4), 990–1012. https://doi.org/10/gdtmhw

Bowden, V., Gond, J.-P., Nyberg, D., & Wright, C. (2021). Turning back the rising sea: Theory performativity in the shift from climate science to popular authority. *Organization Studies, 42*(12), 1909–1931. https://doi.org/10/gnrzdw

Bretos, I., & Errasti, A. (2017). Challenges and opportunities for the regeneration of multinational worker cooperatives: Lessons from the Mondragon Corporation—A case study of the Fagor Ederlan Group. *Organization, 24*(2), 154–173. https://doi.org/10/gjrqdr

Burdín, G., & Dean, A. (2009). New evidence on wages and employment in worker cooperatives compared with capitalist firms. *Journal of Comparative Economics, 37*(4), 517–533. https://doi.org/10.1016/j.jce.2009.08.001

Callagher, L., & Garnevska, E. (2023). Multistakeholder impression management tactics and sustainable development intentions in agri-food co-operatives. *Journal of Management & Organization*, 1–21. https://doi.org/10.1017/jmo.2023.35

Callagher, L., Korber, S., Siedlok, F., & Elsahn, Z. (2022). Metaorganizing collaborative innovation for action on grand challenges. *IEEE Transactions on Engineering Management*. https://doi.org/10.1109/TEM.2021.3135792

Errasti, A., Bretos, I., & Marcuello, C. (2023). Classifying the degree of cooperative multinationality: Case study of a French multinational cooperative. *Annals of Public and Cooperative Economics, n/a*(n/a). https://doi.org/10.1111/apce.12450

Fiore, M., Galati, A., Gołębiewski, J., & Drejerska, N. (2020). Stakeholders' involvement in establishing sustainable business models: The case of Polish dairy cooperatives. *British Food Journal, 122*(5), 1671–1691. https://doi.org/10.1108/bfj-04-2019-0263

ICA. (2017, June 29). *Coops for 2030: A movement achieving sustainable development for all*. https://www.ica.coop/en/media/library/research-and-reviews/coops-2030-movement-achieving-sustainable-development-all

ILO. (2016). *Cooperatives and the sustainable development goals: A contribution to the 2030 agenda for sustainable development* [Document]. International Labour Organization. http://www.ilo.org/global/topics/cooperatives/areas-of-work/WCMS_445131/lang--en/index.htm

Jackall, R., & Levin, H. M. (2021). *Worker cooperatives in America*. University of California Press.

Jaumier, S. (2016a). Preventing chiefs from being chiefs: An ethnography of a co-operative sheet-metal factory. *Organization, 24*(2), 218–239. https://doi.org/10/gf372g

Jaumier, S. (2016b). The big leap: A story of the public accounting firm that wanted to become a cooperative. *Journal of Accounting & Organizational Change, 12*(1), 24–49. https://doi.org/10.1108/JAOC-03-2013-0032

Jaumier, S., & Daudigeos, T. (2021). Resisting work degeneration in collectivist-democratic organizations: Craft ethics in a French cooperative sheet-metal factory. In K. K. Chen & V. T. Chen (Eds.), *Research in the sociology of organizations* (pp. 55–79). Emerald Publishing Limited. https://doi.org/10.1108/S0733-558X20210000072003

Jentoft, S., & Davis, A. (1993). Self and sacrifice: An investigation of small boat fisher individualism and its implication for producer cooperatives. *Human Organization, 52*(4), 356–367. https://doi.org/10/gk4z8d

Khumalo, P. (2014). Improving the contribution of cooperatives as vehicles for local economic development in South Africa. *African Studies Quarterly, 14*(4).

Kociatkiewicz, J., Kostera, M., & Parker, M. (2021). The possibility of disalienated work: Being at home in alternative organizations. *Human Relations, 74*(7), 933–957. https://doi.org/10.1177/0018726720916762

Kreinin, H., & Aigner, E. (2022). From "decent work and economic growth" to "sustainable work and economic degrowth": A new framework for SDG 8. *Empirica, 49*(2), 281–311. https://doi.org/10.1007/s10663-021-09526-5

Kyriakopoulos, K., Meulenberg, M., & Nilsson, J. (2004). The impact of cooperative structure and firm culture on market orientation and performance. *Agribusiness, 20*(4), 379–396. https://doi.org/10/cmc6xr

Lambru, M., & Petrescu, C. (2014). Surviving the crisis: Worker cooperatives in Romania. *Organization, 21*(5), 730–745. https://doi.org/10.1177/1350508414537807

Liu, M., & Guenther, C. (2022). How do incumbents affect the founding of cooperatives? Evidence from the German electricity industry. *Organization Studies*, https://doi.org/10.1177/01708406221107457

Novkovic, S. (2008). Defining the co-operative difference. *The Journal of Socio-Economics, 37*(6), 2168–2177. https://doi.org/10/c3fw9c
Novkovic, S. (2022). Cooperative identity as a yardstick for transformative change. *Annals of Public and Cooperative Economics, 93*(2), 313–336. https://doi.org/10.1111/apce.12362
Paranque, B., & Willmott, H. (2014). Cooperatives—Saviours or gravediggers of capitalism? Critical performativity and the John Lewis Partnership. *Organization, 21*(5), 604–625. https://doi.org/10/gjrqgt
Rai, S. M., Brown, B. D., & Ruwanpura, K. N. (2019). SDG 8: Decent work and economic growth—A gendered analysis. *World Development, 113*, 368–380. https://doi.org/10.1016/j.worlddev.2018.09.006
Ribeiro-Duthie, A. C. (2020). SDG 8 decent work and economic growth. In I. B. Franco, T. Chatterji, E. Derbyshire, & J. Tracey (Eds.), *Actioning the global goals for local impact: Towards sustainability science, policy, education and practice* (pp. 117–133). Springer. https://doi.org/10.1007/978-981-32-9927-6_9
Romeo, N. (2022, August 27). How Mondragon became the world's largest co-op. *The New Yorker*. https://www.newyorker.com/business/currency/how-mondragon-became-the-worlds-largest-co-op
Siedlok, F., Callagher, L., Elsahn, Z., & Korber, S. (2023). Strategy performation to avoid degeneration: How producer cooperatives can achieve social and economic goal. *Organization Studies, 0*(0). https://doi.org/10.1177/01708406231119325
Siedlok, F., Elsahn, Z., & Callagher, L. (2021). Managing internationalisation tensions in producer cooperatives. *AIB Insights*. https://doi.org/10/gh4sbh
Sinkovics, N., Sinkovics, R. R., & Archie-Acheampong, J. (2020). The business responsibility matrix: A diagnostic tool to aid the design of better interventions for achieving the SDGs. *Multinational Business Review, 29*(1), 1–20. https://doi.org/10.1108/MBR-07-2020-0154
Sinkovics, N., Sinkovics, R. R., & Archie-Acheampong, J. (2021). Small and medium-sized enterprises and sustainable development: In the shadows of large lead firms in global value chains. *Journal of International Business Policy, 4*(1), 80–101. https://doi.org/10.1057/s42214-020-00089-z
Slade Shantz, A., Kistruck, G., Pacheco, D., & Webb, J. (2020). How formal and informal hierarchies shape conflict within cooperatives: A field experiment in Ghana. *Academy of Management Journal, 36*(2), 503–529. https://doi.org/10/gfz2fz
Tadesse, Y., Almekinders, C. J. M., Griffin, D., & Struik, P. C. (2020). Collective production and marketing of quality potato seed: Experiences from two

cooperatives in Chencha, Ethiopia. *Forum for Development Studies, 47*(1), 139–156. https://doi.org/10.1080/08039410.2019.1635523

Wiksell, K. (2020). Worker cooperatives for social change: Knowledge-making through constructive resistance within the capitalist market economy. *Journal of Political Power, 13*(2), 201–216. https://doi.org/10.1080/2158379X.2020.1764803

Part III

Teaching Perspectives on SDG 8

15

Embedding Diversity, Equity, and Inclusion (DEI) in International Business Education

Aušrinė Šilenskytė and Matevž (Matt) Rašković

1 Introduction

The necessary shift from rhetoric to implemented action is still largely missing when embedding diversity, equity, and inclusion (DEI)[1] in higher education (Burrell Storms et al., 2020). Education is a transformative vehicle for DEI *and* belonging[2] (Slee, 2019; Williams, 2013), which can address contemporary political, social, and technological trends (OECD, 2023). With the global moral landscape in flux (Fitzsimmons et al., 2023), the slow-paced nature of the academic sector (Burrell

[1] We see *diversity* as the degree of representation of different sociodemographic categories (visible and invisible), *equity* as the provision of tailored opportunities and support, and *inclusion* as the process of accepting and valuing diversity.

[2] "A feeling of safety, acceptance and being valued" in a specific social or work setting (AACSB, 2021).

A. Šilenskytė (✉)
Strategic Business Development Research Group, School of Management, University of Vaasa, Vaasa, Finland
e-mail: ausrine.silenskyte@uwasa.fi

N. Sinkovics et al. (eds.), *International Business and SDG 8*, The Academy of International Business, https://doi.org/10.1007/978-3-031-46802-5_15

Storms et al., 2020) holds the sector back from contributing to a fairer and more just society through DEI-informed educationand curricula (Smith & Schonfeld, 2020). Business schools play a particularly pivotal role in addressing the societal grand challenges (Aragon-Correa et al., 2017; Sewchurran, 2022) operationalised through the United Nations' Sustainable Development Goals (UN SDGs). This role is not limited to UN SDG 4 (Quality Education) but underpins *all* 17 SDGs (Tonegava, 2022), each requiring a separate elaboration. In this chapter, we elaborate on UN SDG 8 (Decent Work and Economic Growth). Regarding SDG 8, international business (IB) and its education with embedded DEI can make a wide-ranging positive social impact that requires talents capable of leading the "Decade of Action" (Van Tulder et al., 2021), thereby ensuring a socioeconomically sustainable future for all.

We discuss *how* to embed DEI practices and principles in IB education with relevance to SDG 8. The literature on *actions* for embedding DEI into IB education remains scant compared to those related to management or marketing (e.g., Riedel et al., 2023), despite 50 years of research on DEI that has advanced our understanding of it within IB (Fitzsimmons et al., 2023). To narrow the rhetoric-vs-action gap, we draw on the conceptual framework of promoting inclusive education for diverse societies, provided by Cerna and colleagues (2021). In particular, we utilise their original framework to discuss (1) programme and/or course curriculum design and (2) classroom interactions through which IB educators can help their students understand both the business case for DEI *and* its moral imperatives (i.e., the social justice perspective) (Ely & Thomas, 2020).

M. (Matt) Rašković
Department of International Business, Strategy & Entrepreneurship (IBSE), Auckland University of Technology, Auckland, New Zealand
e-mail: matt.raskovic@aut.ac.nz

2 Promoting Inclusive Education for Diverse Societies: A Framework

The "wicked" nature of today's global issues (Rašković, 2022) is closely intertwined with the UN SDGs (Van Tulder & Van Mil, 2022). Trying to tackle the complex nature of DEI, Cerna et al. (2021) developed the OECD framework for fostering inclusive education for diverse societies. Inclusivity, in their framework, refers to "the extent to which they [education systems and actors] promote the inclusion of diverse learners" (Cerna et al., 2021, p. 6). Inclusivity is fostered within the context of a particular society, its systems, and the education system within which the higher education institution (HEI) operates.

To achieve inclusive education for diverse societies, Cerna et al. (2021) suggest five steps: (1) governing, (2) resourcing, (3) developing capacity for managing, (4) promoting HEI-level interventions, and (5) evaluating and monitoring diversity. We have adapted their framework, simplifying it (see Fig. 1). Additionally, we have (1) incorporated the concept of belonging (AACSB, 2021), which directly relates to the UN SDG 8 context, and (2) slightly expanded the definition of diversity dimensions to make it more representative of the contemporary IB context. We structure our chapter around the five elements (2.1–2.5) in Fig. 1. Examples provided in each section below support bridging institutional-level policy actions with those taken at the business programme, course, and individual level (by educators). We argue that IB educators, who effectively bridge the distance-diversity nexus (Doh, 2021) and can leverage IB's history of theorising about the diversity of cultures, institutions, and firm unit roles in cross-border operations (Roth & Kostova, 2003; Rousseau & Fried, 2001), are particularly well-positioned to imbue IB education with DEI (Dieleman et al., 2022). Nonetheless, we hope our suggestions speak to business educators across disciplinary silos.

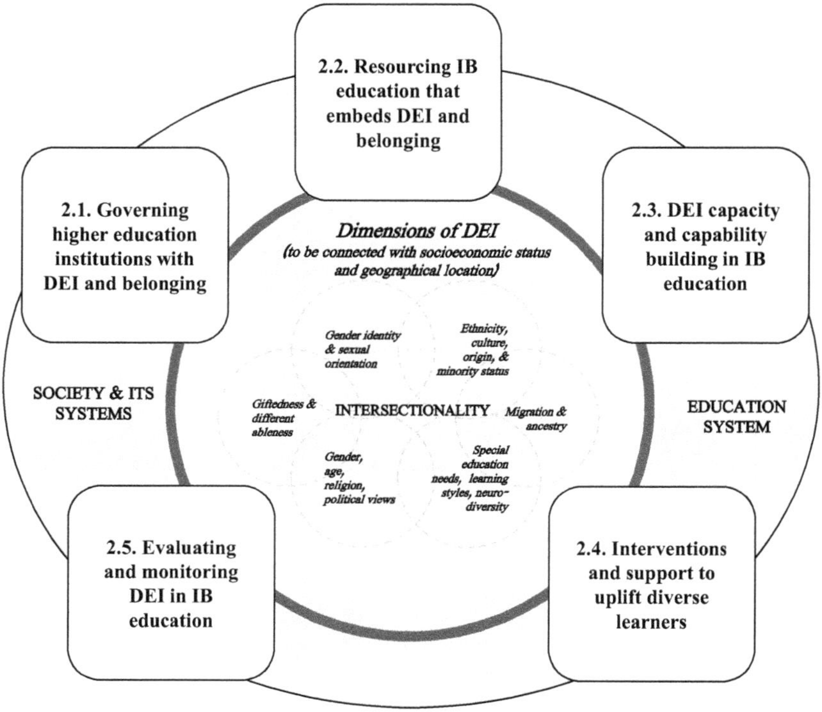

Fig. 1 A framework for inclusive international business education for diverse societies (*Source* Adapted from Cerna et al. [2021])

2.1 Governing HEIs with DEI and Belonging

The role of (supra)national institutions is critical for promoting an education system that adheres to the DEI philosophy (Dobbin & Kalev, 2016). Supranational institutions, such as organisations behind university ranking lists (i.e., QS World University Ranking, Times Higher Education, Financial Times ranking) or specialised accreditation bodies (i.e., AACSB and EQUIS/EFMD), set global standards, including those used for addressing societal grand challenges. For example, AACSB, the premier business accreditation body from North America, has in 2020 included "Diversity & Inclusion" as core values in 66% of its accreditation standards, despite DEI principles already being incorporated into 40% of the accreditation standards previously (AACSB, 2020). When such a stimulus occurs at the supranational level, national higher education accreditation agencies typically follow suit. For instance, the national accreditation agency in Slovenia—NAKVIS—has moved from its primary quality assurance role to include a broader mandate focusing on social impact, touching on inequality and inequities.

While institutional standards may ensure adherence to the DEI philosophy out of compliance, in the long term, the bottom-up approach, which enables the uncovering of the meaning of DEI at multiple levels (Sippola, 2007), is desired. This means that the institutional-level DEI actions are expected to shift from a *discrimination-and-fairness paradigm* in administering DEI (i.e., affirmative action) to an *access-and-legitimacy paradigm* (i.e., the DEI business case), and then, to a *learning-and-effectiveness paradigm* (i.e., diversity as a strategic asset),[3] penetrating business education to programme, course, and individual levels.

Following what is stipulated through compliance or going beyond it, the universities adopt governance mechanisms that instigate DEI in education at multiple levels. Such mechanisms may include *formal DEI-advocating positions*. For example, Grace and Ammerman (2022) advocate the establishment of a cross-functional DEI office at a strategic level (with strategic authority), which is appropriately supported by resources and staff (including learning designers). Along these lines, UC Davis in California, which has one of the most diverse student bodies of all the US universities, has a *DEI office* sitting under the Vice-Chancellor and focusing on fostering belonging; the office supports the integration of DEI goals within faculty, study programme, and course learning goals.

Promoting a DEI-supportive *organisational culture* is the other frequently adopted governance mechanism typically enacted through communication. For example, when presenting the university's values, the Pontificia Universidad Católica del Perú (PUCP) (in Peru) defines itself as a plural and tolerant academic community. The University of Vaasa (in Finland) emphasises that faculty and students, regardless of

---

[3] Please see Ely and Thomas (1996, 2020).

nationality, belong to the university's community, even if some countries are currently at war (UVA, 2022). These actions directly support the implementation of SDG 8 at HEIs because they lead to the establishment of youth employment, education, and training (SDG 8.6), protection of labour rights, and the ensuring of a safe work environment regardless of background (SDG 8.8) (*8 Decent Work and Economic Growth*, n.d.).

2.2 Resourcing IB Education that Embeds DEI and Belonging

Every strategic vision or communicated preference must be supported by appropriate resources (e.g., economic-financial, technological, human, time) vital for their implementation (Riccò & Guerci, 2014). At the HEI level, such an approach is consistent with AACSB's *global* philosophy of fostering DEI and belonging (AACSB, 2021). For faculty members, the availability of needed resources may increase flexibility (Cerna et al., 2021). Table 1 illustrates different kinds of resources and briefly explains how they may support embedding DEI and belonging in IB education.

Creating teaching and learning environments enabled by diverse resources leads to better educational outcomes since education is tailored to individualised needs and engagement through belonging(ness). However, additionally, such environments role-model how graduates can resource and shape their organisations, leading IB to become a decent, home-like workspace that celebrates growth (as a return on their DEI investments).

2.3 DEI Capacity and Capability Building in IB Education

Directing study programmes to grow their DEI capacity and helping the faculty develop their DEI capabilities is essential in order for IB education to become truly inclusive. For this, we need both specialised DEI-focused courses and the integration of DEI principles across the regular curriculum (Hawkins & States, 2021). Figure 2 summarises how

Table 1 Examples of resources necessary for IB education with DEI

Resources	Ways in which they support DEI and belonging in IB education
Infrastructure and space	Designing teaching and learning spaces that cater to diverse learners is essential (Sanger, 2020). For instance, classrooms friendly to neurodiverse learners may include flexible furniture, physical elements that allow shelter, and building a sensory-friendly space (i.e., colours and soundproofing). The importance of space extends beyond the classrooms (i.e., gender-neutral or designated bathrooms, special spaces for child care, etc.)
Resources for different formats of learning	The face-to-face learning format benefits some, but not everyone. Learning in class may be challenging for students with caregiving responsibilities, socioeconomic constraints, or neurodiverse students. Virtual or hybrid learning can help address those needs
Tools for learning	Employing different tools for learning helps address diverse learning styles and caters to neurodiverse students. For instance, the podcast format supports neurodiverse learners (Listenwise, 2021) and allows the introduction of marginalised, especially indigenous, voices (UBC, 2020). The use of diverse teams for group work (Hawkins & States, 2021), storytelling (Rezvani & Gordon, 2021), role-playing, and simulations, especially around global issues (Lutterman-Aguilar, 2003), have all been found to be effective tools in "preparing students for diversity"

(continued)

Table 1 (continued)

Resources	Ways in which they support DEI and belonging in IB education
Diverse learning and teaching materials	DEI and belonging can only be created with learning and teaching materials that reflect different identities, views, voices, and beliefs. For instance, case studies (Hawkins & States, 2021), different types of media, and newspaper articles (beyond Western media) can help highlight issues in different (local) environments. Considering socioeconomic diversity when selecting learning resources (preferably open-source, free-of-charge materials) helps ensure access to learning for everyone
Time	Developing DEI-related competencies for the faculty may take time. Moreover, designing learning activities that allow students to reflect on DEI typically requires personalised feedback and individual attention (Šilenskytė, 2022). Providing sufficient time that supports both students and faculty in enabling needed reflections and considerations of alternative views, or simply for performing deeper discussions, is vital, especially in culturally and ethnically diverse classrooms

such two-pronged DEI in education can be achieved. Figure 2 is based on the Inclusive Pedagogy and Universal Design for Learning (UDL) principles, comprising (1) providing multiple means of engagement ("*why*" of learning), (2) providing multiple means of representation ("*what*" of learning), and (3) providing multiple means of actions and expressions ("*how*" of learning) (CAST, n.d.). Discussing the questions suggested in Fig. 2 (designed based upon a large body of research aiming to address DEI and DEI in education) within each of the three listed domains supports educator teams with spotting actions for DEI development and, thereby, allows them to foster belonging(ness) at the programme and course levels. Such discussions are most effective when they incorporate the context of the relevant society and education system.

It is essential to acknowledge that, while the three domains and the questions under them are presented as separate, they are all highly interlinked and affect each other. For example, embedding DEI at either the programme or course level relies on what Garcia and colleagues (2020) call the inclusion-exclusion paradox. The paradox relates to the performativity of choices regarding "what to include or exclude in our conversations about equity and diversity (as educators)" (Garcia et al., 2020, p. 37). The inclusion or exclusion in learning conversations relates to every part of the curriculum: the learning goals, content, teaching methods, and assessment.

Thus, having one of the learning goals be aimed at uplifting DEI, educators will employ teaching content and methods that recognise the need to hear, respect, and encourage a variety of voices and opinions, including opposing ones (Šilenskytė, 2022). Since the opposition will likely be expressed differently in culturally and otherwise diverse classrooms, educators ought to consider providing various venues, forms, and cues so that opposing views might be expressed in very open but also indirect and subtle ways. As a result, the opposing views may be invited through class discussion and anonymous online voting. Students could also be informed about potential biases they may expose when working in diverse teams (Tavoletti et al., 2022). Case studies and role-playing may be adopted as a "safe way" to explore opposition or build compassion through "stepping into someone else's shoes". Educators should adopt specific behaviours that support the appropriate handling of opposing views: acknowledging the conflict, managing it constructively, diffusing it, and turning it into a valuable learning moment through debriefing and guided (self-)reflection (Bernardo, 2017). Learners who are provided with such role models will be able to manage conflicts in the (future) workplace and create a feeling of respect for their counterparts, regardless of any opposing opinions.

The loop of developing a curriculum with embedded DEI is likely to be closed with the deployment of assessment methods that consider

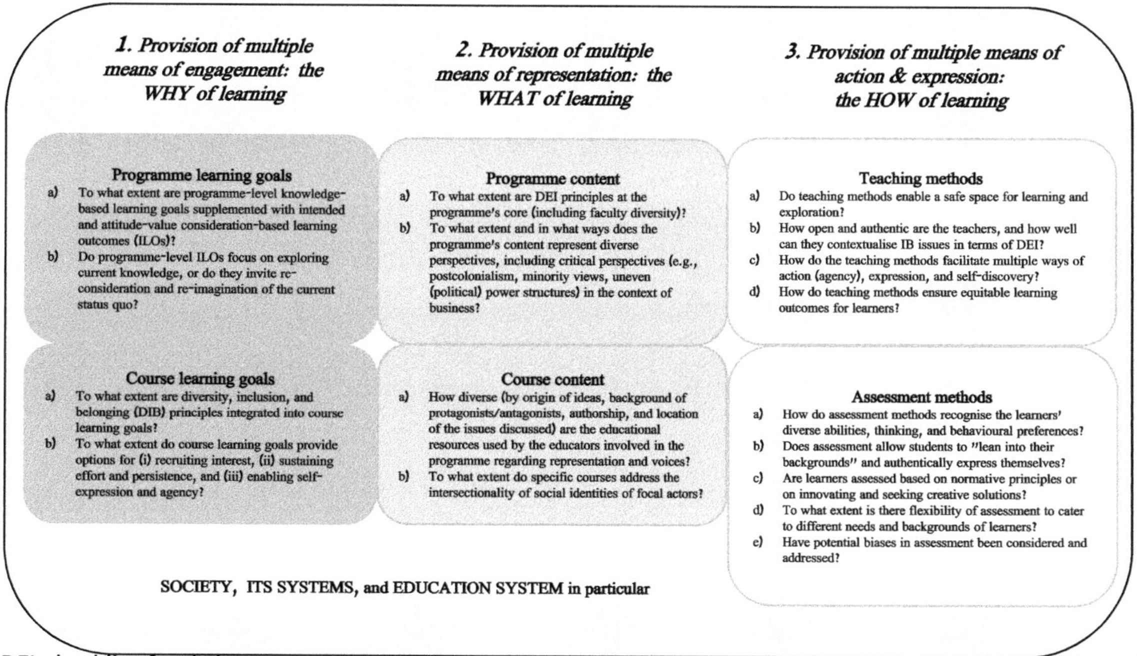

Fig. 2 DEI checklist for (IB) programme managers and educator teams (*Source* Authors' own work based on the UDL principles)

potential biases in the assessment process and allow the evaluation of student learning despite students possibly having different views from those of the educator. Educators may share their power with students by inviting them to select an essay topic or case to be analysed instead of providing them to the students. Educators are encouraged to be open and upfront about their potential and implicit biases (Šilenskytė, 2022). For example, in New Zealand, in front of indigenous students, a *pākehā* (white) educator should be open about their background and *whakapapa* (genealogy) and acknowledge the colonial biases in the IB discipline.

2.4 Interventions and Support to Uplift Diverse Learners

The DEI issues in higher education are *glocal* by nature. Glocal thinking helps to design effective interventions in HEI. The interventions designed with such thinking combine specific local, cultural, and historical needs with the global realities in the contemporary HEI context (AACSB, 2021). However, finding the right glocal balance in the interventions is difficult. For example, DEI initiatives in a North American HEI context predominantly focus on gender and racial diversity (Grace & Ammerman, 2022) but might be less sensitive to the linguistic diversity of non-native-speaking learners. In New Zealand, on the other hand, the primary focal areas are usually ethnicity (not race), ancestry/genealogy, and indigeneity—the latter set against a decolonisation context.

The disbalance in the DEI agenda and its interventions, like the ones mentioned above, could be noticed and addressed through business-school-wide discussions or other activities. Self-reflective exercises can be elevated to the institutional level. For instance, Bentley University carried out such an institutional-level exercise. The racial justice task force at Bentley University engaged *all* of its employees in a comprehensive discovery process focused on cultural barriers to racial equity (Grace & Ammerman, 2022). Understanding what DEI means in the context of a business school within a specific location and the context of a diverse student/faculty body within IB education is a first step in bridging actions at the institutional and individual levels.

After establishing general links between institutional-level actions and student/faculty bodies within the business school, the next step in universal learner-centred equity-focused approaches would be to embed the DEI and belonging principles within every kind of course (Hawkins & Staats, 2021) by utilising a bottom-up approach (Sippola, 2007). There needs to be a strong "people and culture" focus across levels and functional areas, capturing inclusive structures, processes, and investment beyond the corporate slogans mentioned in Sect. 2.1. There also needs to be a strategic commitment to move from diverse faculty representation (usually achieved through targeted hires) to having diverse academic departments or schools with clear leadership and employee pipelines (Wingfield, 2020). Recruitment of faculty needs to be informed by the value of representation (Hawkins & States, 2021) and based on specific skills (i.e., communication) and capabilities (i.e., compassion).

Language and framing play pivotal roles in making DEI initiatives actionable. Hence, adopting an inclusive language policy (i.e., gender-neutral pronouns and non-gender role descriptions) is usually the central step to ensure DEI integration in education (Market Research Society, 2022). Once such language policies are established at the institutional level, they set the guidelines for inclusive practices in every classroom and lecture. Educators typically role-model specific behaviours to students. Thus, staff guidance through policies and training in inclusive language and DEI is critical.

Interventions would be even more powerful if a whole-of-learner approach, which captures not just the learners themselves but also their social support system or lack of it (i.e., family, friends, and community), were adopted. An example of this would be adopting a *whānau*[4]-informed approach to assessment deadlines in New Zealand, recognising the competing demands indigenous student learners face in prioritising family (members') needs.

---

[4] *Whānau* refers to a community connected through common heritage and ancestry (*whakapapa*). It is a flexible and multi-layered concept built on a tribal worldview with physical, socioemotional, and spiritual meaning.

2.5 Evaluating and Monitoring DEI in IB Education

Evaluation and monitoring are essential for DEI principle implementation as they ensure accountability and the possibility of improving the system, actions, and practices even further (Riccò & Guerci, 2014). While regular monitoring of "standard" social-category-type metrics usually happens periodically at most HEIs, more holistic evaluations occur less regularly/frequently. They are often driven by external accreditation bodies (i.e., AACSB, EQUIS/EFMD). In some cases, they can also be prompted by external DEI audits for various reasons, including legal actions.

At a system level, Grace and Ammerman (2022) point to a necessary move from static DEI key performance indicators (KPIs) associated with various types of visible or invisible diversity (in isolation) towards a dynamic and integrated system that is clear, transparent, and active. For example, Stanford University's interactive diversity dashboard is based on its IDEAL DEI survey, which enables users to interact with DEI data in their preferred way, capturing intersectionality, i.e., interactions of different diversity dimensions.

At the programme level, a holistic well-being approach could also be adopted. Such an approach addresses not just typical academic achievement outcomes (i.e., completion rates and learning outcomes across social categories) but a variety of physical, social, psychological, material, and spiritual learner outcomes with intersecting social identities. Diverse outcomes could be compared across institutional, programme, and/or course levels.

At the individual staff member level, group and peer evaluations are common but insufficient to embed DEI and achieve belongingness. To foster inclusivity, handle difficult situations, encourage diverse voices, and promote respect despite opposing views, staff should engage in frequent self-reflection and continuous self-development, including mentoring and shadowing others. As Ravitch (2021) suggests, self-development takes time and is difficult. Educators could allocate time (and be provided with time resources, as indicated in Sect. 2.2) for self-reflection, monitoring their thinking and biases, envisioning their actions in difficult situations, developing their awareness about sensitive,

DEI-related issues, and learning communication techniques that support conversation based on mutual respect and trust (Ravitch, 2021). Peer interactions and support are also central to these efforts.

When educators engage in self-evaluation and continuous self-development, they can avoid significant interaction pitfalls, such as escalating conflict (due to the inability to manage opposing views in the classroom), unjust evaluations (e.g., due to biases regarding someone's verbal communication abilities or accent), or unnecessary misjudgments (e.g., due to erroneous assumptions about a learner's gender or ethnic origin based on their name, that is likely to create painful reactions and feelings of exclusion for those erroneously identified). To ease unwanted reactions when such mistakes happen (and they will happen because we can never reach perfection in DEI issues), educators are encouraged to adopt a life-long learning attitude in their teaching and self-evaluation, showing their humanistic side to the learners (Šilenskytė, 2022).

At the individual student level, students ought to be exposed to evaluating and assessing various DEI-related issues within their business school, IB (Sinkovics et al., 2022), and society. When considering course content, educators may think about integrating the successful examples of multinational corporations from both the Global North and South, having different gender identifications featured in the teaching cases, and having both mainstream (e.g., internationalisation theory or Hofstede dimensions of culture) and critical (e.g., post-colonial theory or critical realist identity theory) perspectives included in the curriculum. Different sources, e.g., The Economist and Al Jazeera, can be used to represent diverse evaluations of the same global issue. Naturally, business courses could integrate DEI-related thematic assessment assignments that point to pressing social challenges, such as modern slavery (Nagar & Hurd, 2020), discrimination, under-representation, social "washing" (e.g., Newbury et al., 2022), pre-judgement and social identities (Raskovic & Takacs-Haynes, 2021; Šilenskytė et al., 2022), human rights (Ruggie, 2007), global versus indigenous views (Salmon et al., 2022), and similar.

Students' evaluations assessing not their views or ability to replicate an established theory, perspective, or viewpoint, but their ability to evaluate critically diverse views and respectfully argue and effectively defend their chosen perspective, would further enliven DEI principles. Students' abilities to evaluate DEI and belonging(ness) in various contexts could also be further enhanced through experiential (Beckem II & Watkins, 2012; Viswanathan et al., 2022), self-directed (Šilenskytė, 2022), and radical or critical (Lyons & Tarc, 2022) teaching approaches. The underlying moral questions behind global wicked problems, which are often driven by diverse needs, preferences, and perspectives of various societal stakeholders (Rašković, 2022), could also be evaluated by observing the phenomenon-oriented nature of IB (Doh, 2015).

3 Conclusion

We have aimed to provide some of our considerations regarding how IB education may support SDG 8 implementation by embedding DEI and belonging principles at various levels of its activities, driven by the motivation that "*business schools occupy a pivotal role in the movement toward a more equitable, just, and inclusive economy. They educate students who enter the global talent market and therefore have the potential to be change agents*" (Grace & Ammerman, 2022, p. 2). We suggest that the rhetoric-vs-action gap can be narrowed by embedding DEI and belonging perspectives within HEIs, study programmes, course design, and the individual level. Utilising the OECD framework developed by Cerna and colleagues (2021), we have elaborated on the specific actions at each level. While some suggestions in our chapter are applicable to business schools in general, we have mainly focused on IB-specific examples. We hope our work sparks discussion and inspires IB educators and education leaders to shift from lofty aspirational rhetoric on DEI and belongingness to implemented actions.

References

AACSB. (2020). *AACSB business accreditation standards: Diversity and inclusion in the standards*. https://www.aacsb.edu/educators/accreditation/business-accreditation/diversity

AACSB. (2021). *Our commitment to diversity, equity, inclusion, and belonging*. https://www.aacsb.edu/-/media/publications/research-reports/deib_positioning_paper.pdf?rev=1876431c9287467f9395358b2810dfbf

Aragon-Correa, J. A., Marcus, A. A., Rivera, J. E., & Kenworthy, A. L. (2017). Sustainability management teaching resources and the challenge of balancing planet, people, and profits. *Academy of Management Learning and Education, 16*(3), 469–483. https://doi.org/10.5465/amle.2017.0180

Beckem, J. M., II., & Watkins, M. (2012). Bringing life to learning: Immersive experiential learning simulations: EBSCOhost. *Journal of Asynchronous Learning Networks, 16*(5), 61–71.

Bernardo, D. (2017). You just had a difficult conversation at work. Here's what to do next. *Harvard Business Review*, pp. 2–4. http://ezproxy.staffs.ac.uk/login?url=http://search.ebscohost.com/login.aspx?direct=true&db=bth&AN=123765762&site=ehost-live

Burrell Storms, S. L., Donovan, S. K., & Williams, T. P. (Eds). (2020). *Teaching through challenges for Equity, Diversity, and Inclusion (EDI)*. Rowman & Littlefield.

CAST. (n.d.). *The UDL guidelines*. Centre for Applied Special Technology (CAST). Retrieved August 17, 2023, from https://udlguidelines.cast.org

Cerna, L., Mezzanotte, C., Rutigliano, A., Brussino, O., Santiago, P., Borgonovi, F., & Guthrie, C. (2021). *Promoting inclusive education for diverse societies: A conceptual framework* (OECD Education Working Papers, 260). https://doi.org/10.1787/94ab68c6-en

Decent work and economic growth. (n.d.). *Global Goals*. https://www.globalgoals.org/goals/8-decent-work-and-economic-growth/

Dieleman, M., Šilenskytė, A., Lynden, K., Fletcher, M., & Panina, D. (2022). Toward more impactful international business education: A teaching innovation typology. *Journal of Teaching in International Business, 33*(4), 181–202. https://doi.org/10.1080/08975930.2022.2137279

Dobbin, F., & Kalev, A. (2016). Why diversity programs fail. *Harvard Business Review, 94*(7), 14.

Doh, J. P. (2015). From the editor: Why we need phenomenon-based research in international business. *Journal of World Business, 50*(4), 609–611. https://doi.org/10.1016/j.jwb.2015.08.002

Doh, J. P. (2021). Distance as diversity: Two sides of the same coin? *Journal of Management Studies, 58*(6), 1640–1643.

Ely, R. J., & Thomas, D. A. (1996). Making differences matter. *Harvard Business Review, 74*(5), 79–90.

Ely, R. J., & Thomas, D. A. (2020). Getting serious about diversity. *Harvard Business Review, 98*(6), 114–122. http://search.ebscohost.com/login.aspx?direct=true&db=bsh&AN=146207724&site=ehost-live

Fitzsimmons, S., Özbilgin, M., Thomas, D. C., & Nkomo, S. (2023). Equality, diversity and inclusion in international business: A review and research agenda. *Journal of International Business Studies, in press*. https://doi.org/10.1057/s41267-023-00642-x

Garcia, S., McCoy, T., & Nguyen, H. (2020). In S. K. Storms, S. L. Burrell, S. K. Donovan, & T. P. Williams (Eds.), *Teaching through challenges for equity, diversity, and inclusion* (pp. 35–44). Rowman & Littlefield.

Grace, B., & Ammerman, C. (2022). How business schools are really doing with diversity. In *Harvard Business Publishing Inspiring Minds* (pp. 1–9).

Hawkins, N., & States, B. (2021). Towards a more inclusive business school. *Harvard Business Publishing Education: Inspiring Minds*. https://hbsp.harvard.edu/inspiring-minds/what-administrators-and-educators-can-do-now-to-drive-progress-on-diversity

Listenwise. (2021). *5 ways listenwise podcasts support students with disabilities*. BLOG. Retrieved August 15, 2023, from https://blog.listenwise.com/2021/10/5-ways-listenwise-supports-students-with-ieps-and-504-accommodations/

Lutterman-Aguilar, A. (2003). Educating about diversity & global issues: A review of simulation games for use in community-based learning programs. *Transformations: The Journal of Inclusive Scholarship and Pedagogy, 14*(2), 101–126.

Lyons, J., & Tarc, P. (2022). How might IB classroom pedagogy 'make a better world ?' (Toward) illuminating a promising IBDP teacher praxis. *Globalisation, Societies and Education*, pp. 1–20. https://doi.org/10.1080/14767724.2022.2142764

Market Research Society, M. S. C. C. (2022). *Diversity & inclusion best practice guides: Use of language*.

Nagar, S., & Hurd, F. (2020). Addressing modern slavery in the IB classroom: Are we doing enough? *AIB Insights, 20*(2), 2–6.

Newbury, W., Rašković, M. (Matt), Colakoglu, S. S., Gonzalez-Perez, M. A., & Minbaeva, D. (2022). Diversity, equity and inclusion in international business: Dimensions and challenges. *AIB Insights, 22*(3), 1–6. https://doi.org/10.46697/001c.36582

OECD. (2023). *Equity and inclusion in education: Finding strength through diversity*. https://doi.org/10.1787/e9072e21-en

Rašković, M. (2022). International business policymaking for a "wicked" world. *Journal of International Business Policy, 5*(3), 353–362. https://doi.org/10.1057/s42214-021-00113-w

Raskovic, M., & Takacs-Haynes, K. (2021). (Re)discovering social identity theory: An agenda for multinational enterprise internalisation theory. *Multinational Business Review, 29*(2), 145–165. https://doi.org/10.1108/MBR-02-2020-0031

Ravitch, S. M. (2021). Equitable teaching takes time and practice. Here are strategies to help. How to prepare yourself—and your students—to discuss race, identity, and equity. *Harvard Business Publishing Inspiring Minds.* https://hbsp.harvard.edu/inspiring-minds/equitable-teaching-takes-time-and-practice-here-are-strategies-to-help

Rezvani, S., & Gordon, S. A. (2021). How sharing our stories builds inclusion. *Harvard Business Review*. https://hbr.org/2021/11/how-sharing-our-stories-builds-inclusion

Riccò, R., & Guerci, M. (2014). Diversity challenge: An integrated process to bridge the "implementation gap." *Business Horizons, 57*(2), 235–245. https://doi.org/10.1016/j.bushor.2013.11.007

Riedel, A. S., Beatson, A. T., & Gottlieb, U. (2023). Inclusivity and diversity: A systematic review of strategies employed in the higher education marketing discipline. *Journal of Marketing Education, 45*(2), 123–140. https://doi.org/10.1177/02734753231159010

Roth, K., & Kostova, T. (2003). The use of the multinational corporation as a research context. *Journal of Management, 29*(6), 883–902. https://doi.org/10.1016/S0149-2063(03)00083-7

Rousseau, D. M., & Fried, Y. (2001). Location, location, location: Contextualising organisational research. *Journal of Organizational Behavior, 22*(1), 1–13. https://doi.org/10.1002/job.78

Ruggie, J. G. (2007). Business and human rights: The evolving international agenda. *American Journal of International Law, 101*(4), 819–840.

Salmon, E., Chavez, J. F., & Murphy, M. (2022). New perspectives and critical insights from indigenous peoples' research: A systematic review of indigenous management and organization literature new perspectives and critical insights from indigenous peoples' research: A systematic review of indigen. *Academy of Management Annals*.

Sanger, C. S. (2020). Inclusive pedagogy and universal design approaches for diverse learning environments. In C. S. Sanger & N. W. Gleason (Eds.), *Diversity and inclusion in higher education: Lessons from across Asia* (pp. 31–71). Palgrave Macmillan/Springer.

Sewchurran, K. (2022). *Sustainability is essential in business education*. AACSB. https://www.aacsb.edu/insights/articles/2022/05/sustainability-is-essential-in-business-education

Šilenskytė, A. (2022). Teaching diversity management online: a learning journey for achieving inclusion. In S. Bustamante, E. Saltevo, M. Schmitz, & M. Martinovic (Eds.), *Shaping a sustainable future. Innovative teaching practices for educating responsible leaders* (pp. 165–184). Nomos Publishing. https://doi.org/10.5771/9783748933090-165

Šilenskytė, A., Kohtamäki, M., & Dhanaraj, C. (2022). Strategy implementation in the transnational MNC: A critical realist investigation of European and Indian unit collaboration. *Journal of Business Research, 152*, 276–289. https://doi.org/10.1016/j.jbusres.2022.07.041

Sinkovics, N., Vieira, L. M., & van Tulder, R. (2022). Working toward the sustainable development goals in earnest—Critical international business perspectives on designing and implementing better interventions. *Critical Perspectives on International Business, 18*(4), 445–456. https://doi.org/10.1108/cpoib-05-2022-0059

Sippola, A. (2007). Developing culturally diverse organisations: A participative and empowerment-based method. *Women in Management Review, 22*(4), 253–273. https://doi.org/10.1108/09649420710754228

Slee, R. (2019). Belonging to an age of exclusion. *International Journal of Inclusive Education, 23*(9), 909–922. https://doi.org/10.1080/13603116.2019.1602366

Smith, D. G., & Schonfeld, N. B. (2020). The benefits of diversity: what the research tells us. *About Campus, 5*(5), 16–23. https://doi.org/10.1177/1086482200005005055

Tavoletti, E., Stephens, R. D., Taras, V., & Dong, L. (2022). Nationality biases in peer evaluations: The country-of-origin effect in global virtual teams. *International Business Review, 31*(2), 101969. https://doi.org/10.1016/j.ibusrev.2021.101969

Tonegava, Y. (2022). Educating in SDGs: What is inclusive and equitable education. In S. Urata, K. Kurd, & Y. Tonegava (Eds.), *Sustainable development disciplines for humanity: Breaking down the 5Ps-people, planet, prosperity, peace, and partnerships* (pp. 55–70). Springer.

UBC. (2020). *Indigenous voices.* https://irsi.ubc.ca/indigenous-communities/indigenous-voices

UVA. (2022). *War in Ukraine—University of Vaasa guidelines.* https://www.uwasa.fi/en/war-ukraine-university-vaasa-guidelines

Van Tulder, R., Rodrigues, S. B., Mirza, H., & Sexsmith, K. (2021). The UN's sustainable development goals: Can multinational enterprises lead the decade of action? *Journal of International Business Policy, 4*(1), 1–21. https://doi.org/10.1057/s42214-020-00095-1

Van Tulder, R., & Van Mil, E. (2022). *Principles of sustainable business: Frameworks for corporate action on the SDGs.* Routledge.

Viswanathan, M., Sreekumar, A., Duncan, R., & Cai, S. (2022). Global virtual immersion in a post-Covid world lessons learned in moving from sympathy to informed empathy in subsistence marketplaces. *Journal of Teaching in International Business, 33*(4), 203–223.

Williams, D. A. (2013). *Strategic diversity leadership: Activating change and transformation in higher education.* Stylus Publishing.

Wingfield, A. H. (2020). We built a diverse academic department in 5 years. here's how. *Harvard Business Publishing Education: Inspiring Minds.* https://hbsp.harvard.edu/inspiring-minds/we-built-a-diverse-academic-department-in-5-years-heres-how

16

The Role of External Context in Enhancing Student Learning Outcomes Through Experiential Learning

Joanne Wright

1 Introduction

By embracing experiential learning approaches (Christ & Burritt, 2019) , business schools are well-positioned to support progress towards the United Nations Sustainable Development Goals (SDGs). This chapter focuses on how international business (IB) educators can enhance student learning outcomes by adopting experiential learning approaches (Johnson & Jordan, 2019). Experiential activities take a 'learning by doing' approach, which encourages students to engage more deeply in their learning by drawing on theoretical, behavioural, emotional, and reflective perspectives (Nagar & Hurd, 2019). Ranging from industry projects to case-based discussions, experiential learning activities can support students to understand complex global dynamics (Nagar & Hurd, 2019; Seow et al., 2019), and also to develop critical thinking and

J. Wright (✉)
The University of Auckland, Auckland, New Zealand
e-mail: joanne.wright@auckland.ac.nz

N. Sinkovics et al. (eds.), *International Business and SDG 8*, The Academy of International Business, https://doi.org/10.1007/978-3-031-46802-5_16

solution-seeking behaviours which help them understand connections between the many challenges that internationalising firms face.

However, many factors can affect the success of experiential learning approaches. For instance, prior work experience (Nagar & Hurd, 2019), and student culture (Zhu & O'Sullivan, 2022) can influence the level of engagement in activities, influencing outcomes. Another challenge lies in developing realistic learning environments, to facilitate student opportunities to engage with the international environment and observe and experience the challenges faced by managers (Aggarwal & Wu, 2019). Creating such a learning context can demand significant resources, which may impose constraints on educator options. Resource constraints can also hamper efforts to scale up experiential activities for larger cohorts. Taken together, it can be inferred that not all learning environments can offer equal learning outcomes.

Drawing on this idea, this chapter suggests that the New Zealand (NZ) small and medium-sized enterprise (SME) context offers heightened opportunities for students to learn about internationalisation through experiential learning activities. Several reasons support this. Firstly, NZ SMEs experience aggravated challenges when internationalising. For instance, enabling students to understand market selection decisions considering NZ's geographic isolation can help students draw connections between strategic decisions (and decision-makers) and subsequent outcomes. Secondly, strong connections and reciprocal relationships between many NZ SME managers and NZ Universities can help facilitate student access to industry leaders. This privileged access provides opportunities for IB educators to establish realistic experiential learning activities, strengthen student learning outcomes, which in the long-term supports progress towards SDG8 (especially SDG8.3—as it relates to small firm growth) as students move beyond tertiary education, to industry.

The activities and observations outlined in this chapter are drawn from a NZ University postgraduate IB programme. Students following this pathway, a taught masters, are predominantly from Asia, moving to NZ for the duration of their programme of study. Some Asian students however are educated in NZ, remaining in the country for their university education. This chapter first highlights in more detail, the uniqueness of the NZ environment, detailing the reasons it offers potential for enhanced student learning outcomes in SME internationalisation through the adoption of experiential learning approaches. The chapter also outlines some practical examples of experiential learning assessments which, upon reflection, highlight strong learning opportunities for students, but also identifies some complexities for IB educators that warrant deeper investigation.

2 What Makes the NZ Context Unique?

NZ is an export-driven economy (Fath et al., 2021) which meets the criteria of an advanced small and open economy (SMOPEC) having a high per capita income and a small population (Skilling, 2020, 2023). Such economies consistently outperform larger economies in terms of gross domestic product (GDP) growth (Skilling, 2018), therefore offering potential insights about growth. Like comparable SMOPECs (e.g., Finland, Denmark, Singapore etc.), NZ has a high proportion of SMEs, which when defined as firms with 49 or less full-time employees (OECD, 2020) comprises around 99% of all firms in the economy (OECD, 2022). Further, around 72% of NZ SMEs have no employees at all (Statistics NZ, 2022), suggesting that growth efforts rest solely on the founder(s) ability to support growth while also maintaining existing operations. Thus, pursuing growth through internationalisation can spread SME resources thinly, challenging survival.

Further, in contrast to its contemporaries, NZ's growth challenges are compounded by geographical isolation. NZ shares no land borders with other countries and lacks proximity to major trading partners. This impacts the ease with which NZ SMEs establish networks in foreign markets, which are necessary to support local market knowledge (Johanson & Vahlne, 2009), knowledge spillovers (Audretsch & Feldman, 1996) and also opportunities to embed in global supply chains (Skilling, 2018). Taken together with the small, open nature of the NZ economy, geographical isolation contributes negatively to productivity performance. Therefore, while NZ has a strong record of establishing free trade agreements, with consecutive governments developing export-focused policies (Kahiya, 2020), NZ lags behind other advanced SMOPECs who drive growth through innovation (Skilling, 2020). NZ's GDP growth, in contrast, is driven by increased labour hours and production output (Skilling, 2020), an unsustainable long-term growth proposition.

These factors contribute to the growth challenges of NZ SMEs, even by comparison to other advanced SMOPECS who share many of the same country and firm size-related challenges. Despite this, many NZ SMEs are successful, with globally recognised brands, suggesting that the above challenges can be overcome. Understanding how NZ SMEs navigate the challenges provides a wonderful and unique foundation for experiential learning for students.

3 Experiential Learning and Context

Kolb's experiential learning cycle (Kolb, 1984) is perhaps the most influential model on experiential learning theory (Morris, 2019). Kolb suggested that for learning to be effective learners must develop four different abilities—concrete experience, reflective observation, abstract conceptualisation, and active experimentation (Kolb, 1984; Morris, 2019). Therefore, to support learning about SME internationalisation, IB educators must develop a learning environment that enables students to engage fully in the SMEs internationalisation experiences, their processes, opportunities, and challenges. However, for successful experiential learning, educators must also provide opportunities for reflection, enabling students to develop their own understanding based on their experiences. This theorising can then be used to guide decision-making and solve problems. Therefore, providing an authentic learning context which is sufficiently realistic to offer students the opportunity to observe and experience SME internationalisation challenges, opportunities, and decision-making processes is a key foundation for long-term learning benefits through this approach.

There is an important distinction between learning *from* experience and experiential learning. Experiential activities are intentionally designed, using formal processes to support learning (Kurthakoti &

Good, 2019). Implemented via a range of approaches like case study discussions and workshops, or industry internships, experiential learning requires the deliberate establishment of the context within which learning can occur (Usher & Solomon, 1999). Learning *from* experience reflects what individuals experience daily.

4 Experiential Learning and the Benefits of the NZ SME Context

The NZ SME context offers students and IB educators a unique and important opportunity to learn about SME internationalisation and enhance learning outcomes. There are several reasons for this. Firstly, the nature of the challenges confronting NZ SMEs, especially those seeking internationalisation, are aggravated, even in contrast to other advanced SMOPECs (for example, Denmark, Sweden, and Finland). These aggravated challenges allow students to observe SME processes and decision-making approaches more readily, enabling students to engage in and experience the way SMEs navigate internationalisation challenges and opportunities. This in turn enables students to reflect on the tension between their experiences and prior knowledge, driving new learning outcomes. For example, through industry projects, students can observe how SMEs navigate geographical and cultural distance, how they establish partnerships even with limited knowledge, and how they can overcome a lack of legitimacy. Secondly, because NZ SMEs are very small, the key decision-makers are limited, creating stronger ties between decisions and subsequent firm-level outcomes. In larger organisations this is often ambiguous because it is often not possible, to identify which decisions lead to observed outcomes.

Thirdly, the NZ SME context is potentially enhanced because of the privileged access and collaboration opportunities with SME managers and NZ universities. A reciprocal relationship often exists between these institutions, with NZ SMEs able to leverage knowledge and research developed through student-based industry projects, in turn providing invaluable hands-on-learning opportunities for students. For instance,

SME managers often have ideas about international growth opportunities but lack the resources to research in detail. Further, NZ SME managers often feel an obligation to engage in IB education, engaging as guest lecturers, and participating in industry projects. These opportunities enable students to interact with industry leaders, developing additional knowledge through experience, often about the entrepreneurial nature of the NZ SME international challenge.

Lastly, experiential learning is not limited to industry projects or internships. Opportunities for experiential learning in theory focused courses also exists. This can be achieved by drawing on valuable NZ SME case studies to support student understanding of theoretical concepts, engaging with founders and managers through guest lectures, and introducing assessments which are focused on the application of knowledge learnt to solve real-world business growth challenges. For instance, helping students to identify the differences between staged internationalisation pathways and effectual pathways can begin to help them unpack the different challenges, and decisions made by NZ SMEs. In general, NZ offers opportunities for IB educators to develop targeted experiential learning activities to understand SME internationalisation.

5 Examples of Practice

Under the broad heading of experiential learning, many techniques are used in business education generally. This chapter provides examples that draw on project-based learning (PBL), and experiential assessments.

5.1 Postgraduate Experiential Learning Example 1

This example falls under PBL, which is described as 'a systematic teaching method that engages students in learning knowledge and skills through an extended inquiry process structured among complex, authentic questions and carefully designed projects and tasks' (Markham et al., 2003, p. 4). PBL creates a strong connection between the student learning opportunities and the context they are embedded in, enhancing learning outcomes.

5.1.1 Course Context and Aim

This course relates to the capstone IB consultancy project, taught over the final 10-week quarter of an 18-month taught master's degree. Students are required to engage in two related courses that run concurrently. The first focuses on capability development—both research and professional skills, and the second is an industry project where the students are assigned to a 'live client' to solve an IB growth challenge. Once assigned to a project, students work onsite with the client three days per week, meeting weekly with their project supervisor for academic and research direction.

The objectives of the programme are three-fold. First, to support the student in developing work-ready capabilities. These capabilities range from developing an understanding of the NZ work context, professionalism in the work context, and conducting purposeful and valuable meetings. For example, students must organise, administer, and document their project kick-off meeting. Second, efforts are made to assign students to a project in an industry they would like to work in post-graduation. This provides students with opportunities to gain exposure in that industry and establish professional relationships. Finally, the project provides students with a unique opportunity to embed themselves in the organisational context, and solve a key IB growth challenge or opportunity, systematically applying concepts learned throughout their master's degree.

5.1.2 Outcome

This course is challenging for all students. However, the rewards are bountiful, supporting the development of an applied understanding of IB concepts in a practical way. Establishing the context and embedding students within the NZ SME work environment provides students with in-depth insight into the challenges and opportunities of growth.

Students become acutely aware of the constraints of limited resources, as they themselves grapple with trying to develop cohesive international business strategies within the boundaries of the SMEs' available resources and capabilities. Student submissions include a 30-minute client presentation and a 12,000-word consultancy report, both are significant submissions, designed to help the students systematically deliver their research findings, apply critical and creative thinking, and develop practical (SMART) recommendations.

As a secondary outcome, students often comment that an unanticipated benefit was the professional skills developed through the course, which, along with the evidence of having experience working in a NZ firm, supported them in securing their first post-master's role.

5.1.3 Assessment Reflection

Supporting the students through this course over several years has been both challenging and rewarding. In general, the transformation of each student in terms of their knowledge and capability is dramatic, and their confidence also greatly improved. For most, this course helps ease worries about transitioning from university to industry. For many, this is their first experience in navigating the messiness and ambiguity of a real business challenge, along with the nuances of the NZ SME work context, which they often find unexpectedly informal and fast-paced. Post project interviews with clients indicate that in many cases student recommendations are taken onboard and implemented, and on occasion with student involvement.

As each cohort enters the programme, alumni are invited to meet and talk to them about their project and programme experiences. It is heartening to hear that students use the frameworks, approaches, and their knowledge in the projects to tackle challenges at work. Thus, through the projects, students develop new, systematic approaches to understanding business challenges, developing long-term capabilities which support them in their careers.

5.2 Postgraduate Experiential Assessment Example 2

The following example outlines an assessment that incorporated an experiential approach within a foundational/theory course.

5.2.1 Course Context and Aim

The course 'Foundations of International Business Strategy' is a 10-week course, part of a taught Master of Management in IB degree. The course is framed by a two-part assessment. Part 1, is a group assignment, requiring the group to develop an IB growth strategy for a NZ SME. The assessment scenario is that as a 'boutique consulting firm' the group must pitch their internationalisation strategy to the SME's Board. Students develop a 10-minute presentation and a slide deck (capturing presentation, evidence, and reference slides). Part 2, an individual assignment, builds on part 1, and requires the student to write an email memo advising the CEO of their recommended foreign market entry strategy.

The aim of these assessments together is for the students to understand firstly how firms internationalise, and how this differs from a strategy to enter a specific foreign market. The NZ SME focus is embraced, increasing the complexities like limited resources. This requires the students to assess if their proposed strategies are feasible and realistic, given the SMEs constraints.

5.2.2 Outcome

Students reflected on the difficulty of the assignment, mostly commenting that while it is easy to develop strategies, developing realistic and feasible strategies is challenging. This assessment encouraged students to think critically about how to overcome resource constraints, in particular financial limitations, knowledge, and limited experience. An important outcome of this experiential assessment was the demonstration of knowledge about course concepts, their application to a real-world context and engagement in higher level thinking and solution seeking at the conceptual/strategic level required at a post graduate level. For our mostly international student cohorts, this assessment is embedded in the NZ SME context, which, provides opportunities for students to improve their understanding of the NZ context.

Because many SME founders and CEOs have strong connections with the university, two of the allocated SME CEOs offered guest lectures during the course. This encouraged deeper engagement by the students and enabled them to draw on their research and ask additional questions. One student commented they sent the CEO a LinkedIn connection request, which was accepted on the same day, along with a message acknowledging the great questions the student asked. These interpersonal connections with business leaders and our student cohorts reinforced the specialness of the NZ SME context.

5.2.3 Assessment Reflection

There is a challenge in creating the conditions that lead to engaged and committed learning, especially in a theory-based course which is typically taught in a traditional lecture style. However, students reflected at the end of this assessment with many highlighting their appreciation in completing an assessment that enabled them to apply knowledge as they were learning it in class. Attendance by NZ SME managers also reinforced to the students that the knowledge they were learning was valid and important in a real-world context.

6 Overall Observations and Reflections

Overall, this chapter suggests that establishing an appropriate context for experiential learning activities can influence long-term student learning outcomes and capability development. In establishing a well-designed experiential learning programme in IB, this can translate to progress towards SDG8, in particular SDG8.3 which relates in part to SME growth. Student feedback and observations throughout the examples above suggest the approach supported the transformation of student experiences into knowledge.

However, several factors appeared to influence learning outcomes. Firstly, if students had been in NZ long-term, their ability to understand the NZ SME context appeared much stronger. Secondly, with predominantly Asian student cohorts, cultural challenges emerged, suggesting that before pushing forward with a 'learning-by-doing' approach, more thinking is required to ensure inclusivity, enabling all students to benefit from experiential learning opportunities. Relatedly, we observed differences in engagement with experiential activities across different cohorts which were accentuated if a dominant culture existed. Therefore, student culture may impact the benefits of experiential activities.

6.1 Level of Embeddedness in the NZ Context

Throughout the covid pandemic, the postgraduate courses discussed above were taught both online and in person. We observed that students who were already in NZ when the borders closed, exhibited greater engagement in the context, and more able to assess research findings strategically. Offshore students in contrast were less engaged in activities, with a focus on applying frameworks, rather than developing knowledge about the practical realities of NZ SMEs. It was not uncommon for example, for offshore students to propose a sensible strategy but one that lacked reality and feasibility given the SMEs limited resource. In one example, a group recommended a SME with 5 full-time employees, establish a manufacturing plant in China to reduce manufacturing costs and enhance logistics.

Past research shows that limited exposure to a culture can lead to confusion for students trying to understand the environment (Zhu & O'Sullivan, 2022). This suggests that having an existing connection with the culture may be important in supporting learning outcomes. With covid behind us, and experiential learning approaches being increasingly adopted, overcoming this challenge is vital to successfully enhancing the learning outcomes of our Asian students. A recently proposed solution (to be implemented) is to develop culture-specific student clubs, pairing late programme students with new students, to help students better understand the culture and opportunities for growth.

6.2 Tension Between Experiential Learning Benefits and Culture

While Western universities are increasingly adopting experiential learning approaches, in the pursuit of enhanced long-term learning outcomes, we identified that not all students benefit from experiential learning, with these approaches less accepted in Asian cultures (Speece, 2002). With Asian students being an important target for many universities this is problematic. Chinese students prefer traditional approaches to teaching, with strategies like repetition and rote learning (Kennedy, 2002). The facilitator role of educators in experiential learning activities, also translates poorly for many Asian students.

Further, we observed that with high proportions of Chinese students, increased demands were placed on teaching availability with feedback requested via numerous channels including emails, online chat sessions, and emails requesting assessment draft reviews. Chinese students also insist on clear and explicit instruction, limiting opportunities for creative thinking. As experiential learning approaches are implemented, deeper thought is required to ensure benefits exist for all students.

7 Concluding Thoughts—Experiential Learning, Context, and SDG8

The benefits of learning about NZ SME growth from within NZ are manifold. The natural context isolates and accentuates SME challenges. However, many NZ SMEs overcome these challenges, embracing entrepreneurial approaches growth, and leveraging relationships to supplement resource constraints. The NZ SME context provides a unique environment to implement experiential learning opportunities that can lead to enhanced student learning outcomes.

Experiential learning, which is embedded in a learning context that provides authentic opportunities for students to gain hands-on-learning opportunities in IB, can enhance long-term learning outcomes. Through purposeful activities, IB students, our industry decision, and policy makers of the future develop critical thinking and solution-seeking capabilities, supporting the stronger alignment of social and organisational goals (Christ & Burritt, 2019). In preparing IB students to connect with real-world challenges, opportunities exist to support long-term progress towards SDG8.

References

Aggarwal, R., & Wu, Y. (2019). Challenges in implementing experiential learning in IB education. *Journal of Teaching in International Business, 30*(1), 1–5.

Audretsch, D. B., & Feldman, M. P. (1996). R&D spillovers and the geography of innovation and production. *American Economic Review, 86*(3), 630–640.

Christ, K. L., & Burritt, R. L. (2019). Implementation of sustainable development goals: The role for business academics. *Australian Journal of Management, 44*(4), 571–593. https://doi.org/10.1177/0312896219870575

Fath, B., Fiedler, A., Sinkovics, N., Sinkovics, R. R., & Sullivan-Taylor, B. (2021). International relationships and resilience of New Zealand SME exporters during COVID-19. *Critical Perspectives on International Business, 17*(2), 359–379. https://doi.org/10.1108/cpoib-05-2020-0061

Johanson, J., & Vahlne, J.-E. (2009). The Uppsala internationalization process model revisited: From liability of foreignness to liability of outsidership. *Journal of International Business Studies, 40*(9), 1411–1431. https://doi.org/10.1057/jibs.2009.24

Johnson, J. E., & Jordan, M. L. (2019). The development of undergraduate international business practicums in small business schools: An experiential learning framework. *Journal of Teaching in International Business, 30*(1), 6–32. https://doi.org/10.1080/08975930.2019.1628686

Kahiya, E. T. (2020). Context in international business: Entrepreneurial internationalization from a distant small open economy. *International Business Review, 29*.

Kennedy, P. (2002). Learning cultures and learning styles: Myth-understandings about adult (Hong Kong) Chinese learners. *International Journal of Lifelong Education, 21*(5), 430–445. https://doi.org/10.1080/02601370210156745
Kolb, D. A. (1984). *Experiential learning: Experience as the source of learning and development* (P. Hall, Ed.). Englewood Cliffs.
Kurthakoti, R., & Good, D. C. (2019). Evaluating outcomes of experiential learning: An overview of available approaches. In *The Palgrave handbook of learning and teaching international business and management* (pp. 33–61). https://doi.org/10.1007/978-3-030-20415-0_3
Markham, T., Larmer, J., & Ravitz, J. L. (2003). *Project based learning handbook: A guide to standards-focused project based learning for middle and high school teachers*. Buck Institute for Education.
Morris, T. H. (2019). Experiential learning—A systematic review and revision of Kolb's model. *Interactive Learning Environments, 28*(8), 1064–1077. https://doi.org/10.1080/10494820.2019.1570279
Nagar, S., & Hurd, F. (2019). Experiential learning in the executive education international business classroom: The importance of context. In M. A. Gonzalez-Perez, K. Lynden, & V. Taras (Eds.), *The Palgrave handbook of learning and teaching international business and management* (pp. 915–951). Springer International Publishing. https://doi.org/10.1007/978-3-030-20415-0_43
OECD. (2020). New Zealand-key facts on SME financing. https://www.oecd-ilibrary.org/sites/a819a8fe-en/index.html?itemId=/content/component/a819a8fe-en
OECD. (2022). New Zealand-key facts on SME financing, 32. https://www.oecd-ilibrary.org/sites/5e4c6af5-en/index.html?itemId=/content/component/5e4c6af5-en#:~:text=SME's%2C%20when%20defined%20as%20businesses,the%20data%20is%20available%20from.
Seow, P., Pan, G., & Koh, G. (2019). Examining an experiential learning approach to prepare students for the volatile, uncertain, complex and ambiguous (VUCA) work environment. *The International Journal of Management Education, 17*, 62–76.
Skilling, D. (2018). *Policy insights for Scotland from small advanced economies*. Reform Scotland.
Skilling, D. (2020). Frontier firms: An international small advanced economy perspective. *Report prepared for the New Zealand Productivity Commission.*
Skilling, D. (2023). *Improving economic resilience enhancing economic resilience of industries and communities to persistent supply chain disruptions.*

Speece, M. (2002). Experiential learning methods in Asian cultures: A Singapore case study. *Business Communication Quarterly, 65*(3), 106–116.

Usher, R., & Solomon, N. (1999). Experiential learning and the shaping of subjectivity in the workplace. *Studies in the Education of Adults, 31*(2), 155–163. https://doi.org/10.1080/02660830.1999.11661409

Zhu, H., & O'Sullivan, H. (2022). Shhhh! Chinese students are studying quietly in the UK. *Innovations in Education and Teaching International, 59*(3), 275–284. https://doi.org/10.1080/14703297.2020.1813603

17

Examining Modern Slavery Through Design Thinking in the International Business Classroom

Swati Nagar

1 Introduction

The 2030 Agenda for Sustainable Development, adopted by all United Nations Member States in 2015, provides a shared blueprint for peace and prosperity for people and the planet, now and into the future. At its heart are the 17 Sustainable Development Goals (SDGs), an urgent call for action by all developed and developing countries in a global partnership. They recognise that ending poverty and other deprivations must go together with strategies that improve health and education, reduce inequality, and spur economic growth—all while tackling climate change and preserving our environment. Of the 17 SDGs, SDG8, Decent Work and Economic Growth (target 8.7- Eradicating Forced Labour/Modern Slavery) is perhaps most pertinent to the discipline of International Business. SDG8 and target 8.7 promote inclusive and decent work for all

S. Nagar (✉)
Discipline of International Business, The University of Sydney Business School, Sydney, Australia
e-mail: swati.nagar@sydney.edu.au

N. Sinkovics et al. (eds.), *International Business and SDG 8*, The Academy of International Business, https://doi.org/10.1007/978-3-031-46802-5_17

while ensuring sustainable economic growth. To realise this goal, the UN has several initiatives to work with governments, industry and academia. Driven by business school deans and the industry, the Principles of Responsible Management Education (PRME) is an example of such an initiative in academia. This initiative aims to ensure business schools provide business students with the skills needed to attend to grand challenges (such as modern slavery) and equip future business leaders with the understanding and ability to deliver change tomorrow.

However, as outlined in this chapter, there needs to be more focus in the business classroom on how firms need to change their strategies, operations and activities to meet the expectations set by SDGs (in particular, SDG8). The paucity of academic discussion on modern slavery also highlights an apparent lack of urgency in the business school curricula to move beyond the traditional focus on the firm towards the inclusivity of all stakeholders necessary to address the grand challenge of modern slavery. To an extent, this limited focus also hinders the development of our student capability by not allowing them to fully comprehend the role of the firm, consumers and the government in ensuring inclusivity and access to decent work, especially for the most vulnerable in our communities. This chapter aims to contribute to this limited literature by proposing how design thinking can be a pedagogical tool to inform and educate students on the grand challenge—modern slavery.

This chapter has seven sections. Following the introduction, the second section presents a brief overview of modern slavery. Sections three and four outline the nature and extent of exploitation in cocoa farming and the chocolate industry, followed by a discussion on modern slavery in the IB classroom. Section five presents an outline of design thinking as a pedagogical tool. Section six presents the in-class activity and assessment, which use design thinking principles in examining the nature of modern slavery in cocoa farming and the chocolate industry. The final section (seven) concludes the chapter by offering key actionable insights.

2 The Nature of Modern Slavery

Though slavery is considered mainly a historical phenomenon, the enslavement of vulnerable individuals remains a reality for millions of workers worldwide (Walk Free Foundation, 2023). According to estimates by the International Labour Organisation (ILO), approximately 50 million people were in some form of modern slavery in 2021 (ILO, 2022). The number of people in modern slavery has risen significantly in the last five years (especially during and post-pandemic). It is estimated that approximately 10 million more people were in modern slavery in 2021 compared to 2016 global estimates (ILO, 2022). It is important to note that there are two distinct forms of modern slavery—forced labour and forced human trafficking (including forced marriage and commercial sexual exploitation). While forced human trafficking has long existed and is a result of organised crime, the rise in the use of forced labour is more a result of globalisation and opportunistic firm behaviour that we have witnessed in the last four decades (Crane, 2013; Samonova, 2019; Stringer & Michailova, 2018a(a)). The contemporary version of this social stain (modern slavery) ranges from pauper wages to forced labour (Burmester et al., 2019; Stringer & Michailova, 2018a). Modern slavery keeps workers in abusive employment (Breman, 1996; Yea & Stringer, 2021). It is one of the most pervasive and insidious parts of the global economy (Michailova et al., 2020; Molchanova, 2019; Raskovic, 2023) moving from child labour in developing nations to migrant workers facing illegal and cruel work practices in the middle of the developed world's metropolises (Hodal, 2019; Major, 2012; Nagaraj, 2020). Given the context of this chapter, it is therefore fitting to discuss forced labour (modern slavery) that is driven by the corporate agenda of lower production costs.

While a global issue, modern slavery is most widespread in developing and least developed economies (Islam & Stringer, 2018; Khattak. et al., 2017). Modern slavery permeates every aspect of our society. It is woven through our clothes, lights our electronics and seasons our food. At its core, modern slavery is a manifestation of extreme inequality. It is a mirror held to power, reflecting who in any given society has it and who does not. This paradox is most visible in the transnational supply chains of several firms. Modern slavery no longer involves the formal legal designation of persons as chattels (Choi-Fitzpatrick, 2017; Hodal, 2019). Still, as noted by Stringer & Michailova, Samonova and Hewamanne, workers in various industries find themselves subject to the complete control of their employers. They are worked until they cannot continue and are discarded (Hewamanne, 2020; Pandit, 2020; Samonova, 2019; Stringer & Michailova, 2018a, 2018b(b)). These workers are primarily invisible, as they often work at a distance, whether geographic, cultural, or socioeconomic (Desai, 2020; Federici, 1975). Also, as these workers mostly come from impoverished socioeconomic backgrounds and are often uneducated, they are more vulnerable to physical and physiological abuse (Hewamanne, 2020; Hodal, 2019; Samonova, 2019; Stringer & Michailova, 2018a). As evident from the work of Stringer and Samonova, modern slavery thrives at the conjunction of poverty and discrimination. Desperate for work, workers from these marginalised racial and minority groups are often employed in high-risk industries creating "disposable workers", often in millions, rendered unfree by the final authority of violence (Bales, 2012, p. 5; International Dalit Solidarity Network, 2020a). These industries may include (but are not limited to) agriculture, transport, cleaning, brick kilns, scrape and metal, construction, local roadside restaurants/cafes, fishing, domestic work, mining and manufacturing (Sampath, 2017; Upadhyaya, 2017; Vaidyanathan, 2020). In certain instances, people are born into "hereditary" slavery if their mother or father is a slave (Samonova, 2019). This exploitative practice is mainly observed in agriculture, where workers are bonded to the landlords'. This is particularly true in the case of cocoa farming. As outlined in section three, cocoa farming is notoriously known for employing workers (often children) from impoverished backgrounds vulnerable to exploitation and prone to debt bondage and other forms of forced labour (Odijie, 2021).

3 Modern Slavery in the Cocoa Farming and the Chocolate Industry

The production of cocoa in West Africa has long been linked to human rights abuses, structural poverty, low pay and child labour (Balch, 2021). Today approximately two-thirds of the cocoa beans used in the chocolate industry are farmed in West Africa, where workers (primarily children) are often subjected to dangerous working conditions (Odijie, 2021). The workers are often employed on a five-year contract by the employers (landlords of the farms), which allows leading chocolate producers (e.g., Nestlé, Hersheys and Mars) to argue that the workers are contracted labourers rather than enslaved workers. However, the contracts produced have little power to protect the workers, as they cannot leave the plantations. In other words, the workers are chattels of the employer for the duration of the contract. While the exploitation on cocoa farms has been well documented by leading academics and media outlets, often causing international outcry, little has been done by the chocolate industry to address the extent of exploitation and abuse that is still prevalent on the farms in West Africa (Odijie, 2021; Whoriskey & Siegel, 2019). The world's leading chocolate firms have continually failed to uproot child labour and exploitative practices from their cocoa supply chains. The representatives from some of the most well-known brands, including Hershey, Mars and Nestlé, cannot guarantee that their supply chains are free of labour exploitation. This is primarily because leading chocolate producers are unable to identify the exact farms (suppliers) where their cocoa is sourced, making it challenging to eradicate modern slavery from their supply chains. As an example, Mars, the maker of M&M's and Milky Way, can trace only 24% of its cocoa back to farms, while Hershey, the maker of Kisses and Reese's, less than half. Nestlé, one of the largest confectionary producers in the world, can trace only 49% of its global cocoa supply to farms. As a result, the odds are substantial that a chocolate bar bought in any part of the world is the product of modern slavery (Whoriskey & Siegel, 2019).

As the industry has struggled to develop a system for monitoring modern slavery on cocoa farms, it increasingly has turned to third parties to tackle the problem. Fairtrade, Utz and Rainforest Alliance are the three leading not-for-profit agencies that certify products that have been produced according to their ethical standards, including a prohibition on child labour and other forms of forced labour. Over the past decade, several chocolate firms (e.g., Whittakers, a New Zealand-owned confectioner) have pledged to buy increasing amounts of cocoa certified by one of the three agencies (Blach, 2021; Whoriskey & Siegel, 2019). While most major chocolate companies seek to buy at least some "certified" cocoa, modern slavery in the cocoa industry will prevail till such time the industry continues to pay farmers a fraction of the cost of sustainable production. An industry that collects an estimated US$103 billion in sales annually has spent only US$150 million over the past two decades to address the issue (Whoriskey & Siegel, 2019). Indeed, the efforts by the industry have been stalled by indecision and insufficient financial commitment to address this wicked problem. Also, with its roots firmly embedded in poverty, eradicating exploitation from cocoa farms is a daunting task not only for the leading firms in the industry but equally a mammoth challenge for local government and independent agencies.

4 Modern Slavery in the IB Classroom

As academics, we are mindful of institutional and industry calls to ensure our students understand and are prepared to respond to ethical issues that are particularly prevalent in business today. These calls are not new, starting with concerns around sweatshop practices during the 1990s and heightened with calls for a paradigm shift in business studies dating back to a decade ago (Holland, 2009). Indeed, based on six principles, the PRME not only recommends the nature of the content business schools will cover with students but also suggests how universities will lead the discussion among industry members around SDGs. Currently, there are over 800 PRME signatories worldwide. It is within a PRME signatory context that the signatories teach a range of IB and Management courses. The aim is to engage students in not creating an awareness of the grand challenges (e.g., modern slavery and labour exploitation) that concern business and society today (Nagar & Hurd, 2020) but also developing much-needed critical skills in our future business leaders to help us keep on track in achieving the targets set by SDG8. Employing a "learning by doing" strategy, the aim is to encourage deep learning. This is achieved by engaging both theoretical and applied content, especially when addressing corporate social responsibility, ethical conduct, labour abuse and exploitation. Although these topics feature in the business curricula, data availability is an issue. For example, disciplines of Organisational Behaviour, Supply Chain Management and Ethics often have a range of case-based examples and journal and editorial articles that discuss such aspects. However, applying the literature from those sources to a traditional IB classroom is often challenging. Indeed, slavery as a contemporary phenomenon has struggled to gain conceptual and definitional clarity and recognition as a current issue in the IB academic domain. This paucity of materials is perhaps because the frameworks and the mainstream literature do not sufficiently address the "dark side" of globalisation. The limited availability of mainstream academic research and teaching resources means that academics often use examples covered in the media. The nature of the material in the media also means that class debates on how the need and desire to achieve the triple bottom line relate to firm strategy and the broader social and institutional environment, potentially the driving force behind modern slavery, remain primarily superficial. From a pedagogical perspective, the need for more academic research and teaching resources on such topics makes it challenging to create awareness and much-needed critical reasoning skills among the business student body (Nagar & Hurd, 2020). Leading IB academics echo the need for more significant discussion and debate on the issue of modern slavery. In addition, there is limited development in understanding modern slavery, specifically, how it can be an outcome of strategic decisions by firms, as well as how firms might develop strategies to tackle modern slavery in their own operations (Phung & Crane, 2018; Yagci & Altay, 2023). Considering the current gaps, the aim of this chapter is to contribute to the existing literature by providing a pedagogical tool to examine the drivers of modern slavery. In doing so, sections five and six propose teaching and learning strategies that create better awareness of this grand challenge in the classroom and encourage students to become more sustainable and conscious future business leaders.

5 Design Thinking—A Pedagogical Tool

Anchored in a human-centred approach, design thinking is an innovative approach to problem-solving a challenge or issue. As a pedagogical tool, design thinking reflects a complex process of inquiry and learning that the students perform in a given context. Students work collaboratively to identify a strategic solution(s) to a grand challenge that may concern a firm, consumers, government or society. Design thinking supports the development of diverse ideas, which are critical for innovation (Grimsgaard, 2023). At its core, the design thinking teaching and learning approach not only helps students learn about core issues through the application but also promotes the development of social, cognitive and behavioural skills (Seigfried-Speller et al., 2022). With innovation and creativity at the forefront of many industries, design thinking is increasingly seen as a critical career skill. Indeed, designing products and services that meet the needs of multiple stakeholders is at the heart of a human-centred design thinking approach (Grimsgaard, 2023). In addition to developing new products and services, applying human-centred design also promises to address community needs while engaging students in meaningful problem-solving work (Seigfried-Speller et al., 2022). As seen in Fig. 1, there are six principles of the human-centred design approach.

In the first step, empathy, the students are introduced to the context and stakeholders (internal and external) that are integral to the context and understanding the grand challenge(s). Following this, in the second step, the students then are tasked with defining the grand challenge and identifying the resources needed to address the challenge. In the third step, the students are expected to generate and evaluate strategic solution(s) for the grand challenge. In the fourth and fifth steps, the students

Fig. 1 Six principles of human-centred design thinking (Adapted from Grimsgaard, 2023)

are expected to collaborate to develop and test a strategic solution for the grand challenge. The aim of the strategic solution should ideally make products or services useful, useable and desirable. When analysing a grand challenge (e.g., modern slavery), the strategic solution should outline ways in which the grand challenge can be best addressed. In the final step, the students are expected to employ storytelling to convey their strategic solution to connect with the stakeholders.

Based on this literature, the author suggests that the human-centred design thinking approach can be applied to examine the most complex problems—such as modern slavery. The section below outlines an in-class activity and assessment that use the principles of design to bring awareness and identify innovative strategic solutions to address modern slavery in cocoa farming and the chocolate industry.

6 Applying the Principles of Design Thinking to Examine Modern Slavery

6.1 Modern Slavery—The Hidden Iingredient in Chocolate

Using the example of cocoa farming and the chocolate industry, the activity is designed to inform and encourage critical thinking on the nature of modern slavery among students. It suits a wide range of senior undergraduate (Year 3) and postgraduate courses (MBA and Taught Masters). The nature and extent of slavery seen in the supply chains of an everyday product, chocolate, make it a perfect example of the design thinking pedagogy addressed in this chapter. While this activity is designed for international business courses, it can be used in any other business course where understanding firm responses to modern slavery is essential. The author uses this activity in their undergraduate courses for teaching and assessment. The activity highlights the nature of modern slavery prevalent in cocoa farming and the chocolate industry and asks the students to critically analyse the role of the firm, government and independent agencies (e.g. WalkFree Foundation, International Cocoa

Initiative, World Cocoa Foundation) to prevent such exploitative practices. The suggested activity can be utilised in various ways; for example, as independent learning tasks before class or to facilitate the carrying out of a series of exercises over multiple weeks covering topics on sustainable production and consumption, ethics and modern slavery/labour exploitation.

The section below presents how the activity informs in-class discussion and a strategic design assessment to address the issue of decent work and modern slavery (SDG8 and target 8.7). The activity has the following learning objectives. First, the activity is designed to inform/create an awareness of the nature and extent of modern slavery prevalent in different industries (primary and manufacturing). The second objective is to use design thinking to identify the drivers of modern slavery in cocoa farming in West Africa (particularly Ghana) and the chocolate industry. In doing so, the students examine the supply chain in the chocolate industry from farm to table and propose strategic solutions to ensure transparency and decent work practices. The third objective is to develop the students into conscious consumers and future business leaders that can help address this grand challenge.

6.1.1 Activity Aim—Class Discussion

Using the principles of design thinking pedagogy, the activity follows the six steps of design thinking (refer to Fig. 1) to engage our students to examine and understand the issues around labour exploitation within cocoa farming and analyse the supply chain of the chocolate industry. This format is used in our Global Social Impact course (Undergraduate Year 3).

Step 1 (Context): To set the scene and establish a connection with the issue that is modern slavery, the students are provided with a set of resources that consist of academic articles, industry and media reports on modern slavery in cocoa farming. The aim is to introduce students to the industry context, the stakeholders and the widespread nature of exploitation in sourcing and manufacturing an everyday product, chocolate. The resources specifically highlight the nature of bonded labour often used on farms in West Africa to harvest and process cocoa. Using examples of leading MNEs (e.g. Nestlé or Hersheys), the readings also highlight the fragmented nature of and the lack of governance in the supply chains of these firms.

Step 2 (Problem Statement): To begin their analysis, the students are divided into teams (five students per team), and they are asked to consider a range of stakeholders, including but not limited to the workers on the farms, the producers (often the landlords), the firm and the consumers. Upon identification of key stakeholders, the students are asked to choose a minimum of two stakeholders. The aim is to encourage them to identify a key issue concerning the identified stakeholders and develop a problem statement. The students are encouraged to keep the workers at the core of their problem statement.

Step 3 (Idea Generation): In this phase, teams are asked to undertake independent research to develop an in-depth understanding of their chosen stakeholders. In most cases, the students consider producers (cocoa farming) and associated practices, the workers (the drivers and nature of labour abuse/exploitation), the role of the firm (governance of supply chains), government and independent agencies and their contribution to recognising and possibly taming modern slavery and hyper-production. The intention here is to develop a detailed understanding of the problem and ideate a possible solution(s). This part of the activity is perhaps the most critical in the design thinking phase as it encourages the students to be creative to design innovative solution(s) to help govern modern slavery.

Step 4 (Strategic Solution): Upon idea generation, the students are asked to debrief and present strategic actions. These strategic actions include policies to assist and protect the workers on the farms, better governance of supply chains, the role of local and international governmental and independent agencies to ensure that the interests of the most vulnerable are represented and the role of consumers in aiding sustainable production and consumption practices. The students often create poster boards, narratives and murals to present their strategic solution.

6.1.2 Assessment—Strategic Design

The assessment is a project-based exploration of modern slavery in the supply chain of the chocolate industry. The students can choose one of the three firms from the list—Whittakers (a New Zealand-owned confectioner), Mondelez International (Cadbury) and Nestlé. The students work in groups of four-six as consultants hired to analyse the strategic issues around sustainable production faced by the firm. They examine the nature of modern slavery that exists (and to what extent) in the supply chain of their chosen firm. The students use design methodology to conduct an internal analysis of the firm and examine the industry context (external analysis) before developing their problem statement and, subsequently, strategic solutions for the identified problem. In addition to identifying key strengths of the design thinking approach, the students are also expected to discuss the limitations of design thinking as an analytical tool to examine modern slavery. The students are expected to apply relevant strategic concepts, frameworks and models covered in their degree to identify the key operational challenges and propose strategic solutions to address competing pressures of value creation while meeting the moral imperatives of being ethical and sustainable. As an outcome, the students are expected to create a 10 min pitch to present their strategic solution together with their business report. At the end of the semester, the students offer strategic solutions to industry representatives. The aim is to bring real-world industry expertise into the classroom. Our INTB709 Strategic Design course (Undergraduate Year 3) uses this assessment.

6.1.3 Pedagogical Outcomes

The in-class discussion and the assessment seek to achieve the following pedagogical outcomes:

• Creating Awareness and Developing Knowledge (Cognition): One of the primary objectives of using cocoa farming and the chocolate industry is to create awareness of the nature and the extent of modern slavery in the sourcing and manufacturing an everyday product, chocolate. The in-class activity and assessment are examples of how firms have failed to take corrective action to limit exploitative practices in their supply chains in an industry known for poor resourcing and production practices. The class discussions and the assessment aim to help students understand how the pursuit of value creation and lower production costs have failed to achieve sustainable/ethical production practices in the industry. In the case of Whittakers, it allows them to know how the firm has created a point of difference by ensuring that they have 100% traceability across their supply chain and go-to-market distribution channels. The students also understand how the firm's journey conveys an ethos towards sustainable production and ensuring that the workers in their supply chain are treated fairly. This has also allowed Whittakers to build a more socially conscious brand image with their consumers in New Zealand and internationally. As consumers of the product chocolate, the students also often establish a close identity with the context and propose strategic solutions that can help address the grand challenge of labour exploitation where global brands have failed.

Instilling a Sense of Purpose and Collective Action (Behavioural): One of the key reasons for using the chocolate industry as an example is that the students find it easy to connect with the context and the firms in the industry. As the students uncover the extent of exploitation prevalent in the supply chains of leading firms, they develop a sense of purpose to develop strategic solutions to help protect the most vulnerable in our society. During the course, they also create a can-do attitude and demonstrate the ability to think laterally and collaboratively to solve a grand challenge. Their strategic solutions suggest how leading brands can take a more sustainable approach to sourcing and producing a product loved by millions of consumers worldwide. The students also demonstrate a sense of pride in suggesting ways in which the industry and consumers can take collective action, which can lead to cross-cutting outcomes for the workers, leading firms and the industry as well as consumers. The student engagement and feedback on the in-class activity and assessment design have been positive, with several students stating that the discussions in class, together with the course work, have provided them with vital insights and a platform to develop solutions for key social challenges that will continue to shape their future. This is an important outcome.

Creating greater awareness and providing students with a platform to present strategic insights not only makes them informed consumers, but such activities also allow the students to build much-needed knowledge and skills as our future business leaders who are sensitised to the dangers of labour exploitation in international business and who are better able to ensure that human rights risks are minimised.

7 Conclusion

Typically design thinking has been used to examine business strategy challenges. However, its application as a pedagogical tool to address cross-cutting problems such as modern slavery is limited. This chapter demonstrates how design thinking principles can be employed to encourage students to understand the causes and drivers of modern slavery and develop strategic solutions that help promote sustainable and ethical practices in cocoa farming and the chocolate industry. In doing so, the activities discussed in this chapter are designed to not only create awareness of modern slavery but also to instil better judgement and critical reasoning skills. The aim is here to develop the next generation of business leaders who are not only sensitised to the precarious nature of labour exploitation in international business but are also equipped with the knowledge to develop strategic solutions to ensure that we remain *on track* to help address and minimise such human rights violations and risks. The discussion in this chapter will also ideally spark a conversation and encourage fellow educators to reflect on our role in developing curricula and innovative pedagogical tools that examine responsible business practices.

References

Balch, O. (2021, February 12). Mars, Nestlé and Hershey to face child slavery lawsuit in US. *The Guardian*. https://www.theguardian.com/global-development/2021/feb/12/mars-nestle-and-hershey-to-face-landmark-child-slavery-lawsuit-in-us

Bales, K. (2012). *Disposable people—new slavery in the global economy (Vol* (3rd ed.). University of California Press.

Breman, J. (1996). *Footloose labour—Working in India's informal economy*. Cambridge University Press.

Burmester., B, Michailova, S., & Stringer, C. (2019) Modern Slavery and International Business Scholarship: The Governance Nexus. *critical perspectives on international business* 15. https://doi.org/10.1108/cpoib-02-2019-0011

Choi-Fitzpatrick, A. (2017, April 28). Cruelty or keeping it in the family? What I learned from India's slaveholders. *The Guardian*. https://www.theguardian.com/global-development/2017/apr/28/what-i-learned-from-india-slaveowners-austin-choi-fitzpatrick

Crane, A. (2013). *Modern slavery as a management practice: exploring the conditions and capabilities for human exploitation Academy of Management, 38*(1), 49–69. https://doi.org/10.5465/amr.2011.0145

Desai, K. (2020). Exploitation and liberation: Case study of women workers in surat's unorganised sector. *Social Change, 50*(1), 12–27. https://doi.org/10.1177/0049085719901051

Federici, S. (1975). *Wages against housework*. New Clarion Press.

Grimsgaard, W. (2023). *Design and strategy—A step-by-step guide*. Routledge.

Hewamanne, S. (2020). Surveillance by another name: The modern slavery act, global factory workers, and part-time sex work in Sri Lanka. *Journal of Women in Culture & Society, 45*, 653–677. https://doi.org/10.1086/706471

Hodal, K. (2019, February 25). One in 200 people is a slave. Why? *The Guardian*. Retrieved 5 January 2020, from https://www.theguardian.com/news/2019/feb/25/modern-slavery-trafficking-persons-one-in-200

Holland, H. (2009). Is it time to retrain B-schools. *New York Times*. Retrieved from 29 October 2019 https://www.nytimes.com/2009/03/15/business/15school.html

International Dalit Solidarity Network. (2020a). *UN experts raise concern over caste-based slavery*. Retrieved 2 February 2021, from https://idsn.org/un-experts-raise-concern-over-caste-based-slavery/

International Dalit Solidarity Network. (2020b). *Vulnerable workers in supply chains need urgent protection to survive impact of Covid-19*. Retrieved 2 February 2021, from https://idsn.org/vulnerable-workers-in-supply-chains-need-urgent-protection-to-survive-impact-of-covid-19/

ILO. (2022, September 12). 50 million people worldwide in modern slavery. *ILO*. Retrieved 18 July 2023 https://www.ilo.org/global/about-the-ilo/newsroom/news/WCMS_855019/lang--en/index.htm

Islam, T., & Stringer, C. (2018). Challenges of achieving social upgrading in Bangladesh's apparel industry. *Society and Business Review., 15*,. https://doi.org/10.1108/SBR-07-2018-0068

Khattak, A., Stringer, C., Haworth, N. & Benson-Rea, M. (2017). Is social upgrading occurring in South Asia's apparel industry? *critical perspectives on international business*, 13(3), 226–243. https://doi.org/10.1108/cpoib-11-2015-0051

Major, A. (2012). *Slavery, abolitionism and empire in India, 1772–1843* (Vol. 6). Liverpool University Press.

Michailova, S., Stringer,C., & Mezias, J. (2020) Letter from the editors: Special issue on "investigating modern slavery: how ib scholarship can contribute". *AIB Insights*. https://doi.org/ https://doi.org/10.46697/001c.14362

Molchanova, V. S. (2019). Modern Slavery in India: the essence, forms, distribution. *Slavery: Theory and Practice, 4*(1), 20–28. https://doi.org/10.13187/slave.2019.1.20

Nagar, S., & Hurd, F. (2020). Addressing modern slavery in the IB Classroom: Are we doing enough? *AIB Insights, 20*(2). https://doi.org/10.46697/001c.13543

Nagaraj, A. (2020, January 9). *Indian slavery survivors swap life of bondage for seat in boardroom at tea plantation*. https://news.trust.org/item/20200109095732-0rc77

Odijie, M. (2021, October 27). Slavery in West Africa: Understanding Cocoa farming is key to ending the practice. *The Conversation*. https://theconversation.com/child-slavery-in-west-africa-understanding-cocoa-farming-is-key-to-ending-the-practice-170315

Pandit, A. (2020, March 16). Reporting of crime a must in new anti-trafficking bill. *The Times of India*. https://timesofindia.indiatimes.com/india/reporting-of-crime-a-must-in-new-anti-trafficking-bill/articleshow/74644233.cms

Phung, K. & Crane, A. (2018). 'The business of modern slavery: Management and organizational perspectives'. In J. Clark & S. Poucki (Eds.), *The SAGE handbook of human trafficking and modern day slavery*, pp. 177–197, SAGE.

Samonova, E. (2019). *Modern slavery and bonded labour in South Asia—A human rights-based approach*. Routledge.

Sampath, G. (2017, July 14). It's not help, it's work. *The Hindu*. https://www.thehindu.com/opinion/op-ed/its-not-help-its-work/article19273135.ece

Seigfried-Spellar, C, K., Laux, C., & Mentzer, N., (2022). Integrating a Human-Centered Design Approach in a Human Trafficking Hackathon, *Irish Journal of Academic Practice, 10*(1). Article 3. https://doi.org/10.21427/p2ve-rc51

Stringer, C., & Michailova, S. (2018a). Tackling modern slavery, the ugliest phenomenon of our times: An invitation to the IB scholarly community. *AIB Insights, 18*(2), 4. https://doi.org/10.46697/001c.16840

Stringer, C., & Michailova, S. (2018b). Why modern slavery thrives in multinational corporations' global value chains. *Multinational Business Review* 26. https://doi.org/10.1108/MBR-04-2018-0032

Raskovic, M. (2023). Taming wicked problems through international business policy: Recommendations for addressing modern slavery. *Critical Perspectives on International Business, 19*(4), 1742–2043. https://doi.org/10.1108/cpoib-09-2021-0081

Upadhyaya, K. P. (2017). *Poverty, discrimination and slaveryThe reality of bonded labour in India, Nepal and Pakistan* London: Anti-Slavery International https://www.antislavery.org/wp-content/uploads/2017/01/1-poverty-discrimination-slavery-final.pdf

Vaidyanathan, R. (2020, 17 November). Indian factory workers supplying major brands allege routine exploitation. *BBC*. https://www.bbc.com/news/world-asia-54960346

Walk Free Foundation. (2023, July 20). *The global slavery index, walk free foundation*. https://www.walkfree.org/global-slavery-index/

Whoriskey. P & Seigel, R. (2019, June 5). Cocoa's Child Labour. *The Washington Post*. https://www.washingtonpost.com/graphics/2019/business/hershey-nestle-mars-chocolate-child-labor-west-africa/

Yagci, S., & K., & Altay, N. (2023). Impact of modern slavery allegations on operating performance. *Supply Chain Management, 28*(3), 470–485. https://doi.org/10.1108/SCM-08-2021-0387

Yea, S., & Stringer, C. (2021). Caught in a vicious cycle: Connecting forced labour and environmental exploitation through a case study of Asia-Pacific. *Marine Policy, 134*(14), 104825. https://doi.org/10.1016/j.marpol.2021.104825

Part IV

Practitioner Reflections on SDG 8

18

SDG 8 and the Case for Local Value Creation in Africa's Food Value Chains

Jason Archie-Acheampong

The global food system provides us with a lens to view some of the grand challenges facing societies today. Roughly 63% of the world's poorest are involved in agricultural value chains (World Bank Group, 2023) and approximately 30% of global greenhouse gases (Crippa et al., 2021) can be attributed to agricultural activity. Efforts to reduce poverty and halt climate change can be intrinsically linked to the production, distribution and consumption of food. In 2019, 884 million people were said to be employed within the agricultural industry, that is approximately 20% of the global workforce (FAO, 2020). Achieving the Sustainable Development Goals (SDGs) is only going to be possible if we are to design solutions that prioritise smallholder farmers and the contexts in which they produce the majority of the world's food. The SDGs offer a framework for organising these developmental challenges into practice-oriented actions, whilst setting a multi-stakeholder agenda to address

J. Archie-Acheampong (✉)
Agrica UK, London, England
e-mail: jason@agricacapital.com

Producers Direct, London, United Kingdom

N. Sinkovics et al. (eds.), *International Business and SDG 8*, The Academy of International Business, https://doi.org/10.1007/978-3-031-46802-5_18

these. The role of the private sector (e.g. Small medium enterprises, multi-national corporations and financial institutions) can be critical in mobilising the resources and capital needed to facilitate decent work opportunities, promote economic growth and reduce poverty. This can be seen across global food systems.

The commercialisation and trade of agricultural goods and food have the power to improve the outcomes for some of the world's under-served workers and communities. Whether it is Ivorian farmers supplying coconuts to the European retail market, crop diversification schemes aimed at improving the incomes of smallholder farmers and West African food entrepreneurs commercialising underutilised indigenous food crops, most of these producers operate in contexts of insecurity, retaining very minimal value from the wealth generated through global food production. If the private sector is to fully realise its potential in being able to tackle some of the global challenges facing societies today, there must be a global multi-stakeholder effort to address the disparities that exist in who benefits from the value created in our global food system.

1 Unlocking Jobs for Local People

Producing finished goods locally at source can help facilitate decent and productive employment through the creation of jobs for local people. As it currently stands, there is a disparity in the role the Global South plays vis-à-vis the Global North in the production of food. The former is mostly characterised by the planting and harvesting of the raw materials that go on to be processed by food manufacturers, mainly in the Global North. As a result, skilled jobs are more prominent in the Global North, whereas the more manual, labour-intensive roles are concentrated in the Global South. By 2030, Africa will be home to the world's most youthful populations. Therefore, if we are to achieve SDG 8 for reducing the percentage of youth not in employment, education, or training, then the private sector will need to play a key role.

Fruit processing companies headquartered in the UK with manufacturing subsidiaries in less economically advanced countries can improve their resilience and competitive advantage with this strategy by spreading their supply risk across a number of locations. Producing finished goods in the Global South will also facilitate productive employment and can offer decent work opportunities for a domestic workforce. Businesses successfully doing this need to be celebrated and can be used as case studies for others to learn from. In contrast, if most food products continue to be manufactured outside of the countries that produce the raw materials, there will be a missed opportunity to create decent and productive employment for some of the world's poorest. By producing locally, countries are able to diversify their economies and improve their resource efficiency. Policy makers therefore are instrumental in creating and enabling an environment in which countries in the Global South retain more value from the food they produce.

2 Locally Produced Goods for the End Consumer

Creating value at source through the production of finished goods is not always a simple task. There are challenges to achieving this that sometimes go beyond national and international regulatory regimes. For instance, consumer-driven factors, such as preserving product quality, may drive a firm's decision to locate the production of finished goods outside of sourcing countries, and instead closer to consumer markets. The coffee sector is a good example. Leading coffee producers and exporters of coffee beans are typically found in the Global South, whereas roasting and value addition predominately occur in consumer markets in Europe, where a premium is paid for the finished goods. The moment coffee is roasted and bagged, it begins to lose its flavour profile. The shorter the distance the roasted coffee has to travel until it reaches supermarket shelves, the better the tasting experience for the consumer. This is one reason why most value addition occurs in Europe and America, closer to the end consumer. Moreover, the consumer demand in African-producing countries is much lower than Europe and Asia, thus not warranting investments into local roasteries and domestic processing capabilities. However, in other value chains, processing raw materials into finished goods at source could happen without compromising the final product quality and with local market demand for the finished product. The chocolate industry exemplifies this. For example, Ghana and Ivory Coast taken together are the world's leading producers of cocoa. Yet, they continue to retain very minimal value from the global confectionary industry. This phenomenon can also be observed within the cashew industry. Although 57% of the world's raw cashew is produced in countries across Africa, the continent only processes 10% of the global volume (ACA, 2021). This is slowly changing as governments in Africa fervently act to create policies that better support domestic food production through government-backed investments and subsidies. The current Ghanaian government's flagship economic programme 'One District, One Factory' (1D1F) embodies this ambition. This programme set out to finance the establishment of processing and production factories in all districts across Ghana. The intended outcome was to create more local jobs and drive wealth creation through local value addition. Additionally, by producing finished goods on the continent it would facilitate regional trade between countries in the continent and reduce trade dependencies with countries outside the continent. For this to happen, regulatory policies are necessary in creating an enabling environment for African SMEs.

3 Facilitating Regional Trade

An international regulatory environment that is equitable and champions domestic value addition is needed, if we are to achieve the SDGs. The African Free Continental Trade Agreement represents an attempt by African nations to enhance regional trade, making it the world's largest single market. But it still remains to be seen the extent to which this is to be sustainable and/or achievable. As it currently stands, there is very limited infrastructure and transport solutions to make inter-trade seamless and inexpensive across Africa. We need to move beyond a global food system where sweet potato is produced in South Africa, shipped to Europe only to then be shipped back into Africa in the form of sweet potato chips. The responsibility does rest with domestic and foreign governments to promote 'development oriented' policies that favour indigenous businesses. Ultimately, for many people in the world, access to food is determined by the price and availability. If the local infrastructure does not exist nor is it robust enough to make food affordable and readily available, it brings into question the utility of local value addition. For instance, many food and beverage manufacturing companies, set up as a result of Ghana's 1D1F programme, have failed to meet its daily output expectations due to inconsistent supply of raw material. This has brought many factories to a standstill. If local value addition is to take place in Africa at a level that is sustainable and meet regional food demands, then investing in all aspects of the supply chain is going to be critical.

4 Better Financing

To encourage domestic job creation in the Global South, domestic SMEs require better support and investment. Agricultural SMEs face a significant barrier in accessing the finance required to see them grow. This curtails any efforts for agribusinesses and producers to diversify and improve resource efficiency. Agricultural investments, particularly those across Africa, are generally perceived as high risk, and, as a result, many SMEs in the sector fail to scale up their operations. Most of the time, these SMEs also cannot afford high-interest bank loans. For many financiers, the sector is too high risk and where investments are made, these are geared towards large-scale agricultural projects or tech enabled/driven ventures. For countries to develop the national capacity to feed their population and create jobs locally is going to require better support for those businesses usually excluded from traditional financing schemes. We therefore need greater equity in the global financing space. Bamboo Capital, AV Ventures, Ag Dev Co are examples of specialist financing bodies focused on tackling this and partnering with the private sector in doing so. The British International Investments, a UK development institution, recently launched the Growth Investment Partners in Ghana to address investment gaps for SMEs. This also provides SMEs with the opportunity to access flexible financing options. Such initiatives are going to be instrumental towards unlocking employment opportunities and facilitating economic growth in underserved markets.

References

ACA. (2021). *Creating an enabling policy environment for the cashew industry in Africa, a necessity*. African Cashew Alliance. https://www.africancashewalliance.com/en/news-and-info/blog/creating-enabling-policy-environment-cashew-industry-africa-necessity

Crippa, M., Solazzo, E., Guizzardi, D., Monforti-Ferrario, F., Tubiello, F. N., & Leip, A. (2021). Food systems are responsible for a third of global anthropogenic GHG emissions. *Nature Food, 2*(3), 198–209. https://doi.org/10.1038/s43016-021-00225-9

FAO. (2020). *World food and agriculture—Statistical yearbook 2020*.

Group, W. B. (2023). *Expanding market opportunities and inclusive private sector engagement in agribusiness*. https://www.worldbank.org/content/dam/Worldbank/document/Trade/CompSector_Agribusiness.pdf

19

European Migration, Where Are We Going and How to Improve Integration?

Wilhelm Brunner

1 European Migration—Decent Work and Economic Growth Context

In 2022 alone almost 220,000 migrants[1] came to Germany as asylum seekers. One would think that such an inflow would satisfy the need for labourers. However, like all European countries, Germany has regulated access to the labour markets that is so restrictive, that one could summarise it as "access but no access" for asylum seekers.

[1] https://ec.europa.eu/eurostat/statistics-explained/index.php?title=Annual_asylum_statistics#Main_countries_of_destination_.E2.80.93_Germany.2C_France.2C_Spain_and_Austria.

W. Brunner (✉)
ORS Group AG, Zürich, Switzerland
e-mail: wbrunner@orsservice.at

N. Sinkovics et al. (eds.), *International Business and SDG 8*, The Academy of International Business, https://doi.org/10.1007/978-3-031-46802-5_19

While only 20–30% of the applicants[2] will be granted asylum and get work permits, the German labour market alone needs an additional 400,000 skilled labourers per year to maintain its production level.[3] Adding 100,000 legal labour migrants to Germany in 2022[4] leaves the most powerful European economy with 230,000 labourers per year short.

The political intention is to keep asylum seekers from joining the labour force until their legal asylum cases are concluded with positive results. Reaching such decisions on asylum cases is a tedious and time consuming process. On average, an asylum case takes two years to be decided upon in most European countries and most decisions are negative (in 2022, two thirds of asylum seekers received a negative decision). Once an asylum seeker receives the final negative decision, the legal status of residency is ended, and they must leave the host country instantly. However, in reality only 20% of those who should leave the country really do so, because of lack of travel documents from their home countries.

Upon entry to the host country, an asylum seeker is asked many questions during interviews on different levels and by different authorities. One question is not on any list: What education and/or professional qualification do you have?

This question would imply that the respective host country would like to integrate someone into their society. Instead, at that early stage, the bureaucrats follow the following rules and principles: During the asylum process, access to the labour market is very restricted, if not impossible or even illegal. Tax payers' money cannot be spent on integration while the legal asylum procedure is still ongoing and has an uncertain outcome (in fact, the probability of a negative result is much higher). The involvement of the public employment services is not desirable under these

---

2 https://ec.europa.eu/eurostat/statistics-explained/index.php?title=Annual_asylum_statistics#Decisions_on_asylum_applications.

3 https://www.reuters.com/world/europe/germany-wants-attract-400000-skilled-workers-abroad-each-year-2022-01-21/.

4 https://www.bamf.de/SharedDocs/Anlagen/DE/Forschung/BerichtsreihenMigrationIntegration/MonitoringBildungsErwerbsmigration/mobemi-halbjahresbericht-2021.pdf?__blob=publicationFile&v=6.

circumstances because the asylum seeker will most likely be asked to leave the country. Further, from a political point of view, it is hard to argue to integrate asylum seekers, when there are still unemployed local residents in the host country. As the question implies an interest in the asylum seeker for integration, it is seen as a "pull factor" for additional "unwanted migration" through the asylum channel.

There are many consequences of the restrictions of asylum seekers not being integrated in the host country. Millions of migrants are waiting for the decision on their legal asylum cases without any or very little contribution to the economy or society in the host countries. The increased spending on social welfare and health for all asylum seekers is a burden on the fiscal national systems being topped by enormous expenses for the legal system (staff working on asylum application procedures at all levels including appeals' courts, office space etc.). When asylum seekers are forced to enter the "black labor market" lacking opportunities to join the workforce legally, it is lowering the quality of the work environment and putting additional pressure on entry wages of legal labourers in the primary labour market. Apart from being lured into the illegal labour market, the lack of meaningful occupation increases criminal activities among asylum seekers. The selection of labourers according to skills/education/qualification for interested employers is not possible due to the restrictions of bureaucratic rules. Hence, the needed trainings in language and other skills never happen on this level.

2 "Wanted" Versus "Unwanted Migration"

Currently, asylum seekers are defined and considered as migrants for a humanitarian reason. After the positive decision on the asylum application, asylum seekers become a recognised refugee; the labour markets in the target country opens up. This channel is frequently abused because of the fairly unbureaucratic way at the beginning of the journey to Europe. However, due to its abuse, the system has become overloaded and ineffective to make fast decisions or bring those with negative asylum decision back home. Thus it has been labelled ""unwanted migration".

The past and current focus has been to decrease the “unwanted migration”, where migrants with any reason to come to Europe use the asylum channel to do so. At the same time, governments have eased some of the rules for “wanted labour migration” in an attempt to make Europe a serious competitor for the skilled labour force in third countries (facing competition primarily from USA, Canada and other industrialised countries across the globe).

The “wanted migration” of labour, known for the intake of Turks, South Italians, citizens of the former Yugoslavia, North Africans and people from the former (British or French) colonies in the 60s of the last century, to still the hunger for factory workers was a success for different industries. The industrial power of Germany, North Italy, France and Britain was built on the foundation of this migration.

The downturn of the European economies with fierce competition from Japan (in the 80s) and lately China (just to name two examples) has led to unemployment and protective labour migration laws in Europe.

The principally successful labour integration in the years of the “Deutsches Wirtschaftswunder” (Germany’s economic miracle after the Second World War) to name just one example, has a “dark” side as well. The first generation of migrant workers that arrived was integrated quickly into local industries. The need for a social and cultural integration was often neglected. Many of the first labour migrants never learned the language of their host country and started to live in a separate society of their own. Their children often spoke the local language for the first time, when starting school at six, because their parents (especially their mothers) never had access to integration classes with language training and other relevant topics.

Until today, the host societies and the migrants’ societies live at a higher risk of poverty and social exclusion.[5] Further, because of its economic contribution and the opportunity to select migrants according to criteria (level of education, skill set, knowledge of languages etc.) the wanted labour migration is the preferred channel.

[5] https://ec.europa.eu/eurostat/statistics-explained/index.php?title=Migrant_integration_statistics_-_at_risk_of_poverty_and_social_exclusion.

3 Let the Migrants Choose the Regular over the Irregular Way

How could we make the wanted labour migration channel also the preferred channel for migrants who, up to now, choose to ask for asylum rather than seeking work permits from their home countries?

In 2021 the overall number of wanted migrants that entered the German economy legally (obtained work permits for Germany in their home countries) was merely 100,000 with granted work permits to non-residents of Germany/EU.[6] According to the head of department for international labour migration of the German"Bundesagentur für Arbeit" (federal agency for employment), Alexander Wilhelm, whose department administers and has to approve all work permit applications from abroad, the bottleneck for increasing the number of legal labour migration is the lack of administrative capacities at the consulates of the Republic of Germany around the world (Interview, January 30th, 2019). The German Ministry of Foreign Affairs would need to more than double its personnel and cost for visa consulates across the world for reaching or getting even close to satisfying the need for international migrant workers for the German job market in the upcoming years.

4 The Wanted and Legal International Labour Migration—Next Steps

If the wanted and legal international labour migration in Europe is the preferred way to attract workforce from abroad, several steps need to be taken. A strategic master plan how to re-channel migrants from the inefficient asylum to a managed labour migration channel is need. However, foremost, countries need to identify the need of workforce by categories (industry, services, agriculture etc.) and a set of criteria (education, professional qualification, language, social etc.) for selective migration.

[6] https://www.bamf.de/SharedDocs/Anlagen/DE/Forschung/BerichtsreihenMigrationIntegration/MonitoringBildungsErwerbsmigration/mobemi-halbjahresbericht-2021.pdf?__blob=publicationFile&v=6.

Europe will face strong competition from other industrial areas and therefore must promote the advantages of the European labour market in comparison to other competitive target markets. Countries have to build the resources around the world to give access to information and application procedures at consulates. Serious preparation efforts for entering the European labour markets (professional and cultural training, language programs etc.) have to be established or expanded. Partner countries must be identified and the labour migration to Europe as well as the re-integration into the home countries have to be secured on highest state levels. Home countries should have benefits from such international programs, such as introducing training centres, give access to training opportunities to locals as well, train the trainers, provide local job opportunities and scheduled re-integration programs. Long before the first wanted labour migrants will be welcomed, social issues, such as cultural networks, need to be established in the host countries or family programs (allowing to bring their families with them) need to be considered. Along this theme affordable housing in the host countries for hundreds of thousands of people need to be provided. It is highly advised that existing programs are analysed and lessons learned from successes and failures. And above all, coordination of activities among European countries is needed to avoid the cannibalisation of efforts.

5 Combination of Channels—Is This the Way to Go?

Looking at the high numbers of needed labour in Europe, it is difficult to imagine that those numbers can be achieved by reorganising the legal labour migration channel only.

It is understandable that the legal way allows for better selection and matching the demands with the needs more accurately thus reducing the risk of failures of integration. However, the risk of not entering the job market in the host country after a lot of money is spent on search, identification, preparation and training in the home country should not be underestimated. Many reasons can interfere with the previously made decision of entering such a program for international labour migration (e.g. personal reasons such as family issues, health issues, local offers, change of mind etc.) and may reduce the achievable numbers quite harshly.

So why not include the already locally residing asylum seekers to master the challenge in introducing millions of needed labourers into the European labour market?

Most prominently the legal experts are heavily against such a mixture of channels. In one way, there is the need to safe-guard the asylum process for it is the guarantee for humanity in our civilised societies, when the unspeakable horrors keep occurring. In another way, it is also against humanity to keep someone from the opportunity to develop or find meaning by being useful and work. There is also the concern that opening up the labour market to asylum seekers will create a "pull factor" inviting even more migrants to use the asylum channel to come to the European labour market—without meeting the selection criteria for a more successful integration.

While many use this argument to do little or nothing for any improvement on any channel of migration, there are examples of a different approach already in place and could be a "best practise" for other countries. Switzerland is known for its robust economy, expensive watches, beautiful countryside and high standard of living. It is also known for having one of the highest percentages of migrant workers in the job market in Europe.[7] The Swiss migration policy (including asylum law) is generally speaking as restrictive or open as any of its neighbouring countries such as Germany, Italy, or Austria in regard to labour integration: there is no general access to the Swiss labour market for asylum seekers. However, the Canton Berne introduced an innovative model for the care and integration of asylum seekers "against" all common restrictive measures and laws in 2019. The program is called "Neustrukturierung des Asyl- und Flüchtlingsbereichs (NA-BE)" (new structure of the asylum and refugee sector[8]). It requires from care givers a holistic approach towards social care with integration in mind. Upon arrival of

[7] https://ec.europa.eu/eurostat/statistics-explained/index.php?title=Foreign-born_people_and_their_descendants_-_labour_market_indicators#Overview.

[8] https://www.rr.be.ch/de/start/beschluesse/suche/geschaeftsdetail.html?guid=75e9f58ec2744bb89687c3ad122b290e.

an asylum seeker in the canton of Berne, the asylum case is still pending, as it is with all asylum seekers being sent from the Federal State Secretary of Migration (SEM) to the doors of any canton of the Swiss Federation. Yet, the canton Berne concluded that no matter of the outcome of the legal asylum case, most asylum seekers will stay in the canton of Berne (or Switzerland) anyway. Facing this reality the "Regierungsrat" (highest executive body of a canton) of the canton Berne, after passing a popular vote and introduction of a new law by the local parliament, asked care givers to include not only social but also integration services for asylum seekers. The goal of all care giving services is to place refugees into the local Swiss job market .

20

Post Brexit Trade and Investment and the Implications for Scottish Businesses: Some Reflections

Jonathan Slow and Holly Sherrie

1 Introduction

The issue of Brexit has been discussed extensively across the media and it is fair to say there have been some very polarised views both for and against it. It is not our intention in this paper to rehearse those arguments again, but we do wish to consider what the implications might be beyond the high-level media speculation, and in particular for Scottish businesses.

The implications of Brexit are likely to be felt for a long time. One of the arguments in support of Brexit was that of the Singapore-upon-Thames model whereby the UK would be able to offer a much lighter regulatory climate and businesses low tax rates as an alternative to the

J. Slow
University of Southampton, Southampton, UK
e-mail: Jonathan.Slow@scotent.co.uk

H. Sherrie (✉)
University of Strathclyde, Glasgow, Scotland
e-mail: Holly.Sherrie@scotent.co.uk

N. Sinkovics et al. (eds.), *International Business and SDG 8*, The Academy of International Business, https://doi.org/10.1007/978-3-031-46802-5_20

EU, comparable to Singapore within Asia. However thus far, the benefits of this type of model in the UK haven't yet materialised. The unfolding of Brexit is an ongoing process and it may take a number of years to understand its full effect. Therefore, even as businesses react to those issues, the legacy may last. It is also likely that the implications of different economics will compound and, therefore, we must look at Brexit as one issue alongside COVID-19, given they will both have a long-lasting impact on the Scottish economy.

We are perhaps uniquely positioned to discuss some of the material; working in economic development and with Scottish Enterprise having a core part of its remit in trade and investment activities means there is significant interest both at a practical and operational level.

Although there is much material available on Brexit and how it may be impacting businesses, the economic analyses are still only coming through periodically. And inevitable delays between data gathering and publication can be crucial in a fast-moving environment.

Moreover, material from businesses, especially in Scotland, has been less regularly analysed systematically. Therefore, in this reflection piece, we explore some of the material available to us; the aim is to present the impacts so far on Scottish businesses based on a combination of published and proprietary evidence.

It is also easy to assume that Brexit only impacts exporting activity. The impact, however, is much wider and covers imports and investment, particularly inward investment. In this note, we will explore each of these activities in the context of the data.

In the next section, we will briefly outline the data sources we have used. The final three sections reflect on the evidence we have for exporting and outward investment, importing and inward investment respectively.

2 Data Sources

Due to the recentness of Brexit and the time scales over which research is undertaken, it is perhaps not surprising that papers are only now starting to be published. These papers have been important steps in our understanding of the numerical impacts of Brexit and particularly with regard to the counter-factual: what might have happened had Brexit not happened? However, important as these papers are, we recognise that, inevitably, they are a partial picture; to present a more complete reflection of the impact of Brexit on businesses, particularly the more nuanced operational impacts, we need to look beyond published academic material.

In Scotland, we are fortunate to have access to a wide range of data sources both from the UK Office for National Statistics, HMRC, and data provided regularly by the Scottish Government. Some of these sources are updated frequently—e.g. the Scottish Business Insights and Conditions Survey is published fortnightly (using Scottish weighted data) and the UK version is published weekly. Although not all questions are asked in each wave, the data are suitably frequent to provide a solid longitudinal picture we are looking to establish. We use these sources regularly to deepen our evidence-base. This material is further supplemented by the wide coverage of business surveys, helping to triangulate the material we have and enable a story to emerge.

However, as these data are questionnaire-based, they can have some limitations—e.g. of coverage. For this reflection piece, we can go further, using internal Scottish Enterprise research and data that build on conversations between Scottish Enterprise staff and the businesses they engage with. This unique, proprietary, data source provides valuable insights that are perhaps not easily identifiable from other sources; they also enable a clearer elucidation of the impacts on the business and what this can mean operationally. It might be reflected that the external data give us a very strong contextual and dynamic base to work with; the internal data provide a cornerstone for developing the best support to businesses.

The rest of this note explores the findings of our analysis from this range of data.

3 Trade—Exports and Outward Investment

3.1 The Link Between Trade and Economic Growth

The link between trade and economic growth is well evidenced. According to the World Bank, trade is an engine of growth that creates better jobs, reduces poverty, and increases economic opportunity. Recent research shows that liberalisation of trade increases economic growth by an average of 1.0 to 1.5 percentage points, resulting in 10 to 20 per cent higher income after a decade. It is therefore important that we are able to assess the impact that Brexit might have had on both the UK and Scottish economies.

3.2 Exports

It can be argued that some of the export trends started before Brexit day. Evidence from the Bank of Spain shows that post-2016 and the vote to leave, European businesses were already looking to place orders elsewhere within Europe and away from UK suppliers. The impact would not have been immediate given existing contracts but the logical approach for businesses would be to reduce risk and the added uncertainty of the Article 50 discussions and what the eventual trade deal might be would only have added to this. Although perhaps hard to quantify or even qualify this would undoubtedly have impacted Scottish businesses.

Then, in the immediate aftermath of 'Brexit Day', exports fell precipitously, while the new systems 'bedded-in'. However, recovery happened within six months and some normality returned: businesses reported exporting levels 'around normal' during 2021; but some evidence appears to suggest that the recovery may have been less than expected in the light of economies moving out of the COVID-19 period, and that the sales to the EU were perhaps lower then would have been seen had the UK still been in the EU.

Another element worth noting is the decisions that some Scottish businesses took to step back from exporting altogether and focus on the

UK market: so far, the data suggest that the number of exporting businesses slowed more in Scotland post-Brexit before recovering again by 2021. However, it should also be stressed that this change in exporter numbers came at the same time as a global pandemic which undoubtedly will also affect the numbers.

More widely, there has been a fall in the variety of goods exported to the EU. It is possible that some of this change is directly down to trading regulations and complexities; other elements might be down to companies considering serving European markets in a different way. This aspect will be explored further below.

When considering exporting, the sectoral element is critical. Scotland has performed well in export terms since Brexit, and this has been down to products such as whisky and petroleum within the food & drink and oil & gas sectors. These sectors continue to support Scottish export totals but as we move towards Net Zero and continue to reduce carbon emissions, further changes may take place to the structure of Scotland's exports.[1]

As exporting to the EU has become more difficult post-Brexit, it can be argued that exporting to non-EU countries has perhaps become easier. There is some evidence of exporters 'shifting' markets and/or exploring locations they would not have previously considered but this is still relatively early stage.

As Scottish businesses become more accustomed to the new trading relationships with the EU, the proportion of those companies reporting trading challenges has fallen although they still exist. For example, businesses exporting to the EU regularly mention issues due to the volume of paperwork and customs checks; the time to complete and/or review relevant paperwork with partners; transportation costs, including port delays; and over and above all this the management time absorbed in getting products to market. The impact of these challenges has been felt more acutely by smaller businesses in general.

Businesses have perceived a change in their relationships with some EU customers and feel they are having to 'work harder to stand still'

[1] It can also perhaps be argued that Scotland benefits from a consistent framework of support for exporting businesses or those considering exporting, see Scottish Government (2017, 2022) and Slow and Fletcher (2017, 2018).

in terms of servicing current contracts and to win new business. This is made even more difficult as many businesses struggle to recruit appropriate staff, putting pressure on existing staff; a situation made more complex with some businesses losing EU nationals who returned home after Brexit.

3.3 Outward Investment

Some businesses have used Brexit as an opportunity to reconsider their supply chains and how they serve key markets, including those in Europe. One of the options some are exploring is outward investment: having a presence in an overseas market. The number of businesses actively pursuing outward investment is currently relatively small but there has been increased interest in doing it—e.g. for businesses that use imported raw materials/semi-finished goods who through a joint venture may be able to reduce costs through importing to the UK and then re-exporting to the EU.[2]

Other businesses are considering new ways to approach manufacturing—e.g. accessing 3D printers to manufacture directly in/near market but using proprietary designs that remain here. Outward investment may also provide opportunities to address some of the issues resulting from employees returning to the EU or being unable to recruit, although the evidence on this is a little less clear at present.

4 Trade—Imports

Brexit-related impacts on imports are perhaps sometimes overlooked relative to exports. However, given the international nature of many supply chains, they are important. The contribution of imported goods to supply chains varies considerably but can be significant: changes can result in significant disruption and increased costs. Many Scottish exporters need imports as part of their production process.

[2] For an explanation of some of the thinking that businesses may undertake to consider an overseas location of operations see Slow, Fletcher and Slow (2019).

It is perhaps difficult to ascertain the overall impact of Brexit on imports as the early part of the post-Brexit period other events were also preventing global trade from flowing smoothly—e.g. shipping containers being expensive, in short supply, and in the wrong place; the Ever Given ship grounding in the Suez Canal; and the general disruption from COVID-19 in many economies. Further, some businesses stockpiled supplies at the end of 2020 'just in case' there were issues when Brexit came into effect and this probably reduced the import-related impact. So, although it is difficult to disentangle all the effects, it is likely that Brexit did have some effect initially on Scottish imports.

As global trade has recovered and many bottlenecks in supply chains have reduced, imports to the UK and Scotland have returned to a more normal situation. However, the composition of imports has changed: we now import more from the rest of the world relative to the EU. On current trends, this is likely to continue. The implications of this are not yet clear.

Businesses are also selectively considering and, in some cases, changing their supply chains to make them the most resilient they can be. We have seen businesses look more globally for inputs while others are looking to increase UK sourcing. This trend and the increase in digitalisation of supply chains as much as possible are coincidental with, rather than the result of, Brexit and have been accelerated by the impacts of COVID-19 but they provide another lens to consider whether to purchase from EU suppliers in the medium term.

5 Inward Investment

Brexit appears to have had little impact overall on inward investment to Scotland. Scotland's historically strong performance and inward investment is still evident and the interest in and appetite to invest here remains high. That major change has not happened is perhaps unsurprising when often the main reasons businesses cite for locating here are linked to workforce quality; this has not changed because of Brexit. Even with potential trading changes over the longer-term due to Brexit, the domestic conditions for businesses seeking to invest in Scotland remain strong.

Sectoral contributions are again important here and Scotland is fortunate to have a strong presence in digital companies and renewable technologies both of which have seen significant investment flows in recent years and these trends are set to continue.

And while we should perhaps exercise a little caution given the length of time it can take for inward investment projects, there is no current evidence of a let up an interest in Scotland as an investment destination.

6 Conclusion

This paper has reflected on some of the impacts to date of Brexit on Scottish trade and investment. Overall, it is too early to say what the long-term implications will be. It is perhaps worth bearing in mind that data on trade will also be affected by the significant unexpected risks that have shocked the global economy including COVID-19 and the war in Ukraine.

However, evidence suggests that sales to the EU remain lower than that if the UK was still a member and the variety of goods exported has fallen. It is likely that Brexit did have an initial effect on importing, and although having now returned to a more normal situation, the composition has changed with more imports now coming from the rest of the world relative to the EU. Scottish businesses have found ways to adapt and innovate where they can, and that process will continue to evolve as respective governments (UK and Scotland) introduce new fiscal and monetary policies.

As for inward investment, evidence shows little impact for Scotland as it remains a desirable investment destination. Despite the turbulence of the last few years, Scottish trade continues to play a key role in economic growth.

References

BCC calls for action as exports remain in limbo. (2022). *British Chambers of Commerce*. Retrieved May 31, 2023, from, https://www.britishchambers.org.uk/news/2022/07/bcc-calls-for-action-as-exports-remain-in-limbo.

British Chambers of Commerce. (2022). *Export growth now stagnant for 1 year as BCC sounds warning on trade.* Retrieved from British Chambers of Commerce: https://www.britishchambers.org.uk/news/2022/04/export-growth-now-stagnant-for-1-year-as-bcc-sounds-warning-on-trade

Bromley, S. (2022). *SME insights report: What challenges are small businesses facing in 2022?* Simply Business. https://www.simplybusiness.co.uk/knowledge/articles/2022/07/small-business-insights-report-2022/

Department for International Trade, DIT national survey of registered businesses' exporting behaviours, attitudes and needs 2021 (2022). Retrieved May 31, 2023, from, https://www.gov.uk/government/statistics/dit-national-survey-of-registered-businesses-exporting-behaviours-attitudes-and-needs-2021.

Du, J. (2023). *Business Confidence, TCA adaption, and export performance.* Enterprise Research Centre.

Du, J., Satoglu, E. B., & Shepotylo, O. (2022). *Post-Brexit UK Trade—An update.* Aaston Business School.

Ernst and Young. (2023). *EY UK Attractiveness Survey 2023: UK including Scotland Spotlight.* Ernst and Young.

Jeffrey, A. F., & David, R. (1999). *Does trade cause growth?* American Economic Association. https://www.jstor.org/stable/117025

Freeman, R., Manova, K., Prayer, T., & Sampson, T. (2022). *UK Trade in the Wake of Brexit*. European Commission.

FSB. (2022). *"Let's make this a small business summer", firms urge, as sectoral confidence gulf grows and insolvencies spiral.* Retrieved May 31, 2023, from, https://www.fsb.org.uk/resources-page/let-s-make-this-a-small-business-summer-firms-urge-as-sectoral-confidence-gulf-grows-and-insolvencies-spiral.html.

Grey, C. (2021). *Brexit Unfolded: How no one got what they wanted (and why they were never going to).* Biteback Publishing.

Grogan, J., Hunsaker, S., Portes, J., Reland, J., Rutter, J., & Stowers, S. (2023). *Where next? The future of the UK-EU relationship.* UK in a Changing Europe.

Gutiérrez, E., Lacuesta, A., & Machuca, C. M. (2021). *Brexit: Trade diversion due to trade policy uncertainty* [Working paper, Bank of Spain]. Madrid, Spain.

HM Revenue and Customs. (2023). *OTS custom table*. Overseas trade data table—UK Trade Info (https://www.uktradeinfo.com/trade-data/ots-custom-table/)

Hopkins, P. (2023). *Supply chain opportunities for Scotland and policy development evidence.* Scottish Enterprise. Document details | Reading Room for Scottish Enterprise (https://www.evaluationsonline.org.uk/evaluations/Search.do?ui=basic&action=show&id=795).

ICAEW Business Confidence Monitor (BCM): Scotland. ICAEW. (2023). https://www.icaew.com/technical/economy/business-confidence-monitor/scotland

International traders cautiously optimistic for the year ahead. (2022). *Institute of Directors*. Retrieved May 31, 2023, from, https://www.iod.com/news/global-business/iod-press-release-international-traders-cautiously-optimistic-for-the-year-ahead/.

OECD. (2022). *Trade and value added database*. https://www.oecd.org/sti/ind/measuring-trade-in-value-added.htm

Office for Budget Responsibility, Economics and fiscal outlook: October 2021 (2021). Retrieved May 31, 2023, from, https://obr.uk/efo/economic-and-fiscal-outlook-october-2021/.

Philips, M. (2019). Brexit: Could "Singapore on Thames" become reality? Cambridge University law Society. https://www.culs.org.uk/per-incuriam/brexit-could-singapore-on-thames-become-reality

Scottish Enterprise. (2023). *Feedback from Scottish Enterprise customers.*

Scottish Government. (2023). *BICS weighted Scotland estimates: Data to wave 82.* BICS weighted Scotland estimates: Data to wave 82–Gov. Scot. (https://www.gov.scot/publications/bics-weighted-scotland-estimates-data-to-wave-82/)

Scottish Government. (2022). *A trading nation—progress review 2022.* Scottish Government. Edinburgh.

Scottish Government. (2017). *Enterprise and skills review: Report on phase 2.* Scottish Government. Edinburgh.

Slow, J., & Fletcher, M. (2017). *Increasing the number of Scottish exporters: The ACE model and its application by Scottish enterprise.*

Slow, J., & Fletcher, M. (2018). *Increasing the number of Scottish international businesses.*

Slow, J., Fletcher, M., & Slow, F. (2019). *Moving beyond exporting: Strategic internationalisation models.*

The World Bank. (2022). *Trade Overview.* The World Bank. Retrieved 16th August from Trade Overview, (https://www.worldbank.org/en/topic/trade/overview)

21

SDG 8—A Reflection on Policies, Programmes and the Gaps Within

J. P. Jagdev

1 Introduction

One of the most important factors behind the success of any information technology (IT) and Information Technology Enabled Services (ITeS) is the strength of skilled human resources available in the geographical area of operation. Successful IT industries have developed in cities where there are large pools of technical workforce. My organisation is a leading ITeS and Management Consulting firm in Bhubaneshwar, a class two city in India. We have always been struggling to source personnel of various talents as smaller cities provide less attraction to migrants. Frequently, we were forced to recruit untrained resources and train them up at our cost to meet our requirements. Casing scarce human resources often created competition and friction with our fellow entrepreneurs. When we heard the news that the state is investing heavily in training and skill development of young people to create the kind of human

J. P. Jagdev (✉)
Parameter Softwares (P) Ltd, Bhubaneswar, India
e-mail: jp.jagdev@outlook.com

N. Sinkovics et al. (eds.), *International Business and SDG 8*, The Academy of International Business, https://doi.org/10.1007/978-3-031-46802-5_21

resource base we need, we were naturally elated. We hope we will be able to institutionally access a pool of interested, skilled resources.

This piece is about our personal experience of absorbing the youths of our state, skilled in the various trades of lower-level ITeS competences.

2 Background

2.1 National Response to SDG 8 (Decent Work and Economic Growth for All):

The National Institution for Transforming India (NITI) Aayog (i.e. commission in Hindi) in one of its document states "India has embarked on the journey to attain the SDG goal 8 Decent Work and Economic Growth for all". Programmes like Make in India, Startup India, Skill India and Digital India have the underlining principle of creating employment opportunities for the country's youth. The NITI Aayog serves as the apex public policy think tank of the Government of India, and the nodal agency tasked with catalysing economic development, and fostering cooperative federalism and moving away from bargaining federalism through the involvement of State Governments of India in the economic policy-making process using a bottom-up approach.

2.2 Ministries and Its Certification and Implementing Arms:

The Government of India, to expedite economic development, has a dedicated ministry, the Ministry of Skill Development and Entrepreneurship *(*https://www.msde.gov.in/*)*. Organisations like National Skill Development Corporation (https://nsdcindia.org/), Sector Skill Council (https://msde.gov.in/en/organizations/nsti), Sector Skill Council (https://nsdcindia.org/sector-skill-councils), National Council for Vocational Training (http://ncvt.co.in/index.html) were formed as independent organisation to deal with specialised cohorts. Similarly, the state of Odisha formed the Odisha Skill Development Mission and

Skill Development Authority (https://skillodisha.gov.in/). These organisations were given the express mandate to encourage entrepreneurship and develop skilled manpower for the industry. They use other government departments and expert public and private agencies to implement training schemes designed to facilitate participants' entry into the job market.

Schemes:

The schemes target people by geography, the extent of social and economic marginalisation, barriers to access opportunities, gender, and disability to ensure that no one misses out on the opportunities provided to be a part of the country's economic resurgence. Examples of organisations that offer such programmes include Pradhan Mantri Kaushal Vikas Yojana (PMKVY), Deen-Dayal Upadhyaya Grameen Kaushal Yojana (DDU-GKY), Jan Siksyan Sansthan (JSS), Advanced Vocational Training Scheme (AVTS), Craft Instructor Training Scheme (CITS).

The initiatives offered range from basic to high-end skills. The available courses are listed on this website (https://nsdcindia.org/nos).

Implementation:

Various empanelled agencies get assigned to train a specified number of people for a trade/ skill within a pre-determined period. It varies from trade to trade. The deliverables are based on the nature of the scheme. The trades/courses offered under the schemes can be residential or a non-residential programme. Some programmes include a placement.

Responsibilities/Deliverables:

The broad responsibilities include to create awareness, mobilise the candidate, establish a training centre, provide training as per the suggested syllabus, provide accommodation if it's a requirement, conduct assessment tests by the certifying agency and help them with placement opportunities or entrepreneurship supports as the scheme specified.

Outputs:

Thousands of certified students are churned out by these agencies. The government in its official website states that several millions of young people have been skilled under state sponsorship and this number is steadily growing. At face value, this is an impressive number and can be interpreted as proof that the state strategy towards promoting sustained, inclusive and sustainable economic growth, full and productive employment and decent work for all is successful.

3 Outcomes/Experiences

To ensure sustainable economic development and equitable distribution of wealth, it is necessary that people get access to decent work and entrepreneurial opportunities. The availability of skilled and efficient human resources in a particular area plays a big role in spurring a country's economic activities and in attracting foreign direct investment. Realising this, the government tried to go beyond enhancing basic literacy skills and invest in skills needed by industries at its different lifecycles. However, to fully evaluate the success of these efforts, it is necessary to examine whether the participants in these programmes have indeed transitioned into employment. Also, it would be important to analyse to what extent recruitment into industry jobs happened through the centres that reported that they trained and certified large numbers of people.

For a full assessment of the effectiveness of these initiatives, a survey of all stakeholders involved in skilling these beneficiaries would be necessary.

As a practitioner in the IT industry, specifically in the ITeS space, we require large numbers of skilled labour to serve our clients to whom we offer business process outsourcing and digitisation services. In the last 5 years we engaged closely with skilling centres, namely Arohan Foundation Tech-Mahendra, Bandhan Bank, Nyati Foundation, Jibika group of Schools, Magic Boxout and the skill development centre managed by the Indian Oil Corporation. We estimate that these centres inducted over

1000 people. Yet, we only identified a handful of prospective employees with the necessary skills.

The following is an illustrative example. We were informed that a skilling centre had 30 trained candidates that were about to graduate. We asked their management to send the trainees to have a physical visit to their potential workplace before attending the interview. Out of 30, only 12 people came for the workplace visit. Out of the 12, only eight reported to the interview and only two were employable. The two candidates that we employed soon after left citing the high workload as a reason. There is no information whether the 30 initial candidates ever entered or succeeded in the job market.

This experience raises a few questions:

1. What deters candidates who went through the training from visiting their perspective workplace?
2. Why did candidates who came to the site visit not come to the interview?
3. Why did the candidates who came to the interview not qualify?
4. Why do candidates who qualify not report to work? Why do candidates who report to work quit after one month?

Answering these questions may help identifying systemic gaps. This observed trend is worrying as the training and skilling efforts made by the state cost billions of rupees. A sophisticated programme evaluation would be necessary to determine the effectiveness of these initiatives and the extent to which they contribute to the SDG8 mandate.

3.1 Stakeholders' Insights:

Conversations with several stakeholders may provide some insights that may inform further analysis.

Candidates:

The motivations of candidates who go through these programmes vary. Many are not aware of their latent aptitude for a particular skill, and they don't know which skill training would be best suited for them. They also don't know how to strategically plan a career. Conversations with several candidates revealed that they only took up the training because it was offered to them free of charge. Others wish for employment that is not physically and mentally challenging. Although migration is seen by some as a path to upwards social mobility, others worry that leaving their social context would lead to isolation.

Parents:

Parents play a very important role in making their children derive benefits from the schemes offered by the government. Many parents are not able to help their children identify the skills they have aptitude for.

Trainers:

The trainers are made to deliver the training content and the practical training mechanically and exactly as per the syllabus prescribed by the government. It offers no scope for them to innovate or customise the training as per the situation or context.

Skilling Agencies:

These initiatives represent a very lucrative opportunity for skilling agencies. They don't have an incentive to deviate from the norm or engage in content innovation to achieve higher outcomes.

Administrative Departments Involved in Managing the Scheme/ Programme:

Government programmes are frequently designed top-down with little scope for customisation. Although they tend to consult academic institutions, the content of the programmes is too broad and does not allow the development of specialist skills. Practitioners and entrepreneurs are seldomly consulted in the curriculum design phase. As a result, these programmes yield more political dividend than economic integration.

4 Conclusion

To make the schemes more effective, the top-down rigid design would need to be replaced by a more inclusive approach. Such an approach would take into consideration the specific needs of the industry, employer expectations, the latent aptitude and aspiration of candidates and the society surrounding them. Skilling alone in isolation or as a prescription from the top will not be sufficient to meaningfully contribute to SDG8.

Index

N. Sinkovics et al. (eds.), *International Business and SDG 8*, The Academy of International Business, https://doi.org/10.1007/978-3-031-46802-5

www.ingramcontent.com/pod-product-compliance
Ingram Content Group UK Ltd.
Pitfield, Milton Keynes, MK11 3LW, UK
UKHW020833290926
15470UKWH00004B/1329
9783031468018